Teaching Developmental Writing
Background Readings

Teaching Development in Fourth

Teaching Developmental Writing

Background Readings

Susan Naomi Bernstein

Shippensburg University of Pennsylvania

Bedford/St. Martin's   Boston   ◆   New York

For Bedford/St. Martin's
Developmental Editor: Amanda Bristow
Production Editor: Bridget Leahy
Production Supervisor: Dennis Conroy
Marketing Manager: Brian Wheel
Editorial Assistant: Erin Durkin
Copyeditor: Susan Zorn
Text Design: Claire Seng-Niemoeller
Cover Design: Lucy Krikorian
Composition: Karla Goethe, Orchard Wind Graphics
Printing and Binding: Malloy Lithographing, Inc.

President: Charles H. Christensen
Editorial Director: Joan E. Feinberg
Editor in Chief: Karen S. Henry
Director of Marketing: Karen Melton
Director of Editing, Design, and Production: Marcia Cohen
Managing Editor: Elizabeth M. Schaaf

Copyright @ 2001 by Bedford/St. Martin's

Manufactured in the United States of America.

5 4 3 2 1
f e d c b a

For information, write: Bedford/St. Martin's, 75 Arlington Street, Boston, MA 02116
(617-399-4000)

ISBN: 0–312–25815–1

Acknowledgments

Linda Adler-Kassner, "Just Writing, Basically: Basic Writers on Basic Writing." Copy-
right © 1999 by Journal of Basic Writing, The City University of New York. Re-
printed from Volume 18, Number 2, by permission.
Eleanor Agnew and Margaret McLaughlin, "Basic Writing Class of '93 Five Years Later:
How the Academic Paths of Blacks and Whites Diverged." Copyright © 1999 by *Jour-
nal of Basic Writing,* The City University of New York. Reprinted from Volume 18,
Number 1, by permission.
Gloria Anzaldúa, "How to Tame a Wild Tongue," from *Borderlands / La Frontera: The
New Mestiza* © 1987 by Gloria Anzaldúa. Reprinted with permission.
Libby Bay, "Twists, Turns, and Returns: Returning Adult Students." *Teaching English
in the Two-Year College,* March 1999. Copyright © 1999 by the National Council of
Teachers of English. Reprinted with permission.
Susan Naomi Bernstein, "Instructional Note: Life Writing and Basic Writing." *Teaching
English in the Two-Year College,* May 1998. Copyright © 1998 by the National Coun-
cil of Teachers of English. Reprinted with permission.

*Acknowledgments and copyrights are continued at the back of the book on pages 377–
78, which constitute an extension of the copyright page. It is a violation of the law to
reproduce these selections by any means whatsoever without the written permission of
the copyright holder.*

Preface

U nderprepared students arrive in our classrooms with a variety of needs; perhaps the most pressing is the need to learn skills that they can immediately apply in their writing for other college courses, for work, and for everyday life. To succeed, they need to see writing as "real" and connected to their experiences and goals. *Teaching Developmental Writing: Background Readings* has been designed with both students' and teachers' needs in mind. The descriptions of pedagogy and practice offered in this text show that the teaching and learning of developing writers takes place in a variety of contexts and under a variety of circumstances. *Teaching Developmental Writing: Background Readings* is one of a series of English titles published by Bedford/St. Martin's that includes extracts from professional readings. In addition to developmental writing, other books in the series include essays on teaching argument and on teaching literature, among other disciplines.

Much has changed since my work began on the first two *Background Readings* ancillaries that accompanied Anker's *Real Writing* and Kirszner and Mandell's *Writing First,* from which this book was adapted. Research and practice in the field of developmental writing have greatly expanded in the last several years. For instance, this ancillary includes a significant focus on diversity issues. There are now separate chapters entitled "Writing and Race, Class, and Gender" and "Teaching ESL." Diversity-focused articles also may be found in the new chapters entitled "Basic Writing: Student's Perspectives"; "Writing and Reading"; "Writing and Adult Learners"; and "Basic Writing and the Writing Center."

Perhaps one of the most critical questions raised by the additional chapters is: What is the purpose of the developmental writing course? A lively discussion ensues about whether students ought to be learning how to write academic discourse, learning how to develop their own writing voices and styles, or learning some combination of both of these strategies. An additional issue addressed by the selections is the impact that technology continues to make on our profession. There is recognition of the fact that access to technology is not universal and is largely dependent on stable social conditions and available economic resources. Moreover, throughout the selections in *Teaching Developmental Writing: Background Readings*, students' own writing is cited to add perspectives to teachers' classroom experiences. In this way, we can see the profound impact that pedagogy and practice may have on perhaps our most important goal: the growth and development of our students as writers and critical thinkers.

Teaching Developmental Writing: Background Readings also answers the questions that we ask every day in our work as teachers. How can we design courses that truly meet our students' needs? How do we create an environment in which a culturally diverse student body can thrive? How can we accommodate students with different learning styles? How should we approach assessment at both the classroom and institutional levels, and, perhaps most significantly, how do these issues affect our day-to-day teaching? I have selected readings that can help us address these questions, both as individual teachers and as a community, and have organized them into fourteen useful, relevant chapters. The editorial apparatus is divided into practical sections. The chapter introductions present a context for the selections and offer a range of perspectives on the issues to be discussed. The reading headnotes present the authors as practitioners and identify the most important features of the article. The "Classroom Activities" sections provide suggestions for creating classroom projects based on ideas or concepts from each reading. The "Thinking about Teaching" sections allow room for professional reflection and action, offering ideas for contributing to the professional discussions taking place in our hallways, offices, staff meetings, and elsewhere in our institutions—and in the forums of our journals, conventions, and Internet listservs. Finally, an end-of-book bibliography provides the reader with more sources of information for further reading and research.

As developmental writing teachers, we often find that our status seems marginal, outside the larger conversations taking place in the rhetoric and composition community. Moreover, the needs of our students, if not the complicated nature of our working conditions, often prove more urgent and immediate than abstract theoretical arguments. How can we create a supportive working environment for students who may be under extreme economic and personal pressures that we can only begin to imagine? How can we be effective teachers if we spend our professional lives as "freeway fliers," rushing across town and across communities to our varied and different classrooms? Although *Teaching Developmental Writing: Background Readings* does not provide easy solutions to these dilemmas, it does present a range of perspectives offered by experienced teachers and emphasizes practical approaches to the everyday problems of our classrooms and our institutions. Each article invites us to examine classroom practice and to take part in professional discussions about our students and our teaching.

Acknowledgments

At Bedford/St. Martin's, I would like to thank Chuck Christensen, President, Joan Feinberg, Editorial Director, and Karen Henry, Editor in Chief, for their commitment to providing teachers with the best possible tools for meeting the needs of their students; Denise Wydra, who first suggested this project in the spring of 1996; Michelle Clark, who carefully nurtured and served as editor of Susan Anker's *Teaching REAL WRITING: Background Readings*; Talvi Laev, who guided me through *Background Readings for Instructors Using WRITING FIRST;* and Amanda Bristow, editor of *Teaching Developmental Writing: Background Readings*, for countless discussions and critically important feedback as this major revision was shaped and reshaped.

I would also like to thank the people in my personal and professional life who continue to make an extraordinary difference: Francie Blake of the Community College of Philadelphia for her thoughtful discussions on the needs and aspirations of community college basic writing students; Linda Fellag of the Community College of Philadelphia for her critical perspective on teaching reading and writing to recent immigrants in the ESL classroom; Ann Green of St. Joseph's University in Philadelphia for her insightful work on writing and race, class, and gender and for her perspectives on the writing center as an activist site for such work; Amy Winans of Susquehanna University for her careful questions about teaching and writing; Angela Graham, who gracefully gave her first lessons on the writing process a quarter of a century ago, when she was my teacher in senior high school English, and who continues her inspired mentoring in well-earned retirement; James Wrable for invaluable insights on the subject of critical thinking; Aaron Bernstein, my brother, for good humor when it was needed most; Missy Starcher, my niece, for her encouragement and support; Elley Cormany, my late mother-in-law, for the memory of her patience and strength; my students, for all that I learn from them as we grow together as writers; and most of all, my spouse, Stephen Cormany, who, when all else fails, lends courage and inspiration for all my writing moments and more. I dedicate this revision to him with love and admiration.

SUSAN NAOMI BERNSTEIN

Contents

1 Basic Writing: Teacher's Perspectives   1

Mina Shaughnessy
Some New Approaches toward Teaching   2

"A teacher must know deeply what he is teaching—what is arbitrary or given, and what is built upon the skills the student already possesses. This is his preparation."

William B. Lalicker
**A Basic Introduction to Basic Writing Program Structures:
A Baseline and Five Alternatives**   14

"A greater understanding of the alternatives will help you determine [which model is] most suited to your [basic writing] program's theories and goals, most achievable with your institution's mission and resources, and most successful for meeting the literacy challenges of your basic writing students."

2 Basic Writing: Student's Perspectives   26

Linda Adler-Kassner
Just Writing, Basically: Basic Writers on Basic Writing   27

"Afterwards when I look at it . . . I'm, like, that wasn't what I was trying to say at all. And I try to put it in different words or I'll just try to rewrite it out later on and it just doesn't work and I'll have to sit there and I'll have to work at it for a while."

"You look at us and you think that we don't know anything. You think that teaching us how to write can't help us cause we're not going to change our lives by reading some essays. But we all want to do well in this class. Can't you just tell us what you want us to write about?"

"I decided to begin with a class-wide engagement in letter writing. Because it is short and yet a complete unit of discourse—and because it has a place in the real world of most students—writing letters seemed an auspicious way to introduce students to writing that transcended skills instruction."

"Often as instructors, we avoid assigning life writing because we fear the results may be too 'personal' to assess objectively. Yet we run the risk of shutting down an important opportunity for facilitating potentially transformative writing experiences for students in basic writing classrooms."

"One of the important ideas to be considered here is that the ability to analyze materials thoughtfully is one that grows gradually over time. In basic writing and regular composition courses we have the opportunity to give students assignments that will begin this process, allowing them to practice the more complex reasoning tasks they will be expected to handle in their upper division courses."

8 Critical Thinking   177

Richard Paul and Linda Elder

**The Elements of Critical Thinking (Helping Students
Assess Their Thinking)**   177

"There are two essential dimensions of thinking that students need to
master in order to learn how to upgrade their thinking. They need to
be able to identify the 'parts' of their thinking, and they need to be able
to assess their use of these parts of thinking...."

Stephen D. Brookfield

**Understanding Classroom Dynamics:
The Critical Incident Questionnaire**   181

"In my own teaching, [Critical Incident Questionnaires] give me good
information about students' readiness for a particular learning activity. This, in turn, helps me pace the course. CIQs also help me curb my
tendency to equate silence with mental inertia."

Glynda Hull and Mike Rose

**"This Wooden Shack Place":
The Logic of an Unconventional Reading**   189

"Specifically, we will analyze a brief stretch of discourse, one in which a
student's personal history and cultural background shape a somewhat
unconventional reading of a section of a poem. We will note the way the
mismatch plays itself out in conversation, the logic of the student's
reading and the coherent things it reveals about his history, and the
pedagogical implications of conducting a conversation that encourages
that logic to unfold."

9 Collaborative Learning   203

Richard Raymond

Building Learning Communities on Nonresidential Campuses   204

"The [following] narrative, I hope, will honestly expose the errors—
strategic and pedagogical—as well as ground our feelings of success. I
hope, too, that this story will encourage the many four- and two-year
colleges whose nonresidential campuses make learning communities
seem improbable consider developing them."

"In small peer groups, students are more inclined to ask questions and help each other clarify their thinking. After working in small groups, students are prepared to engage in more complex discussion of texts."

"Instructors variously reported that students have more confidence in their writing when using the lab and develop self-esteem by working at their own pace to accomplish writing tasks. Among other reasons cited: students respond well to computer-based instruction; working on a computer provides variety and adds interest; computer-related assignments increase student involvement with their own education."

"Although we had not properly anticipated it, electronic technology changes one's instructional habits—changes everything from the nailed-down seating arrangement to the absence of the semicircle of faces that surrounded the big desk."

"I remember being caught speaking Spanish at recess—that was good for three licks on the knuckles with a sharp ruler. I remember being sent to the corner of the classroom for 'talking back' to the Anglo teacher when all I was trying to do was tell her how to pronounce my name."

"When I first entered the multicultural, multiethnic classroom setting, I was unprepared. I did not know how to cope effectively with so much 'difference.'"

"It is time for English instructors, when faced with students from radically different cultural backgrounds and whose needs differ from those of mainstream students, to stop blaming the high failure and attrition rates solely on bilingualism, substandard schooling, low self-esteem, lack of familiarity with SAE, and/or lack of motivation—it is time to look beyond these factors and work to mitigate all the barriers that all minority culture students face."

12 Teaching ESL 276

"If the goal of ESL composition instruction is to help students become proficient writers of English, it must provide a learning environment which both allows students to gain confidence in their ability as writers and transfers the ultimate responsibility for their development as writers from teachers to students."

"As indicated by the majority of these ESL students' autobiographies, the students would like their American teachers to understand their struggle with learning the new language, literacy skills, and academic content at the same time. One way of building the understanding is for teachers to learn about the students' native language and literacy backgrounds."

13 Placement and Assessment 300

"More than many issues within the field of composition studies, writing assessment evokes strong passions."

"Teachers in ENG 098 know that the students, by their own admission, are asking for some help to get ready for college writing. No developmental writing teacher begins class with the view that the first order of business is to prove to the student that he or she was indeed placed correctly. Our best students are the ones that ask us to help them learn, and now in no other class on campus can a teacher assume with as much confidence that this is precisely what every student in the ENG 098 class wants."

"This paper, then, explores what we now see as our failure in assessing Mica's work and speculates on how we might reconceptualize the assessment of writing, particularly the writing of culturally diverse students."

"Few settings offer a richer diversity of voices as the community college writing center. If functionally healthy, the writing center provides a dynamic setting where diverse voices can be heard, varied perspectives explored, and myths about discourse and writing dispelled."

"Each week, my work in the writing center presents me with at least a couple of the dilemmas that I describe with Marcus. I have come to call them questions of autonomy and voice, since their implications go well beyond issues of 'appropriateness' or academic format."

Basic Writing: Teacher's Perspectives

What is "basic writing"? This chapter introduces you to ways in which this question has been framed by professionals in the past quarter century. We begin with Mina Shaughnessy, who defines basic writing from a teacher's perspective. Shaughnessy bases her definition on her classroom observations of urban open-admissions students in the 1970s. She is a firm believer in "buil[ding] upon the skills the student already possesses."

William B. Lalicker, writing almost twenty-five years after Shaughnessy, looks at basic writing from the point of view of a writing program administrator. His article describes the advantages and disadvantages of several program models. He urges readers to create a program that is "most achievable with your institution's mission and resources." Seen together, these two articles give readers a sense of the beginnings of basic writing as its own academic discipline — and of our discipline's future in the twenty-first century.

Some New Approaches toward Teaching[1]

Mina Shaughnessy

Many thinkers and teachers in the field of developmental writing trace their roots to the work of the late Mina Shaughnessy. Founder of the Journal of Basic Writing *(1975) and author of* Errors and Expectations *(1977), she examined the question of where it is "best to begin a course in basic writing."*

Above all, Shaughnessy stresses respect for students — building on their strengths rather than focusing exclusively on weaknesses or deficiencies. As a teacher of city college students, she weighs in with her own ideas about where to begin a course in developmental writing. She assumes that her students are not unskilled but rather inexperienced.

Teaching Basic Writing

I

The term "basic writing" implies that there is a place to begin learning to write, a foundation from which the many special forms and styles of writing rise, and that a college student must control certain skills that are common to all writing before he takes on the special demands of a biology or literature or engineering class.[1] I am not certain this is so. Some students learn how to write in strange ways. I recall one student who knew something about hospitals because she had worked as a nurse's aide. She decided, long before her sentences were under control, to do a paper on female diseases. In some way this led her to the history of medicine and then to Egypt, where she ended up reading about embalming — which became the subject of a long paper she entitled "Postmortem Care in Ancient Egypt." The paper may not have satisfied a professor of medical history, but it produced more improvement in the student's writing than any assignments I could have devised.

Perhaps if students with strong enthusiasms in special fields were allowed to exercise themselves in those fields under the guidance of professors who felt responsible for the writing as well as the reading of students, we could shorten the period of apprenticeship. But clearly this is not the way things are, and students who need extra work in writing are therefore placed in courses called Basic Writing, which are usually taught by English teachers who, as specialists themselves, are inclined to assume that the best way to teach writing is to talk about literature. If such talk will stimulate the student to write, however,

---

[1]Note that although Shaughnessy uses the referent pronoun *he* throughout the article, she herself notes that she was writing in less enlightened times. In a footnote to *Errors and Expectations,* Shaughnessy offers: "After having tried various ways of circumventing the use of the masculine pronoun in situations where women teachers and students might easily outnumber men, I have settled for the convention, but I regret that the language resists my meaning in this important respect. When the reader sees *he,* I can only hope *she* will also be there" (4).

then it will serve most students at least as well as mummies, for the answer to improved writing is writing. Everything else — imaginative writing texts, thoughtfully designed assignments, elaborate rationales for teaching writing this way or that — is merely part of the effort to get writing started and to keep it going.

There are many views on the best way to do this and there is some damning evidence piled up against some of the ways that once seemed right. Since English teachers are often considered both the victims and the perpetuators of these apparently mistaken approaches, it becomes important for them to try once in a while to think away everything except the facts and insights that their experiences with students as writers have given them.

The following pages are my effort to do this.

II

Writing is the act of creative reading. That is, it is the encoding of speech into lines of print or script that are in turn decoded into speech by a reader. To understand the nature of writing, and therefore the way writing can be learned, it is necessary to understand the connections and distinctions between speech, writing, and reading and to identify the skills that are implied in the ability to write.

For most people, speech is easy and writing is difficult; the one is inevitable, the other acquired, generally under conditions that seem to violate rather than use the natural learning abilities of people. Because of this violation, learning to write requires almost as much undoing as doing, whether one is involved with those skills implied in the encoding process itself (handwriting, spelling, and punctuation) or those skills that are carried over from speech to the page (making and ordering statements).

Beyond these two types of skills, there is an additional opportunity in writing that distinguishes it both as a skill and as a product: the opportunity to objectify a statement, to look at it, change it by additions, subtractions, substitutions or inversions, the opportunity to take time for as close and economical a "fit" as possible between the writer's meaning and the record of that meaning on the page. The typescript of a taped discussion is not, therefore, writing in this sense; it is, rather, a repetition on the page of what was spoken. And the goal in writing is not simply to repeat speech but to overcome certain disadvantages that the medium of sound imposes upon speech. (In speech, time says when you are finished; in writing, you say when you are finished.)

Writing thus produces a distinctive circuitry in which the writer continually feeds back to himself (as writer and reader) and acts upon that feedback at any point and for as long a time as he wishes before his statement is finally put into circulation. This opportunity for objectifying a statement so as to "work" on it is the distinctive opportunity of writing, and the central goal of any writing class is therefore to lead the student to an awareness of his power to make choices (semantic, syntactic, organizational) that bring him closer and closer to his intended meaning. Ideally, this opportunity should free the writer because it increases his options; it should give him pleasure because it sharpens his sense of what to say and thereby his pleasure in saying it; and it should make him feel comfortable with so-called mistakes, which are simply stages in the writing process. Unfortunately, the fact that writing can by its very nature produce a more precise and lasting statement than speech has led teachers to expect (and demand) a narrow kind of perfection which they confuse with the true goal in writing, namely, the "perfect" fit of the writer's words to his meaning. Teachers, in other words, have not only ignored the distinctive circuitry of writing — which is the only source of fullness and precision — but have often shortcircuited the writing activity by imposing themselves as a feedback. Students, on the other hand, have tended to impose upon themselves (even when bluebook essays do not) the conditions of speech, making writing a kind of one-shot affair aimed at the teacher's expectations. Students are usually surprised, for example, to see the messy manuscript of pages of famous writers. "You should see how bad a writer Richard Wright was," one of my students said after seeing a manuscript page from *Native Son*. "He made more mistakes than I do!" Somehow students have to discover that the mess is *writing;* the published book is *written.*

A writing course should help the student learn how to make his own mess, for the mess is the record of a remarkable kind of interplay between the writer as creator and the writer as reader, which serves the writer in much the same way as the ear serves the infant who is teaching himself to speak. No sooner has the writer written down what he thinks he means than he is asking himself whether he understands what he said. A writing course should reinforce and broaden this interplay, not interrupt it, so that the student can use it to generate his own criteria and not depend upon a grade to know whether he has written well. The teacher can help by designing writing situations that externalize the circuitry principle. The teacher and the class together can help by telling the writer what they think he said, thereby developing an awareness of the possibilities for meaning or confusion when someone else is the reader.

But if the student is so well equipped to teach himself to write and the teacher is simply an extension of his audience, why does he need a teacher at all? The answer is, of course, that he doesn't absolutely need a teacher to learn to write, that, in fact, remarkably few people have learned to write through teachers, that many, alas, have learned to write in spite of teachers. The writing teacher has but one simple advantage to offer: he can save the student time, and time is important to students who are trying to make up for what got lost in high school and grade school.

To help in even this limited way, a teacher must know what skills are implied in the ability to write what is called basic English and he must understand the nature of the difficulties students seem to have with each of them. The following list is a move in that direction.

HANDWRITING   The student has to have enough skill at writing to take down his own dictations without getting distracted by the muscular coordination writing requires. If a student has done very little writing in high school, which is often the case, he may need to exercise his writing muscles. This is a quantitative matter — the more of anything he copies, the better the coordination. Malcolm X's exercise of copying the dictionary may not be inspiring enough for many students, but if a student keeps copying something, his handwriting will begin to belong to him. Until then, he is likely to have his problems with handwriting mistaken for problems with writing.

SPELLING AND PUNCTUATION   To write fluently, a student must feel reasonably comfortable about getting the words and punctuation down right, or he must learn to suspend his concern over correctness until he is ready to proofread. If he is a bad speller, chances are he knows it and will become so preoccupied with correctness that he will constantly lose his thought in order to find the right letters, or he will circumlocute in order to avoid words he can't spell. A number of students enter our classes every semester so handicapped by misspelling and generally so ineffectively taught by us that they are almost certain not to get out of basic writing. It is a problem neither we nor the reading teachers have willingly claimed, but it presses for a solution. The computer, which seems to hold great promise for misspellers, is still a laboratory. The Fidel chart, so successfully used by Dr. Gattegno in teaching children and illiterate adults to read, has not yet been extensively tried in college programs such as ours.[2]

Students are generally taught to think of punctuation as the scribal translation of oral phrasing and intonation. Some students have, in fact, been taught to put commas where they breathe. As a translation of voice pauses and intonations, however, punctuation is quite crude and almost impossible to learn. Commas can produce as long a pause as a period, and how much time does a semicolon occupy? Most students solve the problem by working out a private punctuation system or by memorizing a few "rules" that often get them into more trouble than they are worth (like always putting a comma before "and").

In the end, it is more economical for the student to learn to translate punctuation marks into their conventional meaning and to recognize that while there are stylistic choices in punctuating, even these choices are related to a system of signs that signal grammatical (or structural) information more accurately than vocal spacing and intonation. The marks of punctuation can in fact be studied in isolation from words, as signals that prepare a reader for certain types of constructions. Whether these constructions are given their grammatical names is not important, but it is important that a student be able to reconstruct from a passage such as the following the types of constructions he — and other readers — would expect:

Sentence fragments, run-ons, and comma splices are mistranslations of punctuation marks. They can occur only in writing and can be understood once the student understands the structures they signal. This suggests that punctuation marks should not be studied in isolation from the structural units they signal. For example, when the student is experimenting with the ways in which information can be added to a subject without creating a new sentence (adjectival functions), it is a good time to look at the serial comma, the appositional commas, and the comma in the nonrestrictive clause.

MAKING SENTENCES   An English-speaking student is already a maker of statements that not only sound like English but sound like him. Because he has spoken so many more years of sentences than he has written, however, there is a gap between what he can say and what he can write. Sometimes the writing down of sentences is in fact such a labor that he loses his connection with English and produces a tangle of phrases he would never speak. Such a student does not need to learn how to make statements but how to write them at least as well as he speaks them. Other students with foreign-language interferences may have to work on English sentence structure itself, but even here their speech is doubtless ahead of their pens. Learning to write statements, therefore, is at first a matter of getting the ear to "hear" script. Later, when the writer wants to exploit the advantages that writing has over speech, the advantage of polishing and perfecting, he may write things he would not be likely to say, but this happens after his pen has caught up with his voice. Students who have little confidence in their voice, or at least in the teacher's response to that voice, have often gone to a great deal of trouble to superimpose another voice upon their writing — sometimes it represents the student's version of a textbook voice; sometimes it is Biblical; sometimes it is a business letter voice — but almost always it seems to keep the writer from understanding clearly what he wants to say. The following sentence, which seems to be a version of the textbook voice, illustrates the kind of entanglement that can result:

> In a broad sense admittance to the SEEK program will serve as a basis of education for me in terms of enlightenment on the tedious time and effort which one must put into all of his endeavors.

A student will usually not abandon this acquired voice until he begins to recognize his own voice and sees that it is safe to prefer it.

There is another skill with sentences which affects the quality of a student's theme as well as his sentences. It involves his ability to "mess" with sentences, to become sensitive to the questions that are embedded in sentences which, when answered, can produce modifications within the sentence or can expand into paragraphs or entire essays. It involves his awareness of the choices he has in casting sentences, of styles in sentences. As Francis Christensen has illustrated in *Notes toward a New Rhetoric,*[3] the sentence is the microcosm. Whatever the writer does in the sentence when he modifies is in principle what he does in paragraphs and essays. The principle of coordination and subordination can be learned there. The foundation of a paragraph, a chapter, a book is there. It is tempting to say that a student who knows his way around the sentence can get anyplace in writing. And knowing his way means working on his own sentences, not so much to polish them as to see how much of his meaning they can hold.

But for many students, putting sentences on a page seems a little like carving something on stone: an error cannot be ignored or skimmed over as it can be in speech. It is there forever. "Everything has to be exactly right," explained one of my students, "and that makes me nervous." The page disconnects the student from his product, which will appear alone, before strange eyes, or worse, before the eyes of an English teacher who is a specialist at finding mistakes. To make matters worse, most students feel highly mistake-prone about sentences. They half remember prohibitions about beginning with certain words, but they aren't certain of which words or why (probably the result of lessons on sentence fragments). In short, they feel they are about to commit a verbal sin but they aren't certain what sin it is. In such a situation, it seems safer to keep still. It is not unusual to have students at the beginning of the semester who sit through several class periods without writing a word, and when they explain that they don't know how to begin, they are not saying they don't have an idea. They are saying they are not certain which are the "safe" words to begin with.

Students who become observers of sentences and experimenters with sentences lose their fear of them. This experimentation can take many forms. Sentences can be examined as if they were separate compositions. A sentence such as the following by Richard Wright can be written on the board without reference to its context:

> Those brave ones who struggle against death are the ones who bring new life into the world, even though they die to do so, even though our hearts are broken when they die.

Students can talk about the way the sentence is built; they can try to imitate it or change it; or they can try to build a paragraph by expanding some part of it.

There is a kind of carpentry in sentence making, various ways of joining or hooking up modifying units to the base sentence. Suffixes added to make adjectives or adverbs, prepositions, "wh" words like where, when, who, which, etc., the double commas used in appositional constructions — all of these can be seen as hooking devices that preserve us from the tedium of Dick-and-Jane sentences. As a form of sentence-play, students can try to write fifty- or one hundred-word sentences that contain only one independent clause. Once discovering they can do it, they usually lose their inhibitions about "real" sentences. Some even move from carpentry to architecture. This sentence was written by a student who was asked in an exam to add information to the predicate of the sentence: "The problem will be solved."

> The problem will be solved with the help of the Almighty, who, except for an occasional thunderstorm, reigns unmolested, high in the heavens above, when all of us, regardless of race or religious differences, can come together and study this severe problem inside out, all day and all night if necessary, and are able to come to you on that great gettin' up morning and say, "Mrs. Shaughnessy, we do know our verbs and adverbs."

ORDERING SENTENCES   Order is an arrangement of units that enables us to see them as parts of something larger. The sense of orientation that results from this arrangement creates a pleasure we call understanding. Perhaps because writing isolates a reader from everything except the page, whereas speech is supported by other gestures and by the right of the audience to query and disagree, we seem to be more tolerant of "disorder" (no clear pattern) in speech than in writing. The talker is not, therefore, committed to knowing where he is going in quite the way that a writer is although he often gets someplace in a way that turns out to have order to it. The writer, however, puts himself on the line, announcing where he is going to go before he sees how he is going to get there. He has to move in two directions at the same time — ahead, point by point toward a destination he has announced but never been to, and down, below the surface of his points to see what they are about. Sometimes, having decided on or having been given an overall arrangement (or plan) that seems a sensible route to where he is going, the writer hesitates to leave the security of this plan to explore the parts of his paper. Result: a tight, well-ordered but empty paper. At other times, the writer stops to explore one point and never gets back because he cannot get control over the generating force of sentences, which will create branches off branches off branches unless the writer cuts them off. Result: a wilderness.

The skill of organizing seems to require a kind of balance between the demand that a piece of writing get someplace along a route that is sufficiently marked for a reader to follow and the demand that there be freedom for the writer to explore his subject and follow where his questions and inventions take him. The achievement of this balance produces much of the "mess" in writing. Often, however, teachers stress the "administrative" aspects of writing (direction and procedure) over the generative or even assume that the generative is not a part of the organizing skill. This assumption in turn seems to lead to the formulation of organizational patterns in isolation from content (pyramids, upside-down pyramids, etc.) and the efforts to get students to squeeze their theme materials into these patterns. I do not mean to say that restrictions or limits in writing are necessarily inhibiting. They can be both stimulating and liberating, as the sonnet illustrates. But the restrictions I speak of here merely hint at forms they are unable to generate, leaving the reader with the feeling that there is a blank to be filled in but with no sense of how to do it.

Because of this isolation of form from content, students have come to think of organization as something special that happens in themes but not in themselves, daily, as they think or talk. They do not notice that they usually "talk" a better-organized paper than they write, that they use illustrations, anticipate questions, repeat thematic points more effectively in conversation than in writing, whereas the conscious effort to organize a theme often cuts them off from the real content of the theme, giving them all the organizational signposts but no place to go. In talking, they are evolving order; in writing, they often feel they must impose it.

This is not to say that developing a paper is as easy as talking but simply that the difficulty lies not in fitting an amount of raw content into a prefabricated frame but in evoking and controlling the generating power of statement. Every sentence bears within it a new set of possibilities. Sometimes the writer chooses to develop these possibilities; sometimes he prefers to let them lie. Sometimes he decides to develop them fully; at other times, only slightly. Thus each step in the development of a base or thesis statement must inevitably send the writer into a wilderness of possibilities, into a fecundity as dense and multiform as thought itself. One cannot be said to have had an idea until he has made his way through this maze. Order is the pattern of his choices, the path he makes going through.

The initial blocking out of a paper, the plan for it, is a kind of hypothesis which allows the writer to proceed with his investigation. Any technique of organization, however, that ignores the wilderness, that limits the freedom of the writer to see and make choices at every step, to move ahead at times without knowing for certain which is north and south, then to drop back again and pick up the old path, and finally to get where he is going, partly by conscious effort but also by some faculty of intellection that is too complex to understand — any technique that sacrifices this fullest possible play of the mind for the security of an outline or some other prefabricated frame cuts the student off from his most productive thinking. He must be allowed something of a frontier mentality, an overall commitment, perhaps, to get to California, but a readiness, all along the way, to choose alternative routes and even to sojourn at unexpected places when that seems wise or important, sometimes, even, to decide that California isn't what the writer really had in mind.

The main reason for failure in the writing proficiency test at City College, a test given to all upperclassmen, has not been grammar or mechanics but the inability to get below the surface of a topic, to treat a topic in depth. The same problem arises in bluebook essays. It is the familiar complaint of students: "I can't think of anything more to say." They are telling us that they do not have access to their thoughts when they write. A part of this difficulty may be related to the way they have learned to write. And a part of the answers may lie in our designing assignments that make the student conscious of what the exploration of an idea is and how this exploration relates to organization.

GRAMMATICAL CORRECTNESS Correctness involves those areas of a dialect where there are no choices. (The "s" on the present tense third-person singular is correct in standard English; the use of a plural verb with the subject "none" is a choice; the comparison "more handsome" is a choice but "more intelligenter" is incorrect.) Native speakers of a dialect are not concerned with correctness; they unconsciously say things the correct way. Non-native speakers of a dialect must consciously acquire the "givens" if they want to communicate without static in that dialect. This is a linguistic fact that seems at the outset to put speakers of a nonstandard dialect at a disadvantage. But it is a strange logic that says having access to one dialect is better than having access to two, particularly when we know that every dialect or language system sets limits on the ways we can perceive and talk about the world.

Unfortunately, this is not the way speakers of other dialects have been encouraged to think about their dialects, with the result that writing classes and writing teachers seem to put them at a disadvantage, creating either an obsessive concern with correctness or a fatalistic indifference to it. The only thing that can help the student overcome such feelings is to help him gain control over the dialect. It is irresponsible to tell him that correctness is not important; it is difficult to persuade him after years of indoctrination to the contrary that "correctness" plays a subordinate role in good writing; but it is not impossible to give him the information and practice he needs to manage his own proofreading.

The information will inevitably be grammatical, whether the terminology of grammar is used or not. But it is more important to remember that the student who is not at home with standard English has most likely had several doses of grammar already and it hasn't worked. For reasons that he himself doesn't quite understand, the explanations about things like the third-person "s" or the agreement of subject and verb haven't taken. He is not deliberately trying to make mistakes but for some reason they keep happening. What he often does not realize, and what the teacher has to realize is that his difficulties arise from his *mastery* of one language or dialect, and that changing to another often involves at certain points a loss or conflict of meaning and therefore difficulty in learning, not because he is stubborn or dumb or verbally impoverished but because he expects language to make sense. (The student, for example, who finally told me he *couldn't* use "are" to mean something in the present because it was too stiff and formal and therefore faraway, and the Chinese student who could not make a plural out of sunrise because there is only one sun, were both trying to hold on to meaning, as Will James, the cowboy author, was when he continued to use "seen" for the past tense because it meant seeing farther than "saw.")

These are obviously grammatical matters, but this does not mean they require the traditional study of grammar. The question of what they do require is widely debated. Certainly it should be apparent that teachers working with students who have black dialect or Spanish or Chinese or some other language background should be familiar with the features of those languages that are influencing their students' work in Standard English. This should be part of the general equipment of us all as teachers. And the new insights that come from the linguists should also be ours. But none of this information will be of much use if we simply make pronouncements about it in class. Students cannot be expected to get more help from memorizing two grammatical systems instead of one, and the diagrams in transformational grammar are still diagrams. The acquisition of new information will not automatically make us better teachers. To make this happen, we need to develop a sharp sense of the difference between talking and teaching. We need to design lessons that highlight the grammatical characteristics of a dialect so that the student can discover them for himself. (It is one thing to tell a student about the "s" in the third-person present singular; it is another for him to discover the power of that schizophrenic letter which clings so irrationally to its last verb to mark its singularity while it attaches itself to nouns to mark their plurality, and then, confusing things further, acquires an apostrophe and marks the singular possessive.) We need to devise ways of practicing that the student enjoys because he is able to invent rather than memorize answers. We need, finally, to teach proofreading as a separate skill that uses the eye in a different way from reading and places the burden of correctness where it belongs — at the end of (rather than during) the writing process. To do things for the student that he can do himself is not generosity but impatience. It is hard work for a teacher not to talk, but we must now be very industrious if we want our students to learn what we have to teach.

III

I have been speaking about the skills that seem basic to writing, but basic writing courses that prepare students for college writing are actually concerned with a rather special kind of prose called exposition, a semiformal analytical prose in which the connections between sentences and paragraphs surface in the form of conjunctive adverbs and transitional sentences. More simply, it means the kind of writing teachers got B's and A's for in college, a style whose characteristics they have now internalized and called a standard.

Teachers of basic writing are thus responsible for helping their students learn to write in an expository style. They must also give them practice in writing to specification (i.e., on a special topic or question and in a certain form) since many assignments require it. The question of how to reach such objectives and at the same time give each student a chance to discover other things about writing and about his individual powers as a writer troubles many teachers and creates many different "positions." Where, for example, on the following list, ranging from highly controlled to free assignments, it is best to begin a course in basic writing:

1. paraphrase

2. summary

3. exegesis of a passage

4. theme in which topic sentence and organizational pattern are given

5. theme in which topic sentence is given (includes the examination question which is usually an inverted topic sentence)

6. theme in which subject is given

7. theme in which form is given — description, dialogue, argument, etc.

8. theme in which only the physical conditions for writing are given — journal, free writing, etc.

Teachers take sides on such a question, some insisting that freedom in anything, including writing, cannot exist until there is control and that this comes through the step-by-step mastery of highly structured assignments; others insist that students must begin not with controls but with materials — the things they have already seen or felt or imagined — and evolve their own controls as they try to translate experience into writing. Meanwhile students confuse the issue by learning to write and not learning to write under almost all approaches. I prefer to start around #7, with description. But then, I have to remember the student who started a research paper on mummies before she could manage her sentences. "Positions" on curriculae and methods are somehow always too neat to say much about learning, which seems to be sloppy. They tend to be generalizations about students, not about the nature of the skills that have to be mastered, and the only generalization that seems safe to make about students is the one they persistently make about themselves — that they are individuals, not types, and that the way to each student's development is a way the teacher has never taken before. Everything about the teacher-student encounter should encourage a respect for this fact of individuality even though the conditions under which we must teach in large institutions often obscure it. Books do have to be ordered and teachers do have to make plans. But perhaps the plans need not be so well laid that they cannot go awry when the signals point that way. A teacher must know deeply what it is he is teaching — what is arbitrary or given and what is built upon skills the student already possesses. This is his preparation. But he cannot know about his student until both meet in the classroom. Then teaching becomes what one student described as "simply two people learning from each other."

In the confusion of information on methods and curriculae that comes to us from publishers — and from each other — it is probably important to emphasize this single truth.

Notes

1. Reprinted by permission from *A Guide for Teachers of College English* (New York: Office of Academic Development, CUNY, 1970).
2. Caleb Gattegno, *Teaching Reading with Words in Color* (Educational Solutions, Inc., New York, 1968).
3. Francis Christensen, *Notes toward a New Rhetoric* (New York, Harper & Row, 1967).

Classroom Activities

Have students generate lists of three to five rules that they have learned about writing (this may be done individually or in small groups). Then compile the separate lists into one long list that will be distributed to the entire class. You may wish to use the following questions as a starting point for class discussion:

- Is there more than one way of stating the same rule?
- Are some rules more difficult to understand than others?
- Which of the rules seem contradictory?
- Which rules seem helpful?
- Are there writing situations in which these rules may be broken?
- What are the consequences of breaking the rules?
- What are the choices that writers can make about how to compose their writing?

Thinking about Teaching

As you read the essays in *Teaching Developmental Writing: Background Readings,* you are encouraged to keep a journal to record your reactions to the readings and to write down student responses to class activities. Think about sharing your journal entries with other teachers — and especially with your students. The pedagogy that Shaughnessy advocates implies engaged involvement between students and teacher. Journaling with your students can be an important means of creating an engaged classroom.

Record your impressions of your students' responses to the above activity. Were you surprised by their lists or by the discussion of rules? What ideas from the lists or from the discussion can you use in class?

Shaughnessy, writing in the mid-1970s, lists the following skills as critical for "the ability to write what is called basic English": spelling and punctuation, making sentences, ordering sentences, and grammatical correctness. Can you think of any others (some examples might be keyboarding and awareness of audience and purpose)? Are there any skills that you would eliminate or revise from Shaughnessy's list? What has changed since Shaughnessy first wrote this article?

Shaughnessy suggests that one way of answering the question of where it "is best to begin a course in basic writing" may be for teachers to evolve a working metaphor of their own practice. "There is a kind of carpentry in sentence making," Shaughnessy writes, "various ways of joining or hooking up modifying units to the base sentence." What metaphors would you use for your own practice of writing and of teaching writing? Why do you find those metaphors particularly helpful or descriptive?

A Basic Introduction to Basic Writing Program Structures: A Baseline and Five Alternatives

William B. Lalicker

William B. Lalicker is the Director of the Composition Program at West Chester University and is involved with the Philadelphia Writing Program Administrators. In 1999, Lalicker conducted a survey on the Writing Program Administrators' listserv in order to determine the different kinds of basic writing program models at a variety of institutions. From these results, he was able to describe a "baseline" model of a basic writing program and five "alternative" models. He listed the advantages and disadvantages of each model, as well as such important features as credit status, placement, and grading. These descriptions give

*us a sense of the variety and scope of the programs in place and the
program options available at various institutions.*

In January 1999, I conducted a brief survey of writing program administrators to determine the alternative structures for basic writing programs. My query on the Writing Program Administrators listserv
asked respondents to identify their basic writing program structures
according to five models I'd identified from a general search of scholarship on the subject. Respondents not only described their basic writing
programs as variants of the five models; they provided useful insights
concerning the advantages and disadvantages of each model in their
specific institutional contexts. (Examples of basic writing programs
herein, when not otherwise cited, are taken from that listserv survey.)
The following is a summary, a kind of primer, about those models and
their features.

Although the appropriateness of each model relies strongly on a
combination of site-specific conditions such as the institution's mission, its demographics, and its resources, no pattern emerged linked to
the generic type of college or university in question. Institutions of every type have developmental writing programs. One might expect research universities, comprehensive state universities, liberal arts colleges, and community colleges to favor particular models according to
institutional type, but such seemed not to be the case. Individual institutional needs — and, possibly, the theoretical or epistemological assumptions driving the writing program — seemed to be a stronger determinant.

Basic writing program directors, then, should be able to borrow
from a range of structural alternatives in designing the best possible
program for their students. The introduction below will begin by describing a baseline approach — the "prerequisite" model. (Since critiques
of this model, especially of its placement and grading systems, are pro-
lific in basic writing journals, I will refrain from extensive analysis
and will simply describe this system in order to provide a starting point
for comparing the alternatives.) I will use a parallel descriptive structure to sketch the key features of alternative approaches.

Baseline: The Prerequisite Model

- *Description:* This is the "current-traditional" approach to basic
  writing. This model assumes that basic writers are provisionally
  allowed to enter college despite literacy abilities that are sub-
  college-level. Writers may earn their way into the college-worthy
  elite (signified by admission to standard composition) by successfully completing the basic writing course; the course frequently
  focuses more on grammatical conformity than on rhetorical
  sophistication. Many institutions have used this model for
  decades. Some examples of this model still rely on grammar-drill

workbooks and limit the scope of student writing to the paragraph level; others attempt to apply more progressive rhetorical theory within a structure unchangeable due to local political or budgetary limitations.

- *Credit status:* The prerequisite model carries with it the assumption that basic writing isn't really "college-level" writing. Although this assumption seldom if ever prevents the college or university from collecting tuition for the course, it usually prevents the institution from awarding college credit. Typically, the three credit hours of the basic writing course are allowed to count toward full-time enrollment status for a student's financial aid qualification, but do not count toward the number of credit hours required for a degree, and do not count as part of the general education core.

- *Placement:* Initial placement is usually determined by locally decided threshold scores on a standardized national examination (ACT-English, SAT Verbal, or infrequently the Nelson-Denny test). A locally developed writing examination — usually a short, timed, impromptu, no-revision-allowed essay — administered near the start of classes may influence placement. Although the timed impromptu essay has its champions (see White), most in the field find alternatives preferable (see Harrington). More rarely, a portfolio of writing solicited as part of the admissions application, or high school grades, may also be used. (For two useful surveys of the most common approaches to placement, see Huot, and Murphy et al.)

- *Grading:* Students may earn a grade on the regular A-through-F four-point scale, or may take the course pass-fail. Grading may be affected by a heavily weighted exit examination, sometimes a test of isolated grammatical questions. Additionally, a number of institutions dictate a higher minimum passing grade: if D is the minimum passing grade in most (that is, "college-level") courses, a C may be the minimum grade for a student to complete the basic writing prerequisite and continue to standard general-education composition.

- *Advantages:* This system can be simple to administer and staff, due to its compatibility with standardized placement, mechanical grammar drill, and Scantron-ready exit exams. Depending on the degree of mechanical standardization in the placement and exit exam practices, this system may be inexpensive to provide. Moreover, it powerfully refutes accusations of grade inflation and general mollycoddling of underprepared students. (Some educators and politicians apparently see this as a "tough love" system: applying this basic writing hazing, we'll have done our students the good service of preparing them for the rigors of academic discourse.)

- *Disadvantages:* Stigmatizing elements of system, and arbitrary-appearing placement and exit exams, can raise resentment in students and parents. Lack of graduation and general education credit raises similar resentments. Outcomes of this approach to basic writing may not be theoretically or epistemologically compatible with outcomes being assessed for the composition program as a whole, especially if the composition program is driven by progressive rhetorical theory.

Alternative 1: The Stretch Model

- *Description:* "Stretch" programs serve basic writers by allowing them to complete a typical introductory standard composition course over two semesters instead of one. After taking this two-semester version of English 101, students take other general-education writing courses as required by the institution's standard curriculum. The stretch program might be numbered as, for instance, ENG 100 and ENG 101, retaining the standard composition course number but adding a prerequisite for some students (the system at Arizona State University, a prominent stretch model). Alternatively, it might be numbered, for example, ENG 99 and ENG 100, with the two courses together carrying general education credit equal to (and substituting for) ENG 101. Some stretch models structure the course as a truly integrated one-year version of introductory composition; others make the basic writing course a discrete prerequisite for standard composition, but allow that prerequisite to carry general-education, elective, or graduation credit.

- *Credit status:* A stretch sequence typically carries general-education credit — but requires students to have three additional composition credit hours compared to students not in the developmental sequence.

- *Placement:* Standard placement methods (SAT Verbal score, writing exam, entrance portfolio, or sometimes pre-enrollment writing sample or high school grade).

- *Grading:* Standard options — may be regular grade; may be pass-fail; or first course in sequence may be pass-fail, with second course being regular grade (to keep number of regular-grade general education credit hours equal for basic writers and nonbasic writers).

- *Advantages:* Number of credit hours and resources devoted to composition remains essentially unchanged from system in which some students are required to take a basic writing prerequisite to standard composition. Faculty roles, number of faculty credit hours taught, and general logistics remain the same as in the baseline programs. Moreover, more faculty may be willing to teach the basic writing course once it's declared 100-level and credit-bearing, since some faculty (like some students) bring a sense of stigma or fear to any course called 0-level. Placement methods are flexible; options are essentially the same as for any other model. Not only students and faculty, but also parents, may find less stigma when starting with general-education credit-bearing, 100-level courses. In the stretch model, all students begin English Comp as university students — members of the academic community — rather than as nonqualifying, 0-level, pre-college-level outsiders. Yet basic writing students get the extra practice they need. Basic writing students begin work on the same general-education objectives as standard comp students, but have more time to reach those outcomes.

- *Disadvantages:* Simply renaming ENG 099 as ENG 100, and then requiring basic writing students to take ENG 101, doesn't necessarily change the substance and perception of a course that is often ghettoized and stigmatized. Also, students are required to earn three additional credit hours to graduate, compared with students not in the basic writing sequence. Although additional required credit hours are a feature of almost any basic writing model, the promotion of basic writing to credit-bearing status in the stretch (or any) model doesn't prevent basic writers (or their parents) from resenting that requirement, especially if it means extra tuition to pay. And a credit-bearing basic writing course may be illegal in states where legislators (or in institutions where administrators) mandate an absolute requirement that students with low SAT, ACT, or Nelson-Denny scores take 0-level courses.

Alternative 2: The Studio Model

- *Description:* A "studio" program typically allows all students to begin their general-education English Composition in the standard comp course, but places certain students in small required group sessions to supplement the work in that standard course. The studio course runs concurrently with the standard comp course and may have the same instructor, a different instructor, or may use teaching assistants or Writing Center tutors. Studio sessions, consisting of six or eight students, discuss grammatical and rhetorical issues from the composition course and do writing workshops to improve the essay drafts assigned in the standard course.

- *Credit status:* Regular general-education credit, although typically the course earns only one credit hour. May be analogous to a science "lab section" — a fourth credit hour added to a three-hour course.

- *Placement:* At the institution that initiated the studio model (the University of South Carolina), students are placed by recommendation of their composition instructors during the second week of the standard comp course. Instructors use two student writing assignments, plus portfolios of writing submitted upon university admission, to decide whether students are assigned to a studio. Some students self-select the studio to improve their skills. However, students might be placed in the studio course by any of the standard methods (SAT Verbal score, or locally designed writing examination, for instance).

- *Grading:* Studio sections are usually (but not necessarily) pass-fail; work in the studio section is assumed to influence the comp course grade indirectly (work in studio section leads to better work and a higher grade in the comp course).

- *Advantages:* Studio sections can mitigate stigma by allowing students to get general-education credit and take standard composition concurrently with raising ability levels for basic writers; many parents and students currently complain that taking basic writing before standard comp (the prerequisite approach) puts them "behind schedule" toward graduation. The studio model unites the curriculum of basic and standard comp: the writing outcomes of basic writers and standard comp are the same, with assessment in the comp section only. This enforces the notion that basic and standard composition students are all working equally and collaboratively toward fluency in academic discourse and critical discourse consciousness (rather than segregating basic writers in a simplistic linguistic world where grammatical conformity dominates). According to Grego and Thompson of the University of South Carolina, "the Studio program gives body and voice to a part of the academic institution which is working to see the personal and interpersonal aspects of learning as part of the 'thinking' that constitutes academic discourse" (81).

- *Disadvantages:* At some institutions, it could be logistically tricky for the registrar to allow students to enroll in a class two weeks into a semester. (Presemester placement, as in the intensive model described below, would solve this problem, albeit with the reintroduction of some stigma and stress for parents and students.) If the studio course is one credit hour, this will significantly reduce (by two-thirds) the number of credit hours generated now by basic writing (reducing course-generated income that supports faculty and programs — an issue in some departments). Studio sections might cost more than the three-hour-requirement system on a per-student basis if the three-hour basic writing course section is larger than eighteen. (An instructor in the studio model teaches only eighteen students if there are six students per studio; but if an instructor teaches three eight-student studio sections, the total of twenty-four students is larger than most basic writing three-credit sections.) The studio system places heavy responsibility for placement on instructors, if the South Carolina placement system is adopted. (This isn't necessarily bad; as Susanmarie Harrington notes concerning placement, "The newer models rely on teacher expertise to sort students into appropriate courses" [53]; William Smith defends this approach based on his experience at the University of Pittsburgh [142–205]. But I tend to share the view of Richard Haswell and Susan Wyche-Smith, whose work with the system at Washington State University leads them to emphasize the care and training such instructor-reliant placement requires [204–07].) Finally, the studio model may not be an option where non-credit-bearing "remedial" writing is required based on entrance test score or other placement measures.

Alternative 3: The Directed Self-Placement Model

- *Description:* "Directed Self-Placement" might be called "Basic Optional": advisors and the writing program administrator (or basic writing director) suggest or persuade, rather than require, designated students to start with basic writing rather than standard English Comp. In fact, directed self-placement isn't really a model in the structural sense: it can be used with a wide variety of course and credit arrangements. But the attitudinal change it seeks to foster in students — that basic writing is something students choose because they know they need it, rather than something forced upon them — may make a number of creative and effective course structure alternatives politically possible, even palatable, in the eyes of some constituencies (students, parents, faculty, administrators). (See Royer and Gilles for a complete description of the model and its effects at Grand Valley State University.)

- *Credit status:* At Grand Valley State University (Michigan), which has pioneered this model, students may choose to take ENG 098, a three-credit-hour, non-general-education-credit course. Programs have the option of using this model with 100-level elective basic writing courses offering general education credit.

- *Placement:* The writing program administrator at Grand Valley State addresses an assembly of all incoming students during orientation, directing them to respond for themselves on key statements defining their literacy levels. Students consider statements such as "I read newspapers and magazines regularly." "In high school, I wrote several essays per year," and "My ACT-English score was above 20" (analogous to "My SAT Verbal score was above 490"). Then, for students who answer "No" to the questions, he makes the case for ENG 098 instead of standard comp, and students sign up for the course in which they believe they belong.

- *Grading:* The basic writing course may be traditionally graded or pass-fail.

- *Advantages:* Students take responsibility for their own literacy — and for their own placement in English Composition. This may lead students to resent their placement less, and to motivate themselves more energetically in whatever writing course they choose. Placement is less expensive and time-consuming: no local testing systems or portfolio assessment necessary. As the subtitle of the Royer and Gilles article concludes, "Directed Self-Placement Pleases Everyone Involved" (65).

- *Disadvantages:* Although Grand Valley State's conclusion is that the students who should have been taking developmental comp all along tended to place themselves in it, there is the possibility that some students who would benefit from the developmental course would avoid basic writing. Some students may self-place inaccurately, be overwhelmed by early academic expectations, and perform more poorly in standard comp and other university writing tasks. If self-directed placement leads to significantly fewer basic writing sections, a loss of income-generating credit hours or critical program mass may lead to a marginalized program without resources to serve its constituency. Directed self-placement may depend upon an enhanced Writing Center (and a commitment to an enhanced Writing Center budget) to provide support to students who might receive extra instruction through basic writing but are placed in standard comp. Finally, the "optional" quality of self-directed placement may not be legal in states where legislators (or campus administrators) mandate placement in "pre-college-level" writing based on test scores or other standardized measures.

Alternative 4: The Intensive Model

- *Description:* The "intensive" model offers two kinds of standard composition sections: the regular sections, plus "intensive" sections that include additional instruction time or writing activities tailored for basic writers. To some degree, the intensive model is a variation on the studio model, usually differing from the standard studio model in two ways. First, in intensive-model basic writing, students start in special intensive composition sections from the first day of classes, based on common placement methods such as test scores or portfolio ratings. Second, in the intensive model, students usually are part of one five-credit class group, while in the studio model, students from several different sections of standard composition come together at random in the studio lab sections; each structure leads to different pedagogical possibilities.

- *Credit hours:* Intensive sections of comp generally offer five credit hours for the course, rather than the standard three-credit-hour sections. All sections — intensive and standard — carry general-education credit.

- *Placement:* Any placement system may be used; institutions presently using the intensive system tend to use SAT Verbal scores for placement.

- *Grading:* Students in intensive sections get regular grades, counting for five credit hours for the initial general-education composition course, rather than the standard three credit hours.

- *Advantages:* Writing program administrators at two of the noted programs using this system (Illinois State University and Quinnipiac College) endorse the intensive model; Mary T. Segall says that the intensive model has removed the basic-writing stigma and increased motivation (38–47). The system also may remove the complaint about prerequisite basic writing delaying the start of general-education comp, may integrate students into mainstream academic writing situations more quickly, and may help unify basic writing and English Comp writing standards and assessment outcomes. Students who are part of a unified classroom group for all of the work that five credit hours implies may find it easier to collaborate with the stable community of student-colleagues. The two-credit-hours' worth of added work in each intensive section is focused on the tasks of one course section (unlike in the studio system, where studio work may include students comparing perspectives from slightly differing course sections).

- *Disadvantages:* In a five-credit-hour system, one-third fewer credit hours would be generated by basic writing than are generated in a prerequisite basic writing system (with possible budgetary consequences). Five-credit courses might be logistically tricky to work into instructors' nine- or twelve-credit-hour loads (and adjunct faculty at many institutions are paid by three-credit-hour course), necessitating some special prorated pay arrangements or overtime salary. If credit is awarded for intensive courses, this policy may violate state or institutional mandates that low-performing entrants take non-credit-bearing "remedial" writing.

Alternative 5: The Mainstreaming Model

- *Description:* "Mainstreaming" essentially eliminates basic writing classes and puts all students, no matter what their apparent writing ability, into standard comp classes. Students address deficiencies in their writing through their own initiative in the Writing Center or use other tutoring options (including increased one-on-one help from professors in conferences).

- *Credit:* Regular general-education credit — basic writers take standard composition.

- *Placement:* No placement into basic writing necessary.

- *Grading:* Same as in standard composition.

- *Advantages:* "Mainstreaming" — teaching special needs students (in this case, basic writers) in standard classes — has been championed in many levels of education for social reasons, mainly the elimination of the "outsider" status of a segment of the student population. Some mainstreaming schools (such as the City College of New York) adopted mainstreaming for the philosophical view that all students should be part of a united community without stigmatized segments (before the CCNY trustees eliminated basic writing in an anti-remedial-education move). In practical terms, there is some evidence that mainstreamed students improve their writing faster when immersed in the higher-level academic discourse of the standard comp class. Some institutions (such as Essex Community College in Maryland) claim that basic writers placed in basic writing classes are ultimately less successful in college writing tasks than basic writers who skip basic writing and go into standard comp (Adams 22–36) (although this may be an argument for "directed self-placement" rather than mainstreaming). Mainstreaming eliminates costs of basic writing placement.

- *Disadvantages:* Some basic writing students might find them-selves overtaxed in standard comp classes, with possible conse-quences ranging from poorer overall student writing performance to decreased retention and graduation. Instructors in standard comp classes would need to be prepared to do more diagnostic work and one-on-one tutoring. Mary Soliday and Barbara Gleason at CCNY warn that mainstreaming requires increased tutoring support and faculty development to meet the needs of basic writers (22–36). Inadequately supported Writing Centers would likely be overwhelmed by demand for service, and might need increased and sustained resources. Alternatively, the regular general-education comp courses might have to lower established standards and expected outcomes, or be revised with an eye toward what has been basic writing instruction (possibly serving basic writers adequately, but more prepared writers less appropriately than under the status quo). Mainstreaming would mean the elimination of basic writing; in some cases, this may mean the elimination of basic writers, especially in jurisdictions where basic writing is mandated for low-scoring students — a violation of many institutions' missions to serve disadvantaged populations or broad regional needs. In some systems, mainstreaming means the loss of budgetary dollars generated by basic writing credit hours (erstwhile basic writing students would be taking three fewer credit hours).

Which model should you adopt? Should you copy the key features of a typical system as described here, or design a variant by playing mix-and-match? A greater understanding of the alternatives will help you determine the answer most suited to your program's theories and goals, most achievable with your institution's mission and resources, and most successful for meeting the literacy challenges of your basic writing students.

Works Cited

Adams, Peter Dow. "Basic Writing Reconsidered." *Journal of Basic Writing* 12.1 (Spring 1993): 22–36.

Grego, Rhonda, and Nancy Thompson. "Repositioning Remediation: Renegotiating Composition's Work in the Academy." *CCC* 47.1 (Feb. 1996): 62–84.

Harrington, Susanmarie. "New Visions of Authority in Placement Test Rating." *WPA: Writing Program Administration* 22.1/2 (Fall/Winter 1998): 53–84.

Haswell, Richard, and Susan Wyche-Smith. "A Two-Tiered Rating Procedure for Placement Essays." *Assessment in Practice: Putting Principles to Work on College Campuses.* Ed. Trudy Banta. San Francisco: Jossey-Bass, 1995. 204–07.

Huot, Brian. "A Survey of College and University Writing Placement Practices." *WPA: Writing Program Administration* 17.3 (Spring 1994): 49–65.

Murphy, Sandra, et al. Report to the CCCC Executive Committee: Survey of Postsecondary Writing Assessment Practices. 1993.

Royer, Daniel J., and Roger Gilles. "Directed Self-Placement: An Attitude of Orientation." *CCC* 50.1 (Sept. 1998): 58–70.

Segall, Mary T. "Embracing a Porcupine: Redesigning a Writing Program." *Journal of Basic Writing* 14.2 (Fall 1995): 38–47.

Smith, William. "Assessing the Reliability and Adequacy of Using Holistic Scoring of Essays as a College Composition Placement Technique." *Validating Holistic Scoring for Writing Assessment: Theoretical and Empirical Foundations.* Ed. Michael M. Williamson and Brian Huot. Cresskill, NJ: Hampton, 1993. 142–205.

Soliday, Mary, and Barbara Gleason. "From Remediation to Enrichment: Evaluating a Mainstreaming Project." *Journal of Basic Writing* 16.1 (Spring 1997): 64–78.

White, Edward M. "An Apologia for the Timed Impromptu Essay." *CCC* 46.1 (Feb. 1995): 30–45.

Classroom Activities

Encourage students to reflect on their own education by thinking about the six models for basic writing that Lalicker presents. In order to offer a more relevant approach to the idea of an educational model for students, you might ask them to respond to the following prompts:

- Describe your experiences with studying writing and reading in grade school, high school, or GED or ABE programs. What was the best experience you ever had with writing? What was the worst? What made these experiences memorable?

- Compare your previous experiences with writing to your basic writing course(s) in college. What differences do you see? What similarities? Are the expectations for writing in college similar or different than in your previous education? Why or why not?

- How does your education in writing compare or contrast to your education in some other discipline(s) (math, science, social studies, and so forth)? What similarities do you see in how these disciplines are taught? What differences? How are these similarities and differences important to your education as a whole?

Thinking about Teaching

In your teaching journal, reflect on your students' responses to the above questions. What surprised you or otherwise jogged your thinking? How can you use your insights about this discussion to help shape activities in your classroom?

Examine the baseline model and the alternative models represented in Lalicker's article. Which model(s) seem to be used in the institution(s) in which you teach? Does this model seem to be appropriate for the student population and the mission of the institution? Why or why not? Do you have questions about how the model came to be used in your institution?

Can you conceptualize another kind of model, one not described in Lalicker's essay? What would that model look like? How would a new model benefit students? How would it facilitate teaching? Are there any details that Lalicker left out of his descriptions of the models? What are they?

As appropriate, share your reflections and questions on the above issues with students, faculty, and administrators. What kinds of questions does your institution need to ask about basic writing? Why?

2

Basic Writing:
Student's Perspectives

W ho are basic writing students? Whether you are a first-year or a veteran teacher, this chapter will help you think through your own response to this question. We already know that, for a variety of reasons, basic writing students arrive in our classrooms underprepared to write for first-year composition courses. Some students, for instance, may have graduated from underfunded inner-city or rural high schools; other students may be returning to school after several years away and need extra support as they begin college. Still other students come to college from GED or ABE programs; and a growing number of students claim English as their second language. Whatever the reasons, as Linda Adler-Kassner argues, the voices of basic writing students need to be heard if we want to better understand their needs as writers. Adler-Kassner presents interviews with basic writing students at the University of Michigan–Dearborn as a primary form of research.

Ann E. Green, in "My Uncle's Guns," creates the voice of a fictional basic writing student who lives, works, and writes in a white, working-class farming community in Pennsylvania. The main character writes as a "personal narrator" much like one assigned in many basic writing courses. The narrator comments on her own writing process throughout her story. Green presents critical issues of social class and region that affect the interactions of basic writing teachers and students. Her short story urges the reader to consider how social class is constructed and represented in basic writing classrooms — and in the writing process itself.

Just Writing, Basically:
Basic Writers on Basic Writing

Linda Adler-Kassner

Linda Adler-Kassner is an Assistant Professor of Composition at the University of Michigan–Dearborn. She is coeditor with Gregory R. Glau of the Conference on Basic Writing's Basic Writing e-Journal <http://www.asu.edu/clas/english/composition/cbw/journal_1.htm> and has published articles in the Journal of Basic Writing (JBW), College Composition and Communication (CCC), Teaching English in the Two-Year College (TETYC), *and elsewhere. She has also edited (with Robert Crooks and Ann Watters)* Writing the Community: Concepts and Models for Service-Learning in Composition. *In the following excerpt from her longer article, Adler-Kassner continues the work begun in "The Dilemma That Still Counts" (coauthored with Susanmarie Harrington). In seeking to answer the question "Who are basic writers?", Adler-Kassner includes the self-descriptions of student writers. The voices of students "Tom" and "Susan" inform her analysis throughout the article.*

Back to Basics: Defining Basic Writers

Who are basic writers? In "The Dilemma That Still Counts," we examined the ways in which basic writers (and basic writing) have been defined through twenty-odd years of basic writing research. We argued that while "basic writing" remains an essential concept in the academy, we must work to clarify what the term means in order to act upon it, particularly in light of political actions like those recently taken within the CUNY system. Among the issues we posed for further investigation in our article was learning more about how basic writers (or, more appropriately, students labeled basic writers within particular institutions) defined themselves. How do they understand their experiences with writing and reading? Do they find particular features in their writing to be problematic? Do they contest their labeling as "basic writers"? Do they perceive their skills and challenges differently than the university does?

In order to find out how basic writers at my institution answered these questions, my colleague Randy Woodland and I interviewed sixteen students chosen randomly from the eighty who placed into our basic writing course during the fall semester of 1998. The questions that we asked students in our interviews reflected the two approaches which Susanmarie and I presented as widely prevalent in basic writing research in "The Dilemma That Still Counts." Cognitively based studies, we wrote, were concerned with writers' individual processes as they wrote and read. The processes which writers bring to producing or decoding texts are the subjects of study. Thus, in designing this current study Randy and I asked students to bring in examples of past writing that they particularly liked and to talk with us about them, and asked questions that prompted students to reflect on their composing processes. Susanmarie and I also suggested that a later trend in basic writing scholarship is toward culturally based studies, which examine the writer in relationship to larger cultures (like the academy). In this light, a writer is seen as within a broader matrix of literate processes, some or all of which might come into play during their encounters with academic texts. This approach is reflected in questions directed to UM-D students about their writing and reading histories and those about their perceptions of writing and reading requirements that they will encounter in college.[1] The interview protocol was divided into four basic areas . . . :

I. *Existing writing*. In the letter inviting students to talk with us, we asked if they had a paper (or several papers) that they particularly liked, and if they would bring those with them to the interview so that we could talk with them about the essays.

II. *Experiences with and ideas about writing and reading*. These included questions about students' families and family histories with writing and reading; students' histories with writing and reading inside and outside of school; students' present writing and reading habits; students' experiences with writing and reading in school; about connections between writing and reading outside and inside of the classroom; and about how students defined key terms related to writing and reading.

III. *Expectations for college*. Here, we asked students if they had a planned major and, if they did, what it was. Additionally, if they had a major in mind, we asked what they expected would be required of them in courses in their major.

IV. *Conceptualizations of and expectations for writing*. Questions here fell into two general areas: those related to the basic writing course (including "what is a basic writer?"), and the specific writing and reading expectations in their proposed or prospective majors.

Students' responses to these questions have helped us develop a better understanding about how they approach postsecondary education, how they imagine the role of writing in that education, and how they see themselves in relation to what they imagine the academy to be. They also provide the foundation for a compelling argument about the responsibilities that institutions (and the teachers who are a part of them) have toward students who are identified as basic writers. Helping students to contest and, ideally, to overcome their status as basic writers is an implied goal of most basic writing courses.[2] But these interviews suggest that to really help students develop a sense of that definition and the means to overcome it, we need to do more than imply. In fact, we need to explicitly help students understand and act on what all of this means in *our specific institutional contexts*. We might even make the questions "what does it mean to be a basic writer *here,* and what does it take to not be one?" part of the "subject" of our basic writing courses.

To illustrate these findings, I'll ground the discussion in portions of interviews with two writers, Tom and Susan.[3] In some ways, these two writers are typical of UM-D's basic writing population. Like most of our students, they came from inner-ring suburbs of Detroit and commuted to UM-D from homes where they lived with two parents or guardians. Both came from homes where some writing and reading took place, although writing and reading was not a main focus in either home. Tom was unusual in that neither of his parents had completed a two- or four-year degree, but was typical in that at least one of his parents had attended (if not completed) community college.[4] Both described themselves as fairly good students.[5] Neither writer professed a great love of writing or reading outside of the classroom (although Tom said he enjoyed science fiction novels); in this respect, they were also quite representative of the other students whom we interviewed.

After taking the UM-Dearborn placement exam, both Tom and Susan received two scores of 2 (out of a possible score of 6) on the exam. According to the scoring guidelines, a "2" essay

> has significant weakness of one or more kinds: Development of ideas may be weak with few specific details to support main ideas. Paragraphs may be relatively short and loosely organized with inadequate transitions. The overall organizational pattern may be loose or not apparent. There may be a pattern of major grammatical errors or numerous misspellings.

Most writers who take basic writing at UM-D receive scores of 2 on their exams, and in this light Tom and Susan were also fairly representative. Their responses to questions about writing in college were also fairly typical of the basic writers whom we interviewed, and they nicely foreground some of the most interesting findings to emerge from our discussions with basic writing students.

Tom's and Susan's Interviews

Tom

Like the vast majority of students on our commuter campus, Tom still lived at home. His father was recently retired from "Ford's";[6] his mother worked at the Kmart Headquarters in Troy, Michigan. Tom said neither he nor anyone in his family did a lot of writing or reading outside of school, although he did enjoy "making up a story and writing about it" and he liked science fiction. Once, in school, he got to write a science-fiction story as a paper, which he enjoyed. But most of his high school writing and reading he found tedious — reading a book and writing reports, and doing "analyzing." Tom could name only one book he enjoyed reading in high school, *To Kill a Mockingbird.*

At UM-D, Tom planned to major in Computer Information Systems, a major housed in the College of Engineering and Computer Science. When I asked Tom if he thought he'd have to do a lot of writing or reading for his major, he said, "I don't believe so," although he hadn't talked to anyone to get a sense of whether his impression was correct. He did think he'd have to do a lot of math, "and . . . research with the books and the computer books and stuff," but since he was "into computers," he didn't think he would be "handed a book and [told,] 'Here, read this.'"

When I asked him to describe his writing, Tom said, "I can get creative, but it's mostly just like science fiction stuff that I like to come up with." As a writer, he said, "I'm only doing it 'cause I have to, and I have to get a good grade on it." Tom thought he would learn "how to write essays, you know, essays, papers," in basic writing. Additionally, he thought he'd learn to

> try to keep focus on certain points and use proper grammar, which I was never really good with anyways, but . . . actually, it's the grammar that I don't really care for. I learned a lot of it, but I just can't remember.

Susan

Susan also graduated from an inner-ring suburban high school. Susan's dad was "kind of self-employed," and her mother was a nurse. She said her family did some reading and writing — her mom "[wrote] e-mails a lot and read magazines a lot," and her stepfather read the newspaper. She didn't do a lot of writing or reading. She had a creative writing class in school that she liked, but they didn't do a lot of writing the first semester, and had "a journal" in the second. "It wasn't really a writing class. It ended up being a relationship class." She liked her ninth grade English teacher, who "really pushed you, and made you understand [reading in the class]."

Susan thought she would major in business at UM-D, but wasn't really sure. Susan expected to write papers in college, and that those papers would be "so much different [from high school] . . . everything [in college] is just more intellectual and you have to think more and go, you know, deeper into things and explain yourself . . . and just have things to back it up."

When I asked her if she thought of herself as a good student she didn't answer directly. Instead, she said, "I know what I want to do and I know what I have to do, so. . . ." As a writer, Susan said, "I think I have a lot to say . . . but I don't know how to write it. I don't know how to put my words together and write it down and make it flow good and make it sound right. I can't do that." She said her writing now was

> really shaky . . . 'cause I'll have to sit there and I'll have to write something over and over again 'cause it just doesn't flow right and it doesn't make any sense the first time I write it, so I have to sit there and I have to really work at it.

I asked her if it came out, but it wasn't what she was thinking, and she said,

> Exactly. . . . Afterwards, when I look at it . . . I'm, like, that wasn't what I was trying to say at all. And I try to put it in different words or I'll just try to rewrite it out later on and it just doesn't work and I'll have to sit there and I'll have to work at it for a while.

Sometimes she continued to work at it; sometimes, she gave up because she found it frustrating. "Being a writer," Susan said, was "being creative about what you say and being able to write it down; having it make sense and come together and having people read it and understand it and know what you're talking about. . . . The thoughts [in your head] come out right." "Learning to write" meant "just developing the skills that you need to get all your words down, all your thoughts out and get them out properly, and just brainstorming and putting it all together and writing it down." In the basic writing course, Susan hoped to learn "better writing techniques, how to get everything out properly, and how to write it down and make everything flow."

Included in Tom's and Susan's responses are three compelling issues that came up with most of the writers whom we interviewed: their understanding of the term "basic writing," their expectations for writing and reading in other college courses, and their conceptualizations of writing. For those who have worked in basic writing for any length of time and/or those versed with basic writing literature, these issues may sound familiar. However, hearing them expressed from students' perspectives led me to think carefully about the responsibilities that we have toward basic writers as teachers and as representatives of the institutions where we teach.

Issue #1

Basic Writers on "Basic Writers": What's in a Name?

> Teachers often label students "remedial," "marginal," "at risk," "basic," or "illiterate": labels given by the judges, not the judged.
> — Alan Purves, "Clothing the Emperor"

What do the words "basic writer" mean to you?

> Just writing simple. Just well, yeah, that's important for jobs and communicating with other people, that's the same thing there.
> — Tom

> Basic writer. I guess just a person who writes, probably someone who just, you know, writes things just . . . like their given assignment and they'll just write it down. But I think a writer is actually somebody who does writing and writes a lot.   — Susan

Among the questions that Susanmarie and I raised in "The Dilemma That Still Counts" is whether basic writers contest the label that had been attached to them as a result of their performance on some kind of assessment measure (like our composition placement exam). But Tom and Susan, like every other writer we interviewed for this study, don't know what "basic writer" means. I don't mean that they don't know what it means to *be* a basic writer — they certainly know that they're not taking first-year composition. But they don't know that they are *called* basic writers, or that the course they're in (ours is called "Writing Techniques") is spoken of in the field as a "basic" (or "developmental") writing course.

I think that this is a dilemma for several reasons. In a recent essay, Peter Mortenson raised questions about the ethics of using subjects anonymously in our research. I see this as an extension of that problem — here, the issue of "basic writing" itself is anonymous, at least (as Tom, Susan, and Alan Purves suggest) to the people who are labeled that way. In fact, many basic writing researchers and teachers have worked long and hard to help erase the stigma that we think students must feel when they are placed in basic writing courses. Some researchers, for instance, attempt to identify the ways in which basic writers are multiply literate, despite the labels that have been affixed to them based on performance on a measure like a placement exam. Their positions are clear: these writers have abilities outside of the classroom; their performance in the classroom is affected by the ways that they approach their work (and those approaches, in turn, are affected by any number of internal and external circumstances).

We have taken these more complex labels into the classroom, as well. Many basic writing instructors (and I include myself here) have been shaped by the ideas of Mina Shaughnessy and her intellectual descendants (Perl, Hull, Rose, Bartholomae, and so on). We have developed a number of skillful ways to talk about literacy (or literacies) so that students don't feel they are failures, don't see their experiences as isolated, and don't feel that the literacies that they bring to the academy are "bad." In the mythic story of basic writing, we say that this different way of talking about basic writers and their abilities works against the deficit model that has framed writing instruction since the end of the nineteenth century, pointing to the creation of English A at Harvard University while gnashing our teeth and wringing our hands.

Sometimes, as in some of my own classes, we use texts (like *Lives on the Boundary*) with which we hope basic writers will identify — that they will read and say, "Aha! That person's experience is like mine!" Because the texts are always carefully chosen (again, like *Lives*), the hope is that students will then understand that they bring something different — not bad, but different — to their learning, and need to find ways to fit that "difference" into writing in this context. But this approach, which certainly isn't one that only I use, still elides the question of what it means to be a basic writer in the specific context in which these writers find themselves. In a sense, it asks students to participate in a system of values that surrounds a particular "reading" of *Lives on the Boundary*. Yet one of the tenets of recent culturally based approaches to basic writing work is the notion that these writers do not share (some) of the same values reflected in academic discourse. Thus, the logic here is inconsistent: Shared interpretation, to some degree, is based on shared culture. And basic writing scholarship has suggested that these writers do not participate in this culture. Therefore, they might not share interpretations held by members of this culture.[7] (Additionally, imagine the dizzying connections between these things! Is one academic institution like another? Yes, in some ways. Is UM–Dearborn in 1999 like Loyola or UCLA in the mid-1960s and early 1970s? In some ways yes, and in some no. But why should we expect students to make the rather abstract connections that we might see between that circumstance and theirs?) Since we — since *I* — sometimes don't tell basic writers *exactly* what it means to be a basic writer (in this time and place), these students are left to their own devices to figure out what basic writing is, and what makes them basic writers.

Meanwhile, while we talk with students about their multiple literacies inside the classroom, we're talking about them as "basic writers" outside of it, as in this article. I'm a member of the Conference on Basic Writing. I subscribe to the *Journal of Basic Writing*. But the idea of the "basic writer" and all of the characteristics associated with it are invisible to the students themselves.

One could make the argument that I'm quibbling over issues of mere semantics, but I don't think I am. After all, how can basic writers contest their labeling *as* basic writers (and then refute it as well) if they don't know that this is what they're called? Certainly, they can tell us that they know more than they have been labeled as knowing; they might say that they're better at writing in different contexts — they can say a lot of things. But if language is power (and I believe that it is), not giving students the language to talk about themselves (or, at least, their labels) and their situations seems to me an act of withholding power. . . .

Notes

1. These questions were also shaped, in part, by Deborah Mutnick's outstanding study of basic writers described in *Writing in an Alien World*. Questions asking writers to define some terms ("basic writer," "learning to write," "being a writer") were asked by Mutnick, and were used in our study with her permission.
2. This notion of basic writing and basic writer is in some ways reflected in (and is a reflection of) the research in basic writing. Often, the pedagogy in basic writing courses is influenced by research which focuses on helping students work through issues that have resulted in their placement in basic writing courses. While the analysis in that research probably stems from specific institutional contexts (like this article's does), the ideas in it are meant to be generalizable (as the ideas in this article are). But we must ask ourselves: Does the need to construct "basic writers" and "basic writing" as

semihomogenous categories lend credence to an avoidance of specifically defining those categories? While this issue is outside the scope of this article, it will be taken up by the larger study of which this research is a part.

3. These names, along with all other student names in this article, have been changed.

4. While we did not ask specifically about parents' education levels, most students told us something about their parents' educational backgrounds. Two students had at least one parent with an advanced degree; five had at least one parent with a four-year degree; four had at least one parent with a two-year degree; three had parents with no higher education. Among those who didn't specifically identify higher education experiences of their parents, three had at least one parent in what might typically be considered a "blue-collar" job (e.g., working on the line in a stamping plant); three had at least one parent who worked in what might be considered a "white-collar" job (e.g., nursing).

5. Admission to UM–Dearborn is quite competitive — generally, students are in the top ten percent of their high school classes. For this reason, it is not surprising that Tom and Susan described themselves as fairly good students.

6. Typically, blue-collar workers at Ford Motor Company (or those related to them) refer to the company as "Ford's"; employees in more "professional" positions (e.g., managers or engineers) refer to it as "Ford."

7. Of course, this is a point raised in Glynda Hull and Mike Rose's article "This Wooden Shack Place: The Logic of an Unconventional Reading" as well.

Classroom Activities

Create a "literacy narrative" assignment for students. Invite them to reflect on the topics that Adler-Kassner asked her own basic writing students to reflect on in their interviews. Have students consider how their own family and educational histories of reading and writing affect their position as basic writing students. Questions based on Adler-Kassner's research could include the following:

- Existing writing: Is there a paper you have written that you particularly like? What do you especially like about it?

- Describe your family background and your family's history and experiences with reading and writing.

- What is your own history with reading and writing, inside and outside of the classroom?

- What are your present reading and writing habits?

- How do you define key terms related to reading and writing?

- What are your expectations for college? Do you have a planned major, and if so, what is it? What expectations do you have of the requirements of your major?

- What are your conceptualizations and expectations for writing in college?

- What is a basic writer?

- What are the specific writing and reading expectations in your proposed or prospective majors?

- How do you understand your experiences with reading and writing? Do you find particular features in your writing to be problematic? Do you contest your labeling as "basic writer"? Do you perceive your skills and challenges differently than the university does?

Thinking about Teaching

Conduct your own research with students based on the above questions. What similarities do the students seem to share? What differences? Write your reflections in your journal and consider revising them for publication. Share the results with your students in class.

Push your research one step further. What assumptions underlie the above questions? Can you think of questions that you would add or eliminate in your own research project?

Consider how your institution defines basic writers. How is the basic writing program set up? How many courses does it include? Are there separate courses for ESL and native speakers? How does placement work? How are the courses set up? Does each teacher use a common syllabus or common textbooks? What assumptions does your institution seem to make about basic writers? Do you believe these assumptions to be correct? Why or why not? As appropriate, share your reflections and questions on the above issues with students, faculty, and administrators.

My Uncle's Guns

Ann E. Green

Ann E. Green is the director of the writing center and an Assistant Professor of English at St. Joseph's University in Philadelphia. Her recent publications include "'Learning' and 'A Girl and Her Thoughts': Two Stories of Writing, Race, Social Class, and Cultural Difference," in The Personal Narrative: Writing Ourselves as Teachers and Scholars, *ed. Gil Haroian-Guerin and Xin Liu Gale, Calendar Island Press, 1999; "In Conversation with Community: Writing, Social Class and Feminist Pedagogy," in* Teaching Working Class, *ed. Sherry Linkon, Massachusetts University Press, 1999; and "Selling Out: Reflections of a Farm Daughter" (nonfiction), in* Calyx: A Journal of Art and Literature by Women *(Summer 1996), reprinted in* Present Tense: Art and Literature by Young Women, *ed. The Young Women Writer's Collective, Calyx Press, 1997. In her short story "My Uncle's Guns," Green creates a first-person narrative from the point of view of a basic writing student from a working-class and poor white community in rural Pennsylvania. As the narrator tells this story, she includes metacognitive comments that demonstrate the frequently ignored impact of social class differences on students and teachers.*

My uncle, who is not really my uncle but my father's best friend since grade school, bought an antique gun from the First World War. We saw it when we went over to my uncle's house to visit. Dad and T.J. were talking, having conversations with long pauses, while I watched out the living room window.

> I'm not sure how these essays are supposed to start. You said in class that a narrative should tell a story. How much of the story do I have to tell? Should I put in a reflection now? Should I tell you about smoking? Growing up, I watched men have conversations with each other filled with these long moments of silence where they smoked. One of them would light another cigarette or refill his pipe or, on a special occasion, smoke a cigar. If they didn't smoke, they chewed, either wintergreen Skoal or a pipe stem or a long piece of hay. Dad smoked a pipe with Old Hickory Tobacco until he quit farming. T.J., according to Dad, used to have every vice imaginable and then some, but he had quit smoking both cigarettes and cigars, almost entirely stopped chewing tobacco, and even cut back on his drinking since his heart attack. Every time I watch Dad talk, I remember how he smoked. Should this be part of the story?

While I was looking out the window, two deer appeared from the woods and strolled out into the yard. Although T.J. and Dad hunted together every year, T.J. fed wild animals, birds and rabbits, deer and even stray dogs in his back yard. The two deer went to pick at the food that had fallen from the bird feeders. One was a good-size doe, the other a late-born fawn with spots on its rump yet. When I walked up to the window to get a closer look, the deer spooked and leaped over the stone wall separating the lawn from the woods. Dad said, "Damn it, T.J., where's your camera?"

"Don't own one. If I shoot something, it ain't going to be for a god damn picture, anyway." He paused and slowly stood up from his recliner. "Come here, I'll show you what I'll shoot it with come December."

Dad and I went into T.J.'s spare bedroom to his gun cabinet, and he pulled out the WW I gun, a rifle whose stock had been cut off and refinished, evidently as a deer hunting gun. T.J. said, "It's my gun from the First World War." And then he laughed long and hard at his own joke. His laugh, as usual, drowned out any other sound and ended with a

couple of snorts after which he laughed again. T.J. hadn't seen any combat after he enlisted. His ROTC scholarship paid for Penn State, but
instead of sending him to Korea where the fighting was, the Army sent
him to West Germany as a stretcher carrier in a medical unit. For the
Army, it hadn't been bad, T.J. said. They spent most of their time moving the mobile medical unit along the East German border, to practice
in case of a communist attack.

My father took the gun from T.J.'s hands. "Nice job cutting it back.
Craig .340."

The gun didn't look any different to me than the dozens of other
guns I'd seen and handled. I didn't hunt, or at least I didn't shoot, but I
occasionally had gone out for turkey with Dad in the spring. We'd never
even seen one, but it was beautiful in the woods at dawn.

At twelve, my first date was a picnic on roast woodchuck in a field
near home; the gun that shot the chuck was a bolt-action 30.30. Everyone in my class took the Hunter Safety course in sixth grade, before it
was legal for us to hunt at twelve. All of my boyfriends and a good
many of my girlfriends owned guns for shooting or hunting purposes,
and school was canceled for the first day of buck season in December.
In the fall, I was late home from dates because any boy I was with
would use the drive home as a good opportunity to spotlight deer, to
see how many there were before hunting season.

> Are these the kinds of details that you mean when we talk in class
> about significant details? How am I supposed to know which details are
> important to you?
>
> I feel like I have to tell you all the details about deer hunting so you
> won't think we're simple or backward or country, getting all excited
> about looking at somebody's gun. Even though you assign us those Tim
> O'Brien stories with lists, you really don't think we'll write like that do
> you? And you would tell us we were too repetitive if we did. You're not
> from around here, and I can see you don't like us sometimes when we go
> outside on break from class and smoke and talk too loud about how we
> hate our jobs.
>
> You look at us and think that we don't know anything. You think that
> teaching us how to write can't help us cause we're not going to change
> our lives by reading some essays. But we all want to do well in this
> class. Can't you just tell us what you want us to write about?

As Dad looked the Craig .340 over, peering down the barrel, checking to see if it was loaded, he said, "Let's try the son-of-a-bitch out in
November at the fireman's shoot-in and pig roast." We left then, in our
pickup, complete with spotlight and gun rack in the cab. Dad had to get
home to go work as a janitor at 7 A.M. , while I had to make it in early to
run the drive-by window at the bank. We saw twelve deer in a field on
the way home, and nothing was unusual.

In fact, the night that it happened I had gone to the fair with Dad
and his new woman, Louise. It was about time Dad found somebody
else, and I was glad it was Louise, who was younger than Dad but older

than me by quite a bit. I'd seen what other kinds of women men found after their first wives.

> I'll cut Louise out of this paper later, because I know that you'll think she's extra, just one more person who's not really in the rising action of this story, but right now it's important to me that she stay in here. Most of the time I'm too busy trying to figure out how I'll pay for my next class and my car insurance to sit around and think about how I feel about somebody who's important in my life, but not a pain in my ass in some way. Louise has just been a fixture, a nice addition to Dad's life that makes him leave me alone more.

I rode down to the fair that night with Dad and Louise, knowing that I'd most certainly see somebody I knew and come home with whoever was there. T.J.'s volunteer fire company had beer at its fair, so it was a big event. It was high school reunion week, but nobody had called me to go as a date. I guess after this long, everybody brought their wives. What I didn't expect at the fair was that Mike would show up, looking better than the last I'd seen him, appearing between the clam and the beer tents while Dad brought Louise and me beers. He wasn't wearing anything Army. Evidently he no longer needed to show his pride in the uniform by wearing it to public events. He came over and asked Dad how he was and what he was doing since he wasn't farming. Mike nodded to Louise, but he was looking me up and down, checking to see if I had a wedding band, if weight had settled on my legs or on my ass, trying to see if the rumor about me taking college classes could be true. Dad said, "Mike, are you staying with your folks? Could you run Maria home on your way?"

I was mad that Dad was passing me off on Mike, even if I did plan on staying later. I could find my own way home and always had.

"I'll take her home. No problem," Mike said, grinning at me. "Does she have to be home at any particular time these days?"

We all laughed, because even when there were particular times, I had often missed them. Mike and I had another good long look at each other. No beer belly. No visible scars. Lines around his eyes. Teeth still straight and white. The Army has good dental.

> The good dental is an important detail, and you probably don't know that. If you're on welfare, you get dental, same if you're in the Army, but if you work loading potato chips on tractor trailers you don't get dental, the bank gets some dental (because otherwise who'd deposit their paycheck with a teller-girl minus a front tooth?) but if you're self-employed or working in a stone quarry, you don't get dental. First thing that goes on people round here, makes them look older than they are, are teeth. That's why kids in Head Start are fluoridated almost to death. Mary, from our class, her kid is in Head Start, and she says they make those kids brush their teeth twice in the three hours they're there. It's like that Head Start teacher believes Mary's teeth are bad because she doesn't brush them, not because her Mom raised her on potato chips

and soda. If those kids don't look poor, if they have good teeth, a decent set, they might just make it.

"How's the babies doing?"

"Fine. Growing like weeds. They're still in Texas. This is a short trip, just me seeing Mom and Dad and going to the reunion. Karen's pregnant again, and she don't travel too good."

I remembered the one time I'd seen Karen, she was a dishwater blond with circles under her eyes and a crooked, white smile. Mike had met her at basic training in Oklahoma. Mike just came back from that last ten day brutal basic training hike in the desert and proposed. They were married before he was shipped to Germany, and they were in Germany when Mike got shipped to Saudi. She had stayed in Germany, praying that what was at first a conflict wouldn't last too long, and then praying that the war wouldn't kill him before their first child was born.

We decided to go get a drink at our favorite bar, the Tea Kettle, because it had been a good place to skip an afternoon of school when we were growing up. It seemed like a perfect place to fill Mike in on the local gossip.

Mike was driving a familiar car, his Dad's ancient, rust and white colored Ford Fairlane, the passenger seat littered with the usual collection of empty cigarette packages, a partially filled bottle of oil left over from a previous oil change, and an oil filter wrench. Mike threw the junk into the back seat on top of a light-weight fluorescent orange hunting vest with the license pinned in the back and an ancient red hunting cap. I smiled because the clutter in the back seat was so familiar. The extra flannel shirts and jumper cables didn't seem to have moved in the years since I'd ridden with him.

You said something in class about Tim O'Brien and parataxis. Is that a list or something? Does this description of Mike's back seat count? Should I describe the flannel shirts? Do you even know what an oil filter wrench looks like?

At the Tea Kettle, we started drinking shots and went through our high school classmates, listing births, deaths, marriages, divorces, and affairs. We'd each graduated with about seventy people, most we'd known all our lives, and we had talked about almost everybody when I started asking him about his time in the Gulf.

"It was lots of sand and way too hot," he said. "But in that way it was like Oklahoma and basic all over again. MRIs and sweat. No black widow spiders, though. Did I tell you about that?"

"No. Don't we have black widow spiders around here? The males have the red hour glass on their backs?"

"No, the females. They bite their mates after they have sex and kill them."

"But what about the Gulf? Your Mom told Dad that you were in the actual fighting and some of the digging of the bodies out of the bunkers after stuff was over."

"It wasn't that big a deal. The hardest thing was losing the barracks to the Scud. I knew those people to speak to. . . . They were Pennsylvanians, reserve, not career military. Stupid loss, shouldn't have been there.

"But anyway, I was on maneuvers in the Oklahoma desert," Mike continued. "Last ten day stretch of basic. The Army has convinced you, you can't brush your teeth unless somebody else says it's O.K. and shows you how, and we're supposed to be out surviving in combat conditions. I'm in my tent putting on socks . . ."

"Putting on socks?"

"Yeah. We had to march ten miles back and my feet are blistered, so I'm putting on a pair of these stupid army issue socks. I'm pulling the left sock on and I feel this sharp pain, and I look down and there's a god damn black widow spider stuck to my leg. And we'd been told there are no black widow spiders in the Oklahoma desert, no dangerous spiders at all."

"Wait a second. No bad spiders. How in the hell did it end up on you then?"

"Christ, I don't know. But this drill sergeant has been giving me shit since the beginning, saying that it don't matter if my father was in Asia, that I'm such a smart ass that I'm not going to make it through basic. And since I think I'm so god damn intelligent, I should try for an ROTC scholarship in the Air Force, and just look at war on a computer screen, like Space Invaders. He's been busting on me for weeks, and now he's not going to let me finish basic. Or he's not going to believe me, and by the time he does I could be dead."

"Why are they such sons-of-bitches?"

"Right now you can only be career Army if they keep moving you up the chain of command. Career Army means retirement at thirty-eight and a new life. This weekend warrior shit means dying whenever somebody who's been away for a while forgets the rules and has an accident and you're in the line of fire or in the tank that he mistakes for the enemy."

I don't know if this is the kind of dialogue that you say "reveals character." We said "fuck" a lot more than I'm writing down now, but you probably don't want that in a paper. It's probably one of those things that a professional author can use, but that we can't yet. Like we have to get good at knowing how to use big words first, before we can write like we talk. See, for me the spider symbolizes what Mike's life has been like, something always biting him on the ass at a crucial moment and screwing things up, but I don't know if you'll get the spider comparison. It doesn't seem "realistic," but it's what he said really happened, so it must be true.

Is this the language of "the oppressed" that you've been talking about in class? Like that guy who taught those peasants, those peasants probably said "fuck" in Spanish a lot, too, but that probably wasn't included in their essays, right?

"So, anyway, you're still in the Army," I said, motioning the bartender to give me another chaser. "So what did you do about the spider?"

"Well, the Army gives you this stuff that freezes on contact. Why not just a bottle of bug spray, I don't know. So I'm hopping up 'n' down and grabbing the can from my kit, dumping stuff all over, and the spider's trying to beat a hasty retreat and I'm hopping after it, knocking the tent down, till I finally freeze the sucker. I'm trying to figure out . . ."

The door to the Tea Kettle slams, and Candy Dimock, now married to a Brown, bursts in, talking before she's in the door.

"There's bodies in the road. Please come help. They're dead. We think they're dead, but we're not sure. Bodies . . ."

"What bodies, Candy?" I ask, but people are already standing up and pushing forward. "What road, where?"

"Up the hill," she says. I had seen her from a distance at the fair grounds earlier with her husband. They must have been driving home and seen something. "Danny went to call the state cops, the ambulance."

"Run over?" I ask. Candy says, "Blood in the road. I don't know . . ."

Mike grabs Candy by the arm. "Come show us where you saw them," he says. "We'll see if we can help. Maria, you know CPR, right?" He pulls Candy toward the Ford and throws open the back seat door for her. Reaches around and pulls a thirty-thirty out from underneath the hunting clothes. "Get in," he says, and pushes Candy inside, handing me the rifle. "There are shells in the glove box." Other people are getting into their cars, some still holding their beers. Some are unpacking knives and deer rifles from beneath their back seats. They are waiting to follow us. I fasten my seat belt and open the glove compartment while Mike gets in the car. When I open the glove box, Mike's grandpa's service issue revolver tumbles out with boxes of shells, pink registration information, and their Family Farm insurance card. Mike backs up fast, while I start slipping long yellow-colored bullets into the chamber of the thirty-thirty, load it and put the safety on. Candy says, "Maria, do you remember two-man CPR in case we need it? I can't remember how many breaths per second . . ."

"How far," Mike asks, voice calm. He doesn't wait for an answer before he says, "Load the Colt, too."

I am already filling the Colt from the other box of bullets. The only gun I have shot on a regular basis. Friday nights shooting bottles filled with water and watching them explode. Saturday nights shooting mailboxes at midnight driving too fast, throwing beer bottles at the mailboxes if it wasn't your turn with the gun.

"Here," Candy says, but at first we see nothing. Then we spot the white in the ditch, the unmoving white in the ditch.

I remember (from first aid class):

—gun shot wounds are to be treated as puncture wounds;

—knife wounds also puncture (don't remove the knife);

—cover and try and prevent bleeding with direct pressure.

Mike gets out of the car with the thirty-thirty, metal glinting, catching the light from a car pulling up behind us. Others pull up behind us, also get out. Slowly. Moments drag on and on. I hold the forty-five. The bodies are end to end in a ditch by the road side. Blood has run from the man's chest onto the road and pools on the asphalt. In the headlights, it's not clear whether the woman's sweatshirt is gray or white. She lies on her side, and I can see that she was shot from the front because the exit wound on her back is big enough for me to put one of my hands in.

"Two," Mike says, his hand gently lifting the man's dark hair from his neck as he feels for the carotid pulse.

My fingers probe the woman's neck for the artery, any sign of life. Their clothes are red and maroon, fresh and bright, partly dried blood. Her eyes are wide open, but she is dead. It is silent as we gather around the bodies, not moving them. Sticking the guns back in the vehicles, finishing the beers, lighting cigarettes, waiting for the cops. No one recognizes the two dead.

We found out later it was a lover's triangle involving newcomers. The guy who did the killing went to the fair with his ex-girlfriend. She wanted to be friends and invited him to come with her to meet her new boyfriend. The old boyfriend was in the back seat of the car, pulled out a gun, shot through the seat and killed the boyfriend. She stopped the car, turned around, and said, "What the hell is going on?" and was shot in the chest. He panicked, threw the bodies in the ditch and drove off. Threw the revolver and its clip out at different places on his way out of town, but was caught before he hit the interstate because a cop stopped him and noticed the blood and rips on the passenger seat. The cops found the clip the first day, on the five mile strip of two lane that was most likely, but they couldn't find the gun. T.J.'s fire company cleaned up from the fair and then helped hunt for the gun. T.J. found the weapon three days later, ten yards from the road, in the rain. He knocked over some strands of purple and white vetch with a branch when the stick hit the gun. It was his sixtieth birthday, and after he found the gun, all the state cops shook his hand. His picture, holding his walking stick and grinning, was in the local paper.

That night, after we'd talked to the cops, Mike drove me home and finished telling me about the Gulf.

"Since I'm in for twenty years and already served almost half, they stuck me in a tank with more firepower than you'd ever imagine, guarding some West Point son-of-a-bitch commander who'd never even sweated in a desert. He was trained in jungle warfare, a kind of leftover. It was just miles and miles of tunnels, sand, and oil. And we were going to suffocate them in their bunkers anyway."

As I sit here trying to write this story, I try and remember what was said about a good narrative, what a good narrative consists of, but I don't have a conclusion in this story, just more fragments: Dad and T.J. hunted deer and came back empty-handed; Mike's mother sent over a venison roast from one of their deer; we ate the venison roast today at noon, with potatoes. And I don't have any questions for peer reviewers, because now that I'm in these night classes with these eighteen-year-olds, they don't understand my life anyway. At least in the continuing ed classes we had a variety of experiences, like shitty jobs or boyfriends, and shared ideas about good writing, like no comma splices and clear words. These girls can't even tell the difference between a Honda and a Ford, a double barrel shot gun and a pellet gun, or even, a buck and a doe. Some of them aren't even sure what their major is, while I'm trying to get enough algebra in my head to pass chemistry, qualify for the nursing program.

The assignment sheet said that this narrative should contain reflections, reveal something about ourselves and how we were changed by an event. But how should I be changed by finding a couple of bodies on a strip of two lane a couple of miles from home? Should I have a moral about how guns are dangerous and bad and nobody should have them anymore? Should I lie and tell you that I'll never be around guns anymore, that I'll be a good girl now and stay away from violent people and places?

How can I explain to you or to the other people in class that I finally decided that the noise I'm hearing outside the window as I write this isn't firecrackers, but gunfire. And that the phone just rang, and I talked to my neighbor who apologized for shooting his gun off, although it's ten on a Sunday night. I told him no big deal and he said, "I'm sorry for what I done, but I needed to do that, or I'd have to go somewhere and hit somebody." I don't tell him that Dad's not here, and that I'm trying to finish writing an essay.

And that he scared me.

And that while I've been listening to the shooting, I've propped the twelve-gauge at the front door and the thirty-thirty at the back.

Classroom Activities

Ann E. Green's short story resembles a "think-aloud protocol" in that the narrator includes metacognitive comments about her writing process, her teacher and the other students, and her story itself. Invite students to include their own metacognitive comments in a draft of their next essay or short story. What were they thinking about as they were writing? How might that thinking be included as part of a revised version of their text?

"My Uncle's Guns" is a story that foregrounds differences in social class and cultural and regional origin between teachers and students.

Have students write an essay or short story that highlights social class, race, gender, region, and/or other cultural differences in the lives of the characters. Students can also try writing their essay or story first from their own perspective, and then from the perspective of a teacher or other authority figure.

Give students "My Uncle's Guns" as a reading assignment and ask them to respond to what seems interesting about the form and content of the story. Do the narrator's comments on her own story seem appropriate? Are cultural differences important to an understanding of the story? What else seems striking about the story?

Thinking about Teaching

Record your students' responses to any of the above classroom activities. What issues seemed to be important for the students in discussing the structure of the narrative? What concerns do students have in discussing cultural differences? What insights did students provide on the relationships between students and teachers in a basic writing classroom? Share your reflections with students. In your journal, or in discussion with other teachers, disclose your own assumptions about your relationships with your students, and about cultural differences. Which issues are easy for you to discuss, and which are difficult? How do you account for this difference? For instance, how do you interpret the following statement by Green's narrator: "You look at us and you think that we don't know anything. You think that teaching us how to write can't help us cause we're not going to change our lives by reading some essays. But we all want to do well in this class. Can't you just tell us what you want us to write about?"

Write a short story or personal narrative about a classroom incident from your perspective as a teacher. Then write about the same incident from the point of view of a student. What differences do you notice? How can those differences help inform your classroom practices? As appropriate, share your reflections and questions on the above issues with students, faculty, and administrators.

3

Adapting the Writing Process

S ometimes the most difficult part of teaching developing writers is convincing them that good writing is the result of a process — that there is nothing magical about it. Good writing comes from the writer continually asking the following questions: Why am I writing? For whom am I writing? What do I want to say? How can I clarify my meaning? How can I identify and avoid errors that confuse my meaning? The articles in this section invite students to consider the writing process in forms that require a strong sense of audience and purpose: personal letters and life writing. As writers directly engage their readers, they are encouraged to slow down and focus on each step of the process.

To demonstrate his own approach to writing as a process, Gregory Shafer discusses how he wrote his assignments with his students. Shafer's students critiqued his writing — and thus came to understand that revision includes more than simply proofreading for errors. Bernstein includes a sample of student writing in her description of her life writing assignment. As part of the writing process, students reflected on the criteria for evaluating life writing and suggested how the teacher might evaluate writing that is extremely personal. To understand how life writing may be contextualized in larger social and cultural issues, the students read widely for this assignment.

Using Letters for Process and Change in the Basic Writing Classroom

Gregory Shafer

Gregory Shafer is a Professor of English at Mott Community College in Flint, Michigan. His publications include articles in English Journal *and* The Humanist. *He is also the regional coordinator for the Michigan Council for the Arts and has received four Excellence in Education awards from the Kellogg Foundation. In the following article, Shafer describes how his students learned about the writing process by writing letters to both personal and public audiences. Shafer also participated in this process of letter writing, and the results were significant for both students and teacher. Letters from colleagues follow this article, illustrating once again the potential for using letter writing to teach various aspects of the writing process.*

> The curriculum in Developmental English breeds a deep social and intellectual isolation from print.   — Mike Rose (211)

> Basic writing, alias remedial, developmental, pre-baccalaureate, or even handicapped English, is commonly thought of as a writing course for young men and women who have many things wrong with them.
> — Mina Shaughnessy (289)

Introduction

I never truly understood the discontent of the developmental writing student until I had the chance to teach a remedial writing class designed for students who have "significant weakness in basic sentence structure." It was during the opening day that I began to sense the isolation and alienation to which Rose and Shaughnessy refer. As a class, the students were unlike the frenetic and rather optimistic group that filled my college-level composition classes. Rather than walking in with smiles and eager anticipation, there was resignation and sober resolve — an atmosphere reminiscent of children waiting to be disciplined. It was the first time I had entered a class devoid of casual banter, and I sensed an almost tangible foreboding as I greeted students who sat stoically, eyes focused on books or the desks below.

Later, after collecting their writing samples, I began to further understand the unique and anxious perspective many of these "remedial students" have. "I never liked english," wrote one student, in response to a questionnaire. "It was always to prove what I couldn't do," she said. Added a second respondent, "I hated the workbook exercises. I couldn't get the hang of it."

Helping such students to "get the hang of it" — to feel that they had a voice worthy of respect — was my main goal as I prepared for a first foray into this basic writing course. From the start, I was convinced that the class would only be successful if it could transcend the deluge of skills exercises that remove these students from what Stephen Judy calls "writing for the here and now" (101). While acknowledging the acute lack of formal writing experience the students brought to the class, I also had to recognize the wealth of personal experiences, the sophisticated linguistic abilities they wield and have possessed since childhood. I was determined to allow these students to join what Frank Smith has called the "Literacy Club" — a place where language instruction is inclusive, personal, and predicated upon relevance. Of course, we all want our students to enjoy a democratic environment, but the idea of Smith's "Literacy Club" begins with the premise — like a club — that participants will be allowed a certain acceptance and autonomy as members. Indeed, both children and adults appreciate clubs because they can join with others to engage in fun and meaningful activities — activities where each member is respected as an active voice, where each individual parades certain abilities while collaborating with more experienced members to enhance specific skills. Thus, Smith asserts, learning in a club is almost invariably "collaborative," "effortless," and "no-risk" (21). It is a celebration of communal engagement and sharing, whether people share their love of cards, plants, or in this case, reading and writing.

Letters

The question was what to do with the developmental students — students who seemed scarred from years of failure and apathy. Writing would have to be the foundation of the course, but it would have to be a writing that was neither intimidating nor too lengthy — a writing that was accessible, that assured students an opportunity for success. It had to entice while still working on a practical level, something that made sense to a class of mostly working-class pupils.

I decided to begin with a class-wide engagement in letter writing. Because it is short and yet a complete unit of discourse — and because it has a place in the real world of most students — writing letters seemed an auspicious way to introduce students to writing that transcended skills instruction. Most of the class indicated that they had experience in writing short letters and felt a certain comfort in exploring the various ways the medium could become a theme of the course.

With the general concept of letter writing established, the class began with personal letters as an introductory assignment. In describing the possibilities, I was adamant about stressing the choices writers had and the latitude available to explore both personal and fictitious topics. Many wanted to compose personal letters to loved ones who were either dead or who had moved away, while others contemplated the idea of penning a series of letters that would become chapters of a fiction story. What was most edifying for me as an instructor was the ebullience, the alacrity, that permeated the class not long after I suggested topics and presented a sample. Within minutes, I could feel an effusive energy, as faces became illuminated with potential for writing. Clearly, these were students who were both ready and willing to compose. Much of the second half of class would find me stepping aside, facilitating the flurry of ideas as they whirled from student to student.

From the introductory moments of that day, I continued to act as catalyst, providing ideas, personal examples, and encouragement. Day two, then, became established as a workshop session, a chance for students to continue brainstorming and planning so that each could present a detailed plan or proposal for the letters they would compose. As with the opening day, students worked assiduously, methodically, honing their topics and grafting new ideas onto their original plans. Shantel, who was a single parent of five, planned to write a letter to the father of her children, a man she had not seen in almost five years. Malique, in contrast, had decided to write a letter that was "long overdue" to the woman he had been dating for the past two years. Jackie, in a third contrast, decided to write some very personal words to her deceased grandfather, a man she had loved like a father until his death at sixty-eight.

As class concluded for the week, I could see the dramatic change in atmosphere, a fulminating sense of enthusiasm pervading the discussions. Many students were beginning to write opening paragraphs, asking about going to the writing center to "get started," or about the specific length for the first draft. Next week, the rough draft would be due, and many were ready to write. Indeed, as I reviewed the class for the week, I thought of Mike Rose and his contention that developmental writers "know more than their tests reveal but haven't been taught how to weave their knowledge into coherent patterns" (8).

The Rigors of the Process

The process of moving from idea to rough draft is perhaps one of the most chaotic and exciting stages in composition — especially as it relates to basic or developmental writers. Suddenly, sentences are taking their place on paper, interacting with other sentences, forming paragraphs, changing plans, and acting as catalysts for new directions. Process. Journey. As we joined to share our rough drafts, I continued to reiterate these words. Many students were frustrated, finding the transition from idea to draft a very daunting and messy endeavor. "It's not coming out the way I planned, and I get new ideas I don't know what to do with," lamented one student. Others found the idyllic prose they had in their heads failing to make its way neatly onto their papers. "This isn't as good as I thought," said another. Many were frustrated as they confronted the fact that writing is not a linear, step-by-step process. Now came the process of revision, of working with the organic and unwieldy character of creating prose.

We devoted the beginning moments of the rough draft session to forming small groups, reading each other's papers, and offering suggestions for possible revision. For many, it was the first time an essay of theirs had ever been revised or critiqued. Many were discouraged and found their peers focusing on annoying spelling errors rather than the development of ideas. All of the old memories associated with red ink and derisive comments were resurfacing and creating a contentious atmosphere. Thus, after about fifteen minutes of small group work, I told the class to form a circle with their desks, so we could share our work as an entire class.

Writing with One's Students

It was during this time that I recognized the significance of Donald Murray's admonition that "writing begins when teachers give their students silence and paper — then sit down to write themselves." With most of the class in a rather irritated and frustrated mood, it was an ideal time to use my own letter as an introduction to the plans and questions I had for my own writing — and to the role they could play in helping me to revise. The key, I thought, was moving the class beyond cosmetic changes. The students were devoting too much of the session to discussing surface errors and spending too little time on the solid but incipient ideas in their letters. It was a special opportunity to read and discuss my composition and invite students to discuss the ways I could reach my goal for the letter.

This whole class critique involving my letter was perhaps the turning point in the way the class thought about writing. While many of the students still harbored a reductive view of writing as a process of finding errors, the class discussion of my letter — to my recently deceased father — helped highlight the more compelling reasons one has to write. At the same time, the movement toward content helped show participants the importance of transcending errors and focusing instead on the evolution and improvement of message or substance.

Because of the emotional content, many distanced themselves from petty arguments over subject/verb agreement and were motivated instead by the message I had for my father. At the same time, I was beginning to understand what Frank Smith meant when he argued that anyone who hopes to teach writing must first "demonstrate what writing does and demonstrate how to do it" (31). To this, I would add, teachers must take risks with their students and illustrate the way emotion and writing coalesce to serve very personal needs. Thus, as I began to read the letter, I was learning as well as teaching, opening up and changing the way students perceived writing.

This experience also reminded me of the importance of risk taking and the role teachers play in making it possible. As I read my letter and asked students for suggestions about revising, I recognized the sensitive position I was in as a writer and how protective I felt about the letter in front of me. How, I wondered, would I react if students negated the essence of the letter, focusing instead on comma splices or apostrophe use? Would I become a bit alienated, a bit disconcerted, if the gist of the discussion was about rules rather than the passion that emanated from the prose? Would such an approach tend to make writing irrelevant? Would it truncate the creative process? Such questions enhanced my ability to teach these developmental students from a more empathetic position. At the same time, it brought me back to the theme of the writing club and the idea that one must participate in a writing club if one is to lead it.

The critique session involving my letter lasted for twenty minutes and again placed the spotlight on the need for process and revision. Students who earlier were ready to edit rough drafts for spelling and then prepare them for submission were now aware of the way one can use writing for expression and to clarify questions about life and death dilemmas. As they poured over my two-page letter, pensively evaluating the message, I sensed that they better appreciated their roles as companion writers in a process rather than as editors who search feverishly to expunge error. Like any good reader, they were sensitive to my endeavors and seemed to thrive in their new, more holistic approach. As the discussion moved from observations to questions about specific parts of my paper, we began to better demonstrate the goal of any good writing conference: improvement of one's whole draft.

"Did you really feel that angry toward your father?" From the first questions, students were focused on content, on the message and its efficacy in communicating my true feelings. "I like the realism of the letter," suggested Kaleb. "You can tell that this is real. People just don't make this stuff up." Part of the reason why students transcended issues of surface structure was a set of questions I gave them before we started. Based on the idea that writing conferences should be a sharing of perceptions and constructive suggestions, the questions asked students to identify the best qualities in the writing, the questions they had about the writing, and any suggestions for improvement. "Don't you want to communicate your love for him too?" asked a student in making a suggestion for improvement. "I don't know if you want it to be this cold," added another. Clearly, as we continued to read and discuss the letter, the students were demonstrating an understanding of process and change in writing. We had taken a step forward.

Thus, as we concluded class, we agreed as a group to read and revise our papers for the next session, placing special emphasis on the specific objectives we had for our letters and the way those objectives could be best accomplished. After doing a short class critique on my paper, students better understood the need to set aside questions of spelling and focus instead on the substance of the work — on the use of organization, style, and diction to enliven the personal feelings held by the author. We left class that day with what clearly seemed to be the active, collaborative, inclusive spirit that epitomizes the idea of Smith's "Literacy Club."

Process and Change

The next class session demonstrated further evidence of this spirit when most of the students entered with revised, completed drafts as well as a renewed sense of the writing process. Shantel, who had grappled with her letter to the estranged father of her children, had made great strides in putting aside entanglements concerning grammar and spelling, to compose a very moving two-page letter.

"I just want you to know," she wrote in this second draft, "that your kids are still your kids no matter how far you distance yourself from them. Time and space can't change some things," she added. Later, she concluded with a very moving and poignant effluence of feeling, telling her estranged lover that "I still think about you and tell good things to our children. I remember the good times [. . .] ."

Other drafts seemed to highlight the same kind of clear, dramatic direction. Gina's letter, which had gone through three revisions since the opening discussion, was transformed into an incisive, moving missive to her deceased mother. As with Shantel, Gina had extricated herself from nettlesome questions involving usage and mechanics, and had, in the process, composed a letter that captured the loneliness and loss she felt.

"You always be special," she wrote. "I'll always speak to you, when I go to sleep, when I deal with problems, when I feel wonder about my life."

Both revisions, it is important to note, were the result of a vigorous, recursive, unencumbered writing process — one that allowed students to see themselves as authors in a community or club of writers, rather than as patients in a clinic for the syntactically or mechanically impaired. Where Rose laments the stultifying effects of reducing writing to questions of correctness, these students felt liberated to put expression first, treating their letters as serious drafts rather than objects for correction. For once, ideas and expression — passion and memories — took precedence over the conspicuous inexperience they demonstrated in generating polished prose. And as we engaged in small group critiques, adhering to the set of questions they answered for my letter earlier, we continued to learn about writing by doing it, by perceiving ourselves as writers, and collaborating in its evolutionary process.

Punctuation and usage, it is instructive to note, become more comprehensible and relevant when associated with holistic writing. Thus, as we formed groups of three and began to read and discuss the letters in small groups, we could consider the context in which errors were made. Deneitha's letter had frequent errors in spelling, but with her work flowering into a complex story about two estranged lovers, the misspellings seemed ancillary and insignificant. Of course, she would have to consult a dictionary and proofread more carefully, but such editing concerns were being handled after the essence of her piece had been written — after she had the chance to immerse herself in the empowering experience of creating a story and perceive herself as a writer.

Sondra Perl has suggested that even inexperienced writers bring a sophisticated knowledge of the writing process to the composition experience. During her study of remedial writers, she found that all students "displayed consistent composing processes; that is, the behavioral subsequences prewriting, writing, editing appeared in sequential patterns that were recognizable across writing sessions and across students" (31). In fact, as I observed students reading and critiquing in small groups, I noticed an assiduous attention to the evolutionary character of writing. Shantel's paper had problems with syntax as well as organization and spelling. And yet, her readers focused on her message and how it could be made more coherent as well as correct. Their efforts at keeping the focus on Shantel's goals allowed the process to continue while errors were eliminated. "You need to be more specific as to what he did and why he left," wrote one reader. "And you also need to reread your first two sentences. It wasn't clear to me, cause a word might have been missing."

A second reader agreed, highlighting the interesting ideas as well as the lack of clarity in certain spots. "This is going to be good. It's getting better too. But you have to watch for the fragments. Some of your ideas are still kind of fragmented and so it's not understandable."

From that second critique session came a final revision which was done on a computer. Later the next week, selected students made copies of their letters for the entire class to read and evaluate. For some, the final draft represented up to six revisions of work.

Marcus's final paper was perhaps most emblematic of the development that occurs when one is allowed to write and revise without the cumbersome drone of the grammar guardian filling the air. His letter to his deceased friends from a gang war evolved from clumsy, indelicate writing, to a forceful series of letters that blended the dialect of the street with terse and even opulent prose: "You went in a lightning strike of gun fire, and I miss you all cause you're no longer at my back. The streets are still frigid with the feel of your deaths, but that don't mean, I can't warm up to the memory of your friendship. Good bye."

Wrote Andre, another student who was also a veteran of the streets and the problems and temptations they represent: "I'm writing to you, Ma, because you were there to keep me in the house and far from the 'boys' that wanted me for their 'family.' I can't thank God for the past or future till I give you this letter for being my best friend forever."

Such is the kind of vigor and passion that I found in these developmental writers after several revisions and a thorough journey through the writing process. With mechanics put in perspective, and with each student free to experiment and take risks, correctness seemed to coalesce with clarity.

New Visions of Developmental Writers

Again, it is important to return to the concept of the writing club and the medical metaphor that has traditionally pervaded the teaching of developmental students. "Teachers and administrators," argues Mina Shaughnessy, "tend to discuss basic-writing students much as doctors tend to discuss their patients [. . .]" (289). With the sick, there must be a prescription, but for those who are well, there is guidance, encouragement, and an invitation to succeed through the writing process. In the same spirit, there is a concomitant need to envision a writing club, one that makes composition a group activity rather than a mandate from teacher to student. As my students completed their first letter, replete with rough draft and critique sheets, I realized that their abilities far transcended my expectations and that my role was as catalyst, not only in helping them to read and edit, but also to use the stages of writing, so that editing was postponed until ideas had been formulated and writers began to believe in their work.

Letter writing, I should note, is invaluable not only for its short, holistic character but also for the many political and liberating opportunities it offers. Not long after the class completed the introductory letters to friends and family, it began an exploration of the newspaper and the possibility of writing letters to editors and selected columnists. Many, lamentably, did not know what an editorial was, while even fewer understood the difference between an opinion and a fact. For many, there was confusion as to how one could question the newspaper, since it only printed the "truth." In this case, I found it helpful to refer to Nietzsche's famous quotation that "there are no truths, only interpretations" (25). At the same time, I read and explored the newspaper with the students and discussed the idea of political agendas, power, and the place students have in shaping them. In the end, I found this type of letter writing, with work, can also transcend the academic and awaken the fledgling iconoclast.

As we moved on to other writing endeavors, students became increasingly more familiar and confident with their writing and the stages it entailed. Working within the recursive stages of the writing process — allowing for mistakes and learning from them — facilitates a meaning-first approach, one that permits students to work through their weaknesses as they compose. "Writing," contends Peter Elbow, "is like trying to ride a horse which is constantly changing beneath you" (25). As with college-level writers, my developmental students learned to write by mounting the horse, grappling with the problems, and constructing short but holistic letters. And while their weaknesses far exceeded the average student, their engagement in writing helped them to recognize why clarity is needed and how the process works to make that clarity a reality.

Works Cited

Elbow, Peter. *Writing without Teachers*. New York: Oxford UP, 1973.

Judy, Stephen. *Explorations in the Teaching of English*. New York: Dodd, 1974.

Murray, Donald. "First Silence, Then Paper." *FForum*. Ed. Patricia Stock. Upper Montclair: Boynton, 1983. 227–33.

Nietzsche, Friedrich. *The Use and Abuse of History*. New York: Bobbs, 1949.

Perl, Sondra. "The Composing Processes of Unskilled College Writers." *Cross Talk in Comp Theory: A Reader*. Ed. Victor Villanueva. Urbana: NCTE, 1997. 17–42.

Rose, Mike. *Lives on the Boundary: A Moving Account of the Struggles and Achievements of America's Educationally Underprepared*. New York: Penguin, 1989.

Shaughnessy, Mina. "Diving In: An Introduction to Basic Writing." *Cross Talk in Comp Theory: A Reader*. Ed. Victor Villanueva. Urbana: NCTE, 1997, 289–296.

———. *Errors and Expectations: A Guide for the Teacher of Basic Writing*. New York: Oxford UP, 1977.

Smith, Frank. *Joining the Literacy Club*. Portsmouth: Heinemann, 1988.

Responses

Response to "Letter Writing in the College Classroom"
by Elaine Fredericksen

Dear Elaine:

The research is convincing and copious. Students bring rich and imaginative linguistic skills to our writing classes, whether they are labeled advanced or developmental. Too often, however, we fail to acknowledge this linguistic acumen, choosing instead to treat students as if they are sick and in need of our prescription. Thus, Mina Shaughnessy reminds us, medical metaphors dominate the language while teachers and administrators tend to discuss basic writing students much as doctors tend to discuss their patients [. . .]" (289). They are remedial and in need of diagnosis or a trip to the clinic. Only recently have we begun to speak of the amazing ability they bring to the writing process.

That's what is so valuable and illuminating about your essay, "Letter Writing in the College Classroom." Rather than listing the ways letters can promote better skills exercises in isolation, it begins with the premise that all students are ready to write — that they bring linguistic knowledge to the writing context. And as a result, you invite students to join an activity that is rife with pleasure, both aesthetic and social. They are told, implicitly through the approach, that composition is about self-actualization and authentic communication. In short, you treat them as competent language users, people who have something important say.

Why is this important? Frank Smith suggests that all learning is predicated upon the context in which we learn and those people with whom we are studying. Thus, if we are immersed in a setting that tells us that writing is an arcane, irrelevant activity — one filled with cumbersome prewriting exercises — we are likely to eschew it as one would anything that is unpleasant. In the same way, if we are led to believe that composition is not personally empowering but simply an act of academic imitation, we are again likely to venture elsewhere for life affirming experiences. All learning, contends Smith, pivots on who we think we are and who we see ourselves as capable of becoming (11). We learn, he continues, from the individuals or groups with whom we identify (10).

What is exciting, Elaine, about your letter writing use is its efficacy in creating a nurturing environment. True social exchange, you argue, stimulates students and their readers. Hence, your assignments revolve around what students can do in a setting that is based upon the worlds they inhabit. Because choices emanate from class population and student interest, relevance is virtually assured. In the process, so is true, active, thoughtful participation. The writer is made an active agent. Writing and existence converge.

Along the way, students acquire a variety of lessons about learning. Perhaps the most important of these is the value of the students' voice and personal perspective. With letter writing, composition becomes an extension of one's life. One of the most useful aspects of your essay is the divisions you create for different writers in various contexts. Letters can be used not only for business communication but as a way to express one's feelings or pose questions about a grade. In short, students become major players in a class that is decidedly bottom-up in its approach. The impetus for the letter — whether it is a reflective self-assessment or a fictitious missive to an author — radiates from the students and serves their needs. Relevance is assured.

Of the many interesting ideas you present, none is more helpful than the reflective pieces you assign. In asking your pupils to ponder and assess their progress and performance, you are again emphasizing the need for student engagement. In those contexts, the students are perceived as writers who are in control of their work and cognizant of its strengths and weaknesses. Such involvement is essential in designing a class that fosters student autonomy and creativity. With each letter representing a significant part of the grade, the students learn not only to take responsibility for their work but to appreciate the chaotic, capricious character of the writing process. Rules and injunctions are replaced with introspection and assessment. I especially enjoyed the first piece you include from one of your students. It's reminiscent of Peter Elbow and reveals the kind of progress that can be made when students are extricated from stifling mandates for correct writing:

> I forced myself to write professionally during the first draft. That's always a mistake; it came out lifeless and stilted. But fortunately, good prose isn't written. It's rewritten.
>
> The essay became my own when I stopped trying to write a good English 101 paper. I let myself have fun and put all my bizarre and seemingly unconnected ideas onto the page. This free-writing process gave me a clear theme that I could expand into an actual essay (9–10).

Such student autonomy is invaluable. In many ways, it represents a break with the paradigm that tells instructors that their duty is to initiate students into the world of academic discourse. Such an approach relegates students to the job of imitation and follower. Instead of creating and developing new prose through a personal journey, the writer becomes a scribe, a disciple of the instructor, who in his omniscient role is the purveyor of truths. In this setting, little is really learned because the pupil is never allowed to invent and learn through the process of trial and error. No voice is ever forged because the entire goal of the class is not personal voice but academic allegiance.

"[. . .] teachers," you write toward the end of your essay, "can at least help students recognize that they each have a distinct voice and some truths worth communicating" (p. 283). Yes, they can, but only if the assignments — whether they are letters or five paragraph essays — emanate from the student and include that student in the production of the piece. This approach begins with a view of writers that is inclusive and aware of their linguistic abilities. Once we acknowledge the wealth of language that is brought to the college classroom — and respect the universal need to use language for self-empowerment and discovery — we can begin to design classes that have the kind of success that you experienced.

What is especially good about letter writing is its departure from the impersonal world of the academy. With students practicing a form of discourse that is familiar and nonthreatening, writing becomes an activity that is fun and enriching — something worth exploring. From that point, as you so eloquently suggest, assignments can develop and diverge into letters to authors, to literary characters, and to other writers. They can, in short, serve the higher level thinking skills while remaining accessible to the writers in our classrooms — a goal that is progressive and still very practical.

Sincerely,

Gregory Shafer
Mott Community College
Flint, Michigan

WORKS CITED

Shaughnessy, Mina. "Diving In: An Introduction to Basic Writing." Villanueva. 289–296.

Smith, Frank. *The Book of Learning and Forgetting*. New York: Columbia UP, 1998.

Villanueva, Victor, ed. *Cross Talk in Comp Theory: A Reader*. Urbana: NCTE, 1997.

*Response to "Using Letters for Process and Change
in the Basic Writing Class" by Gregory Shafer*

Dear Greg:

Your article pleased me immensely by supporting my belief that classroom letter writing is good pedagogy. My own article gives a brief history of letter writing in the classroom and highlights a number of recent studies on its usage in first-year composition courses, but it lacks the specificity of your account of experiences with basic writers.

Whereas I concentrated mainly on letters that actually get sent, I like your idea of letter writing as personal expression of, for example, feelings about a missing partner or deceased parent. This reminds me of the ancient teachers' use of *progymnasmata,* or rhetorical exercises, where students wrote according to a formula in order to practice style. Many of the exercises stressed *copia,* or copiousness. That is, they served as a means to get students to write a lot, assuming that more writing meant more practice which led to better writing fluency. Certainly with basic students, this makes sense. When teachers assign an essay, students tend to ask, How long do you want this to be? This contrasts sharply with the effusive energy you report among your students whose emotions dictate how much they will write.

You describe how your students discover the way emotion and writing coalesce to serve very personal needs and the move they make to writing editorials or letters to editors. This seems appropriate to me because it replicates the move from personal to academic that is so important for college writers — and so vital to their success. You also emphasize content over correctness, an approach that many theoreticians applaud. I agree that letter writing provides motivation for self-correction. Students recognize from the start that letters have audiences (even, surprisingly, letters that never get mailed). Awareness of a reading other, a recipient, stimulates them to write clearly and correctly. If a classmate says, I don't get this part, the student willingly makes changes. I wish young writers felt this way about all their writing tasks.

Recent interest in reflection, stirred by Kathleen Yancey and others, suggests the next logical step you might take with your students. After their initial epistolary exercise (or exercises), they could compose a letter of reflection which they actually send to the teacher. This letter would be a place for students to consider what happened to them as they wrote and revised the earlier assignment. Can they talk about the change of focus? Can they articulate the benefits of revision? What did they learn from the exercise? Is their work finished? Will they mail the letters? Why or why not? When the teacher reads and responds to their reflections, a dialogue ensues which extends the classroom discussion into written form, thus providing both a strong sense of audience and additional writing practice. It also reinforces the rapport already established in the classroom.

I really like the idea of reflection and a responding voice. Your article gave me opportunity for both, and I thank you.

Sincerely,

Elaine Fredericksen
The University of Texas
El Paso, Texas

Classroom Activities

Invite students to follow the steps in Shafer's assignment for writing personal letters. As Shafer describes, try giving students time to write rough drafts in class and to then share their drafts with the whole group in order to work on revision. Be sure to share drafts at each stage of the process, including a reading of final copies on the day that the last revised version of the letters is due.

Once students are comfortable with writing personal letters and sharing them with peers, consider extending the assignment to include letters to the editors of local newspapers. Students will need to see copies of such letters, as Shafer suggests, to gain a sense of the genre. Be sure to workshop several drafts of the letters to take students through the writing process and to sharpen their sense of audience and purpose.

Consider beginning a lengthy correspondence with another group of students, either by using the method Shafer suggests or via e-mail. Students can correspond with each other, across classrooms at the same institution, across classrooms at different institutions, and so forth. The letters can discuss reading or writing assignments that students may have in common, college survival strategies, or other issues of personal, academic, or political interest.

Thinking about Teaching

Consider following Shafer's model: Write the assignment with your students and follow each step of the process, including writing and workshopping rough drafts. Try writing personal letters, letters to the editor, and letters to colleagues so that students can observe the differences and similarities in your writing process for different audiences and purposes.

Read the responses at the end of the article. Invite colleagues to correspond with you throughout an entire semester. You might want to trade observations of your students' progress, compare assignments, or discuss pedagogy. At the end of the semester, review the letters to see how critical issues were addressed and what ideas could be implemented in a subsequent semester. As appropriate, share your reflections with students, faculty, and administrators — and consider coauthoring an article with a colleague.

Instructional Note: Life Writing and Basic Writing

Susan Naomi Bernstein

Susan Naomi Bernstein has published two previous Background Readings *ancillaries and has written for* TETYC *and* Thirteenth Moon *(a feminist literary journal) . Her conference presentations include sessions on basic writing pedagogy at the Modern Language Association and the Conference on College Composition and Communication, as well as at many regional conferences. She has taught basic writing at an urban community college and a rural state university, and currently teaches in the English Department at St. Joseph's University in Philadelphia. Her article examines the transformative nature of life writing for students of basic writing, and suggests how the writing process might be enacted in a sample assignment.*

A basic writing student from Cambodia writes about an essay which she is composing:

> This essay is about my parents during the Civil War. At last I finally was able to write about how they survive. And also one of the essays that brought me tears, anger, and frustration. And for that I learned something . . . .

The student writes these reflections as part of an ongoing correspondence to a student enrolled in another basic writing class at her community college. Both students are engaged in learning to write as non-native speakers of English and use the correspondence as an opportunity to reflect on cultural and historical issues related to events and observations in their own lives. Because the students understand that I am engaged in "research as a systematic reflection of [my] teaching . . . in an attempt to become a more effective" instructor (Blake 5), they know that I am also an audience for this correspondence. From this work, all of us learn that life writing takes on different forms in different contexts.

As the students and I study life writing in basic writing courses, we experiment with composing in a variety of genres; we also read literary autobiographies. Our criteria for choosing these autobiographical texts is as follows. First of all, the rhetorical situation must be clear; audience, purpose, and occasion for writing must be apparent. Also the sense of the writer's involvement with historical, cultural, and social issues should be of primary importance. The text itself must be persuasive — motivating the reader to take action or to be convinced of a particular point of view. Moreover, there needs to be a sense that the writer is still in process, much as society is still in process. There should be a strong indication of the need to continue to work on social problems beyond the historical moment when the text ends. Such life writing includes Maya Angelou's *I Know Why the Caged Bird Sings;* the anonymous *Go Ask Alice,* the diary of a teen-age drug user; *The Autobiography of Malcolm X;* Anne Moody's *Coming of Age in Mississippi;* and Elie Weisel's *Night.*

Life writing, in order to be persuasive, needs to be socially and rhetorically conscious rather than nostalgic or rooted in idealistic interpretations of an ahistorical past. Writing assignments that are generated from such readings are rhetorically driven, as students are urged to consider the needs of their readers as they tell their stories. Yet, since no one should have to confess her past in order to succeed in a basic writing course, I invite the students to consider the following three options as they begin one particular aspect of life writing, the narrative assignment:

1. Autobiography: For the autobiography, write a personal story about a significant event (or series of events) in your own life. Select an event that holds importance for you. Moreover, choose an event that will communicate the significance of your experience to the reader.

2. Biography: For the biography, write a story about an event (or series of events) in the life of a friend, relative, or acquaintance with an interesting experience to relate. You will need to interview this person to collect the necessary details. You also may think of this option as a kind of oral history. In the past, students have written successful essays by interviewing Vietnam veterans; recent immigrants to the United States; parents, grandparents, or others who remember historical events and/or life in your community in past decades.

3. Fiction: Invent your own story — fiction, science fiction, fables, fairy tales, and so forth would all be appropriate for this option.

But what if students confronted with such an assignment still choose to disclose events so intensely autobiographical that the reader cannot help being moved or disconcerted by them? How is a teacher to evaluate such potentially critical self-disclosures? I decided to ask students to write to me about this issue. Might I grade life writing without grading lives? After reading their responses, I wrote back to the students as follows:

Your suggestions for evaluating Essay #1 closely parallel the established grading criteria: structure, organization, grammar, punctuation, spelling, length, understanding of audience, communication of message and/or point of view. I was urged not to grade essays on the writers' opinions or on their life stories — but on how the ideas themselves are expressed. Everyone has lived through something difficult, I was reminded, but it matters most how the writer portrays his/her experiences. As you revise the final copy of Essay #1, keep these criteria clearly in mind.

In a recent semester, basic writing students in my course read Elie Weisel's *Night* and reflected on how oppression had figured in their own lives or the lives of family or acquaintances. The student cited in the introduction created a particularly memorable essay, recounting her family's experiences in a Cambodian concentration camp in the late 1970s:

> Soon my father was able to build a small hut for the three of us. Soon he was force to live separated from my mother and I at another camp. At this time I was almost three years old, left to the care of the elderly while my mother left home at early dawn to work at the rice plantation. There she was to excavate dirt with a hoe to make a water canal for rice or sometimes the soldiers would put a limit for her. For days she had to be able to dig up at least 6 to 8 tree trunks that were about two or three times her size. If she couldn't finish, tomorrow she would be forced to work with higher limitations. At this point she was also pregnant. At noon she was allowed to come back in the camp at the mess to feed me and herself. Unfortunately there nothing to eat but porridge (rice soup), porridge that mostly filled with water and vegetable and a few seeds of rice in a bowl. At the rice plantation, every chance she got, my mother tried to find any small animal such as apple snail, frog, or fish etc . . . just satisfied our hunger at night.

When the student read this paragraph aloud to her classmates and me, time seemed to stand still. "Is something wrong?" the student asked in response to the silence that greeted her reading. This question at last moved us to language. We noted the way in which the writer selected details, so that the reader felt at once a part of the scene. Moreover, we praised how such pointed description allowed the reader to gain empathy with the characters of the narrative, to begin to understand this experience of a Cambodian concentration camp.

On hearing this piece, some students were persuaded to continue working on oral histories of oppression. In particular, one student chose to interview his grandfather who, as an American soldier near the end of World War II, participated in the liberation of Buchenwald. His grandfather, the student related, had not spoken much of his wartime experiences, and the student looked forward to this project as a way of setting down his grandfather's memories:

The orders then came in to take the concentration camp of Buchenwald. That was one of the first times I was afraid for my life, stated [my grandfather.] This was because the entire place smelled of death, and when he went into the barracks he pulled out a cigarette to calm himself down, every man in the room rushed him trying to get a smoke. Out of fear he threw the pack into air to let them fight it out. He's not sure but he thinks one or two might have died in the fighting.

Again, students reacted powerfully to this piece in light of their new-found knowledge of Cambodia, as well as their reading of Weisel's *Night*. This particular class of urban community college students included people from a variety of cultural backgrounds, from students in their late teens who had recently graduated from high school, to returning adult women in their forties and fifties who had earned the GED. A broad range of life and educational experiences was represented, several audiences within one heterogeneous grouping. The students responded to these stories of oppression and survival with not only the shock of discovering histories previously unexamined, but also with empathic recognition: These are important stories, the students expressed over and over again. We need to know about them in order to understand our own life histories and our own experiences with racism and oppression, in order to understand the positions of cultures other than our own living in the United States and in our communities. Such understanding deepened the category of life writing beyond the usual narratives of "prom night" or "what I did on my summer vacation," allowing students to make connections between seemingly unrelated historical events and their own lives.

Often as instructors, we avoid assigning life writing because we fear the results may be too "personal" to assess objectively. Yet we run the risk of shutting down an important opportunity for facilitating potentially transformative writing experiences for students in basic writing classrooms. The self, in these shifting contexts, continually refigured in terms of reading and writing, becomes an identity that moves and changes with the demands of the course and the needs of the audience — and the writer — and which is immersed in the material conditions of social life. By these means, life writing becomes persuasive, as the students and I have the opportunity to challenge our thinking regarding the nature of "personal" experience. According to Francie Blake, such work allows "students to claim their own education" by actively reclaiming their own histories (Blake 6). As we examine the exigencies for engaged learning in basic writing classrooms, life writing can become a crucial part of this process.

Work Cited

Blake, Francie. "Identity, Community, and the Curriculum: A Call for Multiculturalism in the Classroom." *The Journal of Developmental Education: A Publication of the ESS Division of the Community College of Philadelphia* 2.2 (1997): 3–7.

Classroom Activities

Present students with the options suggested by Bernstein in the narrative assignment. Be sure to carefully explain the differences among autobiography, fiction, and nonfiction. Read examples of each genre in class and have students discuss the important points of each approach. Why might writers choose to fictionalize their lives? Why might they wish to write autobiography or to write the biography of someone else? Include this discussion as part of the prewriting process for writing a narrative assignment. You might also wish to have students write in imitation of one of the writers that they read for the course.

Discuss grading criteria for personal narratives. Have the students read samples of exemplary narratives and invite them to discuss the qualities of a good narrative. At each step of the writing process, have students identify those qualities in their own and peers' papers. Invite students to join you in creating a list of grading criteria for their narrative assignment based on principles of sound rhetorical structure and on the qualities they identified as critical throughout each step of the writing process.

Invite students, if they are willing, to hand in duplicate copies of their narrative assignment. If facilities exist, compile the narratives into a booklet that can then be copied and used later in the course and in subsequent semesters. The booklet will allow students to see their own and others' work in the final stage of the writing process and will suggest possibilities for writing a narrative in subsequent semesters.

Thinking about Teaching

Write a series of entries in your teaching journal that document each stage of the students' writing process for the narrative assignment. What steps of the process seemed to go particularly well? Which steps were difficult? Did students seem to make important discoveries along the way? As appropriate, share this entry with students, teachers and administrators.

Based on students' discussion of grading criteria, write a journal entry or initiate a discussion with other teachers on how to grade a personal narrative. How should teachers respond when students write about difficult personal experiences? What kinds of suggestions can teachers make for revision that will honor those experiences and foster growth in student writing? Perhaps start an online discussion on a listserv to see how other instructors have dealt with this difficult issue.

4

Writing and Reading

This chapter highlights recent research on basic writing and reading. The results of longitudinal studies cited here emphasize the interrelationship between writing and reading for student success in introductory and advanced college courses. In addition, teacher-researchers share their classroom discoveries and assignments in their own basic writing and reading courses.

Marilyn S. Sternglass suggests that student progress in reading, writing, and analytic thinking is best measured over time. She sees writing as a critical mode of learning and recommends that students begin working with analytic reading at the very beginning of their first course in basic writing. Because basic writing students generally do not enjoy reading, Dianne Goode believes that a combined course in reading and writing can best meet students' needs. Students in such a course experience the joys of reading as they learn to write. Her article offers a model course that she taught at a community college in North Carolina.

In another longitudinal study of former basic writing students at a regional state university, Eleanor Agnew and Margaret McLaughlin present evidence that reading seems to play a greater role than writing in attrition rates. They also discuss how race and social class can affect retention and success rates for former basic writing students in more advanced college courses.

The Changing Perception of the Role of Writing: From Basic Writing to Discipline Courses

Marilyn S. Sternglass

Marilyn S. Sternglass describes how life and learning intertwine in the educational experiences of her students at the City College of City University of New York. Sternglass began her study with fifty-three students, two-thirds of whom were enrolled in basic writing courses. The study, which won both the Mina P. Shaughnessy award of the Modern Language Association (1998) and the Conference on College Composition and Communication's Outstanding Book Award (1999), highlights several case studies from among this original group of students. Now Professor Emeritus, Sternglass continues to argue that students from distressed backgrounds can successfully complete their studies if given adequate time and attention. In the article that follows, she presents excerpts from her book, A Time to Know Them: A Longitudinal Study of Writing and Learning at the College Level *(1997), that focus on the particular cases of Joan, an African-American student, and Delores, a Latina student. Sternglass suggests that students can make connections between writing and learning through reading and writing. At the end of her article, she provides three linked writing assignments based on a reading of the instructor's choice. Breaking this process into three discrete steps allows for metacognitive awareness of the importance of each step and allows students to conceptualize the important interconnections among reading, writing, and learning.*

Introduction

As students move from basic writing and regular composition courses to a variety of discipline courses, they see the potential role of writing in a changing way. Students find it very productive to use writing as a basis for learning. The relationship between writing and learning has been described as having several stages, although they are not found to be practiced in a neat, linear way. Three stages of examining the relationship between writing and learning are:

1. as recall, primarily of facts

2. as the ability to organize information in an analytic way that leads to synthesis

3. as the ability to apply information to the creation of new knowledge, knowledge that is new to the learner if not to the field.

Students who were followed in a six-year longitudinal study at an urban college on the relationship between writing and learning described their perception of how writing helped them understand the materials in their courses, revealing that course demands frequently influenced the approach they took to responding to writing tasks. I would like to provide some examples of two students' comments and writing in response to these different demands in their work. Both students started at the second level of basic writing. The first is an African-American woman I call Joan and the second is a Latina woman I call Delores.

When regurgitation of facts was acceptable, they spoke of writing as helping them to remember information. For example, Joan's mode of writing was to supply definitions in response to examination questions, carefully using the language of instructors or textbooks. In a paper for a sociology course during her second year at the college, Joan wrote: "Sociology is referred to as the systematic and objective (scientific) study of human society and social interaction. Sociology is more or less the study of interaction within groups in society. A sociologist never studies an individual. He or she may observe or study an individual's interaction within a group or groups" (Sternglass 33). As has been noted in *Women's Ways of Knowing* (1986), Joan was relying on "received knowledge," with authoritative definitions her basis for response. Writing helped her remember these definitions, but she was not yet ready to go beyond them in a setting where this was what was required in examinations and papers.

In a paper for an introductory philosophy course in her second semester, Delores similarly relied on academic language to explain some ideas of William James: "In his piece 'Pragmatism,' William James discusses the truth of ideas. In his work, James made a mere distinction between pragmatists and intellectualists view about the truth of an idea. For intellectualists, as James describes, the truth of an idea is an inert and the same time stationary property of an idea. Intellectualists supposition is that once an individual has reached the truth of anything the process of searching for the truth is discontinued" (Sternglass 44). It seems likely that Delores's unfamiliarity with the concepts of the philosophy course motivated her to protect herself by incorporating the text-jargon in her paper.

When demands for more complex reasoning were asked for, these students spoke of how writing helped them critique ideas, see both sides of issues, and to analyze more deeply the causes and effects of issues. A striking example of how course demands can affect the complexity of the writing can be seen in a paper that Delores wrote in her freshman composition course the same semester that she was taking the philosophy course. In a paper on Orwell's "Shooting an Elephant," Delores offered her own interpretation of the effects of subjugating others on the "tyrant" himself. She wrote:

> Orwell says, "A tyrant needs to wear a mask." Orwell in his essay "Shooting an Elephant," is referring to the kind of behavior that the tyrant must display in front of the people they oppress. Even though they might as well behave differently following their own feelings, they have to behave as expected by the people. Even though tyrants subjugate the people, in some way or another they are also subjugating

themselves by have to let feeling [be] suppress. And at the same time robbing themselves (Sternglass 44–45).

While clearly hostile to the behavior of the tyrants she described, Delores also revealed a compassionate sense of understanding the impact of such behaviors on the individuals involved in such acts. Although not yet deeply involved in her major, psychology, she possessed a sense of empathy that would assist her in her future studies. And, in a composition setting in which the primary readings were literary ones, critical interpretations of such texts were highly valued. By the beginning of her sixth year, close to completing her undergraduate degree in psychology, Joan explained how she had come to understand the difference between dependence on textbook language and the importance of putting ideas into her own words. She said:

> "Writing helps me 'regurgitate' back what I learned, not to mimic back
> to the professor but to apply what you learned from readings. . . .
> Writing helps me remember things because I have to apply concepts."
> No clearer explanation from a student could be imagined (Sternglass).

As students became more knowledgeable in their major areas, and where risk-taking was encouraged, they proposed new relationships among existing ideas, recommended alteration in the way images and stereotypes were presented to the public, and prepared research projects to investigate questions not previously researched. Constructing knowledge took different forms with different students. For Joan, in her fourth year at the college, constructing knowledge manifested itself through the integration of her studies in one discipline with those of another. As a psychology major, Joan had learned many terms that she had used in the analyses of psychological cases. Now, in her world humanities course, she brought in a psychological concept in the analysis of Candide's optimism. Joan wrote, "Pangloss inspired Candide's Optimism because he attributed what we would call in Psychology, a Halo-effect to every experience in life, meaning, there is good in everything and everyone" (Sternglass 54).

Applying a psychological concept was a far cry from her regurgitating the terms in her earlier work in sociology. Delores was able to go further than Joan was in proposing new research in her field to investigate issues that others had not examined. Delores's absorption with the relationships between race and gender led to her to undertake a study on the relationship between skin-color and self-esteem in a special enrichment program available to her at Lehman College of the City University of New York. Her study was titled "Skin Color and Its Impact on Self-Esteem of Latino College Students — Dominicans and Puerto Ricans." She described how writing this report made her feel: "I create it. It's my paper — my ideas, like a birth. There wasn't anything like that before" (Sternglass 57). Her evident pride in her originality and the opportunity to make a contribution to her field is evidence of the potential waiting to be realized by students who begin at basic writing levels. In the six years that it took Joan to earn a Bachelor's Degree, Delores earned both a Bachelor's and Master's Degree.

One of the important ideas to be considered here is that the ability to analyze materials thoughtfully is one that grows gradually over time. In basic writing and regular composition courses we have the opportunity to give students assignments that will begin this process, allowing them to practice the more complex reasoning tasks they will be expected to be able to handle in their upper division courses. A few examples of how this process began for students within basic writing levels will illustrate how this can happen:

In a paper, Ricardo, a Latino student enrolled in the second level of basic writing, demonstrated the activist part of his nature. In discussing Maya Angelou's *I Know Why the Caged Bird Sings,* Ricardo concluded his discussion by examining the larger issue of racism that was considered in Angelou's autobiography:

> Due to Maya Angelou's determination, sense of pride and activism she was able to break new grounds not only in the streetcar system in San Francisco [as the first female operator] but on the struggle to maintain her identity and self respect as a black person. This story could had happen in any period of time from the 1930's to the late 1980's. But no matter what period of time it take place, we have to take charge and be active in order to produce changes that would eliminate the bias and racism forever (Sternglass 79).

Unlike some other students who saw stereotyping and racist comments as harmless because they assumed they could not apply to them, Ricardo not only felt the impact of racist behavior toward himself personally, but he was able to see beyond his own situation to how the larger society would be impacted by such attitudes and behaviors. Even at this early point in his academic career, Ricardo always had a mission to help others.

Also, during her first semester at the college, Chandra, an African-American student enrolled in the second level of basic writing, tellingly pictured her recognition of her complex identity in a paper she wrote in response to reading an essay by Richard Rodriguez:

> Similar to Rodriguez, I felt that when I became a student I was "remade." The language I was used to speaking was based upon slang terms. All of the schools I attended allowed me to speak and write with incorrect English. I learned the correct pronunciation of words in drama class. Recently here at City College, I have gained a new identity which I feel that I don't identify with. I am referred to as an African-American. Similar to Rodriguez experiences, I've never connected myself to this racial minority so I feel guilty representing a culture I knew nothing about. I spent all of my life trying to overcome my race and color in order to produce as a part of the American society. But I have realized, one cannot move forward unless they know where they have been. Now,

I feel like I've missed out on something since I don't know anything about African history or African culture. My peers always viewed me as a "wanna be" white girl because I tried correcting my speech and speak intelligently. When I tried to imitate the slang later in my teens, everyone could always tell I did not belong. I always believed that I had to give up my culture to be taken seriously as an intellectual. I later realized that I didn't (Sternglass 68–69).

For both Ricardo and Chandra, readings that presented issues that the students had had experience with stimulated their reflection and encouraged them to offer responses that were simultaneously analytical and personal. Because these examples address issues of race and culture, it is too easy to insist that only multicultural readings can stimulate such reflection on the part of students. However, other issues such as social, economic, political, or environmental ones, to name just a few, could be addressed in readings to foster such reflection and encourage students to take critical stances.

One question that is frequently raised is, when is it appropriate to ask students to begin analytic tasks? My response would be from the very first writing task and the very first course the student is enrolled in. Of course, the other issues of basic writing need to be addressed, but, in my opinion, they should be addressed within the context of serious, thoughtful writing tasks that challenge the students conceptually as well as linguistically. That leads me to my workshop activity:

Workshop Activity

- Select a reading you might assign to students in your basic writing class.

- Write out three assignments you might give to your students, one asking for recall of facts, one asking for an analytic response, and one moving the students beyond the reading itself.

Handout:

Reading _____

Assignment #1 based on recall of facts:

Assignment #2 asking for analysis:

Assignment #3 asking for ideas or implications that go beyond the reading itself:

Discussion and conclusion

Works Cited

Belenky, M. E., B. M. Clinchy, N. R. Goldberger, and J. M. Tarule. *Women's Ways of Knowing: The Development of Self, Voice, and Mind.* New York: Basic Books, 1986.

Sternglass, M. S. *Time to Know Them: A Longitudinal Study of Writing and Learning at the College Level.* Mahwah, NJ: Lawrence Erlbaum Associates, 1997.

Classroom Activities

Try assigning your class the activities that Sternglass presents in her article:

- Assignment #1 based on recall of facts (What does the text say?)

- Assignment #2 asking for analysis (What does the text mean?)

- Assignment #3 asking for ideas or implications that go beyond the reading itself (What relationships can you draw between the text and what you are learning in your other courses? What relationships can you draw between the text and the "real world"?)

- Discussion and conclusion (Ask students to read their writing to each other in small groups and then to discuss what they've learned with the rest of the class.)

Invite students to keep a "learning journal" that documents their progress over time. At the end of the week, have students write down their responses to the following questions:

- What were the most important ideas I learned (read about, wrote about, observed, etc.) this week?

- Why was this learning important?

- What questions do I have, and how can I answer them?

Documenting their own learning processes allows students to see their progress over time, which Sternglass believes is very important.

Thinking about Teaching

In your teaching journal, keep an ongoing list of what readings or texts seem to promote long-term learning. Which texts work best with particular classes? Which readings don't seem to work at all? If readings or texts seem too difficult for students, continue to experiment with the kinds of questions that will elicit thoughtful writing. As Sternglass suggests, learning for basic writing students often takes place over much longer periods of time than for students with fewer academic and life challenges. However, learning does occur, and an analytic frame of mind should be fostered in students from the beginning of their college education.

Consider doing a longitudinal case study of your own students' processes and progress with writing after they leave basic writing. Working with interviews and papers written for other classes, document the kinds of assignments students undertake and how students continue to respond to and learn from their schooling. Use your findings to evaluate the effectiveness of the basic writing course that you teach. What aspects of your course seem to provide a good foundation for students' continued learning? What aspects of the course might you change, based on your findings?

Creating a Context for Developmental English

Dianne Goode

In the following article, Dianne Goode describes CONCUR ("CONtextual CURriculum"), "an innovative curriculum program" that she taught at Piedmont Community College in North Carolina. "Its purpose," Goode writes, "was to design classes specifically for developmental students, applying the principles of contextual learning." Goode's course was a combined experience in reading and writing that included the publication essays written by students in the class. The collection is now available in Piedmont Community College's library. Goode emphasizes the need for students to feel motivated to read and write. She is especially concerned that students discover the joy of reading, "the thrill of becoming lost in a book." In this regard, Goode believes that students learn more by reading whole texts that they choose themselves, than by reading short articles or brief excerpts from longer texts. By contextualizing their own learning and by becoming involved in a hands-on reading and writing project, Goode argues that students become more competent and empowered readers. Suggestions for how to structure the reading activities for the course are included in this article.

Introduction

D evelopmental students in community colleges typically have a life-long history of avoiding both reading and writing whenever possible, with predictable results. These students need to spend significant amounts of time, over significant periods of time, interacting with text, i.e., reading and writing. In order to motivate them to read and write, the developmental English class needs to provide basic writers with a *context*.

The guiding principles of contextual learning are these:

1. People learn when they have a need that is meaningful and real.

2. People learn through interactions with others.

3. People learn by making approximations which, with practice, come closer and closer to mastery.

4. People learn at varying rates and in various stages.

Each of these four factors contributes to a learning experience which is "whole, meaningful, supportive, and continuous" (Cooper 10).

The rationale for contextual literacy instruction is based on compelling evidence that skill-drill comprehension questions (for reading) or grammar exercises (for writing) have little effect on students' language skills. Every English teacher has confronted the frustration of spending hours on the apostrophe, for example, only to see it misused in a writing assignment a day later. Why is transfer so poor? Psycholinguists argue (Stanovich, Smith, and Gee among others) that language skills are developed over a lifetime of interaction with text. In other words, people learn to read by reading, and they learn to write by reading and writing.

The developmental English instructor, therefore, must find ways to inspire students to do more reading and more writing. Unfortunately, most developmental students have emerged from their years of formal schooling convinced that they are unlikely to derive much personal satisfaction from focused interaction with text. Turning those attitudes around is the instructor's first challenge, and Piedmont Community College took on that challenge with a project called CONCUR.

CONCUR

Piedmont Community College, serving rural Person and Caswell Counties, in the fall of 1997 sought funding through the North Carolina State Board Reserve Fund for an innovative curriculum project which it called CONCUR, for CONtextual CURriculum. Its purpose was to design classes specifically for developmental students, applying the principles of contextual learning.

In North Carolina, community college developmental reading and developmental writing have been combined into developmental English classes, which meet five hours a week. This schedule works well for the extended activities of a workshop classroom. Although originally conceived as complementary elements of a complete course, either the reading workshop or the writing workshop may be offered as a separate class. Workshop strategies may also be incorporated into more structured classes.

Engaging students in literate activity through a workshop classroom model is not a new idea. Published in 1987 and revised ten years later, Nancie Atwell's *In the Middle* explains in detail her implementation of this methodology with middle school students. It works equally well with any age group from elementary to adult.

The context created for the CONCUR developmental English class was a publishing company. From the beginning, class members knew that their papers would be published in a class anthology which would become part of the school library's permanent collection. The title, organization, and layout of the eventual publication were to be decided by the class. As others have noted, the promise of publication is itself both empowering and motivating for student writers (Boese, Byrne, and Silverman 46).

Motivation

An English instructor's best motivational tools emerge from the fact that 1) reading and writing are means of communication, and 2) human beings are social creatures who like to communicate.

The CONCUR students were intrigued by the context of a publishing company, with the accompanying promise that their writing would become public for the world to see. The students immediately perceived this approach as a radical departure from the classroom writing they had done before. They were excited by the opportunity to publish but, at the same time, anxious about presenting themselves well.

Another important part of motivation in a workshop setting is that the topics of communication — the reading, writing, and sharing — must be the student's choice rather than imposed from above. Students will read and write much more willingly if they read and write about what interests them. Empowering students to choose what they read and write about is, therefore, a critical element of the reading/writing workshop approach. As the weeks go by, most class members find themselves reading and writing not just willingly, but enthusiastically.

Grading

Grades for the CONCUR course are determined by points accumulated over a grading cycle, usually two weeks long. The instructor records point values on a sheet called a Weekly Work Plan (WWP) during a summer session or a Fortnightly Work Plan (FWP) during a full-length semester. Students receive points for attending class (5 pts/day; 20 day/cycle); turning in reading journals and vocabulary lists complete and on time (5 pts. each; 20 day/cycle); having homework assignments complete (5 pts. each); participating in class activities such as peer editing or sharing (5 pts. each), and so on. Points total 100 per cycle, which usually involves adding some extra points to those earned.

The FWP provides biweekly feedback to the students about their attendance and effort and makes manifest the close relationship between attendance and effort on one hand and grade received on the other. Each FWP carries its own point total for the cycle as well as cumulative points received over points possible. If a student's cumulative points fall below 85 percent, he or she must meet with the instructor.

Final grades are taken from the FWP cumulative total at the end of the term. Writing workshop papers are not given letter grades, though they may be deemed unacceptable and returned to the writer for additional revision. Since no paper can be considered finished until it has been through the entire writing process of revision, editing, and proofreading, all papers — at least in theory — which do reach that point will be worthy of a satisfactory grade. Lynn Ward, the instructor of the summer CONCUR English class at Piedmont Community College, found that the students' grades reflected on the work plans ended up being the same as they would have received if he had graded papers in the traditional manner.

The Reading Workshop

People who don't read don't enjoy reading. Typically, they have never known the thrill of becoming lost in a book. The key concept in the reading workshop is to get the student to read and keep reading, until he or she finally experiences that joy.

Students in the reading workshop must read a certain number of pages per week in a book and turn in journal entries on their reading; keep an ongoing list of new vocabulary words; participate in class activities such as lit circles; and present and discuss their books with their classmates. Each of these activities accumulates points toward the weekly or biweekly total which, for simplicity's sake, should add up to 100. Again, receiving weekly or biweekly feedback on their progress through the term keeps students in touch with the expectations of higher education. Class activities cannot be made up, so absences have an immediate effect.

Providing Books

In order to gain experience in following a book-length narrative, students must read whole books rather than magazine articles or sports almanacs.

One of the early classes meets at the local public library. Students receive extra credit for getting a library card (or having one already). The instructor visits the library the night before and (with permission) pulls a variety of books to "push" — preferably ones the instructor has read and can wax enthusiastic about. All genres should be included: romance, science fiction, fantasy, horror, biography, real-life adventure, history, mystery, and so on, from both adult and young adult sections. Books by and about minorities will attract interest, and paperbacks are less intimidating than hardbacks.

The next day the class gathers around a table piled high with the books and listens to the instructor's wide-ranging book talk. The instructor models book-choosing by showing the covers, reading from the teaser on the back cover aloud, and then reading from the excerpt on the inside front page. The instructor emphasizes that a book one enjoys reading, even if it's longer, will *seem* shorter than a short book that's boring.

Unfortunately, few public libraries are well equipped for the adult low-level reader. If possible, the college should have a collection of books specifically for developmental students, located in the classroom, main library, developmental lab, or learning center — somewhere that students can have easy access to it. (The Perfection Learning Catalog, 1-800-831-4190, offers a comprehensive list of trade paperbacks coded by interest level and reading level.)

Pages Required and Journal Entries

Students should read fifty to seventy-five pages a week. They should fill out two reading journal entries per week, each one about a paragraph in length. In order to move students toward more critical reading of their books, journal entries should involve more than retelling the plot. Rather, students should reflect, analyze, speculate, evaluate, and so on. A list of open-ended journal-starters is helpful, such as "The author keeps my interest by. . . ." or "This story makes me curious to know more about. . . ." Students should be permitted to abandon any book if they don't like it after reading thirty pages. They still get credit for pages read.

If the classroom is equipped with bulletin board space, students will enjoy seeing their progress on a poster with everyone's names listed vertically and blocks representing pages read across the top. Each week the students can update the poster by coloring in blocks equal to pages read that week. Many will read more than required, and displaying their accomplishment for their friends to see is a matter of pride and friendly competition. At the same time, students who fall behind will have a graphic reminder and perhaps even a little peer pressure to urge them along.

Class Activities

Reading workshop class time provides an opportunity for students to enjoy the social aspects of reading. Here are some of the reading activities used:

- *Silent Reading.* Periodically, a half-hour of silent reading allows students to experience the warm feeling of reading among other readers. *It is imperative that the teacher read with the class.*

- *Book Talks.* At regular intervals, class time should be set aside for students to take turns talking to the class about their current books. Seating should be arranged in a large circle for this activity. Students will call out to one another, "Hey, can I have that book next?"

- *Vocabulary Sharing.* Again sitting in a large circle, students take turns sharing two or three favorite new words they have discovered. The instructor should choose one to emphasize and assign as homework that the students must use that word three times in conversation before the next class meeting.

- *Critical Reading Strategies.* In order to move the students toward a more critical approach to text, the instructor should discuss an analytic strategy and then immediately apply that strategy in a lit circle. For example, students might look at text in order to identify the author's bias, locate logical fallacies, or evaluate the effectiveness of figurative language. As time goes on, the class will accumulate a repertoire of critical reading strategies.

- *Literature Circles.* A lit circle is comprised of students who have all read the same text. A newspaper or magazine article works well for this activity, or a few pages copied from a book. Instructors unfamiliar with literature circles can find a more detailed explanation in Harvey Daniels's book by the same name. Originally conceived for elementary students, lit circles work well with adults as a technique for modeling and practicing critical reading strategies.

When the lit circles are held, students must sit — literally — in a circle. Each student is given a particular role to prepare for the class discussion. Roles may include the summarizer; the questioner, who comes up with discussion questions; the vocabulary finder, who defines unfamiliar words; the connector, who relates the piece to real life, and so on. The instructor may also want to create roles according to critical reading strategies the class has studied. One student, pair, or group may be asked to find examples of biased language in the text, while others look for questionable assumptions, hasty generalizations, dubious statistics, and so forth. After the students have some experience with how a lit circle works, the instructor may prefer to dispense with assigned roles entirely. In effect, all the students become responsible for all the roles.

The instructor may encourage several students to read the same book and then bring them together as a lit circle to discuss it. No book should be imposed on them, however.

Note

Detailed curriculum materials from the CONCUR project, including handouts, are available from the author. Contact Dianne Goode at ladydi@intrex.net.

Works Cited

Atwell, Nancie. *In the Middle*. Portsmouth: Boynton, 1987.

Boese, Peggy, Mary Ellen Byrne, and Louise Silverman. "The Rewards of Publication of Student Writings." *Teaching English in the Two-Year College* 24 (1997): 42–46.

Cooper, J. D. *Literacy: Helping Children Create Meaning*. Boston: Houghton, 1993.

Daniels, Harvey. *Literature Circles: Voice and Choice in the Student-Centered Classroom*. York: Stenhouse, 1994.

Gee, James Paul. *The Social Mind: Language, Ideology, and Social Practice*. New York: Bergin, 1992.

———. "What is Literacy?" *Journal of Education* 171.1 (1989): 19–25.

Smith, Frank. *Understanding Reading: A Psycholinguistic Analysis of Reading and Learning to Read*. 5th ed. Hillsdale: Erlbaum, 1994.

Stanovich, Keith. "Matthew Effects in Reading: Some Consequences of Individual Differences in the Acquisition of Literacy." *Reading Research Quarterly* 21 (1986): 360–407.

Classroom Activities

If possible, have students visit the local public or campus library. Include information about how to obtain a library card for those students who don't have one. Make sure that students are aware of other resources that might be provided by the library (Internet access, services for children, etc.).

Incorporate some of the reading activities suggested by Goode into your own course, including silent reading, book talks, vocabulary sharing, critical reading strategies, and literature circles. Have students record in their journals which of these activities are most effective for them; they will also need to include why these activities are effective, and how each activity contributes to their overall learning process. The goal is to have students continue to make connections between their reading and writing experiences.

Thinking about Teaching

With other teachers (and with students) generate a list of what Goode calls "open-ended journal starters." What devices do you (and others) use in your own journal to prompt your own writing about reading? Which prompts have been particularly effective? Which prompts seem problematic? What new prompts can you invent together? Try posting this question to a listserv for teachers to generate a wider pool of ideas.

Consider publishing a book of your students' writing about reading, as suggested by Goode. How would such a project be feasible in your own classroom? Find out what facilities your campus or local copy center has for duplication of longer manuscripts. You might also consider asking your campus library if it would add a student-generated text to its holdings.

Goode writes: "No books should be imposed on them [students], however." Do you agree or disagree with this statement? In your teaching journal, explore this question in more detail. Recall your own experiences with school-based reading and how you responded to books that were "imposed on" you. How would you evaluate such experiences? Be sure to share your journal ideas with other teachers — and with students.

Basic Writing Class of '93
Five Years Later: How the Academic
Paths of Blacks and Whites Diverged

Eleanor Agnew and Margaret McLaughlin

In the longitudinal study that follows, Eleanor Agnew and Margaret McLaughlin discovered that the retention rate for former basic writing students at their school, Georgia Southern University, seemed to be overdetermined by race and social class. Moreover, successful retention seemed to be more related to reading comprehension than to writing ability. In the introduction to their study, Agnew and McLaughlin cite the following statistics:

> *Of the 28,751 freshmen entering Georgia's public colleges and universities in 1994, 43 percent required remediation. At our own school, a regional university in southeast Georgia, with 14,000 students and an approximate 75 percent European American to 25 percent African American ratio, the percentages become somewhat higher: 52 percent of the entering freshmen were placed in developmental classes in 1995, and in 1996, the number was 45.3 percent. . . .*

Agnew and McLaughlin were concerned with what happened to developmental writing students after they left developmental English. "Among our related questions were the following: 1. How many of these students will graduate and in how long a time period? 2. Are there correlations between the attrition rate and students' first quarter writing abilities?" *The authors discuss the results of their study and offer implications for classroom practice.*

Eleanor Agnew is an associate professor of English at Georgia Southern University who has published in Assessing Writing, JBW, Teachers of English to Speakers of Other Languages (TESOL), *and the anthology* Grading in the Post-Process Classroom. *In addition, she is a coauthor of* My Mama's Waltz. *Margaret McLaughlin also teaches at Georgia Southern and has published previously in* TETYC, Notes on Teaching English, The Journal of College Reading and Learning, *and the anthology* Innovative Learning Strategies.

Background of Our Study

The conflicting reports about the validity of tracking students into basic writing classes provided the impetus for us to examine our own program. During the 1993 fall quarter, we decided to follow the academic progress of the sixty-one students who had been placed in the two basic reading/writing classes we were teaching. We formulated our principal research question as "What happens to our developmental writers after they leave Developmental English?" Among our related questions were the following: 1. How many of these students will graduate and in how long a time period? 2. Are there correlations between the attrition rate and students' first quarter writing abilities?

To address these questions, we followed the academic progress of our students through personal interviews, interviews with their subsequent English instructors, a classification scheme based on three possible levels of academic success, analyses of student writing, and analyses of academic transcripts.

The Subjects

As experienced teachers, we recognized that the students enrolled in our classes for the 1993 fall quarter were quite representative of developmental students at our university. Virtually all of our subjects were recent high school graduates; two-thirds were African American; and SAT Verbal scores ranged from a low of 220 to a high of 410 with a mean score of 350. Questionnaires revealed that most were first-generation college students who entered our classes highly motivated to get out of remedial classes, get going on regular college courses, graduate, and get a "well-paying job." Few of the students had ever read a whole book, and their writing backgrounds were often limited to high school research papers, which they told us they could copy from reference books and get by.

The Class

The subjects of this study were in a team-taught developmental reading/writing class in which a modification of the Bartholomae/Petrosky *Facts, Artifacts, Counterfacts,* model was used. The students read a book approximately every two weeks and kept a reader response journal. They also wrote personal experience essays, an autobiography of about 1500 words, summaries of articles about the subject of the course, "Growth and Change in Adolescence," several essay exams about the books they were reading, and, finally, a documented opinion paper.

At our institution, students must earn a C in the developmental course before they are eligible to take the state mandated exit exams which they must pass before they can enroll in regular college classes. The exit exams are alternate versions of the placement tests that put them in the basic writing course in the first place: an English basic skills test and an impromptu timed essay. Exit essays are anonymously evaluated by two English faculty other than their own instructors. If students are successful in each of these three challenges, they are eligible to enroll in Freshman English I. Those who are not successful at the end of the first quarter may take as many as three more quarters of these developmental classes before they are excluded from the university. Placement and exit criteria for all remedial courses in Georgia are mandated by the University System Board of Regents.

Results

After five years in college, most of our students have not done well in college *overall,* suggesting that their performance in the Developmental English course was not a predictor of future success: for example, some students who did not pass the developmental writing course the first time have had successful academic careers whereas some students who passed the developmental writing course on their first attempt did not perform well in subsequent courses. Probably the most startling finding, however, is that, of those students who were *not* successfully remediated in one quarter, white students have more than twice the success rate in subsequent college courses as black students who *did* pass the course. Although it is impossible to predict what any of these students' experiences would have been without the Developmental English course, the fact that "successful" remediation resulted in a much lower success rate for African-American students than for white students caused us to make a closer examination of the academic progress of both groups of students.

Five years after matriculation, nineteen of the students (31 percent) have graduated, and four more of these high risk students are making steady progress toward a 1999 graduation date. These percentages compare favorably with our institution's average 35 percent graduation rate for all students. When we looked below the surface of these figures, however, we found disturbing discrepancies: 57 percent of the white students have graduated but only 22.5 percent of the black students.[1] Moreover, the sixty-one students' overall academic progress did not correlate with their verbal SAT scores nor with their ability to pass the developmental writing class.

When students' progress is assessed according to race, a distinct difference in academic histories can be seen. Although a handful of African-American students have had uneventful educations over five years, the majority of records display "P's", "S's", "E's," and "D's", which stand for Probation, Suspension, Exclusion, and Dismissal. While certainly not free of "P's", "S's", "E's," and "D's", the academic progress of white students has been smoother. A few had an occasional probation or suspension or exclusion, but none were dismissed from the university for academic reasons.

To discover whether we could find any relation between academic success and the students' first quarter writing abilities, we compared their academic success rates over the five year period with their ability to pass the Developmental English class. In Table 1, we used a simple classification scheme to collapse the four-year academic histories of both African Americans and whites. "Successful" refers to students whose academic histories show no probations, dismissals, suspensions, or exclusions; "rocky" refers to students who are still currently enrolled but who have been on probation, dismissal, suspension, or exclusion; and "gone" refers to those who are no longer enrolled. The academic histories of both races are compared with their first quarter writing abilities as measured by their success in exiting remedial English at the end of the first quarter. About three times as many whites (53 percent) have had "successful" academic histories as blacks (18 percent). Further, of those students who exited and were therefore theoretically ready for regular courses, about twice as many blacks (64 percent) as whites (34 percent) are no longer enrolled at the university.

Low Success Rates for African Americans

According to a recent national study, African-American college freshmen are placed in remedial English courses at over twice the rate of white students, yet they comprise only 6 percent of the graduating population (Gray). Astin reports college attrition rates for African-American students at 49.5 percent and Cortina reports the rate at 73.4 percent (qtd. in Fidler and Godwin 35). Referring specifically to the Georgia system, Presley writes, "Developmental English courses . . . apparently pose the most difficulty for minority students. Black students do not exit the developmental English classes in as high a percentage as other students do. And, once in a regular English class, a lower percentage of black students pass than the passing percentage of other students" (51).

In 1993, the year we began our study, 48 percent of the 828 entering black students at our university were placed in Developmental English classes. At the end of four quarters, 15 percent of the black

Table 1. Comparison of Blacks' and Whites' Five-Year Academic Histories and Success with Basic Writing Course

Total Students Who Passed BW 1st Time	*Total Students Who Did Not Pass BW 1st Time*
Whites: 68%	Whites: 32%
Blacks: 56%	Blacks: 44%
Five Years Later: White Students	*Five Years later: White Students*
Successful: 53%	Successful: 43%
Rocky History: 13%	Rocky History: 29%
Gone: 34%	Gone: 28%
Five Years Later: Black Students	*Five Years Later: Black Students*
Successful: 18%	Successful: 6%
Rocky History: 18%	Rocky History: 23%
Gone: 64%	Gone: 71%

students were dismissed from the university for failure to exit Developmental English. In contrast, 22 percent of entering white freshmen had to take Developmental English classes, and at the end of four quarters, fewer than 1 percent was dismissed from the university for inability to pass the course. To explore possible causes for the disparity between the percentages of black and white students for whom Developmental English barred the gates to higher education is certainly beyond the scope of this study, but a cursory review of the retention literature suggests a number of possibilities.

Fidler and Godwin, referring to several studies which describe high college attrition rates for African Americans, state that "colleges and universities have historically structured their curricula, student services, and campus environment based on a white middle class norm" (35). Jones bluntly says, "In its insistence on hierarchy, racism situates basic writing programs as Jim-Crow way stations for minority students, for the thousands of Black and Latino students who fill basic writing classes across the nation" (73).

A study of African-Americans in the academy found that "only five percent of all college faculty are African-American" (Gray 3A). Hillard sees the paucity of African-American faculty as a big problem for blacks who enter the university. They are taught primarily by white instructors, who may not only have negative attitudes towards black language patterns but who "are ill-prepared to teach students who are unlike themselves" (qtd. in Harrold 17). In *The Agony of Education,* Feagin, Vera, and Imani agree, stating that "the intellectual discourse at traditionally white colleges and universities is for the most part parochial and restricted by subtle or overt Eurocentric interests and biases" (114). Hopkins believes that one reason African-American males in particular have difficulty within the educational system is because teachers have low expectations when they should "be committed to this population, show compassion and understanding and be confident that these students can learn" (112). Wallace and Bell cite a number of other studies which suggest causes for the low retention rates of black students at predominantly white institutions: being a first-generation student; having a low socio-economic status; experiencing a lack of comfortable social context; lacking prerequisite courses; and having difficulty with core courses (308). African-American students' feelings of invisibility and marginalization on white campuses may undermine their scholastic ability and determination to succeed, add Feagin, Vera, and Imani: "The lack of human recognition the students detect in some white peers, teachers, advisers, police, and other campus personnel is serious, for it teaches major lessons about neglect, exclusion, or self-worthlessness" (133). And, despite the fact that linguists and literacy scholars have been urging educators for the past thirty years to accept African-American Vernacular English as a legitimate linguistic variety, the national Ebonics debate in December, 1996, and January, 1997, revealed how widely and deeply the negative attitudes toward permitting its use in the classroom prevail.

Focusing on the Wrong Problems

When we set up our tracking study, the focal point of our interest was our students' emerging writing ability. Our assumption, shared by most academics, was that students' writing skill would be a key determinant of their long-range academic success or failure. The belief that students must be proficient writers before they can tackle the rest of their college work has long been accepted in the academy and is the foundation around which most colleges and universities build their curricula: hence, the ubiquitous first year basic writing course.

However, after five years of following our students, we have to question our original assumptions about the role of writing skill as the primary determinant of college success. In fact, most of the successfully "remediated" students in our study began to falter as soon as they began courses in history, psychology, sociology, or other subjects which were heavily reading-based. We looked specifically at our students' success over five years with the regular college courses, the ones which are more reading-based than writing-based. We calculated the percentages of reading-based or math-based courses our students had passed.[2] The result is a percentage of reading-based college courses passed with a C or better. We considered the students who had passed 80 percent or more of these courses to be "Above Average" in overall college success; those who had passed from 70 to 80 percent to be "Average," and those who had passed from 0 to 69 percent to be "Below Average." Neither the white students nor the African-American students have performed exceptionally well, if we consider that over one quarter of the whites and nearly three quarters of the blacks have been classified as "Below Average."

Yet we saw the same discrepancy revealed in our Table 1: 67 percent of African Americans were "Below Average," compared to 27.3 percent of whites, and only 18 percent of African Americans were "Above Average," compared to 59 percent of whites. Again, the fact that African Americans who had been "remediated" foundered at a much higher rate than whites suggests that we may need to reexamine assumptions behind first year programs designed to help at-risk students succeed in college.

Increasing Emphasis on Reading Skills

Virtually all institutions of higher learning consider basic writing and freshman composition courses to be service courses which *must* be offered in the first year to prepare students for later college work. But perhaps institutions need to pay closer attention to the reading skills of their at-risk students. As mentioned above, many students in our study revealed that before the Fall of 1993, when they entered our course, they had never read an entire book. Although we assigned more books for them to read than they had ever read before, eight weeks of reading was undoubtedly not enough to prepare them well for college reading, as evidenced by the low success rates with reading-based courses. Though writing and reading skills are frequently interactive, in a typical institutional scenario, the two are often distanced from one another and treated as separate skills.

For example, at our institution, students find it easier to exit the first-quarter developmental reading course than the first-quarter developmental writing course because exiting is based on their ability to pass a standardized multiple-choice reading test at the end of the quarter. The majority do pass the first time. But this assessment tool may not be providing a valid measure of the reading skills students will need in higher level courses. Chase, Gibson, and Carson point out that "reading differs significantly across academic disciplines in college in terms of number of assigned pages, text characteristics and function, and student perception of the role of text" (14). They closely examined the reading requirements for four college courses — American History, Political Science, Biology, and English — and found that in American History, for example, students were required to read eighty pages per week. In Political Science, thirty-four pages per week were required, and in Biology, thirty pages of text, five pages of lab manual, and ten pages of study guide were required every week (11). But it was not just the amount of material which was challenging, it was the nature of how that material needed to be processed. The authors write,

> In these university courses, reading was a vehicle for gathering information and ideas which would then be transformed through analysis and synthesis into written exams, essays, and other application activi-

ties, such as labs. Even in the Political Science course, where exams were multiple choice, questions were designed to require the student to make critical judgments and synthesize material from texts and lectures (12).

Underprepared students may be more challenged by reading tasks than writing tasks in their later courses because at our institution, and, we suspect, a number of others, the majority of professors in non-English disciplines do not emphasize writing in their courses, nor do they make writing projects the primary component of the course grade. If they require papers, they tend to be less critical of them than an English teacher might be. Thus, if basic writers finish their required English courses, they will probably never again do as much writing as they did in those early courses. But reading is a task they will face on a daily basis for virtually every course they will take for the duration of their academic careers. Our data suggest that success in college depends more on reading ability and all that it implies — speed, comprehension, and critical thinking — than on writing skills. Institutions should consider strengthening first-year reading programs as parallels to first-year writing programs.

Institutions which serve at-risk students should develop Reading Centers, along with Writing Centers, to offer students support and assistance with their college reading assignments throughout their college years. Robert and Thomson describe how the Student Learning Center at the University of California at Berkeley offers study groups for different subjects which are led by experienced students: "The leader acts as a facilitator by encouraging active discussion and helping students understand lecture and reading material" (10).

Other Risk Factors for Minorities

Of course, literacy skills may be just one of several factors contributing to the high attrition rate of African-American students. Tinto points out in *Leaving College* that cultural, financial, and psychological considerations may also play a role in attrition. Simmons cites degree of maturity, family support, motivation, expectations, and social skills as elements which may influence African-American students' success or failure in college. Furthermore, the emotional and cultural disenfranchisement which blacks experience on white campuses may escalate the drop-out rate. Robert and Thomson write that "it is difficult for minority students to escape the suspicion that they really don't deserve to be at the university and wouldn't be there if they didn't get special (read 'unfair') advantages and a lot of special help" (6). As Tinto states, ". . . the ability of students to meet academic standards is related not only to academic skills . . . but also to positive academic self-concept" (73).

African Americans May Need
More Institutional Support

Colleges and universities must become more aware of the obstacles which African-American students face as they embark upon their college careers. Black students, writes Tinto, "are more likely to come from disadvantaged backgrounds and have experienced inferior schooling prior to college" (73). Robert and Thomson note that minority students at Berkeley "come from families with far less experience with higher education and far fewer resources to support the education of their daughters and sons" (6). They suggest that colleges and universities must work actively to retain these high-risk students by creating support programs which help them to adjust not only to the functional aspects of college life, but to the white college culture.

Although our institution does offer study skills courses, minority tutoring, a Learning Resources Center, and a summer enrichment program for incoming minorities, Robert and Thomson point out that

> it has been a common finding that academic support programs which require the student to initiate the contact are particularly unsuccessful with at-risk and minority students. . . . Seeking academic assistance becomes discrediting, and many students of color may simply choose not to do so. . . . Students confided that they had initially denied to themselves and others that they were struggling academically and often delayed seeking assistance until too late in the semester to recover (6).

We have also noticed that our minority students are reluctant to seek extra help.

When we started our study, it had not occurred to us that racial polarization would emerge as an issue. We simply wanted to learn how our high-risk students fared academically after they left our developmental classes. Near the end of the second year into our study, however, we began to notice distinct differences between the academic progress of our black and our white students, and with each subsequent year, those differences became more evident. We began researching the literature and were dismayed to discover that what we were witnessing at our own institution was a national trend. We now realize how easy it can be for this problem to go unrecognized.

Notes

1. Tables detailing the academic progress of the sixty-one students in the study, both individually and as groups, are available on request. Contact the authors care of the Department of Writing and Linguistics, Georgia Southern University, Statesboro, GA 30460.
2. We excluded physical education courses, study skills courses, grammar and mechanics courses, lower division health, music, theater, or Regents review courses (which help students pass the state-mandated writing and reading exams). We also did not include the required freshman writing sequence.

Works Cited

Adams, Peter Dow. "Basic Writing Reconsidered." *Journal of Basic Writing* 12 (1993): 22–36.

Bartholomae, David. "The Tidy House: Basic Writing in the America Curriculum." *JBW* 12 (1993): 4–21.

———— and Anthony Petrosky. *Facts, Artifacts, Counterfacts*. Upper Montclair, NJ: Boynton/Cook, 1986.

Boylan, Hunter R., and Barbara S. Bonham. "The Impact of Developmental Education Programs." *Research in Developmental Education* 9 (1992): 1–3.

Carriuolo, Nancy. "Why Developmental Education Is Such a Hot Potato." *Chronicle of Higher Education* 13 April 1994: B1–2.

Chase, Nancy, Sandra U. Gibson, and Joan G. Carson. "An Examination of Reading Demands across Four College Courses." *Journal of Developmental Education* 18 (1994): 10–16.

Collins, Terence G. "A Response To Ira Shor's 'Our Apartheid: Writing Instruction and Inequality.'" *JBW* 16 (1997): 95–100.

Elbow, Peter. "Counterstatement." *College Composition and Communication* 44 (1993): 587–89.

Feagin, Joe R., Hernan Vera, and Nikitah Imani. *The Agony of Education: Black Students at White Colleges and Universities.* New York: Routledge, 1996.

Fidler, Paul, and Margi A. Godwin. "Retaining African-American Students through the Freshman Seminar." *Journal of Developmental Education* 17 (1994): 34–40.

Gray, Steven. "Study: Blacks Still Lag behind Whites in College Education." *Savannah Morning News* 27 Feb. 1997: 3A.

Greenberg, Karen. "The Politics of Basic Writing." *JBW* 12 (1993): 64–71.

————. "A Response to Ira Shor's 'Our Apartheid: Writing Instruction and Inequality.'" *JBW* 16 (1997): 90–94.

Harrold, Valerie. "An Investigation of Faculty Attitudes and Oral Communication Programs for African American Speakers of Black English at Selected Two-Year Private and Public Institutions of Higher Education in Michigan. Diss. Wayne State U: 1995.

Hopkins, Ronnie. *Educating Black Males: Critical Lessons in Schooling, Community, and Power.* Albany: SUNY, 1997.

Hull, Glynda, et al. "Remediation as Social Construct." *JBW* 10 (1991): 299-329.

Jones, William. "Pushing against Racism." *JBW* 13(1993): 4–21.

Kelly, Dennis. "College Remedial Courses." *USA Today*, 12 Fcb. 1995: 1D.

National Council of Teachers of English. "Resolutions." *College English* 55 (1992): 40.

Palmer, James C. "Do College Courses Improve Basic Reading and Writing Skills?" *Community College Review* 12.2. (1984): 20–28.

Presley, John. "Evaluating Developmental English Programs in Georgia." *WPA: Writing Program Administration* 8 (1984): 47–56.

Purvis, Dale, and Pamela Watkins. "Performance and Retention of Developmental Students: A Five-Year Follow-up Study." *Research in Developmental Education* 4 (1987): 1–4.

Robert, Ellen, and Gregg Thomson. "Learning Assistance and the Success of Underrepresented Students at Berkeley." *Journal of Developmental Education* 17 (1994): 4–14.

Salzer, James. "Four of 10 Freshmen Unprepared for College." *Savannah Morning News*: 14 April 1997: 1A, 10A.

————. *Savannah Morning News:* 15 May 1995: 1D.

Scott, Jerrie Cobb. "Literacies and Deficits Revisited." *JBW* 12 (1993): 46–56.

Shor, Ira. "Our Apartheid: Writing Instruction and Inequality." *JBW* 16 (1997): 91–104.

Simmons, Ron. "Precollege Programs: A Contributing Factor to University Retention." *Journal of Developmental Education* 17 (1994): 42–45.

Sternglass, Marilyn S. *Time to Know Them: A Longitudinal Study of Writing and Learning at the College Level.* Mahwah, NJ: Erlbaum, 1997.

Tinto, Vincent. *Leaving College: Rethinking the Causes and Cures of Student Attrition.* 2nd ed. Chicago: University of Chicago Press, 1993.

Walker, Reagan. "State May Tighten College Admission." *Savannah Morning News* 17 May 1995: 2D.

Wallace, David L., and Annissa Bell. "Being Black at a Predominantly White University." *College English* 61(1997): 307–27.

Wiener, Harvey S. "The Attack on Basic Writing — And After." *JBW* 17 (1998): 96–103.

Wolcott, W. "A Longitudinal Study of Six Developmental Students' Performance in Reading and Writing." *JBW* 13 (1994): 14–40.

Classroom Activities

Have students make a list of the reading they do in their other courses, and then write a journal entry or brief summary of what that reading involves. For example, what kinds of textbooks do they read? What are some of the differences (if any) that they encounter between textbooks for courses like biology or psychology? What does it mean to "read" a math problem — or a work of art or music? The idea behind this prompt is to help students build a metacognitive awareness of the kinds of reading they are likely to do outside their basic writing course and the kinds of difficulties that they might encounter. Have students bring their textbooks to class to discuss specific reading comprehension issues more intensively.

Agnew and McLaughlin's article brings up sensitive issues of race and social class. They address, in an implicit way, the disparities in preparedness for college that students from distressed communities often deal with as a fact of life. Often, basic writing classes have the most demographically "diverse" enrollments on campus. For students enrolled in largely white campuses, this demographic can be difficult to ignore. Have students write a journal entry or analysis paper about the quality of their preparation for college — and especially for college-level reading and writing. Ask them to consider how cultural factors (such as race and social class) might have an impact on the quality of schooling. Such an assignment builds analytic skills by giving students an opportunity to interrogate the cultural conditions of their own education.

Thinking about Teaching

In your teaching journal, consider the following quotation by Robert and Thomson, as cited by Agnew and McLaughlin: "It is difficult for minority students to escape the suspicion that they really don't deserve to be at the university and wouldn't be there if they didn't get special (read 'unfair') advantages." Although some educators have taken this position (most notably Shelby Steele), others have contended that this statement is based in essentialist, racist, and classist assumptions about who "belongs" at the university and who doesn't, and about whether or not "remedial" courses ought to be offered for college students. How do you respond to this quotation? Do you believe that this assumption is limited to minority students? Why or why not? Discuss your ideas with other teachers and consider raising this topic for discussion in class.

Consider gathering statistics and tracking basic writing students in a study similar to the one conducted by Agnew and McLaughlin. What mitigating factors seem to make a difference in retention and attrition? What needs of postdevelopmental students are not being met by other sectors of your college or university? Perhaps you can join or initiate a task force that is conducting such a study, so that you will have a voice in creating clear goals for the education of postdevelopmental students.

5

Approaches to
Grammar Instruction

Teaching grammar remains a contentious issue in many college and university English departments. Though a number of studies have addressed the question of whether grammar instruction leads to improved writing, there has been little consensus, and teachers of composition still find themselves embroiled in debate as they define their programs and plan their courses. The debate is particularly relevant to the teaching of developmental writers, who some argue suffer simply from a lack of foundation in grammar, usage, and mechanics. The writers in this chapter acknowledge the politicization of the issue. They move, however, to a middle ground: Grammar instruction should be an effective transfer of the rules to students' own writing; in this way, students become more aware of their options as writers. "Practice of forms improves usage," Janice Neuleib and Irene Brosnahan suggest, citing Henry Meckel, "whereas memorization of the rules does not." Rei R. Noguchi agrees that teaching grammatical categories in a way that is more accessible and "operational" can make grammar "a more efficient and effective tool for writing improvement." Constance Weaver, meanwhile, suggests directed activities for teaching grammar in the context of students' own writing.

Teaching Grammar to Writers

Janice Neuleib and Irene Brosnahan

Janice Neuleib and Irene Brosnahan situate their ideas within contemporary arguments about whether or not to teach grammar. They examine findings from research and address the need to teach grammar to undergraduate students, especially those who are studying to be writing teachers. As teachers of English at Illinois State University (where Neuleib is also director of writing programs), they have observed the ineffectiveness of having students simply memorize grammar concepts, especially students "inability to apply grammar to editing problems." To ameliorate such difficulties, they believe it is important to teach students to recognize patterns of errors, "to understand how language works."

At a recent workshop for high school and community college teachers, an earnest young high school teacher explained forcefully to an experienced community college teacher that grammar was of no use in teaching writing. The high school teacher cited the now-famous Braddock, Lloyd-Jones, and Schoer quotation. She said that knowing grammar had no effect on writing ability, insisting that "all the research" counterbalanced any intuitive and experiential evidence the older teacher might have to offer. The young teacher had, however, misquoted the passage; it says: "the teaching of *formal* [emphasis ours] grammar has a negligible or, because it usually displaces some instruction and practice in composition, even a harmful effect on the improvement of writing" (37–38).

Taking the words *teaching of formal grammar* to mean *knowing grammar* is a serious mistake. What the research cited by Braddock et al. indicates is that instruction in traditional grammar over a limited period of time (a semester or less in the research studies being discussed) showed no positive effect on students' writing. In fact, several research studies and much language and composition theory argue for certain types of grammar instruction, when effective methods are used for clearly defined purposes. When writers learn grammar, as opposed to teachers merely "covering" it, the newly acquired knowledge contributes to writing ability.

In separate essays on grammar, both Kolln (139) and Neuleib (148) point out that the often-quoted passage in Braddock et al. was preceded by "Uncommon, however, is carefully conducted research which studies composition over an extended period of time" (37). Few people seem to pay attention to the qualification, however. Also, another 1963 study, one that Kolln reviews, has attracted much less notice than *Research in Written Composition*. Yet that other study, by Meckel, is more extensive and thorough in its conclusions and recommendations than is the Braddock work. Meckel's work shows that major questions still existed in 1963 about the teaching of grammar.[1]

Meckel points to three crucial issues (981): First, none of the grammar studies up to 1963 extended beyond one semester — "a time span much too short to permit development of the degree of conceptualization necessary for transfer to take place." Second, none of the studies had to do with editing or revising, that is "with situations in which pupils are recasting the structure of a sentence or a paragraph." Finally, none of the studies makes comparisons between students who had demonstrated knowledge of grammar and those of equal intelligence who had none.

Meckel's recommendations indicate that studies with systematic grammatical instruction ran too short a time or that the research involved presentation of rules without assured student comprehension. Meckel offers several important conclusions (981): (1) Although grammar has not been shown to improve writing skills, "there is no conclusive evidence, however, that grammar has *no* transfer value in developing composition skill." (2) More research is needed to be done on "the kind of grammatical knowledge that may reasonably be expected to transfer to writing."[2] (3) Sometimes *formal grammar* has meant grammar without application; grammar should be taught systematically with applications. (4) "There are more efficient methods of securing *immediate* [Meckel's emphasis] improvement in the writing of pupils, both in sentence structure and usage, than systematic grammatical instruction." (5) Practice of forms improves usage whereas memorization of rules does not.

In spite of Meckel's work being little known, trends in the profession were confirming his conclusions. The years following 1963 were filled with sentence-combining research that showed statistically significant results on methods that relied on practice with forms (e.g., Mellon; O'Hare). This research culminated in the 1979 study by Daiker, Kerek, and Morenberg in which college students made significant progress in writing, including surface structure and punctuation, without any kind of instruction except in sentence-combining exercises and essay writing. Sentence combining, a method of teaching grammar without explicit grammar instruction, fits with Meckel's earlier conclusion on the effectiveness of practice of forms as opposed to the learning of rules.

Shaughnessy in her 1977 *Errors and Expectations* developed a new method of helping students with writing by using grammar. Working with open-admissions students, she developed a form of grammar instruction that has since been called error analysis. Error analysis fits with Meckel's recommendation that students work only on the errors in their own writing and not on rules external to that writing. Teachers gear instruction only to the needs of the students. Shaughnessy shows many error patterns which teachers can use to understand each student's needs. Shaughnessy offers an approach to error excluding formal grammar instruction, but including grammar at every step.

D'Eloia in the *Journal of Basic Writing* explained the reason for the grammatical approach to basic writing instruction introduced by

Shaughnessy: ". . . something was radically wrong with the research design [of earlier studies which rejected grammar instruction] or with the instruction in grammar itself. . . . They [basic writing teachers] cannot bring themselves to believe that units combining the analysis of a grammatical principle with well-structured proofreading, imitation, paraphrase, and sentence consolidation exercises, and with directed writing assignments could fail to produce more significant results in both fluency and error control" (2). D'Eloia then offers applied grammar activities effective with basic writers similar to those in Shaughnessy's book.

More recently, Bartholomae in "The Study of Error" shows how instructors can discover error-producing language patterns in student writing. He shows that correcting these patterns requires special insight on the part of teachers. Says Bartholomae, "An error . . . can only be understood as evidence of intention. . . . A writer's activity is linguistic and rhetorical activity; it can be different but never random. The task for both teacher and researcher, then, is to discover the grammar of *that* [Bartholomae's emphasis] coherence. . . ." (255).

Harris demonstrates this error-analysis approach to a specific problem. She shows that the fragmented free modifier can indicate linguistic growth. Rather than being a case for the red pencil, the fragmented free modifier is often a chance for a teacher to encourage growing linguistic strength. Being able, however, to recognize such indication of growth and using it to help a student develop requires sophisticated grammatical knowledge on the part of the teacher.

Student-centered approaches similar to those illustrated by Harris and Bartholomae demonstrate how grammar can be effectively used in teaching. Of course, merely covering grammar from a workbook would detract from student achievement. Teaching grammar from a traditional grammar text would be worse. DeBeaugrande explains why grammar texts do not teach students either grammar or writing. He argues that teachers need to understand grammar if they are to help improve students' writing. He attacks grammar textbooks, though, saying that they are written for and by grammarians who find the concepts easy since they "know what the terms mean" (358). He calls for a "learner's grammar" taught by techniques that are accurate, workable, economical, compact, operational, and immediate (364). He illustrates some of the techniques, many of which expand and extend Shaughnessy's and D'Eloia's patterns.

Shaughnessy, D'Eloia, Bartholomae, Harris, and DeBeaugrande all illustrate how grammar instruction improves writing skills. Teachers, however, need grammatical knowledge to use the methods illustrated. To analyze errors and to discover language patterns, teachers need to do more than "cover" grammar. They need to be able to work out exercises of the types illustrated by Shaughnessy and D'Eloia, exercises patterned to students' individual language problems.

Yet, received knowledge in the profession seems to legislate in another direction. A few years ago, every time we did a workshop in the schools, teachers were shocked when we said that studies showed that teaching traditional grammar would not improve students' abilities as writers. More recently we have found many teachers too ready to assume that they can omit grammar instruction because it will not help students to write better. These assumptions are reinforced by journal articles which reject formal grammar instruction.[3]

This dismissal of grammar teaching is unfortunate not only because practice has shown that teachers must know grammar to analyze student errors but also because many questions regarding grammar instruction are worth studying. Fundamental questions concern what kind of grammar is being taught, how it is being taught, and what the rationale for that teaching is. Finally, we as a profession need to ask if we understand grammar and the nature of language.

In our opinion, the preparation of teachers is the crucial issue in teaching effectiveness. A confused teacher increases student perplexity. Arguing against the teaching of grammar in the lower grades, Sanborn tells of a teacher who was confused about the difference between a participle and a gerund: The teacher said "being" in "Being accused of something I didn't do made me mad" was a participle (73). Of course, traditional grammar is replete with ambiguities in its terminology. The term *participle* is ambiguous in that it is both a form term (for a verb) and a function term (modifying a noun, another ambiguity), and the term *gerund* is a function term (functioning in a nominal position) with an implied form (a verb form ending in -*ing*). If our profession had prepared the teacher well, she would have been aware of the ambiguities in the grammar. If some teachers want to teach eight parts of speech in English, for instance, they need to know that the parts of speech are defined neatly, sensibly, and logically by inflectional forms in Latin but that they are defined inconsistently and illogically by mixing form and function in English. Unless teachers are informed about the imperfections of traditional grammar, students will fail to understand it and thereby to learn and retain it.

Superficial retention became painfully obvious to us in a recent survey we conducted in an English grammar course required of upperclass students seeking teacher certification in English. At the beginning of the course, the prospective teachers filled out a questionnaire and took a test in grammar. The questionnaire asked when the prospective teachers had been taught grammar, what kind of grammatical activities they had had, and how they rated themselves on various types of grammatical knowledge. Of the twenty-four participants in the study, twenty-three reported having studied grammar at two or more levels of schooling (elementary school, junior high, high school, college), and fifteen at three or more levels. All reported having learned grammar through a variety of activities such as diagramming sentences, memorizing grammatical terms and labeling parts of speech, identifying and correcting grammatical errors, writing sentences and paragraphs with grammatical forms indicated, and so on. They also rated themselves rather high (mostly 3 or above on a scale of 1 to 5) in most grammatical skills listed, particularly in knowing names of and identifying parts of speech and parts of sentences, standard grammatical usage, and correct punctuation rules and applications.

The results of the grammar test, given with the questionnaire, however, indicated little retention of formal grammatical knowledge and an inability to apply grammar to editing problems. Only three out of twenty-four prospective teachers could accurately name the eight parts of speech — most of them could name four or five (usually noun, verb, adjective, adverb), but function terms like subject and object were mixed in. Most participants could name the two important parts of a sentence and count the number of sentences in a given passage taken from Warriner (58), but no one could accurately count the number of clauses in the paragraph. Some participants even counted fewer clauses than sentences. Although most of these prospective teachers knew what a verb was, only half the group could pick out a transitive verb, and no one could identify an intransitive verb. Only six could find the solitary passive verb in the passage. A prepositional phrase was easily identified, but only two participants correctly picked out an adverbial clause, and only four found an adjective clause. Quite a few people labeled phrases as clauses, apparently not knowing the difference between phrases, clauses, and sentences. Thus, an obvious discrepancy existed between the prospective teachers' perceptions of their formal grammar knowledge and their demonstrated knowledge.

The grammar test also contained two sentences which the participants were to punctuate. They also had to explain their reasons for using each punctuation mark as they did:

1. Please turn off the light its much too bright

2. I was anxious to go shopping but my mother who is usually so organized was taking her time today.

Only seven participants, less than a third of the group, could punctuate sentence 1 correctly; many either used a comma to separate the two clauses and/or neglected the apostrophe for *its*. With sentence 2, almost everyone separated the nonrestrictive clause with a pair of commas, and thirteen of them put a comma before *but*. As for providing the rules of punctuation, only three participants could explain the punctuation in sentence 1 in appropriate grammatical terms, and only one participant could do so for sentence 2. A number of the participants offered explanations involving pauses and meaning, while others misused grammatical terms. For the majority of these prospective teachers, therefore, punctuation rules had not been learned at the conscious operational level. Of course, we realize that the performance of this group of prospective teachers cannot be generalized to all students who have studied grammar, but having taught grammar to similar upperclass students in the last fifteen years, we can say that their lack of formal grammatical knowledge is typical.

We would like to suggest that the first step in increasing teachers' understanding of grammar is to develop a clear definition of the term. Theorists as disparate as Kolln and Hartwell stress the confusion in the definition of grammar. Kolln points out that the Braddock et al. report did not define "formal grammar," so conclusions could not be confirmed (292–293). In addressing this need for definition, Hartwell builds upon W. Nelson Francis's 1954 "Revolution in Grammar" to define five grammars: Grammar 1 is intrinsic knowledge of language rules and patterns that people use without knowing they use them; Grammar 2 is the linguistic science that studies the system of Grammar 1; Grammar 3 merely involves linguistic etiquette, such as calling "he ain't" bad grammar; Grammar 4 is "school grammar," the system that is oversimplified in traditional handbooks and workbooks; Grammar 5, stylistic grammar, uses grammatical terms to teach prose style, in the manner of Lanham, Williams, Christensen, and Strunk and White (Hartwell 109–110). Hartwell stresses that these five grammars often do not match. They are pieces of puzzles that fit into different pictures or that overlap untidily in the same picture. Without being aware of the mismatch between Grammar 4, "school grammar," and Grammar 1, intuitive grammar, many teachers teach Grammar 4 as if it made perfect sense.

We strongly feel that writing teachers need to study the historical background of grammar, be well-acquainted with better descriptions of language (that is, with Grammar 2, linguistic studies, as well as Grammar 5, stylistic grammar), and appreciate relations among different grammars. Still, teachers should not begin to teach linguistics in their writing classes. College level linguistics is not the solution for junior and senior high school students. Rather, when teachers understand how language works, they can make the description of the language accessible to students.

The challenge now is in the area of teacher training and retraining. At the end of the semester, the prospective teachers described in the study above had been exposed to the history of language study and to many of the concepts reviewed here. They went on to learn that to work with basic writers at any level, teachers have to do the hard part. They have to understand stylistic choices, and they have to analyze errors so that they can show students how language works. When teachers do more than "cover" grammar, writers will improve their writing by using the grammar they have learned.

Notes

1. For a thorough review of the research, see Meckel; for a summary of Meckel's findings, see Kolln.
2. Sentence-combining research represents at least one kind of grammatical knowledge that has proved to be transferable to writing. See Neuleib for a summary of sentence-combining research through that date.

3. Hartwell's "Grammar, Grammars, and the Teaching of Grammar" illustrates the sort of dismissal of grammar that encourages this attitude in teachers. Hartwell does mention error analysis, but in his conclusion he calls for a halt to all grammar research. The message teachers often carry from such an article is to abandon grammar instruction of any type.

Works Cited

Braddock, Richard, Richard Lloyd-Jones, and Lowell Schoer. *Research in Written Composition*. Urbana, IL: National Council of Teachers of English, 1963.

Bartholomae, David. "The Study of Error." *College Composition and Communication* 31 (1980): 253–269.

Christensen, Francis. "A Generative Rhetoric of the Sentence." *College Composition and Communication* 14 (1963): 155–161.

Daiker, Donald, Andrew Kerek, and Max Morenberg. "Sentence-Combining and Syntactic Maturity in Freshman English." *College Composition and Communication* 29 (1978): 36–41.

DeBeaugrande, Robert. "Forward to the Basics: Getting Down to Grammar." *College Composition and Communication* 35 (1984): 358–367.

D'Eloia, Sarah. "The Uses — and Limits — of Grammar." *Journal of Basic Writing* 1 (1977): 1–48.

Francis, W. Nelson. "Revolution in Grammar." *Quarterly Journal of Speech* 40 (1954): 299–312.

Harris, Muriel. "Mending the Fragmented Free Modifier." *College Composition and Communication* 32 (1981): 175–182.

Hartwell, Patrick. "Grammar, Grammars, and the Teaching of Grammar." *College English* 47 (1985): 105–127.

Kolln, Martha. "Closing the Book on Alchemy." *College Composition and Communication* 32 (1981): 139–151.

Lanham, Richard. *Revising Prose.* New York: Scribner's, 1979.

Meckel, Henry. "Research on Teaching Composition and Literature." *Handbook of Research on Teaching*. Ed. Nathaniel L. Gage. Chicago: Rand, 1963.

Mellon, John. *Transformational Sentence Combining: A Method for Enhancing the Development of Fluency in English Composition*. Urbana, IL: National Council of Teachers of English, 1966.

Neuleib, Janice. "The Relation of Formal Grammar to Composition." *College Composition and Communication* 23 (1977): 247–250.

O'Hare, Frank. *Sentence-Combining: Improving Student Writing Without Formal Grammar Instruction*. Urbana, IL: National Council of Teachers of English, 1971.

Sanborn, Jean. "Grammar: Good Wine Before Its Time." *English Journal* 75 (1986): 72–80.

Shaughnessy, Mina. *Errors and Expectations.* New York: Oxford UP, 1977.

Strunk, William, and E. B. White. *The Elements of Style,* 3rd ed. New York: Macmillan, 1979.

Warriner, John E., John H. Treanor, and Sheila Y. Laws. *English Grammar and Composition 8.* Rev. ed. New York: Harcourt, 1965.

Williams, Joseph. *Style: Ten Lessons in Clarity and Grace.* Glenview, IL: Scott, 1981.

Classroom Activities

Develop a questionnaire for basic writing students similar to the one that Neuleib and Brosnahan provided for their own students (preservice student teachers). The purpose of the questionnaire is for students to reflect not only on how much grammar knowledge they have retained, but also on how they have studied grammar throughout their schooling. A similar questionnaire for developing writers would provide interesting results for both students and teachers. Students could describe their experiences with the study of grammar or list rules they have learned over the years. You may approach class discussion of the results of these self-assessments by comparing your own experiences with grammar instruction to those described by students.

Thinking about Teaching

Neuleib and Brosnahan suggest error analysis as an appropriate means of teaching grammar to basic writers. If students are able to recognize patterns of error, they will become more adept at editing their work. In this context, it may be useful to collaborate with colleagues to determine which errors are the most common among your population of students. Create a rubric based on categories suggested by Neuleib and Brosnahan. Then exchange student papers and diagnostic tests and proofread for categories of error that seem most prevalent. After this exchange, discuss the kinds of errors that predominate and the best ways to approach such editing difficulties with your students.

Teaching the Basics of a Writer's Grammar

Rei R. Noguchi

The following selection comes from Rei R. Noguchi's National Council of Teachers of English monograph Grammar and the Teaching of Writing. *Noguchi, professor of English at California State University, Northridge, argues that basic writing students learn to edit more effectively not by memorizing grammar rules but by becoming more aware of how grammar functions in their own writing. Accordingly, Noguchi suggests that we move toward teaching the "operational definitions" of grammar terms, as opposed to the "compositional definitions." Noguchi argues that students need to acquire "underlying knowledge" of several major areas of language usage in order to "crack 'the grammar code.'" Those areas include pronoun usage, understanding the sentence as a whole, and the use of presentence elements. Noguchi's strategies can help you teach developing writers to identify and correct "status marking" and "stigma-*

tized" error, which often have significant consequences in real-world written communication.

Cracking the Grammar Code

How can students crack the "grammar code"? How can they gain a working knowledge of basic grammatical categories such as sentence, subject, verb, etc., if such categories are defined in terms of other categories? Isn't it much like looking up the word *structure* in a dictionary and finding the definition "form" and under the entry for *form* finding the definition "structure"? I believe students can crack the grammar code but not by the time-consuming and frustrating methods of the past. The solution lies not in presenting semantic or compositional definitions, which inevitably entail either opaque or interlinking definitions of the categories, but rather in operational definitions. By an operational definition here, I mean a definition which defines by means of what an entity does or can have done to it rather than what comprises the entity. To cite a mundane example outside of grammar, one definition of *water* would be an aqueous chemical compound composed of two atoms of hydrogen and one atom of oxygen. This definition focuses on the composition of the entity and thus resembles many of the problematic definitions found in the study of grammar (e.g., "A sentence is composed of a subject and a predicate"). In contrast, an operational definition of *water* would be a liquid ingested by plants and animals to sustain life, or, perhaps, a liquid used to wash and rinse cars, dishes, etc. Granted, operational definitions are not as impressive or as delimiting as nonoperational definitions. The important point here is that they do not have to be. All that is required of operational definitions is that they work in actual use and that they avoid interlinking technical terms, something which the nonoperational definition of *water* does not do.

The Underlying Knowledge of "Pronoun"

As startling as it may sound at first, all students who have acquired English as a native language (as well as many who have acquired it non-natively) already possess an immense knowledge of the operations (i.e., descriptive rules) of English, including its syntax. This must be so, or they would not be able to produce grammatical sentences in everyday conversation. This knowledge, however, is largely unconscious. Students normally cannot explain the operations, or rules, but the knowledge is nonetheless there and waiting to be tapped. Consider pronouns. Most grammar books state explicitly that a pronoun is a word that "substitutes for a noun." Yet this traditional definition of pronoun is clearly incorrect, or at least incomplete, since a pronoun can substitute not just for a noun (e.g., *boys* → *they*) but also, among other things, a noun phrase (e.g., *the noisy boys in the back of the room* → *they*) or any construction that functions as a noun or noun phrase, including other pronouns (e.g., *he and she* → *they*). Indeed, if students dutifully mastered and meticulously applied the grammar-book definition of a pronoun and only that, they would be unable to identify many pronoun substitutions in the language. Whether grammar books state the definition of a pronoun correctly or completely, fortunately, does not really matter in the end. Native students already unconsciously know the correct version of the pronoun substitution rule; otherwise they could not use pronouns in everyday conversation.

If given the following sentences and personal pronouns, students who are native speakers of English would find little difficulty in substituting the pronoun for the appropriate word or words in the sentence:

1. Jane and Bob bought a book during the trip to San Francisco. (*she*)

2. He and she live in New York City. (*they*)

3. It was the Beatles who first made British rock music popular. (*they* or *them*)

4. That Mary studied hard was very clear to John. (*it*)

5. Most people believe that the world is round. (*it*)

6. Sometimes, exercising can be relaxing. (*it*)

Items 1–6 above illustrate two important facts concerning personal pronouns. First, personal pronouns do, indeed, substitute for a variety of constructions in English. In (1), *she* substitutes for the noun *Jane;* in (2), *they*, for the compound pronoun *he and she;* in (3), *they,* for the noun phrase *the Beatles;* in (4), *it,* for the noun clause *that Mary studied hard;* in (5), *it,* for the noun clause *that the world is round* or, alternatively, for the noun phrase *the world;* in (6), *it,* for the gerund *exercising*. Second, errors involving prescriptive rules (i.e., usage errors) may often occur but errors involving descriptive rules rarely occur. For example, in (3), students may substitute the pronoun *them* for *the Beatles* instead of the more formal *they*. However, this is a very different type of error from substituting a personal pronoun for *made* (a verb) or for *popular* (an adjective). Stated more generally, though students may substitute the incorrect form of a personal pronoun, they will never substitute a personal pronoun for any grammatical category other than a noun, a noun phrase, or a construction that serves as such.

The above exercise with personal pronouns helps point out some significant advantages of operational definitions in the teaching of grammar. If students can substitute pronouns for the appropriate word or words in exercises like (1–6) above and in utterances of daily speech — in ignorance of or, perhaps, despite the inaccuracy or incompleteness of the common textbook definition — then teachers do not really have to teach the definition of pronoun, not even the operational one. Students already have that knowledge. Put in a more general way, teachers cannot teach students what they already know. Although students probably cannot state the operation of pronoun substitution in the metalanguage of grammar, they must already possess the tacit knowledge that a personal pronoun, at the least, is a word that can take the place of a noun, noun phrase, or something that functions as either. (The foregoing is a rough operational definition of a personal pronoun.) Again, without this kind of unconscious linguistic knowledge, students would be unable to make pronoun substitutions for the appropriate words in daily speech.

The fact that students already have such knowledge can also help teachers clarify some facts about English grammar. If students already unconsciously know that a personal pronoun can substitute for a noun, noun phrase, or some construction that functions as either, then they must also know that these elements which accept pronoun substitution are all syntactically (though not necessarily semantically) similar. That is, despite the various forms and lengths which these units take, students already unconsciously know that they function as one category, namely, that of noun. Indeed, precisely because the noun clauses *that Mary studied hard* and *that the world is round* in (4) and (5) above allow the personal pronoun *it* as a proper substitution, teachers can plausibly argue that these constructions, while not having the form of nouns, are functioning as nouns. That is, even though the shapes are different, the function is the same. This fact is important since it means teachers can use pronoun substitution as an operational test for nouns (and vice versa). If a personal pronoun can appropriately substitute for a word or group of words, then the word or group of words is functioning as a noun, regardless of its form. This, in turn, obviates the need to teach formally the definitions of noun, noun phrase, and the other constructions which substitute for nouns. If such constructions allow personal pronouns as substitutions in a sentence, then, operationally, they are nouns.

Reliance on this kind of unconscious underlying knowledge of the language, of course, has always been implicit — and crucial — in the development of transformational/generative grammar and its derivative applications for the classroom. It should come as no surprise that the basic design and the general success of sentence-combining exercises rest greatly on this kind of intuitive knowledge. Indeed, without such knowledge, students would be unable to carry out the instructions (i.e., perform the operations) required of such exercises. Yet, with the exception of a small number of studies (D'Eloia 1977; DeBeaugrande 1984; Noguchi 1987), little has been done to exploit this powerful resource to define grammatical categories for writers, even though the very same resource has been used fruitfully by linguists in their syntactic analyses for the past thirty or so years.

The Underlying Knowledge of "Subject"

An approach capitalizing on intuitive linguistic knowledge can be used to define, for example, the notion of "subject of a sentence." For students, being able to locate the subject of a sentence easily is a valuable skill since several kinds of common stylistic problems require the identification of subjects — for example, errors in subject-verb agreement, unnecessary shifts in person, overuse of nonagent subjects. Locating subjects can most easily be handled by exploiting some descriptive rules of grammar which operate on or interact with subjects. Consider the following declarative sentences and their corresponding tag and yes-no questions:

7. a. Jim and Sue can dance the tango.
   b. Jim and Sue can dance the tango, can't they?
   c. Can Jim and Sue dance the tango?

8. a. The company, which employed many workers and made many different kinds of products, went out of business.
   b. The company, which employed many workers and made many different kinds of products, went out of business, didn't it?
   c. Did the company, which employed many workers and made many different kinds of products, go out of business?

9. a. The cost of the three typewriters and the four clocks will be raised.
   b. The cost of the three typewriters and the four clocks will be raised, won't it?
   c. Will the cost of the three typewriters and the four clocks be raised?

10. a. Tom ate some bad spaghetti and had a stomachache all day.
    b. Tom ate some bad spaghetti and had a stomachache all day, didn't he?
    c. Did Tom eat some bad spaghetti and have a stomachache all day?

11. a. Doing math problems isn't one of Billy's favorite activities.
    b. Doing math problems isn't one of Billy's favorite activities, is it?
    c. Isn't doing math problems one of Billy's favorite activities?

12. a. Whether Sam likes it or not, Janet should telephone David again.
    b. Whether Sam likes it or not, Janet should telephone David again, shouldn't she?
    c. Whether Sam likes it or not, should Janet telephone David again?

Forming the corresponding tag and yes-no questions from the original declarative sentences offers a way of identifying subjects operationally. With tag questions (all the (b) sentences above), the pronoun copied at the end of the tag question refers to the subject of the sentence. Stated more simply, the last word of the tag question stands for the subject. For example, in (7b), the last word *they* stands for *Jim and Sue*, the subject of the sentence; in (8b), the last word *it* stands for *the company*; in (9b), *it* stands for *the cost;* in (11b), *it* stands for the whole sequence *doing math problems* (not just *math*), and, hence, the whole sequence is the subject of the sentence. With yes-no questions (all the (c) sentences above), an auxiliary, or "helping," verb has been moved leftward to occupy a new position. If no auxiliary verb occurs in the original declarative sentence, as in (8a) and (10a), an appropriate form of the *do* auxiliary verb (*do, does,* or *did*) is added instead. The subject of the sentence can be identified relative to the new position of the moved or added auxiliary. More specifically, the (simple) subject is the first noun or noun substitute that stands to the immediate right of the moved or added auxiliary verb. Stated more in everyday English, the subject is the first noun or noun substitute that stands to the nearest right of the moved (or added *do*) word. Thus, in (7c), the noun phrase *Jim and Sue* stands to the nearest right of the moved word *can* and, hence, is the subject of the sentence; in (8c), the noun or noun substitute standing to the nearest right of the moved word *did* is *company;* in (9c), the noun or noun substitute standing to the nearest right of the moved word *will* is *cost*.

Handling Some Exceptions

As with any method dealing with the complexities of English grammar, real or apparent exceptions may occur. The key is to explain them as clearly as possible. For example, sentences like (13a) and (14a) will yield a proper corresponding tag question but not a proper corresponding yes-no question:

13. a. For Tommy to pass now isn't going to be easy.
    b. For Tommy to pass now isn't going to be easy, is it?
    c. *Isn't for Tommy to pass now going to be easy?[1]

14. a. That Jane is a genius is obvious to everyone.
    b. That Jane is a genius is obvious to everyone, isn't it?
    c. *Is that Jane is a genius obvious to everyone?

Conversely, a sentence like (15a) will yield a proper corresponding yes-no question but sometimes a noncorresponding (yet proper) tag question:

15. a. I believe that a good education makes a big difference in life.
    b. *I believe that a good education makes a big difference in life, doesn't it? (instead of the syntactically corresponding "I believe that a good education makes a big difference in life, don't I?")
    c. Don't I believe that a good education makes a big difference in life?

The general problem in (13–15) is that the tag question and the yes-no question give conflicting indications of what is the subject of the original sentence. For example, in (13b), the *it* in the tag question refers to or stands for the infinitive phrase *for Tommy to pass now*, and, hence, the whole infinitive phrase is the subject of the sentence. In (13c), however, the yes-no question is corresponding but ungrammatical. To make matters worse, the first noun or noun substitute occurring to the nearest right of the moved word is *Tommy* and, thus, students may incorrectly identify *Tommy,* rather than the whole infinitive phrase *for Tommy to pass now,* as the subject of the sentence.

Rather than merely viewing the results in (13–15) as contradictory or unrevealing, teachers can exploit such situations not only to sharpen but also to expand their students' skills in employing operational definitions. For example, if in (13b) the last word *it* truly represents a pronominal copy of the subject (i.e., *for Tommy to pass now*), then we ought to be able to substitute *it* for the subject without changing the essential meaning of the sentence. This we can do in both (13a) and (13b) to get *It's not going to be easy* and *It's not going to be easy, is it?,* respectively, thus providing strong evidence that *for Tommy to pass now* is, indeed, the actual subject. Significantly, we can also substitute *it* for the same group of words in the problematic (13c) to get *Isn't it going to be easy?,* again giving strong evidence that *for Tommy to pass now* is the subject of the sentence. (Note that if *Tommy* alone were the subject of the sentence, the corresponding tag question would be the ungrammatical **For Tommy to pass now isn't going to be easy, is he?*). Further analysis, then, shows that the subject of the sentences in (13) is, indeed, the whole infinitive phrase *For Tommy to pass now* rather than just *Tommy* or any other portion of the infinitive phrase. The same line of argument can also be used to explain the discrepancy in identifying the subject in (14).

The discrepancy in (15) can also be explained in a revealing way for students. In (15c), the moved word in the yes-no question correctly indicates that *I* is the subject of the sentence; in (15b), however, the copied pronoun *it* in the tag question refers to *a good education,* and, thus, erroneously indicates that *a good education* is the subject. The cause of the discrepancy here lies more in the *use* of tag questions than in their formation. For example, the tag question that syntactically corresponds to *I believe that a good education makes a big difference in life* is *I believe that a good education makes a big difference in life, don't I?* (If this is offered as a possible tag question to (15a), most, if not all, students will agree.) However, though this is a syntactically correct tag question, we normally do not utter it for reasons having to do with the semantics (i.e., meaning) and pragmatics (i.e., use) of such questions. In contrast to yes-no questions, which seek from the addressee a neutral *yes* or *no* response, tag questions seek a confirmation of whatever the addresser asserts. Put in another way, yes-no questions roughly mean something like, "My utterance here offers you a free choice. I ask you to indicate the choice with a *yes* or *no.*" Tag questions roughly mean something like, "My utterance here asserts something. I ask you to confirm or deny the assertion." In the tag question *I believe that a good education makes a big difference in life, don't I?*, the addresser asserts his or her belief about the importance of a good education in life. However, the meaning of the sentence is strange in that the addresser explicitly affirms his or her own belief (with *I believe*) and then denies or casts doubt on it (with *don't I?*). Because of this conflict between self-affirmation and self-doubt, students often prefer the syntactically noncorresponding tag question *I believe that a good education makes a big difference in life, doesn't it?* We can check this explanation against a comparable tag question, such as *Maria believes that a good education makes a big difference in life, doesn't she?*, which lacks the conflicting beliefs of the addresser and, hence, is more acceptable than **Maria believes that a good education makes a big difference in life, doesn't it?* (Teachers can encourage further exploration of this phenomenon by asking students to substitute other nouns and personal pronouns for the pronoun *I*.) The reason that sentences like (15b) sometimes occur as the tag-question counterparts for sentences like (15a) then is not that students do not know the syntax of tag questions (they do) but rather that they also know something about the semantics and pragmatics (or the meaning and use) of tag questions.

The Importance of Tag-Question and Yes-No Question Formation

What the preceding examples with tag questions and yes-no questions indicate is that students also unconsciously know a great deal more about the categories of English grammar than teachers realize. The very ability to perform the operations of tag-question formation and yes-no question formation presupposes that students already have an underlying knowledge of not only the concept of "subject" but also those of "auxiliary verb," "negative," and "personal pronoun" (and, as we shall see later, also "sentence" and "presentence modifier"). That students have already acquired the concept of personal pronoun (along with the associated concepts of case, number, and gender) is evident in their ability to add the correct noun-equivalent pronoun (with matching case, number, and gender) at the end of the tag question. That students have already acquired the concept of auxiliary verb is evident in their uncanny ability to select, among numerous possibilities within a sentence, the correct word to copy in the tag part of the tag question or the correct word to move leftward in the yes-no question. (The ability to identify auxiliary verbs is further verified when students insert a form of *do* in sentences containing no auxiliary verb. How can they tell that a sentence lacks a movable or copiable auxiliary verb unless they know first what constitutes an auxiliary verb?) That students have already acquired the concept of negative is evident in their ability to add and contract *not* in the tag (or in their ability to negate any positive sentence of English). If students did not possess an underlying knowledge of such categories, they would be unable to produce grammatical tag questions and yes-no questions in everyday conversation.

The Underlying Knowledge of "Main Verb"

The underlying knowledge of native speakers also includes knowledge of the category "main verb." The ability to locate main verbs is important because some highly frequent stylistic errors concern main verbs. These errors involve not only the choice of main verbs (as suggested by the oft-quoted advice, "Write with action verbs") but also their form (incorrect tense, lack of subject-verb agreement, improper tense shifting, nonstandard dialectical forms). Locating the main verb of a sentence, however, is not always easy for students, even when they know the subject of the sentence. Simply asking students, "What is the subject doing?" will not work when, for example, the sentence is passive or the main verb is some form of *be*. Students do, nonetheless, have an underlying knowledge of main verbs. After students have learned how to identify both the subject of a declarative sentence and the correct pronominal form of the subject operationally, teachers can tap their underlying knowledge of main verbs by having students work with sentence frames like A and B below. Frame A isolates the predicate of a sentence in the second slot. If that predicate contains the verb *be*, frame B is then used to separate the linking verb *be* from the passive *be*. In fact, frame B works only with passive sentences and serves to isolate the "real" main verb.

A. They somehow got _____ to _____.

B. But it wasn't me who did the _____-ing.

To locate main verbs with sentence frames A and B, students start with any (declarative) sentence and then use that sentence to fill in the blanks of A and B. The operational test here requires two basic steps:

1. Insert in the first slot of A the subject of the (declarative) sentence in the appropriate pronoun form and insert in the second slot whatever remains of the sentence.

2. If (and only if) the second slot in A has *be* as the first word, try to fill the slot in B with the appropriate word from the original sentence (this word also has to appear in the second slot in A). If this can't be done, don't worry.

To simplify matters here, sentence negatives may be ignored. Although the sentences produced from following the steps above may sometimes be strange, they will, nonetheless, be sentences (keep in mind that, even in real life, people sometimes utter strange but syntactically correct sentences). More important, the resulting sentences will isolate the main verb in the second slot in A or, if the original sentence is passive, the main verb will appear in the slot in B. The previous declarative sentences in (7–12), repeated for convenience below as (16–21) illustrate the isolation of the main verb. The (a) versions are the original sentences, the (b) versions are the results of using frame A, and the (c) versions show the results of using frame B.

16. a. Jim and Sue can dance the tango.
    b. They somehow got *them* to *dance the tango*. (Hence, *dance* is the main verb.)

17. a. The company, which employed many workers and made many different kinds of products, went out of business.
    b. They somehow got *it* to *go out of business*. (*Go* is the main verb.)

18. a. The cost of the three typewriters and the four clocks will be raised.
    b. They somehow got *it* to *be raised*.
    c. But it wasn't me who did the *raise*-ing. (*Raise* is the main verb.)

19. a. Tom ate some bad spaghetti and had a stomachache all day.
    b. They somehow got *him* to *eat some bad spaghetti and (to) have a stomachache all day*. (Two main verbs here: *eat* and *have*.)

20. a. Doing math problems isn't one of Billy's favorite activities.
    b. They somehow got *it* to *be one of Billy's favorite activities*.
    c. But it wasn't me who did the _____?_____-ing. (Since frame B does not work here, *be* is the main verb.)

21. a. Whether Sam likes it or not, Janet should telephone David again.
    b. They somehow got *her* to *telephone David again, whether Sam likes it or not*. (*Telephone* is the main verb.)

Even the troublesome declarative sentences in (13–15), repeated here as (22–24), yield their main verbs, as indicated below:

22. a. For Tommy to pass now isn't going to be easy.
    b. They somehow got *it* to *be easy*.
    c. But it wasn't me who did the _____?_____-ing. (Hence, *be* is the main verb.)

23. a. That Jane is a genius is obvious to everyone.
    b. They somehow got *it* to *be obvious to everyone*.
    c. But it wasn't me who did the _____?_____-ing. (Hence, *be* is the main verb.)

24. a. I believe that a good education makes a big difference in life.
    b. They somehow got *me* to *believe that a good education makes a big difference in life*. (*Believe* is the main verb.)

As shown by the examples above, sentence frames A and B work together to isolate main verbs from declarative sentences. Sentence frame A isolates transitive and intransitive main verbs from the sentence, while sentence frame B separates the main verb *be* from a passivized main verb (i.e., a main verb which occurs in passive form and which occurs after the auxiliary verb *be*). Working in tandem, sentence frames A and B make the isolation of main verbs considerably easier because they operationally remove distracting auxiliary verbs from consideration as main verbs. For example, the active sentence *Bill could have been taking care of his tired feet* becomes in sentence frame A, *They somehow got him to take care of his tired feet,* while the passive sentence *Mary might have been chosen* becomes in sentence frames A and B, *They somehow got her to be chosen* and *But it wasn't me who did the choosing.*

The Underlying Knowledge of "Sentence"

Being able to identify main verbs, main subjects, and auxiliary verbs can, of course, aid students in identifying sentences and defining the all-important notion of "sentence." However, to piece together these elements with others to define a sentence is wasteful of time and effort because native speakers of English already know what a sentence is. That this knowledge already exists, tacit though it may be, is evidenced in the very ability to form grammatical tag questions and yes-no questions. Regardless of the vast numbers of sentences that can be transformed into tag questions or yes-no questions, the key point to keep in mind here is that the operations that form tag questions and yes-no questions work properly only on genuine sentences. While students will have no difficulty in transforming the (a) sentences in (7–12) into tag questions and yes-no questions, they will find the task impossible with such nonsentences as the following:

25. Enjoyed the baseball game on Saturday.

26. Whatever you could do to help my sister.

27. The wind howling through the trees last night.

28. If you came tomorrow afternoon at one o'clock.

29. In order to find a job he liked.

Try as they may, students will find it impossible to form either the corresponding tag question or the corresponding yes-no question for the sequences in (25–29). If forced to write or utter a "corresponding" tag or yes-no question for the sentence in, say, (25), students might come up with one of these constructions:

30. Didn't he enjoy the baseball game on Saturday?

31. Enjoyed the baseball game on Saturday, didn't you?

32. You enjoyed the baseball game on Saturday, didn't you?

Yet even these forced and noncorresponding questions are highly instructive, for they reveal some of the elements which might be added to (25) to make it into a complete sentence. The yes-no question in (30) reveals that (25) lacks a possible *he* subject; the tag questions in (31) and (32) implicitly and explicitly reveal that (25) lacks a possible *you* subject. That is, the very attempt to force a tag question or a yes-no question from a nonsentence offers evidence not only of the existence of a student's underlying knowledge of a (complete) sentence but also the strength of this knowledge.

What ultimately makes tag questions and yes-no questions so useful in differentiating sentences from nonsentences is their ability to mark sentence boundaries. Every sentence, no matter how complex, has two boundaries, one that marks the beginning of the sentence and one that marks its end. (In writing, we can call these two boundaries the left and right boundary, respectively.) Differentiating a sentence from a nonsentence — or, in our terms, defining a sentence operationally — crucially depends upon identifying the two boundaries, since what lies in between them is the sentence. Indeed, one major advantage of using tag-question formation and yes-no question formation as a test for "sentencehood" is that the operations involved visually mark the boundaries of a sentence. Tag-question formation visually marks the right boundary by placing the appropriate tag there (e.g., *isn't he, aren't they*); the yes-no question formation visually marks the left boundary by moving the auxiliary (or adding a *do* form) there. If both boundaries cannot be so marked, then the original sequence falls short of being a sentence.

The following sequences help illustrate the marking of boundaries ("//" indicates a sentence or independent clause boundary):

33. a. //It's a great party//
    b. It's a great party//isn't it?
    c. Is//it _____ a great party?
34. a. //Whatever you say will be okay with Mary//
    b. Whatever you say will be okay with Mary//won't it?
    c. Will//whatever you say _____ be okay with Mary?
35. a. //The man and the woman, neither of whom Ted knows, came from a place called Hamburg//
    b. The man and the woman, neither of whom Ted knows, came from a place called Hamburg//didn't they?
    c. Did//the man and the woman, neither of whom Ted knows, come from a place called Hamburg?

With tag questions, the right sentence boundary is marked even if, for semantic and pragmatic reasons, the wrong subject is copied as the pronoun in the tag, as in (36b) and (37b), or even if the auxiliary verb lacks an accepted negative contracted form, as in (38b) and (39b)[2]:

36. a. //I think Bob is going to Sally's Halloween party in a Dracula costume//
    b. *I think Bob is going to Sally's Halloween party in a Dracula costume//isn't he?
    c. Do//I think Bob is going to Sally's Halloween party in a Dracula costume?

37. a. //We are certain that Janice and her two friends will not get an A in history//
    b. *We are certain that Janice and her two friends will not get an A in history//will they?
    c. Are//we _____ certain that Janice and her two friends will not get an A in history?

38. a. //Dave might finish the assignment over the weekend//
    b. *Dave might finish the assignment over the weekend//mightn't he? (This one is acceptable in certain dialects.)
    c. Might//Dave _____ finish the assignment over the weekend?

39. a. //I'm just being stubborn//
    b. *I'm just being stubborn//am't/ain't I?
    c. Am//I _____ just being stubborn?

With yes-no questions, the left boundary is marked even if the moved element creates an awkward or, to some, an ungrammatical sentence, as in (40c) or (41c):

40. a. //That the rock singer may cut his hair could be a problem//
    b. That the rock singer may cut his hair could be a problem// couldn't it?
    c. Could//that the rock singer may cut his hair _____ be a problem?

41. a. //To be a famous movie star can mean a life without privacy//
    b. To be a famous movie star can mean a life without privacy// can't it?
    c. Can//to be a famous movie star _____ mean a life without privacy?

As one final verification of sentencehood, teachers might enlist students to try a simple operation that is independent of both tag- and yes-no question formation. As all native speakers of English implicitly know (just as all teachers who have used sentence combining as a teaching device explicitly know), sentences can be embedded, or nested, within another. One such embedding environment, or slot, for declarative sentences occurs in (42):

42. They refused to believe the idea that _____.

Although many word sequences will properly fit in the above slot, whatever these sequences are, most of them take the form of a (declarative) sentence. Thus, the (a) sentences in (7–12) can be embedded in (42), as the complex sentences in (43–48) below show:

43. They refused to believe the idea that Jim and Sue can dance the tango.
44. They refused to believe the idea that the company, which employed many workers and made many different kinds of products, went out of business.
45. They refused to believe the idea that the cost of the three typewriters and the four clocks will be raised.
46. They refused to believe the idea that Tom ate some bad spaghetti and had a stomachache all day.
47. They refused to believe the idea that doing math problems isn't one of Billy's favorite activities.
48. They refused to believe the idea that, whether Sam likes it or not, Janet should telephone David again.

In contrast, nonsentence sequences, such as those in (25–29), cannot be embedded in the same environment:

49. *They refused to believe the idea that enjoyed the baseball game on Saturday.
50. *They refused to believe the idea that whatever you could do to help my sister.
51. *They refused to believe the idea that the wind howling through the trees last night.
52. *They refused to believe the idea that if you came tomorrow afternoon at one o'clock.
53. *They refused to believe the idea that in order to find a job he liked.

In most cases, the above method proves easy to use because it provides a controlled syntactic context in which to judge sentence completeness.

The Underlying Knowledge of "Presentence Modifier"

In addition to marking the left boundary of a sentence, yes-no question formation is helpful in identifying presentence modifiers. Being able to identify these modifiers proves useful in writing since a comma is sometimes required to set off the presentence modifier from the rest of the sentence.[3] Although appearing in various forms and lengths, all presentence modifiers share two syntactic characteristics: they occur, as the grammatical terminology suggests, at the beginning of the sentence, and they are movable to some other location in the sentence, whether it be the end or somewhere in the middle (the exact position is unimportant here). The basic problem of identifying presentence modifiers, or really separating them from the rest of the sentence, lies in the variety of forms they take. They can be a word, a phrase, or a clause. The value of yes-no question formation lies in its ability to treat them all alike syntactically. If a presentence modifier occurs in a declarative sentence, yes-no question formation will either place the moved auxiliary to its right or displace the modifier to some other location in the sentence. (The displacement of the modifier occurs because of stylistic reasons and is not a part of the yes-no question rule itself.) In either case, the presentence modifier becomes easily identifiable. The presentence modifier is either everything in the sentence that stands to the left of the moved auxiliary verb (or added *do* form) or everything that moves rightward to some other position in the sentence. The following sentences, containing a variety of presentence modifiers, illustrate the point (the modifiers under consideration are in italics for easy reference):

54. a. *Frankly,* everyone says that my fifth-grade teacher is mean.
    b. *Frankly,* does everyone say that my fifth-grade teacher is mean?
    c. Does everyone say, *frankly,* that my fifth-grade teacher is mean?

55. a. *Consequently,* the whole street was destroyed by the tornado.
    b. *Consequently,* was the whole street destroyed by the tornado?
    c. Was the whole street, *consequently,* destroyed by the tornado?

56. a. *In Los Angeles about this time,* Janine claimed that she saw a flying saucer zoom over her house.
    b. *In Los Angeles about this time*, did Janine claim that she saw a flying saucer zoom over her house?
    c. Did Janine claim that *in Los Angeles about this time* she saw a flying saucer zoom over her house?

57. a. *Things being what they are,* Jerry's mother is very angry at him.
    b. *Things being what they are,* is Jerry's mother very angry at him?
    c. Is Jerry's mother very angry at him, *things being what they are?*

58. a. *Although he has never hit a home run in his life,* Jeremy still loves to play baseball.
    b. *Although he has never hit a home run in his life,* does Jeremy still love to play baseball?

    c. Does Jeremy still love to play baseball, *although he has never hit a home run in his life?*

59. a. *When the food arrives,* we'll start with the pepperoni pizza first.
    b. *When the food arrives,* will we start with the pepperoni pizza first?
    c. Will we start with the pepperoni pizza first *when the food arrives?*

Pedagogically, the main benefit of using the yes-no question to identify presentence modifiers lies in avoiding the laborious and time-consuming chore of presenting all the various types of presentence modifiers. Teachers need not introduce individually such modifiers as adverbial disjuncts, conjunctive adverbs, prepositional phrases, nominative absolutes, and adverbial clauses; nor need teachers differentiate between one-word, phrasal, or clausal modifiers. Syntactically blind to such distinctions, yes-no question formation operationally defines presentence modifiers in one general and easily perceptible way: they either occur to the left of the moved auxiliary or added *do* form or else they get moved from the presentence position.

The Applicability of the Basic Categories

We have now operationally defined a set of basic categories — subject, verb (both main and auxiliary), (presentence) modifier, and sentence (or independent clause). If we take into account other categories that become transparent in tag-question formation, we may supplement the basic set with (personal) pronoun, noun, noun phrase and noun substitute, and negative. While the foregoing categories are by no means all the categories that we might define operationally, they comprise a fundamental set for identifying and correcting many highly frequent and sometimes highly stigmatized kinds of errors. In reducing these errors, some of these categories constitute a starting point; for others, they constitute the crucial category (or categories). The importance and potential utility of these categories become clearer if we distribute them in relation to Connors and Lunsford's (1988) list of the twenty most frequent formal errors:

1. No comma after introductory element (presentence modifier, sentence)

2. Vague pronoun reference (pronoun, noun, noun phrase, noun substitute)

3. No comma in compound sentence (independent clause)

4. Wrong word

5. No comma in nonrestrictive element

6. Wrong/missing inflected endings (verb, noun)

7. Wrong or missing preposition

8. Comma splice (sentence or independent clause)

9. Possessive apostrophe error

10. Tense shift (main verb, auxiliary verb)

11. Unnecessary shift in person (possibly subject or pronoun)

12. Sentence fragment (sentence or independent clause)

13. Wrong tense or verb form (main verb, auxiliary verb)

14. Subject-verb agreement (subject, auxiliary verb, main verb)

15. Lack of comma in series

16. Pronoun agreement error (pronoun, subject, main verb, auxiliary verb)

17. Unnecessary comma with restrictive element

18. Run-on or fused sentence (sentence or independent clause)

19. Dangling or misplaced modifier (presentence modifier, sentence)

20. Its/it's error

The importance and potential utility of these categories also become more apparent when they are placed in relation to Hairston's (1981) "status marking" and "very serious" errors, the two most stigmatized kinds of stylistic errors:

Status Marking

nonstandard verb forms in past or past participle (verb)

lack of subject-verb agreement: *We was* instead of *We were; Jones don't think it's acceptable* instead of *Jones doesn't think it's acceptable* (subject, main verb, auxiliary verb)

double negatives (negative)

objective pronoun as subject (pronoun, subject)

Very Serious

sentence fragments (sentence or independent clause)

run-on sentences (sentence or independent clause)

noncapitalization of proper nouns (noun)

would of instead of *would have* (possibly auxiliary verb) lack of subject-verb agreement, non-status marking (subject, auxiliary verb, main verb)

insertion of comma between the verb and its complement (main verb)

nonparallelism

faulty adverb forms

use of transitive verb *set* for intransitive *sit* (verb)

The Practical Benefits

Isolating basic categories of grammar in the manner demonstrated here, then, produces practical benefits. Aside from its relevance to correcting some highly frequent and stigmatized errors, the method reduces significantly the time expended on grammar instruction.[4] Teachers need not present to students all the customary grammatical categories, only a small set of them. Second, and as a direct result of the first benefit, it creates more time to devote to other matters of writing. While unconventional features of style need attention at some point in writing instruction, they should not be the sole nor the primary area of attention. Third, because the method demonstrated here relies on a body of already acquired knowledge, it requires less effort to present the basic categories. Teachers present — and students apply — what they already unconsciously know. Fourth, the method ties in nicely with a process approach to writing. Just as students can improve paragraphs and whole essays by learning about and partaking more consciously in the process of writing, so too can they improve their sentence mechanics by learning about and partaking more consciously in the process (i.e., the operations) of sentence formation.

Notes

1. The asterisk here denotes an ungrammatical sentence, that is, one which violates the descriptive rules of English grammar.
2. When working with tag-question formation, instructors will sooner or later encounter word sequences which are genuine sentences but which, on first try, cannot be transformed into grammatical tag questions (at least not in all regional or social varieties of English). These cases involve sentences containing modal verbs (a subclass of auxiliary verbs) like *may, might, ought,* and *shall,* which, if contracted with *not,* produce in some dialects or styles the unacceptable **mayn't, *mightn't, *oughtn't,* and **shalln't* (*shalln't* [or *shan't*], for example, being unacceptable in many non-British dialects), or the main or auxiliary verb form *am* (which, if contracted with *not,* results in the unacceptable *amn't*). Although such verbs may not contract with *not* to form grammatical tag questions, in some varieties of English they do appear in *uncontracted* form in tag questions. Thus, for example, *He might come tomorrow* can be transformed into *He might come tomorrow, might he not?* (or, possibly, *He might come tomorrow, might not he?*). Although the

resulting tag question is formal in style, it is, nonetheless, in some varieties of English, a grammatical — and corresponding — tag question. To keep matters simple, instructors should, whenever appropriate, inform students that, if the inability to contract the verb is the *only* problem in forming the proper tag question, then the proper tag question is a formal one (i.e., one with an uncontracted verb in the tag part of the question). One other point needs mentioning. Even though verb forms like *may, might, ought, shall,* and *am* may not be contracted with the negative in some varieties of English, so strong is the pattern to have a contracted verb in tag questions (assuming, of course, the original sentence is positive) that native speakers of English will often substitute for an uncontractable verb a contractable one and usually one that's similar in meaning or time reference. Thus, in informal styles, the following changes will occur: *may, might → won't; ought → shouldn't; shall → won't; am → aren't, ain't.* Teachers and students should view such changes solely as efforts of English speakers to get around the uncontractability problem mentioned above.

3. Some handbooks state that the comma should be inserted only if the introductory phrase or clause is a "long" one, usually set arbitrarily at five or more words; however, students who add a comma even for "short" introductory phrases and clauses can hardly go wrong, given the arbitrariness of what constitutes "long." If students realize that all presentence modifiers are also fragments, then a more general and more acceptable rule is possible: "When a fragment immediately precedes a (genuine) sentence and both are intended to be read as one unit, the fragment is set off from the sentence by a comma." The greatest advantage of this rule is that instructors do not need to define the various kinds of phrases (e.g., prepositional, participial, infinitive) or the various kinds of dependent clauses (e.g., adverbial). When a fragment immediately *follows* a (genuine) sentence and both are intended to be read as one unit, the fragment is often (not always) set off by a comma.

4. Using the same underlying principles but slightly different operational syntactic tests than the ones outlined in this study, DeBeaugrande (1984) reports impressive results in getting college students to identify subjects, number-carrying verbs, verb tenses, and fragments. For example, he states that, with respect to identifying subjects and predicates, posttest scores showed an improvement of approximately five hundred percent over pretest scores (363); the same study found that forty-five students who had been taught an operational test for identifying number-carrying verbs and verb tenses made less than half as many errors in recognition than before treatment (365).

My own work with the approach based on underlying syntactic knowledge shows less spectacular gains but highly favorable responses from teachers who use the approach. In the fall of 1988, I conducted a study which differed significantly from DeBeaugrande's insofar as it contrasted two approaches (i.e., a traditional or conventional approach versus the approach based on underlying syntactic knowledge) and covered a wider range of students with greater variability in writing skills, specifically, one sixth-grade elementary school class, three ninth-grade junior high classes, and two freshman-level and two developmental-writing college classes. As a means of identifying fragments, run-ons, and comma splices, the participating teachers (all of whom taught multiple classes or sections) taught a traditional (usually a traditional grammar) approach to one set of students and the approach based on underlying syntactic knowledge to another set of students.

On the basis of pretests and posttests, the experimental groups (i.e., students taught the approach based on underlying syntactic knowledge) showed about the same positive gains in identifying fragments, run-ons, and comma splices as the control groups (i.e., students taught a traditional approach). At the least, the results indicated that students generally do benefit from exposure to some grammar instruction, whether formal or informal, in identifying the three kinds of sentencing errors. In all likelihood, the lack of differentiation in the results of the two approaches lay in two substantial factors: (1) because the experimental and control groups in the study generally could not be equalized with respect to academic ability without severely disrupting the teachers' normal conduct of classes, the higher-achieving class was always assigned as the control group and the lower-achieving class (or classes) as the experimental group, and (2) because most students in the study reported that they had studied traditional grammar for many years, the control groups (both students and teachers) generally had much more exposure and practice with the traditional method than the experimental groups had with the new approach. Yet, despite the probable influence of these two factors, many students in the experimental groups made significant gains, some comparable to those reported by DeBeaugrande. The most impressive findings, however, lay in teachers' responses to the approach based on underlying syntactic knowledge. An attitudinal questionnaire completed by the five teachers who participated in the study and by three other teachers who had also used the approach during the same period generally showed favorable or highly favorable responses with respect to ease of presentation, economy of time, and overall impression. Further, all believed strongly or very strongly that they could get better results with more practice, and all strongly or very strongly indicated that they planned to use the approach in future writing classes (the latter item on the questionnaire, in fact, received the highest positive score of all, with seven out of eight teachers indicating "very strongly"). Lastly and somewhat strangely, a majority of instructors (five out of seven) perceived the experimental method as bringing better results than traditional methods, even though their students, on the average, made about the same gains with the experimental method as with the conventional method. In light of the other responses to the questionnaire, a likely explanation here is that these instructors interpreted "better results" in the questionnaire item "Did the USK [i.e., the Underlying Syntactic Knowledge] method bring better results than the method(s) you normally use?" to mean better results with respect to time and effort spent. (I wish to thank Jeffrie Ahmad, Linda Beauregard-Vasquez, Pamela Grove, Lynn McDonie, John Peters, Mary Riggs, Ilene Rubenstein, and Anne Lise Schofield for their aid in completing this study.)

Positive responses to the underlying-syntactic-knowledge method also came from students themselves. In a study of developmental writers conducted at Antelope Valley College, Beauregard-Vasquez (1989) found that students who were taught the underlying-syntactic-knowledge method not only made 40.5 percent fewer errors in identifying fragments and 37.9 percent fewer errors in identifying run-ons and comma splices but also, with much less classroom instruction, made greater average gains than a control group taught only traditional grammar. Just as important, students greatly preferred the underlying-syntactic-knowledge method over traditional grammar instruction. On the basis of narrative student evaluations of the method, Beauregard-Vasquez states that students found the underlying-syntactic-knowledge method to be a "fun" and "easy" way to "fix" their papers and that students wished that they had learned the method earlier, or in the words of one student:

> I have gone to many English classes all through my years of school, and I have been taught the same type of skills. . . . But the tag and yes-no question method is by far the most unique and simplified method I have ever been taught. . . . I like the method because it is something new and exciting. It is far better than anything else they tried to teach me. (16)

Beauregard-Vasquez notes that the method seems to give students a greater sense of confidence and helps reduce the "excessive blame they tend to place on themselves for not already knowing grammar," or as stated by another student:

> I'm very excited about this new way of learning grammar. I've always felt that I was the problem when it came to learning; however, I thought that it was a lack of attention or just being unable to soak up the material. But now I know it's not; in fact, it was never me. It was the way the material was presented. (15)

Works Cited

Beauregard-Vasquez, Linda. "The USK Alternative to Traditional Grammar Instruction: A Case Study of Student Writers at A.V.C." Unpublished ms. 1989.

Connors, Robert J., and Andrea A. Lunsford. "Frequency of Formal Errors in Current College Writing, or Ma and Pa Kettle Do Research." *College Composition and Communication* 39 (1988): 388–93.

DeBeaugrande, Robert. "Forward to the Basics: Getting Down to Grammar." *College Compositon and Communication* 35 (1984): 358–67.

D'Eloia, Sarah. "The Uses — and Limits — of Grammar." *Journal of Basic Writing* 1.3 (1977): 1–48.

Hairston, Maxine. *Successful Writing: A Rhetoric for Advanced Composition.* New York: Norton, 1981.

Noguchi, Rei R. "Transformation-Generative Syntax and the Teachings of Sentence Mechanics." *Journal of Basic Writing* 6.2 (1987): 26–36.

Classroom Activities

Have students work together in pairs or small groups to try Noguchi's operational approach. Ask them to bring a draft to the group; you should provide copies of some of the exercises Noguchi lists in this article. First, have students identify the sentence-level errors in each other's drafts; next, working on their own drafts, students can use Noguchi's rubrics (tag questions, yes-no questions marking sentence boundaries, and so forth) to improve their own sentences. As Noguchi suggests, these rubrics enable students to conceptualize different choices for correcting errors as well as to internalize the operational definitions of sentence structure. Finally, as a whole group, students can compare sentences before and after editing, writing original and revised sentences on the board to become more aware of this important aspect of the writing process.

Thinking about Teaching

Reflect on your own notions of "socially approved" grammar in your teaching journal. Noguchi suggests that "violations of the prescriptive rules still result in English sentences, even though the sentences may not be socially approved." The rules of standard written English have been presented as a kind of canonical grammar; not following the "rules" in this sense may be equated with transgressing the social order, which carries political implications. Language usage is often understood as a class marker within and outside of our classrooms. What to teach as "standard" thus becomes a dilemma.

Discussing the concept of "social approval" with other teachers is one way to examine this problem. Also included in this category may be the politically charged issues of the back-to-basics movement and the teaching of Ebonics. To emphasize the rhetorical differences in language usage, teachers may at some point wish to share their insights on these divisive subjects with developing writers. In this context, teachers can present *determining audience and purpose* and *editing* as equally crucial parts of the writing process, thereby demystifying the notion of "perfect" or "correct" grammar.

Teaching Style through Sentence Combining and Sentence Generating

Constance Weaver

As a Professor of English at Western Michigan University in Kalamazoo, Constance Weaver teaches courses in reading and writing and in language arts instruction (reading, writing, and grammar). In addition to Teaching Grammar in Context, *she has recently edited* Lessons to Share: On Teaching Grammar in Context *(1998), a collection of essays that offer a variety of perspectives and practical applications, including grammar instruction for ESL students. Other recent books by Weaver include* Creating Support for Effective Literary Education: Workshop Materials and Handouts *(coauthored with Lorraine Gillmeister-Krause and Grace Vento-Zogby);* Reading Process and Practice: From Socio-Linguistics to Whole Language, *2nd ed.; and* Success at Last: Helping AD(H)D

Students Achieve Their Potential (an edited collection). Throughout the mini-lessons presented in the following reading, Weaver emphasizes the potential for creativity in grammar instruction and demonstrates her enthusiasm for playing with language and ideas.

Teachers who need more background in grammar to adapt and ex pand [the following] lessons or develop their own might find Diana Hacker's *A Writer's Reference* (1995) particularly useful. More realistic in its assessment of how the language is really used by educated people is *The Right Handbook: Grammar and Usage in Context,* by Belanoff, Rorschach, and Oberlink (1993). Both of these would also be excellent references for students at the high school and college levels.

Usually, it works well for the teacher to make transparencies for the concepts being taught, and to use different colored transparency pens to clarify particular constructions, marks of punctuation, and so forth. I prefer to use examples from students' own writing or examples from literature, such as the many published examples in Scott Rice's *Right Words, Right Places* (1993); in practice, though, I all too often find myself concocting short examples that can easily be printed by hand on a transparency. All these lessons can be taught to the entire class or to a smaller group of students, but follow-up application commonly needs to be guided individually. Or to put it bluntly, without further guidance, such lessons will not necessarily transfer to students' own writing any better than traditional grammar book exercises have done; they simply reflect a more efficient use of time than the traditional practice exercises and tests. Students will inevitably need guidance in applying these concepts during revision and editing.

Most of these lessons I have taught with students in various classes at the college level, but particularly with the preservice and inservice teachers in my Grammar and Teaching Grammar class. In working with those enrolled in this course, I have usually had a dual or triple aim: to teach something that could benefit them as writers themselves; to suggest and exemplify something that they might profitably teach to their students, at least in simplified form; and to model possible ways of teaching grammar in context. Here, these suggestions often look like rather formal lesson plans, with goals indicated and the reader addressed as "you." But to emphasize the fact that these lessons represent ongoing experimentation, some lessons or parts of them have been written in a more conversational tone — to share what I have done as a teacher at the college level and sometimes to make suggestions for how my experiments might be modified to achieve goals at other levels. This, I hope, will also emphasize the fact that adaptations will usually be necessary as well as desirable: that we must all to some extent reinvent the wheel of effective instruction in our own classrooms, even while we share our efforts with each other, collaborate with one another, and benefit from others' experiences.

1. Introducing Participial Phrases

GOALS   To help writers see the effectiveness of using present participle phrases, when used as free modifiers. In addition, to help writers
see that they can sometimes move such phrases for greater effectiveness, as they revise. Such lessons are most appropriate for writers who
provide few narrative and descriptive details in their writing, or writers who provide such details in separate sentences, instead of appropriately subordinating some details in modifying phrases.

BACKGROUND   One of the constructions that most distinguishes professional writers from student writers is the participial phrase used as
a free modifier — that is, as a modifier that is not absolutely essential
to the sentence and therefore is set off by punctuation — usually by
commas in prose, but sometimes just by line divisions in poetry
(Christensen and Christensen, 1978). The present participle phrase
commonly conveys action, whether it is used in poetry, fiction, or
nonfiction. Such free modifiers most commonly occur at the end of the
clause, even if they modify the subject of that clause. The second most
common position is before the subject-predicate unit. Least common is
a participial free modifier occurring between the subject and the predicate.

Possible Procedures

1. Put some examples on transparencies and discuss them with
the students. For example:

> I watched the flashing past of cotton fields and cabins, *feeling that I was*
> *moving into the unknown.*   — Ralph Ellison, *Invisible Man* (1952)

> "I wish we could get wet," said Lily, *watching a boy ride his bicycle*
> *through rain puddles.*   — Amy Tan, *The Moon Lady* (1992)

> Father,
> All these he has made me own,
> The trees and the forests
> *Standing in their places.*
>   — Teton Sioux, *The Trees Stand Shining* (H. Jones, 1993)

> *Still laughing,* Mama bustled about the kitchen until her masterpiece
> was complete.   — Phil Mendez, *The Black Snowman* (1989)

> Far below, a sea of purple and orange clouds churned, *dashing like*
> *waves in slow motion against the mountain's green forests and reddish-*
> *brown volcanic rock.*
>   — Tom Minehart, "On Top of Mount Fuji, People Hope for Change"
>   (July 17, 1993)

> The river that used to surge into the Gulf of California, *depositing ruddy-colored silt that fanned out into a broad delta of new land at its mouth,* hardly ever makes it to the sea anymore.
> — Paul Gray, "A Fight over Liquid Gold" (1991)

2. Discuss the placement of the participial phrases. In most cases, the participial phrase is probably most effective as is. However, what about putting the participial phrase before the subject in the second example?

> Watching a boy ride his bicycle through rain puddles, Lily said, "I wish we could get wet."

Is this order perhaps as good as the original, even though the focus has changed? By thus discussing the effects and effectiveness of placing modifiers differently, students develop a sense of style and an ability to suit the grammar to the sense of what they are writing.

3. You might also discuss examples like the following sentences from Richard Wright's poem "Between the World and Me" (1935), wherein two past tense verbs are followed by a present participle phrase:

> The dry bones stirred, rattled, lifted, *melting themselves into my bones.*

> And then they had me, stripped me, *battering my teeth into my throat till I swallowed my own blood.*

Why might the poet have switched from past tense verbs to present participle phrases at the ends of these sentences? How is the effect different?

ADDITIONAL MINI-LESSONS   Students may benefit from follow-up lessons in which they listen to or read more literary excerpts making effective use of present participle phrases. The teacher can encourage the students to find and share examples themselves. Another kind of mini-lesson can involve taking a bare-bones sentence from a student's paper and brainstorming together about details that might be added in free modifying -ING phrases. Similarly, one can demonstrate how to combine already written sentences during revision. See also the following lessons in this category.

2. Using Present Participle Phrases as Free Modifiers

POSSIBLE PROCEDURE   Suggest to writers the option of writing "I am" poems (see Figure 1) in which they equate themselves metaphorically with things that reflect their interests, suit their personalities, suggest their goals. Emphasize the possibility of using present participle free modifiers by sharing examples in which the writer has used them effectively.

Figure 1a. Examples of "I am" poems in which the writers were encouraged to use participial phrases. The top three poems were written by sixth graders and the bottom two by seventh graders.

I am an elegant, proud daisy
Dodging life-taking lawnmowers
Spreading out my leaves and petals
Taking in carbon dioxide
Giving out a gift of oxygen.

Rachel Nieboer

PINTO

I am a widely blotched black and white pinto
Gliding smothly into my rocky canter
Tipping over my green grain bucket
Mouthing my metal snaffle bit.

Jennifer Richardson

I am a young speedy pup.
Bringing aggravation to my family
Eating all in sight
Destroying whatever I can
Chewing away at life.

Chris Colyn

I am a long, rectangular bumper sticker
sticking on a small red car
smelling the horrible stench of the exhaust pipe
telling everyone that my owner loves New York.

Aaron Knox

I am a strong lasting tool.
Nailing friends together
Pounding kindness into the world
Sawing through problems
Sanding rough edges in life.

Helen Karsten

Figure 1b. Examples of "I am" poems. The top two were written by college freshmen encouraged to use participial phrases as free modifiers. The bottom two were written by teachers, under less stringent conditions.

LEAVES IN THE FALL

I am a red leaf
    Floating through the brisk air
    Changing from green to fiery red
    Crumbling after being walked on
    Disappearing after crumbling
    Growing new leaves next year.

Tracey Chambers

I am a soccer ball
    rolling down the field
    bounding off the player's head
    curving around the goalie
    flying through the air
    scoring a point to win the game.

Joel Parsons

I am ten o'clock
    steadily ticking toward noon.
A calculator, tracking my progress,
    planning my future.
I am concrete, a foundation for the
    architecture of my life.
Yet I am also a string instrument,
    vibrating with living melodies
A prism absorbing the spectrum of life
    and tossing out multicolored glints
Hungry, determined, I am my own canvas
    never complete.

Pat Reeves

I am "Four Strong Winds" and the "Moonlight Sonata,"
    melancholy yet serene.
I am a Bilbo's pizza with whole wheat crust,
    tomato bubbly and cheese gooey.
I am 5 A.M., a nun
    greeting the morning solitude,
    grateful for the absolution of a new day.
I am a midnight lover,
    cherishing and tender,
    tracing a smile in the dark
    with my fingertips.
I am a whitewater raft,
    sturdy yet flexible,
    bouncing over hidden rocks
    to rest beyond the whirlpool.

Connie Weaver

3. Creating Participial Phrases and Absolutes through Sentence Combining

GOAL   To encourage writers to use participial phrases (both present and past) and absolute constructions in their writing. Also, to consider the stylistically effective placement of these free modifiers.

Possible Procedures

1. Put the sets of sentences shown in Figure 2 on transparencies, leaving plenty of room to write the changes that the students suggest. It may be helpful to provide a copy of the activity for each student, so that students can more easily focus on the task and keep a record of the sentences they have created. Adapted from Allyn & Bacon's *The Writing Process,* Book 9 (1982), the sentences describe a short nonverbal motion picture titled *Dream of the Wild Horses.*

2. Explain that, for now, you want the sentences in each set combined into a single sentence, with the sentence in capitals remaining untouched and the others reduced to parts of sentences (free modifiers), but kept in the same order. Do the first two or three with the students. If the students reorder the parts of the resultant sentence or choose a different original sentence to leave unchanged (which is common), you can accept these variations but, whenever possible, discuss which version works better in the flow of the narrative. Don't worry, for now, about examining the structure of the newly created parts of sentences; that can be done after the narrative is created.

3. After creating a satisfying narrative, you can call students' attention to the three kinds of free modifiers they have created:

Running dreamily, the herd fades into the distance, *leaving sea and shore undisturbed.* [present participle phrase. The *-ing* in these free modifiers shows that the phrases are present participles. They are verb phrases functioning as modifiers.]

The herd stampedes, *panicked by an inferno.* [past participle phrase] *Singed by the flames and choked by the smoke,* the herd plunges desperately into the sea. [past participle phrase. The *-ed* forms in these free modifiers show that the phrases are past participles. They, too, are verb phrases functioning as modifiers.]

Their fears forgotten, the horses frolic in the waves. [absolute phrase. The absolute has a subject and retains the essence of the verb phrase. Often, the absolute can be restored to a complete sentence by adding *am, is, are, was,* or *were,* as in *Their fears were forgotten.*]

The horses gallop in slow motion, *their manes suspended in twilight, their hooves tracing deliberate patterns in the sand.* [The first absolute consists, in effect, of a subject plus a past participle phrase. The second absolute has a subject followed by a present participle phrase. The addition of *were* would restore each absolute to a complete sentence.]

Figure 2. Sentences for creating participial phrases and absolutes.

1. A HERD OF WILD HORSES RACES ALONG A BEACH.
   Their hoofbeats carve patterns in the sand.
   Their hoofbeats churn the surf.
   [A herd of wild horses races along a beach, their hoofbeats carving patterns in the sand and churning the surf.]

2. Manes are flying
   Legs are flailing
   THE HORSES SURGE FORWARD INTO A DEEPENING MIST.
   [Manes flying, legs flailing, the horses surge forward into a deepening mist.]

3. THE THUNDERING HERD ALMOST DISAPPEARS.
   The herd is veiled by a blue haze.
   [The thundering herd almost disappears, veiled by a blue haze.]

4. Two stallions emerge suddenly.
   TWO STALLIONS BEGIN TO FIGHT.
   [Suddenly emerging, two stallions begin to fight.]

5. THEY REAR ON THEIR POWERFUL HIND LEGS.
   They circle each other in a deadly dance.
   [They rear on their powerful hind legs, circling each other in a deadly dance.]

6. The stallions have fought to a stalemate.
   THE STALLIONS RACE TO THE FRONT OF THE HERD.
   [Having fought to a stalemate, the stallions race to the front of the herd.]

7. THE HERD STAMPEDES.
   The herd is panicked by an inferno.
   [The herd stampedes, panicked by an inferno.]

As these examples illustrate, the participial phrase is essentially a verb phrase functioning like an adjective, to modify a noun. The present participle phrase typically connotes present action, while the past participle phrase connotes completed action or description. The absolute construction is effective for conveying descriptive detail, without giving it the full weight of a grammatically complete sentence.

Teacher Resources

Christensen, F., and B. Christensen. *Notes toward a New Rhetoric: Nine Essays for Teachers.* 2nd ed. New York: Harper & Row, 1978. These essays by Francis Christensen are valuable in helping us understand some of the characteristics of today's prose style.

Figure 2. (continued)

---

8. The herd is singed by the flames.
   The herd is choked by the smoke.
   THE HERD PLUNGES DESPERATELY INTO THE SEA.
   [Singed by the flames and choked by the smoke, the herd plunges desperately into the sea.]

9. Their fears are forgotten.
   THE HORSES FROLIC IN THE WAVES.
   They dive into the depths.
   They surface again.
   [Their fears forgotten, the horses frolic in the waves, diving into the depths, then surfacing again.]

10. The horses are restored.
    THE HORSES MOVE BACK TOWARD THE SHORE.
    [Restored, the horses move back toward the shore.]

11. THE SHORE IS NOW SOFTENED BY TWILIGHT.
    The shore is tinted with muted pinks and lavenders.
    [The shore is now softened by twilight, tinted with muted pinks and lavenders.]

12. THE HORSES GALLOP IN SLOW MOTION.
    Their manes are suspended in twilight.
    Their hooves trace deliberate patterns in the sand.
    [The horses gallop in slow motion, their manes suspended in twilight, their hooves tracing deliberate patterns in the sand.]

13. The herd runs dreamily.
    THE HERD FADES INTO THE DISTANCE.
    The herd leaves sea and shore undisturbed.
    [Running dreamily, the herd fades into the distance, leaving sea and shore undisturbed.]

Daiker, D. A., A. Kerek, and M. Morenberg. *The Writer's Options: Combining to Composing.* 4th ed. New York: Harper & Row, 1990. Intended as a text at the college level, this book is also especially valuable to teachers interested in implementing sentence-combining activities that draw upon the research of Christensen and others.

Killgallon, D. *Sentence Composing: The Complete Course.* Portsmouth, NH: Boynton/Cook, 1987. Excellent book for students, especially at the high school level. . . .

4. Appreciating and Using Absolute Constructions

GOALS   To help writers appreciate the absolute construction as a means of conveying descriptive detail, and to help them become sufficiently aware of the absolute construction to use it in their writing.

NOTE ... Technically the absolute is a phrase, because it's not quite grammatically complete as a sentence. Because the absolute has a "subject" and the *essence* of a verb, it can also be described as a near-clause.

Possible Procedures

1. Locate some effective absolutes from literature. The references cited in the lesson immediately above are good resources, as is Scott Rice's *Right Words, Right Places* (1993). The absolute construction is particularly common in narrative fiction and poetry — even in many picture books for children. Here are some further examples:

> I saw the giant bend and clutch the posts at the top of the stairs with both hands, bracing himself, *his body gleaming bare in his white shorts.*
> — Ralph Ellison, *Invisible Man* (1952)

> Before me, in the panel where a mirror is usually placed, I could see a scene from a bullfight, *the bull charging close to the man and the man swinging the red cape in sculptured folds so close to his body that man and bull seemed to blend in one swirl of calm, pure motion.*
> — Ralph Ellison, *Invisible Man* (1952)

> A sudden blow: *the great wings beating still*
> *Above the staggering girl, her thighs caressed*
> *By the dark webs, her nape caught in his bill,*
> He holds her helpless breast upon his breast.
> — W. B. Yeats, "Leda and the Swan" (1924)

Notice how the three absolutes in the Yeats excerpt keep the reader suspended before the main clause, as Zeus in the form of a swan approaches and then claims the girl.

2. As a follow-up, encourage students to experiment with absolutes in their own writing. As a preparatory activity, you might encourage "boast" poems like this:

> My car is a sleek gray cat,
> its paws leaping forward the instant I accelerate,
> its engine purring contentedly.

3. Often in students' narrative writing, one finds simple sentences like *My car is a sleek gray cat*, sentences that could benefit from including more descriptive detail in absolute phrases. When writers are ready to revise at the sentence level, the teacher can help them consider ways of expanding some sentences through absolutes that convey descriptive detail. Past participle phrases can also add descriptive detail, while present participle phrases are often effective in conveying narrative detail.

Classroom Activities

At the end of the mini-lesson on introducing participial phrases, Weaver suggests: "Students may benefit from follow-up lessons in which they listen to or read more literary excerpts making effective use of present participle phrases. The teacher can encourage the students to find and share examples themselves." Have students locate interesting examples from texts that you are reading in class. Then ask students, working individually or in small groups, to find as many phrases as they can. Have students write their favorite examples on the board; then, as a class, try moving the participial phrases around to experiment with word order. Does the placement of the participial phrase make a difference to the sense of the sentence, or to the power of the language?

Thinking about Teaching

In Figures 1a and 1b, Weaver provides yet another inventive example of using participial phrases in context, the "I am" poem. Consider beginning a meeting or writing workshop for teachers by having each person write his or her own version of an "I am" poem. You can decide as a group which particular version of the participial phrase you would like to try, perhaps referring to copies of "I am" poems from Weaver's examples. Share the poems in small groups or with the whole group, or publish them in a small booklet or electronically. You may also wish to try this activity with students, writing along with them in class and reading the results aloud. Weaver asks us as teachers of writing to pay attention to the many ways language can work so that we can experience the benefits of teaching and studying grammar in the context of reading and writing. The "I am" poems are a creative means of working toward this end.

6

Students' Learning Styles

There is no "best way" to teach or to learn. As you may have discovered in your own classes, in a fruitful learning environment the teaching methods support the learning styles of the individual learners. Learning style may be defined as the way one feels most comfortable and most successful approaching and processing a learning event. Developing writers come to the writing classroom with a complex set of needs generated by their varied learning styles and learning differences.

Similarly, the selections in this chapter offer suggestions for approaching teaching and learning through a variety of interlinked strategies. Jacob C. Gaskins shares a series of learning exercises that he gleaned from a workshop at Landmark College, a school exclusively for students with learning differences. Valerie Ann Krahe presents a breakdown of "the rhetorical situation," a technique she employs in composition classes to address the needs of students with a variety of learning styles. Both of these writers use several methods for teaching and empowering students with diagnosed learning disabilities; furthermore, both suggest that all students, whatever their needs, may benefit from instruction that addresses a range of learning styles.

Teaching Writing to Students with Learning Disabilities: The Landmark Method

Jacob C. Gaskins

Landmark College in Putney, Vermont, as Jacob C. Gaskins informs us, is known nationally for its work with students with learning disabilities. Gaskins, Associate Professor of English and Director of the Writing Center at Southeast Missouri State at Cape Giradeau, attended a training institute in the summer of 1993 to study Landmark's methods of teaching writing to students with learning disabilities. He went looking, he admits, for "The Answer." What Gaskins found was a variety of strategies that were not unlike those used in teaching the writing process in freshman composition courses. He suggests that strategies that are appropriate for students with learning disabilities are also appropriate for their classmates who are not so diagnosed.

In July 1993, I attended a week-long Training Institute for Educators at Landmark College, Putney, Vermont, to study Landmark's methods of teaching writing to students with dyslexia and other learning disabilities. Founded in 1985 as an offshoot of Landmark High School in Boston, Landmark College, with a faculty of 85 and a student body of 250, has earned a national reputation as the only accredited college in the country serving dyslexic and LD [learning disabled] students exclusively. (Fans of television's *The Cosby Show* may remember that the episodes about Theo's dyslexia were produced in consultation with Landmark. A picture of the two consultants with the show's cast is displayed on a bulletin board in the administration building, incidentally, and further down the hall, on another bulletin board, letters from grateful graduates.)

I went to Vermont in search of the Holy Grail, the Impossible Dream, some patented technique that would guarantee success with the sorts of students who were causing me, as director of a writing center at a mid-sized, moderately selective, public university in the Midwest, so much frustration and concern. I hoped that the Landmark Institute would prepare me to meet my obligation to assist these students by teaching me methods that were certifiably effective. In short, I wanted The Answer. Predictably, I was disappointed.

First of all, Landmark has not existed long enough to have compiled a broad enough statistical base upon which to determine exactly how effective its methods are — as MacLean Gander, the institute's director and chair of Landmark's English Department, readily admits.

Yet the yearly Training Institute was definitely worth attending, and I recommend it highly to future participants. Although it didn't provide The Answer, it did show me where answers are to be found — in the literature of our profession, in fact. The principles of the Landmark Method are very much in keeping with current pedagogy and bear a notable resemblance to the principles of writing across the curriculum. The uniqueness of the Landmark Method, if it can be so called, lies in the rigor and theoretical coherence of its application.

A list of Landmark's principles follows, beginning with the ones more generally applicable and concluding with the principles that seem more appropriate in the teaching of students with dyslexia or other specific learning disabilities.

1. *Exploit the inter-relatedness of reading, writing, speaking, and listening.* On the assumption that students will "write like they talk," Landmark faculty help students talk like they are going to write. That is, what students gain by speaking in class "in complete sentences only" (asking and answering questions, incorporating other students' perspectives, marshaling points, expatiating for a real audience) feeds back into their writing. The writing-speaking connection underlies Landmark's curriculum as well; students must take speech and writing classes concomitantly.

Given the emphasis on class discussion, our institute instructor was compelled to explain how he deals with shy students. Among his — and the English Department's — tips, as codified in institute materials: Call on shy students at the beginning of the hour with an open-ended question, and if they can't answer, ask them to call on someone else. Signal students before you spring a question by walking over and standing by their desk. Make an agreement with shy students that they will contribute a minimum of two comments during each class period.

2. *Teach in "micro-units."* To quote the institute handbook: "Break written assignments into stages and assess and respond to each stage (e.g., give feedback or assess students' brainstorms, outlines, etc.)." The simple activity of summarizing could include (a) taking notes, (b) distinguishing "superordinate" and subordinate ideas, (c) identifying the author's purpose, (d) outlining the structure, (e) restating the author's ideas in one's own words, (f) incorporating quoted material, and (g) using logical connectives.

3. *Teach study skills.* "Study skills" is one of four headings (with "writing," "speaking," and "reading") that appear in outlines for each of the five courses that make up Landmark's composition sequence. In both the initial, not-for-credit EN-071 and the final, for-credit EN-102, students are required to "maintain an organizational and study system (e.g., master notebook) for course work . . . and initiate conferences with teachers. . . ." Other requirements change, depending on the level of the course. EN-071 students learn to "take notes from readings that include main ideas and details," and they "demonstrate the ability to use a dictionary, thesaurus, and periodical guide." By the time students reach EN-101, however, they are able to "independently apply a system to identify, incorporate, and retain *course-specific* vocabulary" [emphasis mine].

Although I do not teach study skills explicitly, I have adapted the idea of the master notebook, requiring my students to keep all materials and assignments in a folder which we review periodically to chart progress. In addition, I follow the practice of the Landmark instructor I observed who begins each session by writing an agenda on the board, which presumably helps students stay focused. In any event, such methods promote "metacognition" as well.

4. *Foster metacognition.* "Metacognition" is an umbrella under which a number of now-familiar methods, all pedagogically consistent, are gathered. Teachers foster meta-cognition by explicitly teaching learning skills (a subcategory of which is accommodation to students' individual *learning styles*); by using the *process approach* to teaching writing (Landmark students benefit from analyzing their writing process(es) and monitoring their progress); by encouraging a spirit of *collaboration* between student and teacher; and finally, by using Landmark's *portfolio system* for determining final grades.

As students continually review their progress, instructors must also confer with other faculty about their teaching. Supervising instructors visit classes on a regular basis, and even the individualized writing conference is not sacrosanct.

I asked one instructor if he felt intimidated by the continual monitoring, the feeling of teaching in a fishbowl that instructors at Landmark must experience. "You get used to it," he said. Later, at a meeting of all institute participants, in response to the same question from someone else, the English Department chair explained that, because evaluation is continual and integral, a cog in the machinery, it isn't threatening. Collaboration, again, is the goal.

5. *Teach to automatization.* In Landmark's words: "Have students practice each skill until they are able to use it automatically." This principle and the ones that follow apply more directly to the teaching of writing to LD students in particular.

6. *Teach diagnostically.* At admission, each student at Landmark is put through a full battery of tests: IQ, language ability (reading, spelling, and vocabulary), attention span, short-term memory, and fine-motor control, among others. The tests are useful for distinguishing *processing* problems (e.g., memory, fine-motor, or attention-deficit disorders) from *product* problems (e.g., the student is unfamiliar with the rules governing conventional punctuation).

However, the connection between test scores and writing problems may not be immediately apparent. Diagnosis is not made any easier because a single problem may have multiple causes, and one problem may have several equally reasonable explanations. I quote institute materials: "Diagnostic assessment of writing problems . . . is less a science than an art; and the key factor, for the instructor, is to maintain an open mind and a sense of constant inquiry." Ultimately, the tests serve to confirm what can best be determined by the instructor through perceptive reading and consultation with the student. Instructors observe the students' writing for clues about the nature of their difficulty and solicit input from the students, who are clearly in the best position to describe both the nature of the problems and their etiology.

An illustration of both the role of testing and the importance of consulting with individual students is the case of a twenty-three-year-old from New Jersey with an IQ of 145 whose scores suggested variously ADD (attention-deficit disorder) and a "visual-motor handicap." Neither of these weaknesses was apparent in the typed sample of the student's writing that we saw, an essay about the rights and obligations of American citizenship. The writing was remarkable chiefly for its sophomoric tone. It concluded: "Remember, cooperation is the key. Work together, and everyone stays happy. Screw things up for others and you will be taken behind a Dairy Queen and shot." If anything, the essay was *too well* focused and organized, a form without content. And this, it turns out, was the significant clue, as was the diagnosis of a fine-motor disorder. As this student himself eventually revealed, the physical act of writing was so difficult for him (evident in his awkward script) that he avoided the page as much as possible, composing as much as he could in his head and then transcribing what he could memorize. The length of his essays was thus limited by the capacity of his memory, two pages. He never wrote more than that and those two pages were invariably, inevitably "canned." He had never used writing for learning and never revised, and so his papers were typically stiff and superficial. Efforts at helping this student involved instruction by the ubiquitous process approach.

7. *Teach to the student's strengths and accommodate learning styles.* In Landmark's words: "Teach in a variety of modalities." If the above student's method of compensation was inappropriate, other students are taught more effective ways around weaknesses. For example, students who have "strong visual-spatial abilities" but experience difficulty outlining their thoughts on the page can see logical relationships among ideas more clearly by building three-dimensional models with "construction manipulatives." One student demonstrated how she used Klondikes (plastic, linking blocks) to create a model of her term paper, with supporting ideas literally branching off the three main points, each one color-coded. I also observed students in a creative writing class use different-colored highlighters to mark poems they were studying, each color representing a different focus of attention. At the level of sentence structure and grammar, instructors use Cuisenaire rods as visual aids (square rods in several colors, about the width of a piece of chalk and of ten different lengths used most commonly in the teaching of math). Students who learn "kinesthetically" are invited to "walk through" their papers (sections of the room represent parts of the argument), and students who excel at speaking are encouraged to "talk out" their ideas before composing.

8. *Integrate form and process.* Among the six-inch-thick notebook of materials we were provided was a copy of an article from the January 1987 *College English,* "An Apology for Form; or, Who Took the Form Out of Process?" in which Richard M. Coe argues for reinstating structure to its proper place beside process in the teaching of composition. Form is not "constraining," he argues, but "simultaneously . . . generative" (26). On this theoretical basis, Landmark instructors "place [themselves] within the camp that sees the standard opposition of process and product approaches as a false and unproductive dichotomy." Landmark instructors have no compunction about supplying students with "templates" for thesis sentences and whole essays. They defend the teaching of rhetorical modes: "There is no description without describing, no classification without the act of classifying." The form of a comparison-contrast essay, for example, is itself a generator of content, as students fill in the blanks.

9. *Use bypass strategies.* Students with intractable spelling problems, for example, have much to gain from writing at a word processor, using the spell checker to help them identify and correct errors. "Keyboarding" itself constitutes a bypass strategy for students for whom writing by hand impedes fluency. Using a tape recorder, transcribing their own dictation, is another bypass strategy for students whose difficulties in putting words down on paper are severe enough to be called "dysgraphia." Classroom teachers should bend the rules for dyslexic students, requiring fewer pages and allowing more time for certain assignments.

10. *Be patient.* The writing of LD students is no less complex than the writing of any other student, a process/product of affect and intellect, of self and culture that develops with the person — the problems of LD students are not easily or quickly solved. As a case in point, here is an excerpt from an LD student's term paper on schizophrenia.

> Two well supported hypotheses of how schizophrenia develops, through genetic links and/or environmental causes, are commonly done by scientist [*sic*] and psychologists. These two ideas are genetic links and/or environmental causes. Although they don't seem related they are similar in diagnosing a schizophrenic. In the area of genetics most of the testing was done in the prenatal study of the patient. Lehman took a more biological environmental/genetic view on how schizophrenia is caused.

The student who writes that "hypotheses . . . are commonly done," that "[ideas] are similar in diagnosing a schizophrenic," and that "Lehman took a . . . view on how schizophrenia is caused" is obviously uncomfortable with the language of academic discourse. Studying vocabulary and practicing sentence patterns will not solve the problem by themselves, which, as the Landmark Method suggests, must be approached from several sides at once. What this student lacks is a skill that must be gained chiefly through more reading and more writing (and speaking and listening) at a certain level of sophistication. Acculturating her to the language of academic discourse may involve an initial step backward, first "having [her] focus on achieving success with some types of writing that [she] is able to perform relatively well" — to quote Institute materials about a similar case. And that will take time. Of the five composition courses in Landmark's sequence, the first three are noncredit. And even then, there are no guarantees.

In conclusion, as this list of principles and the two student examples suggest, the Landmark Method relies in most respects on what is already known about the teaching of writing; and indeed, the point was stressed by the chair of the English Department that Landmark's methods are not *ad hoc* but soundly based on a thorough reading of the professional literature. Even when discussing such a "dysgraphia"-defining weakness as bad spelling (for which Landmark faculty might be expected to provide The Answer), our institute instructor only pointed in the direction of more reading, more research on *our* part into a frustratingly large number of possibly appropriate strategies. In *Beyond the "SP" Label: Improving the Spelling of Learning Disabled and Basic Writers* (NCTE 1992), for example, strategies include everything from "Latent Study" (i.e., the student keeps the word in sight by writing it on a card and taping it on the bathroom mirror) to simply "Correcting Misspelled Words" — with a twist (i.e., the student writes "the problem words using a different medium for the difficult spots — changing from ballpoint pen, for example, to crayon") (65).

This is not, however, to deny the uniqueness of Landmark College nor of its students. The differences are obvious — in the elaborate system of diagnostic testing, for one thing; in the expertise and dedication of faculty; and in the uncompromising implementation of measures that, in other places, would be regarded as impractical or impossible. The faculty-student ratio at Landmark is 1:3. Every instructor also tutors as part of his or her teaching load. And classes are kept small: 5–8 students on average.

Equally important to the success of the Landmark Method, the students are highly motivated. (With tuition at $25,000 per year, they would have to be.) Of five students who participated in a panel discussion one afternoon, two had returned to school after dropping out, working a while, then realizing they needed an education to fulfill their dreams. One man explained he'd worked for years as a bellhop because the job didn't require him to write. Other students on the panel told us about handicaps as real as any physical or mental illness. One girl confessed to "doing drugs" (a prescribed regimen that enabled her to focus her attention enough to study), and a young man (married, with a son) told us that he was constitutionally incapable of getting more than three hours' sleep a night. Despite these obstacles, the students were optimistic about their future, and grateful to Landmark, where they were learning, they said, for the first time in their lives.

Works Cited

Coe, Richard M. "An Apology for Form; or, Who Took the Form Out of Process?" *College English* 49 (1987): 13–28.

Landmark College. *Handbook, Workshop on Teaching Writing to Students with Dyslexia or Specific Learning Disabilities.* The Training Institute for Educators, Putney, Vermont, July 19–23, 1993.

McAlexander, Patricia J., Ann B. Dobie, and Noel Gregg. *Beyond the "SP" Label: Improving the Spelling of Learning Disabled and Basic Writers.* Urbana: NCTE, 1992.

Classroom Activities

Many developing writers lack the fundamental organizational skills characteristic of more successful students. They have difficulty keeping track of course materials, charting their progress, and, in general, maintaining focus. Moreover, a poor study system too often translates into poor academic achievement. Try adopting what Landmark terms "the master notebook," which would help students take the course by offering them a management system. Such a strategy would enable you to accommodate students with different learning styles by creating an organized space in which to track movement through the course throughout the semester. Ideally, students would also use this ongoing record to initiate conferences and set goals.

Thinking about Teaching

Compare and contrast your own learning strategies with the list of Landmark's principles provided by Gaskins. Such an exercise will help you compile some useful ideas for dealing with various learning styles and learning differences. Consider including strategies submitted by students. This collection of useful information can be disseminated at presentations given at a faculty workshop organized specifically to discuss learning styles and learning differences. You may also wish to collect all of these sources into a handbook and distribute it to basic writing teachers at your institution or to create a file to which all teachers will have access.

The Shape of the Container

Valerie Ann Krahe

Valerie Ann Krahe teaches English at McDowell Intermediate School in Erie, Pennsylvania. Her work with adult learners is informed by David Kolb's delineation of learning styles (his model is one among many). Krahe believes that an understanding of learning styles has critical implications for teaching adult learners in first-year composition courses. According to Krahe, Kolb breaks the processes of learning into four distinct styles: converger (greatest strength: "practical application of ideas"), diverger (greatest strength: "imaginative ability"), assimilator (greatest strength: "creation of theoretical models"), and accommodator (greatest strength: "doing things"). Krahe then delineates how the writing process would look within each of these four learning styles and makes recommendations for how to apply Kolb's ideas to the freshman composition classroom.

Liquid is the only form of matter that will take the shape of its container. But is high school chemistry the only course where this insight proves useful? Not necessarily! It might also be appropriate in freshman composition. And it might prove most beneficial to the adult learner in that course. Indeed, our adult students should be the containers that shape the content of our course.

But how do we do that? How do we fit the course to the adult student without lowering our expectations or our standards? The answer is: We address individual learning style as we plan our course's activities.

Certain recent writers in education have addressed the issue of learning style, among them Charles S. Claxton, Patricia H. Murrell, and Yvonne Ralston; their views are found in the *ERIC Clearinghouse on Higher Education* publications, *Report #4* (1987) as well as *Research Report #10* (1978). However, I am drawing primarily on David Kolb's Experiential Learning model as well as his delineation of learning styles, as discussed in the essay, "Career Development, Personal Growth, and Experiential Learning," located in the third edition of *Organizational Psychology: A Book of Readings* and in McBer and Company's *Learning Style Inventory: User's Guide*.

But why Kolb? After all, his experiential learning theory is one theory among many. However, this theory of learning acknowledges that learning is lifelong, that one can learn from immediate experience as well as from concepts and books, and that one takes in and processes information in a particular way. How appropriate this is for the adult learner. Because of whatever circumstance, he has been out of the classroom. But experiential learning theory recognizes that he has, nonetheless, continued to learn — in the settings in which he finds himself, and in a way that works best for him, according to a particular "learning style"!

What is meant by learning style? It has been defined as an individual's characteristic method of responding to and processing learning events as he or she experiences them. The ideal learning style would allow the individual to get involved fully in a concrete experience, then would afford him or her the opportunity to detach himself or herself from that experience in order to reflect on it from many different perspectives; then with the help of that "perfect" learning style, the person would create theories from the observations or reflections that were generated, and finally would call upon these theories to make decisions and to solve problems inherent in new concrete experiences. Yet, in reality, learning doesn't happen that way! We develop a particular learning style as a way of adapting to and gleaning information from our environment. We might absorb information either abstractly or concretely; we might process information either actively or reflectively.

From his research, Kolb has labelled four learning styles: the converger, the diverger, the assimilator, and the accommodator. The converger learns by thinking/analyzing and then doing, working most efficiently in systematically planning and logically analyzing ideas and in finding single solutions to problems or single answers to questions — with the practical application of ideas being this learner's greatest strength. The diverger learns by intuiting and then planning/reflecting, working most efficiently in generating ideas, in seeing situations from many perspectives, and in organizing relationships into meaningful wholes — with his/her imaginative ability the greatest strength. The assimilator learns by thinking/analyzing and then planning/reflecting, working most efficiently in combining quite distinct observations into meaningful explanations, in making sure theories are logically sound and precise yet not to the point of practically applying them (discarding the facts if they don't fit the theory) — with the creation of theoretical models this individual's greatest strength. And the accommodator learns by intuiting and then doing, working most efficiently in adapting himself to the specific and immediate circumstance, in fitting the facts to the theory (discarding the theory if the facts don't fit), and in getting information from other people instead of through his own analytic ability — with this person's greatest strength lying in doing things. The freshman composition course for the adult learner, then, should be designed with these four styles in mind.

But how does one do that? After all, even though freshman composition is a required course in most colleges and universities, its "design" is truly a chameleon — changing from one institution to another, even from one instructor to another. The way that has worked well for my adult learners, however, is to present them with "the rhetorical situation in small doses" — that is, focus on a few skills practiced well, with these skills generated from the keystone of the course: the concept of the "rhetorical situation." It is, to me, the hub from which all writing skills extend outward.

The rhetorical situation can be defined as each and every writing situation in which a writer finds himself and over which he has control. It includes three indispensable components, interacting with one another — audience, persona, and content: basically, a writer, after deciding to "write" on a particular topic and deciding on the "reason" for the piece, might begin by analyzing the particular audience, uncovering, at the very least, its previous knowledge on the topic, its present need as regards new information, its general intellectual level, and its already established emotional stance toward the topic. Armed with that information, the writer can then decide on the specific content he needs to present to that audience and when he will do it in the piece, limiting or broadening its range and its complexity, depending on the four "audience" factors mentioned above. After that, the writer can decide which persona will best "suit" that audience and that content: one that is emotionally invested in the content and emotionally committed to the audience, or one that is detached from both, or one that falls somewhere in between. And, related to these three concepts are the corresponding skills that range all the way from controlling diction to employing outside source material.

The job of the freshman composition instructor, then, is to exploit the four distinct styles of the adult learner when presenting the "rhetorical situation in small doses." Although delineating the skills of the rhetorical situation in their entirety is beyond the scope of this piece — that's at least a semester's worth of information! — what follows is a list of suggested course experiences and a discussion of each individual learning style in the context of those experiences.

The course experiences and their sequence are ultimately the instructor's choice; however, it has been my experience that the initial and subsequent lectures work well, especially with time and practice in between. In any case, some course experiences to consider are as follows: initial lecture in which each of the three concepts and its corresponding skills are presented; subsequent lecture in which those same elements are presented again; whole-class activities for "reinforcement" of concept and skills; whole-class criticism of previous students' pieces (with permission) in the context of the particular concept and skills; triad writing groups for students to try their hand in nongraded and collaborative fashion; triad work groups, partner or singular brainstorming sessions, and graded major writing assignments.

For the converger, the preferred course experiences could be put in deductive order, that is, a well-structured though abstract initial lecture on the particular concept and its corresponding skills, and then the presentation of problems with singular solutions or singular skills that need to be mastered. Each major writing assignment should be presented to the converger early on so that he or she can organize the incoming knowledge to solve that one ultimate "problem" and also so that he or she can self-pace the process to complete it. The converger also may benefit from a well-structured subsequent lecture to reinforce those abstract concepts and skills while he is "getting things done" on a particular assignment. Triad writing groups might be appropriate for the converger, as well, to aid him in focusing on specific problems he might be encountering with a particular skill or set of skills.

For the diverger, the preferred course experiences would seem to be those that are generative in nature and require "imagination": whole-class activities to generate ideas as well as whole-class criticism to see different points of view; triad writing and work groups to give and take ideas, and partner brainstorming sessions. Giving the diverger the major writing assignments early on would allow him a concrete situation from which he could consider different perspectives.

For the assimilator, the preferred course experiences might be inductively ordered, that is, allowing him to take part in whole-class activities as well as triad writing and group work in order to focus his energies on the skills or "pieces" — allowing him to see the utility of the skills. Partner brainstorming sessions might precede the major writing assignments so as to further reinforce the usability of the skills and thereby reduce the chance that the skills will be tossed once the theory or concept is presented.

And, for the accommodator, the preferred course experiences could be action-oriented: whole-class activities with a lot of interplay among students and ideas, whole-class criticism with the same, and group writing and group work to keep the accommodator "on task" and to offer him examples that demonstrate what is required or needed to be known. Presenting the accommodator with the major writing assignments early on would prove beneficial to him in that he would be able to experiment and self-pace their completion.

So, liquid is not the only thing that will take the shape of its container. Freshman composition can too — with the help of learning style!

Classroom Activities

Students can participate in the discussion of how best to facilitate their own learning if you first briefly introduce the concept of learning styles. You may wish to design a questionnaire for students based on the characteristics of the four learning styles delineated by Kolb and explicated by Krahe: converger, diverger, assimilator, and accommodator. Such a questionnaire can help students identify their strengths as learners and, in consultation with the instructor, discover new ways to build on those strengths.

Thinking about Teaching

Krahe's focus in this article is adult learners, sometimes referred to as nontraditional students. Such students bring a wide variety of skills, life experiences, and goals to the basic writing classroom, and their needs and concerns may be quite different from those of eighteen-year-old high school graduates. How might Krahe's discussion of learning styles help to inform your own work with adult learners? Together, teachers can discuss the advantages of each sequence of course design and perhaps create a configuration that more closely matches the needs of adult learners at your institution. How might collaborative learning be shaped by the notion of learning styles? What would major writing assignments look like? Would breaking each assignment into discrete parts help to facilitate success across learning styles? You may also wish to consider how the abstract notion of "rhetorical situation" can be made more concrete for adult learners.

7

Writing and Adult Learners

As more adult learners and students of "nontraditional" ages (beyond the usual demographic of eighteen-to-twenty-four year-olds) decide to begin or return to college, many of us will see a shifting population in our basic writing classrooms. Such adult learners may well have different needs and purposes for attending college than their younger counterparts. Balancing child care and other family responsibilities with full-time jobs and college course work can be a critical concern for this population. At the same time, many adult learners, as well as their teachers, report a more pronounced sense of commitment to their education and a more direct sense of purpose than they see in younger students. The presence of adult learners in the classroom can certainly enhance the learning environment for all of our students, as the following arguments demonstrate, often using the writing of returning adult students as evidence.

Many of us have wondered how to create a stronger connection between our course and the lives of our students. The voices of adult learners that speak in the following selections reinforce the notion of the writing process as an everyday problem-solving activity. Sarah Nixon-Ponder and Mary Kay Jackman describe pedagogies that grow out of the real-world experiences of adult learners. Libby Bay discusses a survey of adult learners at her community college; she presents the real-life needs that community colleges must pay attention to if they are to best serve this changing population of adult learners. Throughout this section, each of the writers offers suggestions that can stimulate the learning environment (both in the classroom and beyond) for all of our students.

Using Problem-Posing Dialogue in Adult Literacy Education

Sarah Nixon-Ponder

Sarah Nixon-Ponder is an Assistant Professor at Southwest Missouri State University and has been Assistant Director of the Ohio Literacy Resource Center at Kent State University. In the following article, Nixon-Ponder considers the needs of adult learners as she presents the activity of problem-posing, which "begins by listening for students' issues" and which "can build confidence and self-esteem in [students'] abilities to think critically." This student-centered classroom structure provides opportunities for even the most reticent students to begin to speak. Nixon-Ponder proposes a set of discrete steps that engage "adult learners [who] need the initial structure." Not only do these steps create a real-world framework; they also reflect aspects of the writing process. Students work collaboratively to "describe the content" of a given text, dialogue, picture, or orally presented story, to "define the problem," to "personalize the problem," to "discuss the problem," and to "discuss alternatives (solutions) to the problem." Such collaborative work strengthens real-world skills in solving problems and imagining alternative solutions — skills implicit in the writing process.

A group of women are gathered around a table, deep in discussion. Spreadsheets with schedules, open notebooks with lists, copies of government documents, and a diagram with measurements of a living space are spread before them. The women are discussing several options, looking earnestly at the pros and cons of each, and speaking in detail on specific aspects of one option. While two women are searching for a specific reference in the government documents, another is rapidly taking notes on the discussion at hand. In all aspects this appears to be a professional business planning meeting, right? Close, but not quite. This is a group of women in an adult literacy class who have arrived at a solution to their childcare situation by using a process called problem-posing dialogue.

Problem-posing is a tool for developing and strengthening critical thinking skills. It is an inductive questioning process that structures dialogue in the classroom. Problem-posing dialogue is noted in the works of Dewey and Piaget who were strong advocates for active, inquiring, hands-on education that resulted in student-centered curricula (Shor, 1992). Freire expanded on the idea of active, participatory education through problem-posing dialogue, a method that transforms the students into "critical co-investigators in dialogue with the teacher."

Learners bring to adult education programs a wealth of knowledge from their personal experiences, and the problem-posing method builds on these shared experiences. By introducing specific questions, the teacher encourages the students to make their own conclusions about the values and pressures of society. Freire (1970) refers to this as an "emergence of consciousness and *critical intervention* in reality."

So how is this done? What does it look like? What is the final outcome? Let's take a look at these questions as we walk through the process of problem-posing.

How to Conduct Problem-Posing Dialogue

Problem-posing begins by listening for students' issues. During breaks, instructors should listen to students' conversations with one another and make notes about recurring topics. Based on notes from these investigations, teachers then select and bring the familiar situations back to the students in a codified form: a photograph, a written dialogue, a story, or a drawing. Each situation contains personal and social conflicts that are of deep importance to the students.

Teachers begin by asking a series of inductive questions (listed below) that moves the discussion of the situation from the concrete to the analytical. The problem-posing process directs students to name the problem, understand how it applies to them, determine the causes of the problem, generalize to others, and finally suggest alternatives or solutions to the problem. The "responsibility of the problem-posing teacher is to diversify subject matter and to use students' thought and speech as the base for developing critical understanding of personal experience, unequal conditions in society, and existing knowledge" (Shor, 1992).

Five Steps of Problem-Posing

Auerbach (1990) has simplified the steps of problem-posing. Problem-posing is a means for teaching critical thinking skills, and many adult learners need the initial structure these steps provide in order to build confidence and esteem in their ability to think critically. When beginning to problem-pose, it is important to spend time on each step, for these are all essential components in learning how to critically think about one's world.

Describe the Content

The teacher presents the students with a *code*. Codes are a vital aspect of problem-posing. They *must* originate from the students' concerns and experiences, which makes them important to the students and their daily lives. According to Wallerstein (1983), codes can be

- written dialogues, taken from a variety of reading materials, that directly pertain to the problem being posed.
- role-plays adapted from written or oral dialogues.
- stories taken from the participants' lives and experiences.

- text from newspapers, magazines, community leaflets, signs, phone books, welfare or food stamp forms, housing leases, insurance forms, school bulletins.

- pictures, slides, photographs, collages, drawings, photo-stories, or cartoons.

After the students have studied the code, the teacher begins by asking questions, such as: What do you see in the picture (photograph, drawing, etc.)? What is happening in the picture (photograph, drawing, etc.)? or What is this dialogue (story, article, message) about? What is happening in the dialogue (story, article, message)?

Define the Problem

The students uncover the issue(s) or problem(s) in the code. Teachers may need to repeat the following questions: What is happening in the picture (photograph, drawing, etc.)? What is happening in the dialogue (story, article, message)? Students may identify more than one problem. If this occurs, the teacher should ask the students to focus on just one problem (especially with beginning problem-posers), using the other problem(s) for a future problem-posing idea. Students may identify two problems or issues that cannot be separated and must be dealt with together. This, too, is acceptable just as long as it is the students' decision to work with the two problems together.

Personalize the Problem

At this point, the teacher becomes the facilitator of the discussion, thus guiding the students to talk about how this problem makes them feel and what the problem makes them think about, so that they can internalize the problem. Through discussion, the students will relate the issue(s) or problem(s) to their own lives and cultures. The facilitator should assure that all students are given the chance to share their experiences, understanding as well that some may choose not to share. No one should be made to speak if she/he does not feel comfortable doing so. Learning that others have been in similar situations is very important; this experience will serve as an affirmation to their experiences, lives, and cultures; as an esteem builder; and as a means for bonding with other learners and the facilitator.

Discuss the Problem

The facilitator guides the students toward a discussion on the social/economic reasons for the problem by asking them to talk about why there is a problem and how it has affected them. During this step, it is critical for the facilitator *not* to expound upon personal and political beliefs. This temptation may be very strong during problem-posing dialogue, but resistance to do so is absolutely vital to the growth of the students. Because students' beliefs may differ greatly from those of the facilitator's, students will be more apt to take risks and openly share their beliefs if they believe that this is *their* dialogue and they have ownership in its process.

Discuss Alternatives to the Problem

The facilitator should coach the students into suggesting possible solutions to the problem, and discuss the consequences of the various courses of action. Through discussion, adult students become aware that they have the answers to their problems, especially when they approach their problems and concerns through a cooperative, group effort. Facilitators need to urge the students to search for several alternatives to the problem or issue at hand; the solutions need to be those that can be achieved.

Problem-posing delves deeply into any issue or problem, demonstrating the extent of its social and personal connections. Problem-posing "focuses on power relations in the classroom, in the institution, in the formation of standard canons of knowledge, and in society at large" (Shor, 1992). It challenges the relationship between teacher and student and offers students a forum for validating their life experiences, their cultures, and their personal knowledge of how their world works. Problem-posing is dynamic, participatory, and empowering.

Problem-posing is more than a technique that teaches critical thinking; it is a philosophy, a way of thinking about students and their ability to think critically and to reflect analytically on their lives. Eduard Lindeman, one of America's founding fathers of adult education, firmly believed that the responsibility of adult education was to teach learners how to think analytically and critically; this, too, is the role of problem-posing.

Problem-Posing in Action: Two Case Studies

So what does this look like in an adult literacy education (ABE) program? Let's take a look at two examples from actual literacy programs.

Case 1: An ABE Literacy Class

As an ABE instructor, I was always on the lookout for methods that would promote critical thinking in my class. The students in the program were bright and resourceful adults, and I felt the need to challenge their abilities and push them to question the surrounding world view. I spent many hours listening to my students talk about their lives, experiences, and cultures. Living in the Southwest and being an Anglo woman (many times the only Anglo) among the Latinas/Latinos and Native Americans made me very aware of our differing cultures and lifestyles, but more importantly, it made me see the similar problems that all of us encountered and experienced as people and as women. This awareness made me seek out the problem-posing method.

In one class, in particular, the subject of childcare was always on the women's minds; they discussed the topic before, during, and after class. I introduced this issue in "codes" for problem-posing. Because the topic was extremely relevant to their everyday lives and came from them, not me (as I informed them), it was emotionally charged and personal. They worked through the first three steps quickly and with ease. They related to the pictures I brought in, the short story and newspaper articles that we read, and the story that I shared about my divorced sister and her two children. They brought in relevant reading materials and shared their own stories on the problem of childcare — some of them funny and happy, most of them full of frustration and sadness. Their discussions on the reasons for this lack of good affordable childcare ranged from money issues, to unreliable (or no) transportation, to physical isolation from others, to cultural beliefs about who is qualified to care for someone else's children.

For weeks we worked on this topic. Writing assignments arose naturally as the women wrote their feelings about the discussions in dialogue journals, sharing these with others, and their oral histories became written testaments of their lives. They researched different laws on childcare facilities and they learned about co-operatives, thus reading materials on varying levels of difficulty. They answered their problem by taking this issue into their own hands — into their own control — and discussed reasonable alternatives to this overwhelming problem. Their solution was to organize a system for childcare on their own by sharing their resources. They planned schedules for taking care of each others' children, and those with reliable transportation arranged for carpools. They planned meals for their children and the care keeper(s) using arithmetic to figure amount of food and cost. They discussed discipline problems, and they organized a system for funding their project. They had a problem, and they found the solution for it.

This is problem-posing in action. It is exciting and educational; it is cross-cultural and multicultural because it draws from all of the students' cultures. Additionally, problem-posing builds confidence and community among learners. When I initiated problem-posing dialogue into my ABE class, I had no idea exactly where it would take us. But I believed that my students were able to work through this process and arrive at tangible solutions to their childcare dilemma. All of the basic skills were used. They read different types of materials on different reading levels; they wrote journal entries, oral histories, and letters; they planned schedules, organized carpools, and figured budgets. They learned that they had the answers to their problems, and they learned the steps to take in order to arrive at solutions.

Case 2: A GED Writing & Social Studies Class

In *Empowering Education: Critical Teaching for Social Change,* Ira Shor (1992) discusses different ways to tie problem-posing into all classes: science, health, computers, writing, literature, media, engineering, architecture, and sociology. He begins each class "in a participatory and critical way by posing the subject matter itself as a problem." He asks his students to investigate their knowledge about the subject matter and to think critically about it in an active and reflective way. So, how is this achieved?

I practiced this form of problem-posing in my GED classes. I began by asking the students to think about a specific issue (e.g., What is correct writing? Who sets the standards for correct writing? or What is history? Why should history be studied?). Then I would ask them to write their feelings about this issue, keeping in mind the following questions: What do you think about it? How does it make you feel? Why do you feel this way? What are your personal experiences with this? After the students had time to reflect, we began discussing the topic. If no one volunteered to be the first to share with the class, I would start by talking about my experiences. This would get the dialogue flowing, and others soon willingly volunteered to talk about their feelings and experiences.

Next, I asked small groups of students to compare their responses and explore the similarities or differences in each other's experiences. As a class, we talked about the differences or similarities, what we could learn from them, and how their beliefs could be applied to the class. We tried to figure out ways to make the class materials relevant and meaningful to their studies and their lives. We brought outside materials into the class. We talked about how to make the class theirs — how the curriculum, materials, and instruction could reflect their interests and preferences.

Problem-Posing as a New Concept

This was a new concept for most of my students. Some students had a difficult time with the nontraditional format of the class structure. Most were not used to being asked their opinions or beliefs. They did not believe in themselves; they did not believe that they were capable of helping to build the curriculum of a class, of their class. And of course, a few grasped this idea wholeheartedly and ran with it from the beginning. They became leaders, and they accepted the challenge to change their education. They also helped the others to see the benefits of problem-posing dialogue and the importance of learning to think critically.

As the instructor, I had to learn the art of facilitating the discussions and the cooperative groups. I had to learn to let go of power and control and turn it over to my students, thus becoming a facilitator who guides, shares, and coaches. Problem-posing taught me to trust students, to trust in their abilities, to rely on their resourcefulness and experiences, and to make learning meaningful to them.

Problem-posing enables students to bring to the program their experiences, cultures, stories, and life lessons. Their lives are reflected in the thoughtful, determined, and purposeful action that defines problem-posing dialogue. Moreover, problem-posing is a dynamic, participatory, and empowering philosophy that teaches students how to think critically and examine analytically the world in which they live.

Works Cited

Auerbach, Elsa R. *Making Meaning, Making Change: Participatory Curriculum Development for Adult ESL and Family Literacy.* Boston: University of Massachusetts, 1990.

Freire, Paulo. *Pedagogy of the Oppressed.* New York: Seabury, 1970.

Shor, Ira. *Empowering Education: Critical Teaching for Social Change.* Chicago: University of Chicago Press, 1992.

Wallerstein, Nina. *Language and Culture in Conflict: Problem-Posing in the ESL Classroom.* Reading, MA: Addison Wesley, 1983.

Classroom Activities

Adult learners have a variety of concerns that connect their lived experiences to the world of the classroom. Students can work through the process that Nixon-Ponder describes by selecting a reading or working on a community problem that captures their collective interest, and then following the steps of problem-posing to create connections between the classroom and the "real world." Such an approach may also work as the first step of a research project. For instance, students concerned about welfare reform might consult an article in a local newspaper or from the Internet. Following Nixon-Ponder's steps, students would work together to "describe the content" of the article, "define the problem" suggested by the article, "personalize the problem" in terms of their own communities, "discuss the problem," and "discuss alternatives to the problem." While each step suggests a writing assignment (personalizing a problem, for instance, could lead to a narrative essay), students could work through the entire process collaboratively to gain a fuller perspective of the problem. Each student could then write his or her own researched essay exploring the proposed alternatives. Which solutions are feasible? Which solutions probably will not work? As they complete their research and compose their essays, students should be encouraged to evaluate solutions in terms of the needs and concerns in their communities. This sort of approach creates a realistic purpose for writing, since students use problem-posing to confront problems and to propose action concerning issues that are crucial in their own lives and in the world outside their classroom.

Thinking about Teaching

Adult learners approach the study of writing and reading with varying expectations about education and from the perspective of many different learning styles. Problem-posing dialogue depends on active class discussion to consider the issues at hand. Nixon-Ponder suggests that during the problem-posing process "it is critical for the facilitator not to expound on personal and political beliefs." However, as Nixon-Ponder acknowledges, even the most fascinating lesson plan may not generate significant discussion. You may wish to discuss with colleagues the appropriateness of presenting personal experiences and opinions as part of the classroom conversation. Consider how students might respond. Will some students automatically accept the teacher's position? Will others automatically rebel against it? Will students think that their own opinions are being stifled and become afraid to speak? Or, in conveying your own ideas to students, is it possible to demonstrate respect for all opinions presented in the classroom, even if they are significantly different from your own? Try using problem-posing dialogue as a way to discuss these issues and to create alternative solutions to the problem. This discussion might take place within an electronic discussion group for a broader geographic representation. You may also wish to pose this problem to students as part of class discussion.

When the Personal Becomes Professional: Stories from Reentry Adult Women Learners about Family, Work, and School

Mary Kay Jackman

Mary Kay Jackman, a teacher of returning and first-year students at Southern Methodist University, reminds us that a majority of the adult learners in our classrooms will be women students. Citing research by hooks, Belenky, and others, Jackman discusses the critical needs and issues of this group of students. What makes Jackman's article particularly unique, however, is that she tells the stories of several women and their discoveries upon encountering the writing classroom: Margie, a thirty-three-year-old white woman who finds that "pressures arise" not only from her studies, but "from the multiple roles she must play in her family: wife, mother, sister, daughter"; Ann, a twenty-seven-year-old Hispanic woman who lives with her parents and, "returning to college after a seven-year hiatus, . . . juggles two jobs and four classes"; and Sophie, their teacher, a white woman and a "reentry adult woman learner" herself (and master's degree candidate), who "tell[s] personal stories in class to teach writing" and uses extensive conferencing as a way of "mentoring" her students. As Jackman concludes: "The stories from

Margie, Ann, and Sophie — three out of the hundreds of adult women now returning to colleges and universities — suggest the power of the personal to bring about academic transformations, indeed, to (re)create professional academic realities." Indeed, the strong voices of these adult women learners as they tell their stories can be a motivating force and an inspiration for all our students, as well as for ourselves as teachers.

During the fall semester of 1995, I conducted an ethnographic study of a first-year writing classroom focusing on narrative's role in that particular classroom culture at a mid-size state university. The writing instructor in the classroom I studied engaged in personal narrative as one of her principal teaching techniques, and all nine student volunteer research participants responded to her stories in various ways to build their identities as writers and to accomplish their writing assignments. Thus, in writing the results of my study, I argued for narrative's constitutive and epistemic value in a writing classroom and for the autobiographical anecdote in particular as a bridge between teaching and learning.

In sorting through the mountain of data generated by this project, including all the papers each volunteer wrote for class and the transcripts of each of their three interviews with me, I began to hear another argument about the function and value of narrative taking shape, this one more specifically voiced by three reentry adult women participating in the project: students Margie and Ann, and their instructor, Sophie.[1] That argument centers on adult women learners' necessary and workable narrative negotiation of the personal and professional aspects of their lives in order to reach their academic goals. More so than the younger, traditional students in the study, Margie, Ann, and Sophie relied on stories from their lived experience to make learning and teaching sites both inside and outside the classroom useful and valuable to them.

Unlike younger students, whether men or women, for whom college is an anticipated "next step" after high school, older adult women who reenter college have made a conscious choice to do so, expecting the experience to radically change their lives (Goldsmith and Archambault 12). As a reentry adult woman learner myself, I recognize the truth of that claim. My dissertation research came five years after I had returned to graduate school for the third time, almost thirty years after I had earned my bachelor's degree. Like Sophie and similar to Ann, I anticipated a career change after completing the academic program I had entered; like Margie, I was hoping to feel better about myself when the academic journey was over.

Margie, Ann, Sophie, and I, as nontraditional, reentry adult women learners, constitute the fastest growing segment of the student population in higher learning and continuing education programs (Hayes and Flannery 2). The state university we attended, New Mexico State University, had a total student population in fall 1995 of 15,127, of which 7,479 were men and 7,648 were women. Three years later, fall 1998, the population had increased slightly to 15,409, of which 7,274 were men (a slight decrease) and 8,135 were women (a moderate increase). At New Mexico State women outnumbered men in all age brackets except ages twenty to twenty-four and twenty-five to twenty-nine during 1995, 1996, 1997, and 1998.[2] This is only one institution and one study, but the increase in women students corresponds with research findings that indicate a trend of adult women returning to the academy in increasing numbers (see also Nixon-Ponder; Stoffel; Goldsmith and Archambault; Kiskis).

The point of my going into such detail here is that as more and more adult women return to school, notions about the academy's role in the community, about acceptable academic discourse, and about effective teaching practices in higher education may all be challenged. That is, as the material characteristics of the student body change, the material structure and function of the academy itself become susceptible to change. I make this claim based on the stories I hear from Margie, Ann, and Sophie; from the stories I read in recent studies of returning women students; and from my own experience, in which the personal is often inseparable from the professional, a life-state that traditional academic environments not only devalue but attempt to displace (see hooks, *Teaching*; Kiskis). As you will see, Margie and Ann draw on their lived experiences at home and at work to satisfy writing course requirements, and their instructor, Sophie, turns her lived experiences into autobiographical anecdotes that she purposefully uses to teach writing.

Margie

> *I like writing. . . . I keep a journal at home. . . . The nice thing about a journal is that you don't have to make sense. It's just your thing. . . . It's mostly . . . therapy when I write. . . .* (Personal interview)

> *I've come to realize now that I'm over thirty it's not what you do or what you have that counts in life, it's who you are.* (Unpublished essay)

At thirty-three, Margie is the oldest first-year student participating in the research project. A slender woman with curly, medium-brown hair, dark brown eyes, and an easy smile, she is the only married student in the study and the only mother, aside from the instructor, Sophie.

Margie sees herself as a devoted family woman who is now "gonna do something for [herself]" by returning to school. Working within this self-conception,[3] Margie likes to write in her journal at home, but doesn't consider herself a writer when she enters the first-year writing course. As she explains in her first interview, "A writer is somebody who writes a book." Even though Margie's self-image as a writer is limited to her journaling, she believes writing in her journal "does help [her] with the pressures of everyday," pressures that arise from the multiple roles she must play in her family: wife, mother, sister, daughter.

She made her decision to return to school after almost fifteen years of marriage and after discussions with her husband in which Margie says he told her, "'You can go to college. . . . I know you're smart enough.' And [she] would say, 'Oh, I'm not, I'm not. I didn't learn anything in high school.'" She remembers herself as a lackluster student: "[M]y grades weren't the greatest. I was average always." Unmotivated to learn, Margie remembers being placed in the "lower class" in high school with other students who weren't interested in learning. Unsupported by her parents, Margie says, "I think I ended up just giving up."

Margie's history of giving up in high school, marrying and having children early, and living for her family is common to many women, as is her current desire to learn and live for herself (see Belenky, Clinchy, Goldberger, and Tarule; Goldsmith and Archambault). Margie tells me:

> [N]ow that I'm older, I wish I could go back and really absorb all that stuff that they were trying to teach . . . really have listened so that I could have known more. . . . Now that I've come to college, it's really broadened my way of thinking, and it's boosted up my confidence. It's really made me feel good about myself. I'm thinking of [becoming] a counselor . . . because I really like to talk with children. . . . [A]nd I'm really into health. I like to exercise, so it's kinda like something physical versus . . . counseling, psychology, or something.

She negotiates her desire to be a learner among her family's demands for her to function as wife and mother and among the demands of a university classroom in which she must operate effectively as writer and student. While she has operated as a writer within her family, keeping her private journal for over ten years, Margie must somehow learn to operate as a student there, adding that role to her family-sanctioned roles as mother and wife. In the classroom, Margie assesses her roles and positions as student/writer in relation to the expectations of her instructor, Sophie, and to the abilities of the other students. Reflecting the sense of isolation Mary Miritello identifies among returning adult learners (1–3), Margie laughs as she remarks, "[S]ometimes you think that the person next to you is doing so much better than you are and that they understand so much more than you do, and it makes you feel like, 'Well, am I the dummy here or what?'"

Recognizing the multiple roles she must perform effectively at home *and* at school if she is to attain the success she wants for herself and still keep her family functioning, Margie says,

> [M]y mind is sometimes there with the family, but yet it's [pause] split in the middle. You feel like there's two of you, and one of you has to be this good student and the other one has to be a good, understanding mom. And that makes it a little hard . . . to try to be everything for everybody and make the grade. . . . [Keeping my family together] is like [having] two jobs. You have to juggle everything. You have your kids . . .

and the attention that they want, and you can't give it because you're so busy doing this or that for your classes. . . . But . . . I've learned to juggle a little bit of everything at once.

C. M. Greenwood points out that adult women learners are much more likely than men learners to sacrifice their studies for family obligations (4), implying that a woman's familial roles are much stronger than her role as student. Margie, however, has learned to play multiple roles simultaneously. She does this by taking the classroom home with her and by bringing her family into the classroom and into her writing. She turns her experiences into stories that help her analyze problems, explain concepts, and evaluate circumstances.

Virtually all of Margie's writing in the first-year writing course grows out of her life experiences in some way. For example, in responding to the assignment which asks her to identify a problem and propose a solution to it, Margie chooses the problem of alcoholism in a family and writes about a weekend visit by her sister and brother-in-law and his drunken behavior. Before she decided on that as her topic, however, she discussed it with her husband. He not only helped her decide to write on her brother-in-law's drinking problem, he also helped her remember things that had happened during her sister and brother-in-law's weekend visit, even "the words they used here and there."

Margie's inclusion of her husband as collaborator in her writing and studenting roles seems to be both voluntary and involuntary. Sometime during the year after she returns to school with his apparent encouragement, Margie's husband begins reading her journal. His intrusion into her private space, a place separate and apart from her other positions within the family, causes her to abandon the journal writing for a time. Margie tells me, "I can't really write in it anymore because I know he read it. . . . It's hard for me to get back into that little book and start writing . . . I feel like I gotta be real careful what I write. I can't just let the pen flow." He also periodically looks through Margie's school books and notebooks without asking her permission. When she asks him why, he tells her it's "to see what you're doing at school." Rather than argue with him, Margie shrugs, "Whatever. Let him look if he wants to look. But it's no privacy, and it bugs me; it bothers me." Margie's frustration in negotiating her student/writer roles within her family shows when she comments ironically: "I wish I could just tell him to stop, but what can you do? He's your husband and the father of your three children, so . . . [laughs]."

Margie's painful recounting of the way her husband monitors both her private journal writing and her student writing calls to mind Belenky, Clinchy, Goldberger, and Tarule's work with women whom they identify as "subjective" knowers, some of whom, similar to Margie, are attempting to redefine some of their conventionally assigned family roles. In transition, having moved from silence into a state of received knowledge, such adult women knowers are searching for a "self" of their own within and without the family. As Belenky et al. point out, and as Margie's experiences illumine, a family very often does not recognize or nurture "the budding subjectivist's impetus toward change, redefinition, and application of her new ways of knowing and learning" (79).

Margie, however, finds ways to negotiate and compromise these family and school positionings with her husband, her children, her instructor, her classroom peers, and herself. Her ongoing but largely unacknowledged writer role at home has already evoked some changes among family members. Margie's husband read about himself in her journal; "[He] started making changes on the way he treated me, and he started paying more attention to the kids, so I guess by writing in my journal, it helped my marriage in a way." Thus, at home Margie's writing as wife and mother paves the way for her new role writing as student in the family. In the first-year writing classroom, Margie links writer and student through her family roles, creating a working balance for herself by writing stories about her lived experiences to satisfy course assignments.

In doing so, Margie actively seeks collaboration and feedback on her student writing from family members. Their collaboration and feedback, while acknowledging Margie's writer and student roles and the self-images they evoke, ultimately validate her self-conception as a family woman. The feedback that most strongly influences Margie's self-images as writer and student, however, is the feedback she receives from her instructor, Sophie. Margie remembers Sophie's comments to her: "'I can tell you're a writer.' That made me feel really good when she said that; that made my day." Margie believes Sophie genuinely cares about her students, a teacher quality Margie values highly, since to Margie, it leads to successful learning. She writes in her final, reflective essay,

> I have learned so much this semester and feel I'm leaving this class a better writer and feeling good about myself as a writer. I have always liked to write, but never felt I was any good until I took this class. I know that you Sophie made me feel this way about my writing. I only heard good things come out of you to all of us. You were always encouraging us telling us we were all good writers and I could tell you meant it.

From Sophie, Margie the student-writer receives the encouragement she didn't receive from her parents in high school. Margie says Sophie motivates her to "put out some to learn," just as Margie encourages and challenges her children: "I really make sure my kids apply themselves." Once again, Margie seeks to mesh home and school, family and classroom, breaking the boundaries between them. Her self-conception as devoted family woman remains largely unchanged during the semester; she simply stretches it through her autobiographical writings to accommodate her revised and strengthened self-images as student and writer. Testifying to her self-perceived success as both, Margie says:

> I'm not as dumb as I thought I was. [Laughs] I can honestly say I feel like I'm a pretty good writer, that I'm okay. Before I never thought I was, but now I can. . . . I'm just proud of myself that I can do these things. Sometimes I even think of maybe writing a book, you know?

Ann

> *I've never really cared for English. . . . Even before I started [the English course], I was already panicking. . . . I didn't want to be there . . . because I knew that English is not my subject. . . . And, now that I'm done with it, I don't feel like that anymore.* (Personal interview)

Tall, plump, and pretty with short, curly, brown hair, Ann is twenty-seven years old, unmarried, and living at home with her parents again after staying with a boyfriend for a while. Returning to college after a seven-year hiatus, Ann juggles two jobs and four classes. She is determined to stay in school this time around and earn her marketing degree. In her first interview with me, Ann states, "I decided I better go back. I feel like I'm getting older, and I don't want to regret it later." Ann values independence and seeks a career that will provide a good income so that she can support herself: "I don't want to rely on somebody else to help me with the rent or any other expenses like I did before." She also wants a career that will provide her with a variety of tasks and responsibilities (so she will not be bored) and physical activity rather than desk work (so she will not feel confined).

Ann refers to herself as an impatient person, anxious to complete tasks in a hurry. While acknowledging her reserve and occasional shyness, Ann writes in an early essay that she "get[s] along with people" like her Hispanic grandfather did. In fact, when Ann describes herself, she writes that she is very much like her grandfather: stubborn and sociable with a sense of humor. By specifically linking herself to her grandfather, Ann implies other traits within her self-conception that she attributes to him but that she values in and for herself: a stable, versatile, hard-working, physical laborer. Ann's grandfather "followed his father's footsteps" and worked for a large, local farm for thirty-eight years; he later worked as a school custodian for ten years. Ann's first job, when she was fourteen years old, was in the office of the same agribusiness her grandfather labored for. Ann worked with her mother on that job, where she learned that she didn't like being confined to an office. One of Ann's present jobs is painting schools for the same school district for which her grandfather worked before he died; some of her coworkers were also his. Ann's other job is painting houses with her father and working with him in construction. Thus, Ann's self-conception is located within an established, respected family and community of physical laborers, becoming for Ann what Pierre Bourdieu calls a "habitus," a collection of habits of mind and body, "durable, transposable dispositions" (72) that she has absorbed from childhood.

Within her strong self-conception as a working woman, Ann's image of herself as both student and writer at the start of her first school semester in seven years remains pale and unfocused. Ann doesn't return to school to learn to write; she returns *despite* having to take a writing course. Her self-conception as a single working woman who seeks to better her economic position within her habitus brings her back to the writing classroom and carries her past her initial panic at being there. To Ann, then, taking and passing the first-year writing course is an economic necessity, even though she enters it with the self-image of a fearful, uninterested student and failed writer.

Ann failed an English class in high school after a teacher, ignoring Ann's objecting voice, enrolled her in a literature course. Ann told the teacher she had no background for nor interest in the course, but the teacher put her in it anyway. Ann says, "I had no idea what was going on in [that class]. It just didn't interest me enough, . . . [and] I flunked it." The teacher, who refused to listen to Ann's reasons for not wanting to be in the course, then blamed Ann when she failed. Ann remembers the teacher telling her, "'You didn't put enough effort into it.'" Ann, whose well-established and respected position within her habitus of laborers assures that her voice will be listened to, found her position in high school unsettling and her voice largely ignored.

Ann chose the noncollege track in high school because she didn't think she would ever attend college. She didn't take courses then that would satisfy college entrance requirements later when, at her aunt's insistence and with her aunt's financial support, she did decide to go for an associate's degree in architecture. Switching positions from noncollege laborer to college student for Ann meant taking the precollege courses, or their equivalents, that she hadn't taken in high school, one of which was a basic writing course that Ann remembers as "English 111."

Ann thought she was "doing pretty good" in the writing course; all her papers had come back to her marked "satisfactory" or "revise," which she did. On the final paper, however, "that decided if we pass or fail," Ann failed. Once again, Ann's position and voice as student seemed to work against her; she had no inkling prior to the exit essay that she would fail the course.

Seven years later, after Ann decided to return to college to obtain a marketing degree that will elevate her economic position within her habitus, she realizes that she will have to retake a first-year writing course. She tells me, "I just didn't think I was going to get through that class because I knew that English is not my subject." Ann chuckles as she remembers and voices her initial thoughts: "I am going to take English 111 for the rest of my life!"

Ann acknowledges her fears and discomfort as a reentry adult learner in a clear, strong voice on the opening day of the semester. After she is introduced by another student, Ann speaks for herself from her habitus of laborers, smiling and chuckling with a pleasant, open expression as she lets the whole class know that she doesn't like writing, doesn't like English, and would rather be at work painting schools. Other than this opening vocal performance and her oral report later in the semester, Ann remains virtually silent in the classroom. "I never really participate in class," she tells me. "I'm the type of person that won't say anything. I'll just sit there." While Ann's voice as a working woman can speak confidently on the first class day, her student voice remains mute, perhaps because it has failed her in the past.

Even with her reluctance to speak up in class discussions, Ann, like Margie, successfully completes the required writing course by calling upon her experiences in her family and work environments to help her make sense out of her experiences in the classroom. As Malcolm Knowles reminds us, adult learners are life-centered rather than subject-centered; they generally want to enrich their experiences through learning, not simply satisfy academic requirements (33). Further, unlike children, who perceive experience as something that happens to them, adult learners look at their experiences as *"who they are"* (60). Ann, then, seeing herself as a competent, respected member of her laboring family and habitus, uses that self-conception and the experiences constituting it to work for her as student/writer in the classroom. Like Margie, she tells stories from her lived experience to satisfy course assignments.

She includes stories about her grandfather in her first in-class essay assignment, and in the revised essay portion of her portfolio. She asks her coworkers to tell her stories about her grandfather, and she includes some of them in her revised essay. She uses an anecdote about her grandmother to support some of her claims concerning elderly drivers in her problem/solution paper, and she includes her grandmother in her portfolio's revised essay. Her father and cousins appear in these papers as well, and her mother helps her with ideas for the problem/solution paper. Her own experience of miscarrying a child whose father was a heavy cocaine user acts as the impetus for her research paper on the effect of drugs on pregnant women and the fetuses they carry.

Writing these autobiographical accounts helps Ann negotiate and voice her worker, family-member, and student-writer positions. Doing so allows her to perform effectively as a working woman *and* as a student-writer in the classroom (she ultimately earns a "B" in the course). Consciously carrying her habitus into the classroom, Ann seems to have discovered her student-writer voice among her coworkers. She smiles as she tells me in our final interview:

> I always tell [this one man that I work with], "Oooooh, you're so full of it." And I always tell him, "Oh, I owe it all to you." And he goes, "What are you talking about?" And I go, "In my English class — I just learn from you; you're so full of it, and you keep rambling on and on. So, I learned from you, and that's how I can write my papers now."

Using a voice from her habitus and operating from a temporary position as student-writer, Ann successfully completes the first-year writing course, and, thus, takes a step in an upward economic direction. Ann believes that she probably will not be writing much in her career, but knows she will have to write in one more required writing course before she can attain her degree goals. By semester's end, Ann feels writing is "not so bad after all" and believes she is no longer "hopeless at writing papers." She faces the next writing course with more confidence than she had coming into the first-year course:

> I don't feel like I could just pick something up and start writing about it and it would come out great. But I feel comfortable enough to where if I was asked to write something, that it might take a while, but I could get through it. I just feel a lot more confident than I did before.

Sophie

Ann attributes her newfound confidence in herself as a practical, working writer to her instructor, Sophie. Like Margie, Ann likes the way Sophie "explain[s] everything" and "shows more" than her past English teachers about how to do the assignments. A reentry adult learner herself, Sophie has returned to the university to earn a master's degree in technical writing after raising four sons and working in the automobile industry for more than ten years. She is a graduate assistant in New Mexico State's English department. One of the terms of her assistantship is that she teach a section of writing for the department each semester in which she is enrolled in its master's program.

Sophie characterizes herself to me in our first interview as a writing "mentor" who uses "storytelling teaching" in her classroom. She uses stories from her lived experience to introduce the course's required, sequenced assignments and to model various writing techniques, particularly invention and arrangement. For example, when introducing the first writing exercise of the semester, which is to describe a place important to the writer, Sophie tells two stories about her experiences at Yosemite Park: seeing her first waterfall and being chased by a bear. She tells me later that she uses the stories to teach invention by modeling her invention process — "meditation, listing, and freewriting," and the ways these processes help her recall the experience and help her understand why Yosemite is an important place to her. Engaging the class in discussions about the stories, Sophie also uses them to illustrate description that touches the five senses as well as description that sometimes omits details. As she does with virtually all the autobiographical anecdotes she tells, Sophie asks the students to offer feedback on some aspect(s) of the story. In the case of the Yosemite stories, she asks students to provide more detail and to speculate about different details she could have provided or left out. Sophie's storytelling does not go unnoticed by Margie and Ann; they both respond favorably to the way she "explains."

In addition to telling personal stories in class to teach writing, Sophie also holds conferences regularly and privately with each student to discuss his or her specific writing projects. Sophie says "[my students] talk to me a lot. . . . [I'm] personally involved . . . mostly because I do all of this conferencing. I know a lot about them, so it's not as though they're just people out there in desks. . . . [T]hey know me, too." Like storytelling, Sophie's conferencing helps her "become connected" to her students; it's a teaching method she wouldn't give up, even if she were to teach a four-or-five-course load. "I don't think that I could not be conferencing," she says.

As noted earlier, Margie interprets Sophie's classroom and conference demeanor as a personal expression of care and concern for her students. However, Margie also notices Sophie's commitment to her professional obligations as a writing mentor who comes to the classroom prepared to address specific writing tasks. Margie points out:

> You could tell that she plans what she's gonna come in with, and she doesn't all of a sudden just think of something to say or do. She knows what she's gonna do and then, that's that. . . . She's serious about everything she assigns. That to me is a good instructor. And I like the fact [that] she's not mean, but she means what she says.

Sophie's classroom management, as perceived by the two reentry adult women learners discussed here, demonstrates characteristics of what Wendy Luttrell refers to as "maternal authority" (124), a way of managing classroom dynamics through "love, care, protection, and acceptance" that promotes "mutual, egalitarian, and respectful relationships" and has a positive impact on students (124, 125). Her classroom management also reflects characteristics of the "connected teaching" that Belenky et al. believe is most conducive to women's learning (214–229). Such a teaching method combines the personal with the professional: telling and listening to each other's stories in interactive learning, expressing concern for learners (students *and* their instructor) as individuals with complicated lives, and working within a predictable, intentional structure of task analysis and problem solving. As Margie noticed and Belenky et al. point out, most women want some structure in their learning environments (204). Yet, within that structure, they respond to a dialogic exchange of experience, an "antihierarchical" system in which the learning facilitator is unafraid of bringing personal issues and uncertainty into the classroom (Rich 145). Sophie says,

> I'm not really sure that we do any teaching. Maybe we're just there to encourage them. I'm not sure about that. I'm not sure that any teaching technique has been very helpful. I'm more personal about it [in my classroom]. I suppose I come at it from [knowing] what it's like to be a writer. It's hard. "This is what I do to try to solve the problem for myself. This is a way for you to get started." I hope I'm not telling them this is the *only* way to do it. . . . My main goal is to give them some tools so that

they can fly a little bit — get off the ground, so that later on they can do whatever they want. Since I'm such an ordinary person, I'm not a great scholar or a great writer or anything else, . . . I think that if I can do it, they can [chuckles]. That's my attitude. And I *like* teaching. I like [the students]. They surprise me. I learn a lot.

Summary and Implications

As older, returning students, Margie and Ann are nontraditional adult women learners who must pass the required, first-year writing course with a "C" or better if they are to realize their goals: increased self-esteem and confidence as a writer for Margie, with perhaps a career; a marketing degree, greater personal and financial independence, a higher economic position, and a business career for Ann. Their instructor Sophie, herself a nontraditional, returning adult learner, must effectively teach the required writing course if she is to retain her graduate assistantship and complete her master's degree. As Malcolm Knowles points out, adult learners want to see practical gains; they need to see how what they are learning can be applied to their lives (61), a concept echoed in the connected teaching that Belenky et al. describe (219) and demonstrated by the storytelling teaching that Sophie practices.

Michael Kiskis, who has worked extensively with adult learners, an increasing number of whom are women (57), believes that "most adult students . . . seek out and find material within their studies that can be transported back to their home or work environments to help them make better sense out of experiences they face" (60). Margie and Ann, however, in addition to carrying classroom experiences into their home and work, also transport their family and work environments back to the first-year writing classroom to help them make sense out of the experiences they face *there* as students-writers, just as a "mid-wife teacher" in a "connected class" might encourage them to do (Belenky et al. 219) and just as Sophie *does* encourage them to do. Sophie, while relying on autobiographical anecdotes to teach writing in the classroom, also discusses her teaching with her husband at home. He, too, is an educator, conducting classes on interrogation and interview techniques for law enforcement officers. Sophie has observed his classes and has noticed the way "he makes [the police officers] feel valuable . . . important" by inviting them to "bring their real cases [into the classroom] to talk about." Thus, all three women call upon their families and upon the larger habitus in which they find themselves (Bourdieu 81). They locate usable voices in the classroom that emerge from family and habitus by telling stories from their lived experience to learn more about writing.

Earlier this century, John Dewey recognized the "organic connection between education and personal experience" (25) in any effective learning site. Reflecting over our experiences, reviewing and interpreting their meaning, Dewey believed, is the way we learn (86–87), whether in youth or in adulthood, whether male or female. Malcolm Knowles also emphasizes the importance of including personal, lived experience in formal learning situations, particularly when working with adult learners. Since adults perceive their experience as their identity, according to Knowles, denigrating or denying its inclusion in their classroom learning is often interpreted by an adult learner as a personal affront.

The stories told by the reentry adult women learners discussed here seem to exemplify Dewey's notion of learning through reflection and interpretation of experience and Knowles's notion of learning as an adult as opposed to learning as a youth. That is, Margie, Ann, and Sophie have come to the learning environment (the first-year writing classroom) with widely varied experience compared to the somewhat limited experience of the younger student participants. All three women apply what they are learning to their lives in and out of the classroom. Further, they are responding to both internal and external motivations (Knowles 59–63) in that Margie is looking for self-esteem, a higher quality of life; Ann is looking for career advancement, more money; Sophie is looking for satisfaction as an educator/learner, a master's degree.

Neither Margie, even though she writes in her journal, nor Ann considered herself a writer when she entered Sophie's classroom. By semester's end, both Margie and Ann see themselves as writers. In Ann's case, the role may be a temporary one, but Margie is thinking of writing a book. Both women believe they have learned that they can write, that they are learners, that they are not dumb. In Wendy Luttrell's terms, both women are well on their way to "becoming somebody" (1–3). In terms provided by Belenky et al., both women have moved from a state of silence, through states of received and subjective knowledge, to at least some level of procedural knowledge, in the sense of feeling more in control of their own lives (99).

Margie and Ann believe that they have made this move not only by way of their own motivations but also by way of Sophie's connected teaching, which includes the telling of autobiographical stories by all classroom participants, personal concern for students as manifest in one-on-one conferencing throughout the semester, and professional structuring of classroom activities. Through her use of personal stories that she asks the class to critique and sometimes complete, Sophie becomes a "co-inquirer," an interactive learner with her students, and a mentor who facilitates rather than dominates class discussion — attributes Knowles believes work effectively in adult education (Knowles 31).

The importance of personal, lived experience in adult education cannot be ignored in these women's stories nor in established theories of how learning happens. Both Margie and Ann draw on their lived experience to address writing tasks, to fulfill writing assignments, and to function effectively as writers and students. Sophie routinely uses her own personal experience as part of the "objective conditions" (Dewey

45) of the classroom through her storytelling and through her encouragement of storytelling by her students.

As interactive learners and storytellers, bringing their personal lives into the classroom and carrying the classroom into their homes and jobs, Margie, Ann, and Sophie are challenging boundaries between university and community, between personal writing and academic discourse, and between traditional and *"co-intentional* education" (Freire 56). Dissolving boundaries between the community surrounding the university and the university itself is something Adrienne Rich believes a university should encourage. Rich believes the academy, to be an effective learning center, must address local issues and must listen to the stories of people who live around it (152–153), people like Margie, Ann, and Sophie. Dissolving boundaries between personal writing and academic discourse by using personal experiences to explain and fulfill required writing assignments exemplifies what Ruth Behar recognizes as "a sustained effort to democratize the academy" (1). This is a movement bell hooks would characterize as one of "transgression" (*Teaching* 12) beyond conventional educational and epistemic bounds. Such a movement dissolves boundaries between traditional educational practices, whose historical and theoretical bases rest largely on the teaching of children and youth by teacher-experts, and educational practices in which teacher-student and student-teacher come to know and (re)create reality "through common reflection and action" (Freire 56) as learning equals. With boundaries gone, interactive learning is more likely to occur for *all* learners within the academy, and interactive learners are more likely to discover themselves as "[reality's] permanent re-creators" (Freire 56).

Thus, the stories from Margie, Ann, and Sophie — three out of hundreds of adult women now returning to colleges and universities — suggest the power of the personal to bring about academic transformations, indeed, to (re)create professional academic realities.

Notes

1. These are their chosen research names.
2. These figures are from the office of Institutional Research, Planning and Outcomes Assessment at New Mexico State University, and they came to me through personal e-mail correspondence with research analysts and by way of the office's web site: <http://www.nmsu.edu/research/iresearc/>.
3. This term and the term *self-image* are borrowed from social psychologist Ralph H. Turner. For Turner, *self-conception* refers to "the picture an individual has of himself [*sic*]" (93). One's self-conception, then, according to Turner, is usually perceived by a telling self as being relatively consistent compared to the instability and mutability of various, simultaneously held, self-images.

Works Cited

Behar, Ruth. "Dare We Say 'I'? Bringing the Personal into Scholarship." *The Chronicle of Higher Education* 29 (1994): B1–2.

Belenky, Mary Field, Blythe McVicker Clinchy, Nancy Rule Goldberger, and Jill Mattuck Tarule. *Women's Ways of Knowing: The Development of Self, Voice, and Mind*. New York: HarperCollins, 1986.

Bourdieu, Pierre. "Structures and the Habitus." *Outline of a Theory of Practice*. Trans. Richard Nice. Cambridge: Cambridge UP, 1977. 72–95.

Dewey, John. *Experience and Education*. The Kappa Delta Pi Lecture Series. 1938. New York and London: Macmillan, 1963.

Freire, Paulo. *Pedagogy of the Oppressed*. Trans. Myra Bergman Ramos. New York: Seabury P, 1970.

Goldsmith, Diane J., and Francis X. Archambault. "Persistence of Adult Women in a Community College Re-Entry Program." Research Study. 1997. ERIC ED 409 958.

Greenwood, C. M. "'It's Scary at First': Reentry Women in College Composition Classes." *Teaching English in the Two-Year College* 17 (1990).

Hayes, Elisabeth, and Daniele D. Flannery. "Adult Women's Learning in Higher Education: A Critical Review of Scholarship." Annual Meeting of American Educational Research Association. San Francisco. Apr. 1995. ERIC ED 382 838.

hooks, bell. *Talking Back: Thinking Feminist, Thinking Black*. Boston: South End P, 1989.

———. *Teaching to Transgress: Education as the Practice of Freedom*. New York: Routledge, 1994.

Kiskis, Michael J. "Adult Learners, Autobiography, and Educational Planning: Reflections of Pedagogy, Andragogy, and Power." *Pedagogy in the Age of Politics: Writing and Reading (in) the Academy*. Ed. Patricia A. Sullivan and Donna J. Qualley. Urbana: NCTE, 1994. 56–72.

Knowles, Malcolm. *The Adult Learner: A Neglected Species*. 4th ed. Houston: Gulf, 1990.

Luttrell, Wendy. *Schoolsmart and Motherwise: Working-Class Women's Identity and Schooling*. New York: Routledge, 1997.

Miritello, Mary. "Teaching Writing to Adults: Examining Assumptions and Revising Expectations for Adult Learners in the Writing Class." *Composition Chronicle: Newsletter for Writing Teachers*. 9.2 (1996).

Nixon-Ponder, Sarah. "Determining the Characteristics of Successful Women in an Adult Literacy Program." Research Study. Kent State University. 1996. ERIC ED 392 988.

Rich, Adrienne. *On Lies, Secrets, and Silence: Selected Prose 1996–1978*. New York: Norton, 1979.

Stoffel, Judith. "So, You're a Woman, 38, Back in School, and Writing the 'Research Paper.'" Conference on College Composition and Communication. Cincinnati. 19 Mar. 1992. ERIC ED 345 267.

Turner, Ralph H. "The Self-Conception in Social Interaction." *The Self in Social Interaction*. Ed. Chad Gordon and Kenneth J. Gergen. Vol. I. New York: John Wiley, 1968. 93–106.

Classroom Activities

An important part of Sophie's pedagogy is to "mode[l] her invention process — 'meditation, listing, and freewriting.'" Sophie uses these stories of real-life experiences from beyond the classroom to teach such basics as how "to illustrate description," as well as to revise for details. But the stories also seem to demonstrate how personal narrative can be connected to students' own struggles with the writing process, a potentially critical connection for women adult learners, according to Jackman. As Jackman notes, "Sophie's storytelling does not go unnoticed by Margie and Ann; they both respond favorably to the way she 'explains.'" Several suggestions follow from such pedagogy. Of course, you can tell your own stories orally to your students and have students suggest different details for invention and revision. Students can also relate their own narratives to the class.

However, another effective teaching tool would be to have students write a narrative about a significant experience in their lives outside the classroom, such as Sophie's being chased by a bear at Yosemite Park. As a next step, have students read each other's stories. Then, have students suggest what these personal narratives seem to represent about the writing process. For instance, does Sophie's apparent escape from the bear indicate her ingenuity and her ability to take risks in writing, as well as in real life? Do Ann's experiences as a house painter indicate her perseverance? Do Margie's abilities to motivate her children to "apply themselves" to their schoolwork suggest that she would be a careful reader and thoughtful member of a peer review group? What do students' personal stories seem to suggest about their potential abilities as adult learners? Try discussing these stories in small groups and then as a whole class, in order to compare notes.

Thinking about Teaching

One of the most interesting aspects of Jackman's article is that she uses the technique of narrative herself to emphasize its importance as a pedagogical technique for reentry adult women in the writing classroom. Consider writing for publication a narrative case study similar to Jackman's article. Some researchers have described such a style as a "feminist" approach to research, which considers women's particular cultural concerns as primary. Jackman's bibliography includes germinal texts by bell hooks, Adrienne Rich, Mary Field Belenky, and others who have written about feminist approaches to teaching, learning, and research. Rich, in particular, has written about teaching basic writing students in the SEEK program in New York City in the early 1970s. A selection by hooks on how race and socioeconomic class affect the education of students is included elsewhere in *Teaching Developmental Writing: Background Readings*.

Take a look at some of the books and articles by these writers listed in Jackman's bibliography, and write down your responses to their ideas in your teaching journal. Do you see immediate applications to your own classroom — and in particular, to students who are adult learners? What suggestions about pedagogy seem helpful? What suggestions about pedagogy seem limited to particular times and places? What ideas do these writers inspire in your own classroom teaching? Share your ideas with other teachers, and consider how they might apply as you craft a case study based on your observations of your own students and their progress as writers.

Twists, Turns, and Returns: Returning Adult Students

Libby Bay

Libby Bay is the Chair of the Humanities Division and a Professor of English at Rockland Community College in Suffern, New York. She has published "Teaching in the Community College: Rerouting a Career" in the ADE *Bulletin — on the web at <http://www.ade.org/ade/bulletin/n114/114027.htm> — and served as Northeast Region Chair for the Two-Year College Association, a division of CCCC. Bay's article reports on "a study of 85 adult students over the age of 24" at her college "who responded to a questionnaire sent through the mail." She also interviewed "another ten adult students on campus at that time ranging in age from the mid-twenties to the mid-fifties." By asking questions about student demographics and college experiences, Bay was able to form assumptions about who the returning adult students were at her college — about what kinds of services they would need (for example, counseling and child care) in order to be successful in their studies. Her profile of adult learners reminds us that all learning is contextualized against the very real background of our students' personal experiences and needs.*

Introduction

From early admission high school students to adults in their middle years, with military veterans, displaced homemakers, unemployed breadwinners, and leisure learners in between, college classes are populated in diverse ways. All indications are that older learners will continue to be a large part of the college population, and an even larger proportion of community college student bodies in the future. Thus adult students represent a cohort teachers must continue to welcome, understand, and assist.

This essay reports on a study of 85 adult students over the age of 24, at Rockland Community College, a two-year unit of the State University of New York (SUNY), who responded to a questionnaire sent through the mail, and on interviews with another ten adult students on campus at that time ranging in age from the mid-twenties to the mid-fifties. The research explores the reasons mature persons take a life step once confined to the young, the difficulties and satisfactions they experience, and what colleges can do to respond to their needs. It demonstrates how a small survey can provide data and direction for a single college and indicates how such information can be extrapolated and adapted by other institutions.

Research Method

> More than four out of ten college students nationwide — both under-graduate and graduate — are older than 25, and the number of students 35 and older has more than tripled from 1970 to 1993.
>
> — Layton

In the SUNY system, students in the thirty two-year colleges in fall 1995 had a median age of 23.1. More significantly, the percentage of students in the total student population over 24 was 43.8. The numbers in the four-year state-operated campuses, which are residential rather than commuter, are not as dramatic: a median age of 20.8 with 21.8 as the percentage over age 24 ("Age Group"). At Rockland Community College, the percentage of students over age 24 was 41.5, with a median age of 23 (*Student Data*). In fall 1995, this 41.5 percent represented approximately 2900 students.

Only recently convinced of the need to be data-based in projecting new curricula and revamping old programs, I decided to use a survey to provide additional information to supplement my experiences, impressions, and students' narratives. I developed an easily coded questionnaire with space for comments after each question and for general remarks at the end. The first section sought a profile of the adult learner on the Rockland Community College campus, asking questions about age, gender, ethnicity, income, and family status. These demographical items were followed by questions about previous and present college experience: how much? when? present status? The bulk of the questionnaire elicited information on why college was not a consideration immediately after high school, what occasioned the return, who or what was instrumental in such a decision, what difficulties the adult faced, what satisfactions the student derived from the experience, and what support colleges need to provide to make the transition for returning adults easier (see "Survey").

I also interviewed ten students, two counselors, and one community director and followed the general outline of the questionnaire in these interviews. I was amazed by the number of students who were eager to be interviewed, more astounded at their frankness. If anyone has stories to tell it is the returning adult student.

Background Information

Two hundred questionnaires were sent out in fall 1995 and 85 were returned. Most of the 85 respondents, as expected, were women (78 percent). Except for postwar surges of returning veterans, periodic economic crises, and recent workplace downsizings, the majority of adults entering college have been female. Again, as expected, in a suburban county like Rockland, most respondees were white (a little more than 81 percent). It should be noted that intensive recruitment efforts in the past year and a half attracted an increased number of students of color to campus in 1996–97. Thirty-six percent of the students were between the ages of 24 and 50, 64 percent over 50.

Many of those surveyed were part-time students, and many took evening classes. About 65 percent of the group was married. The median income was $50,000, lower than the median income of Rockland County, which is $62,000. Although Rockland is an affluent county, the college attracts a significant number of students from the pockets of poverty and low income that spread across the region from the Hudson River to the Ramapo Hills.

This quick profile leads to certain assumptions for this, and any, study of returning adults. The gender disproportion has implications for child care services, the kinds of courses the college offers, and the nature of counseling necessary. Since many adult students attend evening sessions — the average age at night is over 30 — it is clear that a full spectrum of courses across the disciplines must be offered as well as adequate support services at night. The economic statistics in a county which has a very high cost of living point to the necessity of disseminating financial aid information to returning adults as well as to high school graduates. The move towards increasing minority student enrollment has resulted in a multicultural curriculum so that older as well as young students are alert to issues of pluralism and diversity both through required courses and the classroom environment. One question in this section revealed that not all adult returnees are first-time students. A number are in college to finish studies that were interrupted; a number seek retraining rather than initial job skills; some are retirees looking for enrichment. These different goals suggest that a college's prescription for success for returning adult students must be as varied as the options offered the recent high school graduate.

The College Experience

When asked, "Why did you decide on college now?" students had a range of choices and could check off as many as were relevant. About 50 percent checked off degree, 30 percent training, 25 percent general interest; fewer than 25 percent indicated social reasons, and a meager 7 percent cited boredom.

From my experience in teaching returning adults, I was surprised that more did not indicate boredom. Certainly in the 1970s, when the first rush of adult women came to campus, many indicated that boredom was the reason. As advisor to Janus, a club that returning adult women formed, I learned that these women felt "incidental" at home once their children were absorbed in friends and high school and their husbands in job activities. These women were seeking something to do in their lives beyond their PTA contacts. Whether this scene has changed in the 1990s or whether the present group of returning adults is more goal directed is something my survey did not make clear.

Each question in the second part of the survey left room for comments, and the comments after this question were more enlightening than simple percentages can indicate: "I want to be somebody," wrote one student. "I was ready for a challenge," declared another. "After doing it my way for a decade, I ended up homeless," acknowledged a respondent. One interviewee dazzled the English teacher in me with her honesty and her mixed imagery: "My life felt glued together with a string," she said, "so I just put a screeching halt to everything."

In the course of reading the comments, I realized that I had asked a good question, but not a complete one. I had skipped an important step by not asking why the students hadn't gone to college immediately after high school. Fortuitously, I discovered a 1992 campus survey, "Reasons for not Previously Attending College," which, coupled with the comments on the 1995 survey, provided a more complete picture. The major reason many students did not lock-step their way through education was money: "Had to work." Sometimes, family responsibility dictated the need for earning money, sometimes a desire for things, sometimes the equation of money with independence. Few in this 1995 survey were living in luxury, but many had been able to attend classes because, over the years, they had accumulated funds, or discovered education loans, or learned about federal and state assistance. Money, however, is still a major concern. One of my interviewees went from a high-paying job to a $5.00 an hour part-time position and was not certain just how long she could manage the economic juggling. Another accumulated so much debt that she was $1,500 in arrears for tuition and had to drop out of school for a year to earn enough to repay her outstanding bills and continue.

Another common reason for not having had college on the agenda earlier was "I just didn't know what I wanted to do," or "I simply wasn't interested," or "College was never an option in my mind." More revelatory were self-scrutinizing comments: "I had no confidence in my ability," "I thought I couldn't do it," "Nobody ever asked me if I wanted to," and "School was an embarrassment for me, a disaster, so why continue?"

I questioned the students I interviewed directly about why college did not follow their graduation from high school. Several mentioned lack of guidance and "little encouragement from friends and family." A significant number had actually dropped out of high school. "High school didn't offer anything to me," one young woman explained. When she mentioned her complaint to her parents, her mother told her, "Perhaps you shouldn't raise your hand so often!" Another who left before graduation admitted. "I had to learn from my mistakes — the hard way." Still another explained that he was eager to see the world, not a classroom, so he joined the Navy. Frankly, he said that he had "messed up" in the Navy, but was glad he had taken a roundabout path because "I wouldn't have taken college seriously when I was 17." A very bright man from a wealthy family in Scotland (how he made his way to downtown Suffern is a long and convoluted story) told me that he did not like the feel of his father's footsteps. Not just these adults, but almost all of our students come to our campuses with baggage. The need for counseling services is heightened when the baggage has accumulated over many years.

In addition to a need for counseling services, workshops in adult development, assertiveness training, and confidence building for returning adult students, it is necessary to raise the consciousness of faculty to the different needs of this population. Faculty study groups might be formed on campus to explore women's ways of knowing and learning, to analyze life cycle development in the middle years, to discuss the incorporation of life experiences into the curriculum without impinging on an individual's privacy, even to develop legitimate ways to give credit for life accomplishments, as colleges such as Empire State College and Regents College do.

In a situation I faced in an honors course, these issues became focused for me. The class was bright, the discussions exciting, but the one mature student in the class refused my invitation to continue in Honors English 102. She found the younger students limited in their experiences and theoretical in their responses to life's difficulties. We finally decided that she would gain more from independent study than the classroom. Another time, a Vietnam veteran I recommended for the honors section of English 102 refused to register. "I'm not a good English student," he told me. I could not convince him that his experiences subsequent to high school had matured him and his writing.

There was no clear indication in the survey of who or what had been influential on the students' decision to return to college. My analysis is that, for the most part, circumstances, necessity, readiness, or general societal encouragement prompted the decision.

To the question, "What difficulties confronted you as a result of your return to higher education?" more than 70 percent acknowledged time as their greatest problem. These are, after all, adults, with multiple responsibilities, so that balancing hours and prioritizing obligations among family, friends, work, and school are no easy tasks. Oddly, I did not include "finances" or "stress" as choices, but from comments of interviewees, I know that students read money into "time." There was no close second to time as a choice, which is revealing and directive. Teaching adult students how to manage time and how to handle stress is just as urgent as the study skills we tend to emphasize. Based on my analysis, I recommend that returning adult students upon reentering higher education have a separate orientation through small group meetings with an experienced counselor. At such a session, managing time, handling stress, balancing family responsibilities, developing confidence, defining goals, should be the agenda. This orientation might well be a prelude to the formation of study circles of returning adults to cope further with these issues, with basic study skills added when necessary.

Although I expected family resistance of one sort or another to be a difficulty (husbands, parents, children), as it had been in earlier days, it was not a factor reflected in the survey. In the interviews, however, and in my experience in teaching returning adults, I heard much about reluctance from family or friends. "For several years I'd been Herbie's wife," one woman told me. "Now I needed to be me." A male returnee, a young grandfather and a maintenance worker at a local high school, experienced cautions from his wife, who could not understand why he would even consider giving up his secure civil service job. A mother of three, whose family had been resentful of her return to school, smiled when she said, "My children call me a nerd because I study so much. But I know they're proud of my grades." There seems to be more acceptance of older students in college now than in the past, but still the students need encouragement from staff on campus to know how to handle discouragement when it surfaces.

Child care, which I anticipated as a difficulty, received only minor response. Not just the age range of the sample, but accommodations already in place in our county and on our campus have alleviated this concern. About fifteen years ago the college established a "Fun and Learn Center" which provides excellent child care at a reasonable cost. Any community college that does not have such a facility is placing its student mothers at a disadvantage. Interestingly, in one of my interviews, an evening session single parent mentioned a related problem: the 8–12 year old. This child is too young to leave home alone; baby sitters are often too expensive. She suggested a "Fun and Homework Room" where children could be left while evening classes met. What a workable idea! Such a resource room could be staffed through a practicum program for students in the early childhood program, thus involving minimal or no cost.

Few adults found the coursework too difficult, the younger students intimidating, or the campus lonely. There was, however, some mention of lack of good advisement and hesitancy about basic skills. Again, though not mentioned, I know from experience that women coming back to school suffer from English and math anxiety so that special support in these areas must be provided. Mediated work at one's own pace in math courses has been very successful on our campus. Special services for returning adult students in the campus writing center on a one-to-one basis have also helped.

On the flip side, answers to the survey question "What have been your greatest satisfactions since you returned?" were encouraging. The choices included good grades, new knowledge/skills, new friends, new sense of self, and approval from family. Almost all of the students checked new knowledge and skills; almost as many indicated new sense of self. More than half were pleased by their grades, almost 40 percent had made new friends, and about 30 percent were receiving praise from their families. One student noted, "I am finding what I learn at Rockland Community College useful at my job and in my daily life." Another said, "People are impressed when I say I'm back in school, and that feels good." Others wrote, "It's wonderful sharing ideas with young people"; "Getting to know the instructors is great"; "The sense of accomplishment is tremendously motivating." A feeling of accomplishment and self-esteem permeated all the interviews, and many of the comments highlighted the community college as the place for another chance.

In a newspaper article, a counselor at Rochester Institute of Technology emphasized, "They're more self-directed and focused" ("Adults Have an Edge"). This accolade for the returning student seems to me to skirt the real issues adult students face as directed and focused as they may be — and, of course, not all are. "Reentry shocks" abound, and it is the primary obligation of the community college to check the fuses. The last question on the survey, then, but hardly the least, was "What can the college do to assist you?" The answers often reflected the need for special services. For a while, we had an office at Rockland Community College called R.I.S.E. (Returnees in Search of Education). It was staffed by a full-time director who not only offered group and individual counseling but organized workshops, helped students plan social functions, sponsored brown bag lunch discussions, and always acted as their advocate. We have an extraordinary honors program at Rockland, for example, but it is geared to the recent high school graduate seeking admission to a prestigious college. The director of R.I.S.E. approached the honors coordinator and asked why returning adults were excluded. He gave all kinds of answers — no high school records to check ability, no SAT's, no full-time commitment, nothing in common with the youngsters, no mobility for a prestigious transfer — but she accepted none of these rationalizations. The R.I.S.E. director insisted on a series of meetings to develop ways returning adults could be included in the program. Not only are returning adults now eligible for honors but the honors coordinator has made special efforts at articulation with schools like Brown, Manhattanville, Smith, and Columbia's School of General Studies, which seek out capable adult students.

Unfortunately, four years ago, the director of R.I.S.E. retired, and the position was left unfilled. Mature students have survived, but they and concerned faculty have felt the gap. Recently, a counselor offered to devote some of her time to returning adults, so now we have S.T.A.R.S. (Services to Adult Returning Students) flashing across the Rockland horizon. This counselor's intention is to coordinate adult needs with other support services offered in the counseling center — transfer assistance, career information, crisis intervention, personal advisement, and substance abuse counseling ("Seeing S.T.A.R.S.").

In addition to the support services, respondents to the survey asked for special sections of certain courses. The college offers a life skills program, which many students take in their first semester as an orientation to themselves, their education, and their goals. Because they are older and occupying "a different space," some returning adults feel they would benefit more from a homogenous age grouping. Although adults do have a different learning style and special needs, because life skills is a course that focuses on development throughout the life cycle, I wonder if, in this instance, the span of generations in the classroom is not reinforcing.

A number of students commented that some faculty are not sensitive enough to the special problems returning adults face. This is a tricky, but important issue. How should an instructor react if a young child is brought to class? What about the businessman who regularly comes to class fifteen minutes late because of his work schedule? Should the woman caring for her aging and ailing mother be excused from an extra assignment? Standards and fairness must be maintained, yet as community college instructors, we are also committed to flexibility and understanding. How do we draw the line, a line that is often perilously stretched by the nontraditional student? These questions need serious consideration as the number of returning adults increases.

Conclusion

As an amateur researcher, I belatedly discovered many questions I should have explored. How the goals of returning adult students change in the course of their education, for example, has always intrigued me, yet I had not included such a question. From my own experience, I know they do change. One woman who came to Rockland Community College to study sociology became a convert to English through her experience in a summer course in American literature, went on to earn a PhD in literature, and is now an English professor. Another whole group of women I worked with years ago came to campus just to "kill time," they said. After a few semesters, most of them decided to matriculate. A young man who wanted only to be a carpenter ended up in my classroom because of an injury on the job that precluded further work in construction. He was initially interested in architecture, but called me several years later to announce his law practice. These stories are legion, and I regret that I did not find a way to draw them out in the survey.

I have always maintained the centrality of the first year of English composition in any student's college experience, yet I did not explore this influence in the study. I would love to know how the returning adult student who often equates writing with grammar responds to our emphasis on process and discovery. I wonder how some of them feel about writing personal narratives and about participating in peer groups? Nothing in my survey probed such questions.

Still, I learned a great deal from the questionnaire, the interviews, and the material uncovered. Some information surprised me: three of my interviewees were "in recovery" from drug and alcohol addiction and alerted me to the large number of students on and off campus in a similar situation. Here, perhaps, lies another mission for the community college. We might well offer expanded educational services to rehabilitation agencies in our respective communities. Many comments pleased me: there was great satisfaction expressed with the courses and the faculty at Rockland Community College. Other things troubled me. Rockland Community College's loss of a dedicated office to assist returning adults is a severe diminution of support services.

For the two-year college, centered as it is on community, second chances, responsiveness to civic as well as economic needs, and service to all who want to be educated, these are hard times. Though I worry that we will be shortsighted in the decisions we make, my optimism that we will do the right thing has not faded. It derives not from the budget decisions we are making or the corporate structures we are emulating, but from the persistence to succeed and the enthusiasm to learn that characterized all the returning adults who were part of this study.[1]

Note

1. My thanks to these people who assisted with this study: Dr. Rita Lieberman, Grace D'Amico, Pat Harnett, Paula Casimir, Lorraine Doyle, Katherine Dillon, Patrick Cosgrove, Jean W. Bruno, Ray Wagner, Rosemary Noonan, Scott Sammut, Sherri Craven, Sherry Ribnett, Mark Wanner, Dr. Charles Secolsky, and Barbara Thelen.

Works Cited

"Adults Have an Edge When They Return to School." *Rockland Journal-News* [West Nyack, NY]. 6 Aug. 1995: B7.

"Age Group and Sex of Students. Fall 1995." Report No. 80–90 and 9–96. Central Staff Office of Institutional Research, SUNY, April 1996.

Layton, Mary Jo. "College Students Getting Older." *The Bergen Record* [Paramus, NJ]. 3 Nov. 1996: A-31+.

"Seeing S.T.A.R.S. at RCC." *RCC Scene.* 18 Mar. 1996: 3.

Student Data Report. Albany Annual Report, Form 22C. Rockland Community College. Fall 1996.

"Survey of R.I.S.E. Program Students: Reasons for Not Previously Attending College." Rockland Community College Office of Institutional Research, 1992.

Classroom Activities

Students can create a research project similar to the one Bay conducted (if on a smaller scale) in order to gather stories from and statistics about returning adult students. The purpose of the research project would be to recommend needed services for returning adult students not already provided by your college or university. To this end, students would need to research which services are already provided, and to what extent. In addition, students could implement some of the research tactics used by Bay. If a survey of former students is unfeasible, demographic statistics could be gathered from the college's admissions office or (if such an office exists) from the office of returning or nontraditional students. Stories could be compiled from interviews with classmates in writing or other courses. Such an assignment would allow students to practice important skills in critical thinking and problemposing for real-life situations (as suggested by Nixon-Ponder in the first article in this section) and to draw conclusions about their findings. The assignment would also give them an opportunity to find out more about the services offered by the college — and about the students it serves. Adult learners will be particularly motivated to take on a project that has "real-world" implications for their own lives as students.

Thinking about Teaching

You may wish to survey your own population of former reentry students to discover how they have used writing in their experiences beyond the basic writing classroom, and what aspects of their writing course were most or least helpful to them. The results of such a study could have significant consequences. How might your own pedagogy change, for example, based on your students' postclassroom experiences? Further, consider how the results of such a study might be used to argue for a particular pedagogy or program for current basic writing students. The implications of your study might have a positive and direct impact on education for developing writers not only in your classroom but throughout the institution. For instance, if your college administration wishes to try a strictly prescriptive approach to grammar instruction, the results of your survey may in fact demonstrate that former developing writers received longer-lasting and more significant benefits from collaborative learning and experience with the writing process. The results could also be shared with students to provide a reality check for the kinds of writing involved in various careers. The results of your survey may also provide significant implications for the needs of adult learners.

8

Critical Thinking

The writers in this chapter see critical thinking as a matter of breaking a whole task into carefully examined parts. Linda Elder and Richard Paul urge teachers to consider important guidelines as students work toward developing their reasoning abilities; Stephen Brookfield breaks down the learning process into individual critical incidents that students use to build profiles of themselves as active, critical learners; and Glynda Hull and Mike Rose take a close look at the critical thinking processes of Robert, a basic writing student at UCLA. Collectively, these writers help to demystify the teaching of critical thinking by providing strategies that take into account the needs — and build on the strengths — that students bring to the basic writing classroom.

The Elements of Critical Thinking
(Helping Students Assess Their Thinking)

Richard Paul and Linda Elder

Linda Elder and Richard Paul are, respectively, Assistant Director and Director of the Center for Critical Thinking at Sonoma State University in Rohnert Park, California. The article that follows is from the web site associated with the Center, called the "Critical Thinking Community" <www.criticalthinking.org>. This web site includes such classroom aids as sample syllabi and booklists for interested instructors. Elder and Paul are interested in critical thinking as it develops for college students. They have written articles that examine critical thinking as it relates to intellectual standards and course content. (A complete list of articles in this series is included in the bibliography at the end of this book.) Elder *and Paul define critical thinking as "the ability and disposition to improve one's thinking by systematically subjecting it to intellectual self-assessment." They divide the process of critical thinking into six stages that become progressively more advanced: the unreflective thinker, the challenged thinker, the beginning thinker, the practicing thinker, the advanced thinker, and the master thinker. The following guidelines are based on what Elder and Paul call "universal standards" for critical thinking. These guidelines have significant implications for the processes of writing and reading in developmental English courses.*

There are two essential dimensions of thinking that students need to master in order to learn how to upgrade their thinking. They need to be able to identify the "parts" of their thinking, and they need to be able to assess their use of these parts of thinking, as follows:

- All reasoning has a purpose.

- All reasoning is an attempt to figure something out, to settle some question, to solve some problem.

- All reasoning is based on assumption.

- All reasoning is done from some point of view.

- All reasoning is based on data, information, and evidence.

- All reasoning is expressed through, and shaped by, concepts and ideas.

- All reasoning contains inferences by which we draw conclusions and give meaning to data.

- All reasoning leads somewhere, has implications and consequences.

The question can then be raised, "What appropriate intellectual standards do students need to assess the 'parts' of their thinking?" There are many standards appropriate to the assessment of thinking as it might occur in this or that context, but some standards are virtually universal (that is, applicable to all thinking): clarity, precision, accuracy, relevance, depth, breadth, and logic.

How well a student is reasoning depends on how well he/she applies these universal standards to the elements (or parts) of thinking.

What follows are some guidelines helpful to students as they work toward developing their reasoning abilities:

1. All reasoning has a **purpose.**
   - Take time to state your purpose clearly.
   - Distinguish your purpose from related purposes.

- Check periodically to be sure you are still on target.
- Choose significant and realistic purposes.

2. All reasoning is an attempt to **figure something out, to settle some question, to solve some problem.**
   - Take time to clearly and precisely state the question at issue.
   - Express the question in several ways to clarify its meaning and scope.
   - Break the question into subquestions.
   - Identify if the question has one right answer, is a matter of opinion, or requires reasoning from more than one point of view.

3. All reasoning is based on **assumptions.**
   - Clearly identify your assumptions and determine whether they are justifiable.
   - Consider how your assumptions are shaping your point of view.

4. All reasoning is done from some **point of view.**
   - Identify your point of view.
   - Seek other points of view and identify their strengths as well as weaknesses.
   - Strive to be fair-minded in evaluating all points of view.

5. All reasoning is based on **data, information, and evidence.**
   - Restrict your claims to those supported by the data you have.
   - Search for information that opposes your position as well as information that supports it.
   - Make sure that all information used is clear, accurate, and relevant to the question at issue.
   - Make sure you have gathered sufficient information.

6. All reasoning is expressed through, and shaped by, **concepts** and **ideas.**
   - Identify key concepts and explain them clearly.
   - Consider alternative concepts or alternative definitions to concepts.
   - Make sure you are using concepts with care and precision.

7. All reasoning contains **inferences** or **interpretations** by which we draw **conclusions** and give meaning to data.
   - Infer only what the evidence implies.
   - Check inferences for their consistency with each other.
   - Identify assumptions which lead you to your inferences.

8. All reasoning leads somewhere or has **implications** and **consequences.**
   - Trace the implications and consequences that follow from your reasoning.
   - Search for negative as well as positive implications.
   - Consider all possible consequences.

Classroom Activities

For Elder and Paul, critical thinking can be broken down into several developmental stages; their work suggests that students can be made conscious of their own thinking and can be made aware of the steps they need to take to develop as thinkers. Copy the list of critical thinking guidelines for students or ask students to find the list on the web <http://www.criticalthinking.org/university/helps/nclk>. Ask them to document how they use these guidelines in their own writing so that they become aware of the metacognitive processes involved in thinking critically about the writing process. By encouraging your students to engage in the process of writing, you are teaching them to "take intellectual command of how they think, act, and react while they are learning," a skill that will help them to become better, more *masterful* thinkers and learners.

Thinking about Teaching

Teachers may wish to examine how critical thinking is implemented in other disciplines. How do math teachers, for instance, approach the idea of problem solving? Is math simply a lecture course, or are students able to work in small groups to solve problems and examine proofs and theorems? How do physics or psychology teachers create "a series of manageable steps" so that students might use critical thinking to explore difficult problems or concepts? It would be useful to compare and contrast strategies used in different disciplines to examine the implications for teaching writing. Teachers from various subject areas could meet to discuss strategies for improving critical thinking. Consider arranging cross-disciplinary classroom visitations to foster a broader perspective. Elsewhere, Elder and Paul emphasize the need to connect critical thinking skills across disciplines. Teachers may wish to investigate whether a focus on critical thinking skills is in fact taking place across the curriculum.

Understanding Classroom Dynamics:
The Critical Incident Questionnaire

Stephen D. Brookfield

For three decades, Stephen D. Brookfield has focused his research on adult learning, teaching, and critical thinking. He is currently Distinguished Professor in the Graduate Education Program at the University of St. Thomas. He is also the author of, among other works, Understanding and Facilitating Adult Learning *(1968) and* Developed Critical Thinkers *(1989), each of which has won the Cyrill O. Houle Award for Literature in Adult Education, and* Becoming a Critically Reflective Teacher *(1995), from which the following selection comes. In this article, Brookfield encourages teachers to thinking critically about their own teaching so that they can, in turn, encourage students to think critically about their own learning. He offers a practical instrument: a student questionnaire. Asking students to reflect on their learning experiences on a weekly basis, Brookfield argues, gets them "in the habit of hovering above themselves and studying the ways they react to different (learning) situations." Students identify "critical incidents" from each week's happenings, noting their own level of engagement in or distance from learning activities and their responses to the teacher's and other students' actions during class. As a semester-end assignment, students write a summary and analysis of their weekly responses. For the instructor, reading, analyzing, and responding to the questionnaire each week offers ongoing opportunities for rethinking pedagogy and content and for clarifying goals and expectations. Brookfield's critical incident questionnaire provides a practical starting point for charting the teaching and learning process.*

In this [article], I want to describe in detail one particular method for finding out how students are experiencing their learning and your teaching.... [T]his one approach — the critical incident questionnaire (CIQ) — ... is the one that has most helped me see my practice through students' eyes. Critical incidents are vivid happenings that for some reason people remember as being significant (Tripp, 1993; Woods, 1993). For students, every class contains such moments, and teachers need to know what these are. The CIQ helps us embed our teaching in accurate information about students' learning that is regularly solicited and anonymously given. It is a quick and revealing way to ascertain the effects your actions are having on students and to discover the emotional highs and lows of their learning. The CIQ provides you with a running commentary on the emotional tenor of each class you deal with.

How the Critical Incident Questionnaire Works

The CIQ is a single-page form that is handed out to students at the end of the last class you have with them each week. It comprises five questions, each of which asks students to write down some details about events that happened in the class that week. Its purpose is not to determine what students liked or didn't like about the class. Instead, it gets them to focus on specific, concrete happenings that were significant to them.

The form that students receive has two sheets separated by carbon paper. This allows the student to keep a carbon copy of whatever she has written. Five questions are asked on the form, with space beneath each question for the student to write a response:

The Classroom Critical Incident Questionnaire

Please take about five minutes to respond to each of the questions below about this week's class(es). Don't put your name on the form — your responses are anonymous. When you have finished writing, put one copy of the form on the table by the door and keep the other copy for yourself. At the start of next week's class, I will be sharing the responses with the group. Thanks for taking the time to do this. What you write will help me make the class more responsive to your concerns.

1. At what moment in the class this week did you feel most engaged with what was happening?
2. At what moment in the class this week did you feel most distanced from what was happening?
3. What action that anyone (teacher or student) took in class this week did you find most affirming and helpful?
4. What action that anyone (teacher or student) took in class this week did you find most puzzling or confusing?
5. What about the class this week surprised you the most? (This could be something about your own reactions to what went on, or something that someone did, or anything else that occurs to you.)

Students are given the last five to ten minutes of the last class of the week to complete this form. As they leave the room, I ask them to drop the top sheet of the critical incident form on a chair or table by the door, face down, and to take the carbon copy with them. The reason I ask them to keep a copy is that at the end of the semester, they are expected, as part of their assigned course work, to hand in a summary of their responses. This summary is part of . . . [a] participant learning portfolio . . . , which documents what and how students have learned during the semester. The portfolio item dealing with the CIQ asks for a content analysis of major themes that emerged in students' responses over the semester. It also asks for a discussion of the directions for future learning that these responses suggested. Consequently, students know that it's in their own best interests to complete these questionnaires as fully as possible each week because they will gain credit for an analysis of them later in the term.

For CIQs to be taken seriously by students, it is crucial that a convincing case be made for using them. In my course outlines, I describe how the method works and justify its use by saying that it will make the course a better experience for learners. As students read the syllabus, they see that inquiry into, and public discussion of, their experiences as learners will be a regular part of the course. At the first class, I explain why I use critical incidents and how they help me make the class more responsive to students' concerns. I also mention how much students will find out about themselves as learners by completing the form.

I try to give convincing examples from earlier courses of how critical incident responses alerted me to confusions or ambiguities that otherwise could have caused serious problems for students. I let them know that what I found out caused me to change my teaching. I also point out that completing the CIQs each week helps students build up important material for the assessed participant learning portfolio. If possible, at the first class meeting, I assemble a panel of former students to talk about their experiences when they took the course. One theme I ask panel members to address is their perceptions of the advantages and drawbacks of the CIQ.

Analyzing and Responding to Data from the CIQ

After I have collected the CIQ responses at the end of the last class each week, I read through them looking for common themes. This activity usually takes no more than twenty minutes. The bus ride from the campus to my house takes about seventeen minutes, and usually, between getting on the bus and arriving at my stop, I have made a reasonably accurate analysis of the chief clusters of responses. I look for comments that indicate problems or confusions, particularly if they are caused by my actions. Anything contentious is highlighted, as is anything that needs further clarification. These comments become the basis for the questions and issues I address publicly the next time we're together.

At the start of the first class of the next week, I debrief students on the main themes that emerged in their responses. Sometimes I type up a one- or two-page summary and leave copies of this on students' chairs for them to read as they come in. At other times, I take two or three minutes to present an opening oral report. If students have made comments that have caused me to change how I teach, I acknowledge this and explain why the change seems worth making. I try also to clarify any actions, ideas, requirements, or exercises that seem to be causing confusion. Criticisms of my actions are reported and discussed. If contentious issues have emerged, we talk about how these can be negotiated so that everyone feels heard and respected. Quite often, students write down comments expressing their dislike of something I am insisting they do. When this happens, I know that I must take some time to reemphasize why I believe the activity is so important and to make the best case I can about how it contributes to students' long-term interests. Even if I have said this before, and written it in the syllabus, the critical incident responses alert me to the need to make my rationale explicit once again.

Using the CIQ doesn't mean that I constantly change everything that students tell me they don't like. We all have nonnegotiable elements to our agendas that define who we are and what we stand for. To throw them away as a result of students' opinions would undercut our identities as teachers. For example, I won't give up my agenda to get students to think critically, even if they all tell me that they want me to stop doing this. I will be as flexible as I can in negotiating how this agenda is realized, but I won't abandon it. I'll ask students to suggest different ways in which they might show me that they're thinking critically. I'll also vary the pace at which I introduce certain activities and exercises, to take account of students' hostility, inexperience, or unfamiliarity with this process. But to abandon the activity that defines who I am as a teacher would mean that I ceased to have the right to call myself a teacher. So if students use their CIQ responses to express a strong opinion that challenges what you're trying to do or how you're trying to do it, you owe it to them to acknowledge this criticism. In doing so, you need to make your own position known, justify it, and negotiate alternative ways of realizing your aims. But you don't owe it to them to abandon entirely your rationale for teaching.

Advantages of Critical Incident Questionnaires

I am a strong advocate of CIQs because of the clear benefits their use confers. Let me describe these briefly.

They Alert Us to Problems before a Disaster Develops

I have always prided myself on my conscientious use of the troubleshooting period to create a safe opportunity for students to make public anything that is troubling them. I regularly invite them to speak up during these periods about anything they find problematic, unfair, ambiguous, confusing, or unethical about the course or about my teaching. These invitations are frequently met with silence and by serried ranks of benign, smiling faces. Not surprisingly, I used to interpret this to mean that things were going along just fine. Indeed, it seemed at times that students were a little tired of this heavy-handed attempt by yours truly to appear fair and responsive. So you can imagine my surprise, hurt, and anger when I would receive end-of-course written evaluations from students saying that my course was of no real use to them, was uninspiringly taught, and was a waste of their time! I had given them ample opportunity to say these things to me earlier and had assured them I wanted to know about any problems they had so that we could work on fixing them. Why had no one spoken out?

This scenario of silent, smiling faces during troubleshooting periods followed by "take no prisoners" final evaluations repeated itself so often that I resolved to find a way to detect early on in a course any smoldering resentments students felt. If I knew about them soon enough, I could address them before they built to volcanic proportions. Using CIQs has helped me do this very effectively. My teaching has certainly not been without its problems, some of them very serious, but I have ceased to be taken by surprise when these emerge.

Behind those silent, smiling faces lies a recognition by students of the power differential that exists between themselves and their teachers. Students are understandably reluctant to voice misgivings and criticisms to people who exercise substantial influence (through the awarding of grades) over their career destinies and their self-concepts. This is as true for teachers who make repeated avowals of their commitment to democratic practice as it is for those who seem more traditionally authoritarian. However, if anonymity is assured, students may be willing to put their concerns in writing. Without anonymity, they are not comfortable voicing their misgivings, fears, and criticisms: they know the risks involved, and most of them have learned to keep quiet for fear of upsetting someone who has power over them.

Using CIQs helps teachers detect early on in a course any serious problems that need addressing before they get out of hand. The CIQ provides a direct, unfiltered account of students' experiences that is free of the distortions usually caused by the power dynamic between teacher and taught. CIQs are particularly helpful in providing teachers with accurate information about the extent and causes of resistance to learning. They also make us aware of situations in which our expectations about appropriate teaching methods and content are not meshing with those held by students. In my own teaching, CIQs give me good information about students' readiness for a particular learning activity. This, in turn, helps me pace the course. CIQs also help me curb my tendency to equate silence with mental inertia. Let me explain.

Many times in the middle of giving a lecture, I have one of those "Beam me up, Scotty" moments. This usually happens when I sense from students' body language that I've lost them. They're looking at the table, at the ceiling, out of the window — anywhere else but at me. Faced with this lack of eye contact, I feel a rising sense of panic. So I stop and ask students if there's anything I can clarify or if they have any questions about what I've just said. When my invitation is met with silence, I feel demoralized and glumly conclude that the session has been wasted. After all, didn't their blank expressions and muteness prove that they had no idea what I was talking about? Yet often after such occasions, I have been surprised and relieved to read in students' critical incident responses how moments in the lecture had been the most engaging moments of the class or how comments I had made during the presentation had been particularly affirming.

They Encourage Students to Be Reflective Learners

A second advantage of the CIQ lies in its encouragement of student reflection. When the instrument is first introduced into a class, students sometimes find the activity of completing the five questions on the form to be somewhat artificial; they feel they are going through some not very convincing motions. Over time, however, they start to notice patterns emerging in their own emotional responses to learning. They tell me that as they go through a course, they have pedagogic "out of body" experiences: by weeks five or six of the course, they are in the habit of hovering above themselves and studying the ways they react to different situations. They begin to jot down notes about critical classroom events and their reactions to them as they occur so that the information is not missed when the CIQs are completed at the end of class.

They Build a Case for Diversity in Teaching

When teachers report back to students the spread of responses to the previous week's classes, a predictable diversity emerges. One cluster of students writes that the most engaging moments for them were during the small group activity. Typical comments are: "I could recognize what others were saying," "I learned something important from a group member," "I felt my voice was being listened to." This same group of people often reports that the most distancing moments were experienced during my presentation. They write: "I couldn't see the point of the lecture," "What you said did not seem to make sense to me," "I'd had a long day and was fighting to stay awake."

Another cluster of responses says exactly the opposite. To these students, the most engaging moments in class were experienced during the instructor's presentation. Typical comments are: "What you spoke about related directly to me," "I enjoy hearing what you think about this," "I really benefit from having things laid out in front of me." This same group usually reports that for them the most distancing moments happened in the small group exercise: "We got off task," "An egomaniac dominated our discussion," "One man felt it was the duty of the rest of us to solve his problems." Again, in picking out affirming actions, one cluster of responses might refer favorably to a teacher's self-disclosure, while another might report this as irritating or irrelevant. One student wrote, about a recent class of mine: "Your willingness to be open with us is wonderful. It makes me feel like being open in return." Another wrote, "Too much psychoanalysis, not enough content — 90 percent of our class is personal disclosure and only 10 percent is critical rigor."

As I read out these responses at the beginning of each new week, students often comment on their diversity. They laugh as they hear how eight people picked out the small group experience as the most engaging moment and how another eight reported the same activity as the most distancing or confusing episode in the class. They tell me that they hadn't realized how the same things could be experienced so differently. Then we talk about the concept of learning styles or situated cognition and about the ways that culture, history, and personality determine how events are experienced. Seeing a diversity of responses emerge every week gives a drama and reality to the idea that different people learn differently.

Each week, I emphasize that my recognition of this diversity lies behind my own efforts to use a range of teaching methods and materials. The important thing about this is that I ground my use of different methods in students' reports of their own experiences as learners in my courses. I could write in my syllabus, and explain at the opening class, that because different people learn differently, I intend to use different approaches. But saying this would mean little to students who believe that everyone else learns the way they do. However, when they hear, week after week, how people sitting next to them have a completely different reaction to what goes on in class, the reason why I use a variety of approaches starts to make sense.

They Build Trust

The CIQ can play an important role in building trust between students and teachers. Students say that the experience of having their opinions, reactions, and feelings solicited regularly, and addressed publicly, is one that is crucial to their coming to trust a teacher. They say they are used to filling out evaluations at the end of courses, but that they view that activity as artificial and meaningless, since they never see any benefits from their efforts. They know that their comments might change what a teacher does with another group in the future, but this is of little importance to them.

However, with the weekly CIQs, students wait expectantly at the start of each new week for the report on the responses to the previous week's classes. They know that during this report, and in the discussion that follows it, the teacher will be talking about what she feels she needs to do and change in her own teaching as a result of what she has learned from the responses. Students say that hearing their own anonymous comments reported back to them as part of a commonly articulated class concern somehow legitimizes what had formerly been felt as a purely private and personal reaction. When they see teachers consistently making changes in their practice, and explicitly demonstrating that they are doing so in response to students' CIQ responses, the feeling develops that the teachers can be trusted.

Sometimes teachers quite legitimately feel that they can't change their practice to accommodate students' wishes as expressed in their CIQ responses. But the very fact that teachers acknowledge that they know what those wishes are, and the fact that they take the time and trouble to explain why they feel they can't, in good conscience, do what a group of students wants them to do, builds a sense that the class is one in which open and honest disclosure is encouraged.

Works Cited

Tripp, David. *Critical Incidents in Teaching: Developing Professional Judgment.* New York: Routledge, 1993.

Woods, Peter. *Critical Events in Teaching and Learning.* Bristol, PA: Falmer Press, 1993.

Classroom Activities

Brookfield suggests that an important purpose of the critical incident questionnaire is to allow students a safely anonymous position from which to articulate what they are learning from the course. Anonymity allows teachers to gauge how students perceive the progress of the course and the processes of their own learning . Students who may feel reticent about speaking up in class are given the opportunity to provide the teacher with crucial information about how the methods and goals of the course are being perceived and enacted.

For Brookfield, critical thinking involves sustained reflection on the process. As students complete the questionnaire each week, they discover patterns in their own learning; connections between critical incidents and ideas may begin to seem less random. With this in mind, devote ten minutes of each class period to writing a critical incident questionnaire. (The students keep a copy, and the instructor sees the anonymous weekly responses.) Students may wish to share these entries in small groups throughout the semester to compare and contrast experiences. At the end of the course, when you ask them to use their critical thinking skills to summarize and analyze a semester's worth of responses, students will have concrete and significant information at their disposal concerning their own learning styles and thinking and writing processes.

Thinking about Teaching

As instructors, we may not feel comfortable with student evaluations that come at the end of the term and offer only numerical ratings or cryptic comments that do not refer to specific course activities. It seems difficult, if not impossible, to learn very much about how students respond to our teaching from these often vague documents. The critical incident questionnaire is one means of ameliorating this process, giving teachers access to student perceptions of the course and of themselves as learners from the very beginning.

Yet Brookfield makes clear that teachers can also participate in the CIQ process by reflecting on their own methods and on their perceptions of critical incidents in the course. Later in his book, Brookfield recommends that teachers also keep their own learning journal as well as fill out the weekly CIQ — and that they share the results with students. Such activities may well demystify the teaching process for students. Further, such a process allows us to continue to learn about what works well for our students and ourselves and what we may consider changing. Engage in this form of teacher research with interested colleagues; meet as often as possible to share responses and exchange ideas.

"This Wooden Shack Place": The Logic of an Unconventional Reading

Glynda Hull and Mike Rose

Glynda Hull and Mike Rose identify literacy — its definitions and its acquisition — among their teaching and research interests. Hull has worked on such issues at the School of Education at the University of California at Berkeley, where she is Associate Professor and Director of the College Writing Program. Rose has taught for many years at UCLA and recounts his experiences in his autobiographical work, Lives on the Boundary *(1989). He has also written* Possible Lives: The Promise of Public Education in America *(1995), a book on his travels to public schools throughout the United States. Hull and Rose bring unique perspectives to basic writing and to the American system of education in general. Their search for solutions to systemic problems leads them to value the unconventional in the processes of reading, interpreting, and critical thinking. Yet these teachers also understand the necessity of student and teacher working together to arrive at shared meaning, as they demonstrate in the case of one student named Robert. "Robert's interpretation" of a poem he is studying "will cause his teacher to modify his reading, and the teacher's presentation of his interpretation will help Robert acquire an additional approach to the poem." In this article, Hull and Rose examine Robert's "unconventional" reading in detail, allowing the reader to follow along as Robert reveals how social class and cultural background affect his critical thinking and close reading.*

This is a paper about student interpretations of literature that strike the teacher as unusual, a little off, not on the mark. When we teachers enter classrooms with particular poems or stories in hand, we also enter with expectations about the kind of student responses that would be most fruitful, and these expectations have been shaped, for the most part, in literature departments in American universities. We value some readings more than others — even, in our experience, those teachers who advocate a reader's free play. One inevitable result of this situation is that there will be moments of mismatch between what a teacher expects and what students do. What interests us about this mismatch is the possibility that our particular orientations and readings might blind us to the logic of a student's interpretation and the ways that interpretation might be sensibly influenced by the student's history.

The two of us have been involved for several years in a study of remedial writing instruction in American higher education, attempting to integrate social-cultural and cognitive approaches to better understand the institutional and classroom practices that contribute to students being designated remedial (Hull and Rose). One of the interesting things that has emerged as we've been conducting this research is the place of reading in the remedial writing classroom, particularly at a time when composition professionals are calling for the integration of reading and writing while affirming, as well, the place of literature in remedial instruction (Bartholomae and Petrosky; Salvatori, "Reading and Writing"). As this integration of reading, and particularly the reading of literature, into the remedial writing classroom continues, composition teachers will increasingly be called on to explore questions of interpretation, expectation, and background knowledge — particularly given the rich mix of class and culture found in most remedial programs. We would like to consider these issues by examining a discussion of a poem that was part of a writing assignment. Specifically, we will analyze a brief stretch of discourse, one in which a student's personal history and cultural background shape a somewhat unconventional reading of a section of a poem. We will note the way the mismatch plays itself out in conversation, the logic of the student's reading and the coherent things it reveals about his history, and the pedagogical implications of conducting a conversation that encourages that logic to unfold.

The stretch of discourse we're going to analyze comes from a conference that immediately followed a classroom discussion of a poem by the contemporary Japanese-American writer Garrett Kaoru Hongo. The class is designated as the most remedial composition class at the University of California; it is part of a special program on the Los Angeles campus (the Freshman Preparatory Program) for students determined by test scores to be significantly at risk. (The SAT verbal scores of this particular section, for example, ranged from 220 to 400.) Mike Rose taught the class at the time he was collecting data on remedial writing instruction at the university level, and though his class was not the focus of his research, he did keep a teaching log, photocopy all work produced by the class, and collect sociohistorical and process-tracing data on several students and tape record selected conferences and tutorial sessions with them. For reasons that will shortly be apparent, a student named Robert was one of those Rose followed: he will be the focus of this paper. Let us begin this analysis with the poem Robert

and the others in the class read; the discussion took place during the
third week of the fall quarter:

And Your Soul Shall Dance

for Wakako Yamauchi

Walking to school beside fields
of tomatoes and summer squash,
alone and humming a Japanese love song,
you've concealed a copy of *Photoplay*
between your algebra and English texts.
Your knee socks, saddle shoes, plaid dress,
and blouse, long-sleeved and white
with ruffles down the front,
come from a Sears catalogue
and neatly complement your new Toni curls.
All of this sets you apart from the landscape:
flat valley grooved with irrigation ditches,
a tractor grinding through alkaline earth,
the short stands of windbreak eucalyptus
shuttering the desert wind
from a small cluster of wooden shacks
where your mother hangs the wash.
You want to go somewhere.
Somewhere far away from all the dust
and sorting machines and acres of lettuce.
Someplace where you might be kissed
by someone with smooth, artistic hands.
When you turn into the schoolyard,
the flagpole gleams like a knife blade in the sun,
and classmates scatter like chickens,
shooed by the storm brooding on your horizon.

— Garrett Kaoru Hongo

The class did pretty well with "And Your Soul Shall Dance." They followed the narrative line, pictured the girl, and understood the tension
between her desires (and her dress) and the setting she's in. The ending, with its compressed set of similes and metaphors, understandably
gave them some trouble — many at first took it literally, pictured it
cinematically. But, collaboratively, the class came to the understanding that the storm meant something powerful and disquieting was brew-
ing, and that the girl — the way she looks, her yearning for a different
life — was somehow central to the meaning of the storm. The class was
not able, however, to fit all the pieces together into one or more unified
readings. And during the discussion — as members of the class focused
on particular lines — some students offered observations or answers
to questions or responses to classmates that seemed to be a little off
the mark, unusual, as though the students weren't reading the lines
carefully. Rose wondered if these "misreadings" were keeping the students from a fuller understanding of the way the storm could be inte-

grated into the preceding events of the poem. One of these students was Robert.

A brief introduction. Robert is engaging, polite, style-conscious, intellectually curious. His father is from Trinidad, his mother from Jamaica, though he was born in Los Angeles and bears no easily discernible signs of island culture. His parents are divorced, and while he spends time with both, he currently lives with his mother in a well-kept, apartment-dense area on the western edge of central Los Angeles. Robert's family, and many of their neighbors, fall in the lower-middle-class SES bracket. He was bused to middle and high school in the more affluent San Fernando Valley. His high-school GPA was 3.35; his quantitative SAT was 410, and his verbal score was 270. In class he is outgoing and well-spoken — if with a tinge of shyness — and though his demeanor suggests he is a bit unsure of himself, he volunteers answers and responds thoughtfully to his classmates.

During the last half hour of the class on the Hongo poem, the students began rough drafts of an interpretive essay, and in his paper Robert noted that his "interpretation of this poem is that this girl seems to want to be different from society." (And later, he would tell his teacher that Hongo's poem "talked about change.") Robert clearly had a sense of the poem, was formulating an interpretation, but he, like the others, couldn't unify the poem's elements, and Rose assumed Robert's inability was caused by his misreading of sections of the poem. Here is Rose's entry in his teacher's log:

> Robert was ok on the 1st third of the poem, but seemed to miss the point of the central section. Talk with the tutor — does he need help with close reading?

Rose decided to get a better look, so he moved his regularly scheduled conference with Robert up a week and tape-recorded it. In the three-minute excerpt from that conference that follows, Robert is discussing the storm at the poem's conclusion — the foreboding he senses — but is having some trouble figuring out exactly what the source of this impending disruption is. Rose asks Robert if — given the contrast between the farming community and the girl's dreams and appearance — he could imagine a possible disruption in her not-too-distant future. We pick up the conversation at this point. To help clarify his own expectations, Rose replayed the stretch of tape as soon as Robert left, trying to recall what he intended in asking each of his questions.

1a   *Rose:*   What do you think . . . what, you know, on the one hand what might the reaction of her parents be, if she comes in one day and says, "I, I don't like it here, I want to leave here, I want to be different from this, I want to go to the city and . . ." [*Expectation:* Robert will say the parents will be resistant, angry — something rooted in the conservative values associated with poor, traditional families.]

1b *Robert:*   Um, that would basically depend on the wealth of her family. You'd wanna know if her parents are poor . . . [*mumbling*] . . . they might not have enough money, whereas they can't go out and improve, you know . . . [Responds with a *qualification* that complicates the question by suggesting we need to know more. This further knowledge concerns the family's economic status, something Rose had assumed was evident.]

2a *Rose:*   OK. OK. [*Acknowledges with hesitation*] From what we see about the background here and the times and the look, what can . . . can we surmise, can we imagine, do you think her parents are wealthy or poor? [*Focuses* on the poem, asking for a conjecture. *Expectation:* Robert's attention will be drawn to the shacks, the hand laundering, the indications of farm labor.]

2b *Robert:*   I wouldn't say that they're wealthy but, again, I wouldn't say that they are poor either. [Responds with a *qualification*]

3a Rose: OK. [*Acknowledges with hesitation*] And why not? [Requests *elaboration. Expectation:* Robert will provide something from the poem, some line that explains the ambiguity in his answer.]

3b *Robert:*   Because typical farm life is, you know, that's the way that you see yourself, you know, wear jeans, just some old jeans, you know, some old saddle shoes, boots or something, some old kinda shirt, you know, with some weird design on the shoulder pad . . . [Responds by creating a *scenario*]

3c *Rose:*   Uh huh . . . [*Unsure about direction,* but *acknowledges*]

3d *Robert:*   . . . for the guys. And then girls, probably wear some kind of plain cloth skirt, you know, with some weird designs on it and a weird shirt. I couldn't really . . . you really wouldn't know if they're . . . whether they were rich or not. Cause mainly everyone would dress the same way . . . [Continues *scenario* leading to an observation]

4a *Rose:*   Yeah. [Sees the purpose of the scenario] That's right, so you wouldn't be able to tell what the background is, right? [*Confirms* Robert's observation and *reflects back*] Let's see if there's anything in the poem that helps us out. (pause) "All of this sets you apart . . ." this is about line twelve in the poem, "All of this sets you apart from the landscape: / flat valley grooved with irrigation ditches, / a tractor grinding through alkaline earth, / the short stands of windbreak eucalyptus / shuttering the desert wind / from a small cluster of wooden shacks / where your mother hangs the wash." [*Focuses* on poem] Now if she lives with her mother in a wooden shack, a shack . . . [*Begins line of reasoning*]

4b *Robert:*   OK. OK. Oh! [*interrupts*] Right here — is it saying that she lives with her mother, or that she just goes to this wooden shack place to *hang* her clothes? [*Challenges* teacher's line of reasoning]

4c *Rose:*   Oh, I see. So you think that it's possible then that her mother . . . [*Reflects back*]

4d *Robert:* [*picks up thought*] washes her clothes probably at home somewhere and then walks down to this place where the wind . . . the wind . . . so the eucalyptus trees block this wind, you know, from . . . [*Elaborates*]

4e *Rose:* [*picks up thought*] so that the clothes can dry.

4f *Robert:* Right. [*Confirms*]

5a *Rose:* Well, that's certainly possible. That's certainly possible. [*Confirms*] Um, the only thing I would say if I wanted to argue with you on that would be that that's possible, but it's also the only time that this writer lets us know anything about where she might live, etc. . . . [*Begins to explain his interpretation* — an interpretation, we'd argue, that is fairly conventional: that the family is poor, and that poverty is signaled by the shacks, the place, most likely, where the family lives]

Certainly not all of Robert's exchanges — in classroom or conference — are so packed with qualification and interruption and are so much at cross purposes with teacher expectation. Still, this stretch of discourse is representative of the characteristics that make Robert's talk about texts interesting to us. Let us begin by taking a closer look at the reasoning Robert exhibits as he discusses "And Your Soul Shall Dance." To conduct this analysis, we'll be intersecting socioeconomic, cognitive, and textual information, bringing these disparate sources of information together to help us understand Robert's interpretation of sections of "And Your Soul Shall Dance," explicating not the poem, but a particular reading of it in a particular social-textual setting.

Here are a few brief comments on method:

Our data comes from the stretch of discourse we just examined, from other sections of the same conference, from a stimulated-recall session (on an essay Robert was writing for class) conducted one week prior to the conference,[1] and from a follow-up interview conducted four months after the conference to collect further sociohistorical information.

To confirm our sense of what a "conventional" reading of this section of the poem would be, we asked six people to interpret the lines in question. Though our readers represented a mix of ages and cultural backgrounds, all had been socialized in American literature departments: two senior English majors — one of whom is Japanese-American — two graduate students — one of whom is African-American — and two English professors — one of whom is Mexican-American. Regardless of age or cultural background, all quickly offered the same interpretation we will be suggesting is conventional.[2]

Analysis

1a–1b

> 1a *Rose:* What do you think . . . what, you know, on the one hand what might the reaction of her parents be, if she comes in one day and says, "I, I don't like it here, I want to leave here, I want to be different from this, I want to go to the city and . . ."
>
> 1b *Robert:* Um, that would basically depend on the wealth of her family. You'd wanna know if her parents are poor . . . (*mumbling*) . . . they might not have enough money, whereas they can't go out and improve, you know . . .

Robert claims that the reaction of the girl's parents to "I want to leave here . . . [and] go to the city . . ." would "depend on the wealth of her family." This qualification is legitimate, though the reasoning behind it is not quickly discernible. In the follow-up interview Robert elaborates: "[If she goes to the city] she's gonna need support . . . and if they're on a low budget they won't have that much money to be giving to her all the time to support her." The social context of Robert's reasoning becomes clearer here. He comes from a large family (eleven siblings and half-siblings), some members of which have moved (and continue to move) across cultures and, to a degree, across class lines. It is the parents' obligation to help children as they make such moves, and Robert is aware of the strains on finances such movement brings — he is in the middle of such tension himself.

2a–4f

This segment includes Robert's qualified response to "do you think her parents are wealthy or poor?" his farm fashion scenario, and his perception of the "small cluster of wooden shacks." As we've seen, we need to understand Robert's perception of the shacks in order to understand his uncertainty about the parents' economic status, so we'll reverse the order of events on the transcript and deal first with the shacks.

> 4a *Rose:* Yeah. That's right, so you wouldn't be able to tell what the background is, right? Let's see if there's anything in the poem that helps us out. (pause) "All of this sets you apart . . ." this is about line twelve in the poem, "All of this sets you apart from the landscape: / flat valley grooved with irrigation ditches, / a tractor grinding through alkaline earth, / the short stands of windbreak eucalyptus / shuttering the desert wind / from a small cluster of wooden shacks / where your mother hangs the wash." Now if she lives with her mother in a wooden shack, a shack . . .
>
> 4b *Robert:* OK. OK. Oh! Right here — is it saying that she lives with her mother, or that she just goes to this wooden shack place to *hang* her clothes?

Those of us educated in a traditional literature curriculum, and especially those of us trained in an English graduate program, are schooled to comprehend the significance of the shacks. We understand, even if we can't readily articulate them, the principles of compression and imagistic resonance that underlie Hongo's presentation of a single image to convey information about economic and historical background. Robert, however, isn't socialized to such conventions, or is only partly socialized, and so he relies on a model of interpretation Rose had seen him rely on in class and in the stimulated-recall session: an almost legalistic model, a careful, qualifying reasoning that defers quick judgment, that demands multiple sources of verification. The kind of reasoning we see here, then, is not inadequate. In fact, it's pretty sophisticated — though it is perhaps inappropriately invoked in a poetic world, as Rose begins to suggest to Robert in 5a. We'll come back to this momentarily, but first we want to address one more issue related to Robert's uncertainty about the income level of the girl's parents.

We would like to raise the possibility that Robert's background makes it unlikely that he is going to respond to "a small cluster of wooden shacks" in quite the same way — with quite the same emotional reaction — as would a conventional (and most likely middle-class) reader for whom the shacks might function as a quickly discernible, emblematic literary device. Some of Robert's relatives in Trinidad still live in houses like those described in the poem, and his early housing in Los Angeles — further into central Los Angeles than where he now lives — was quite modest. We would suggest that Robert's "social distance" from the economic reality of poor landscapes isn't as marked as that of the conventional/middle-class reader, and this might make certain images less foreign to him, and, therefore, less emotionally striking. This is certainly *not* to say that Robert is naive about his current position in American society, but simply to say that the wooden shacks might not spark the same dramatic response in him as in a conventional/middle-class reader. The same holds true for another of Hongo's indicators of economic status — the hanging of the wash — for Robert's mother still "likes to wash her clothes by hand." Paradoxically, familiarity might work against certain kinds of dramatic response to aspects of working-class life.

In line with the above assertion, we would like to consider one last indicator of the girl's economic status — the mention of the Sears catalogue. The Sears catalogue, we believe, cuts two ways in the poem: it suggests lower-income-level shopping ("thrifty," as one of our readers put it) and, as well, the importing of another culture's garments. But the catalogue also carries with it an ironic twist: it's not likely that conventional readers would consider a Sears catalogue to be a source of fashion, so there's a touch of irony — perhaps pity mixed with humor — in this girl fulfilling her romantic dreams via Sears and Roebuck. We suggest that Robert's position in the society makes it difficult for him to see things this way, to comply with this conventional reading. He knows merchandise from Sears is "economical" and "affordable," and, to him, there's nothing ironic, pitiable, or humorous about that. When asked if he sees anything sad or ironic about the girl buying there he responds, "Oh, no, no," pointing out that "some of the items they sell in Sears, they sell in other stores." He then goes on to uncover an interesting problem in the poem. He uses the Sears catalogue to support his assertion that the family isn't all that poor (and thus doesn't necessarily live in those shacks): "She couldn't be really poor because she has clothes from the Sears catalogue." Robert knows what real poverty is, and he knows that if you have enough money to buy at Sears, you're doing OK. He goes on to speculate — again with his careful, qualifying logic — that if she is as poor as the shacks suggest, then maybe the Sears clothes could be second-hand and sent to her by relatives, in the way his family sends clothes and shoes to his relatives in Trinidad. Hongo's use of the Sears catalogue is, in some ways, undercut by other elements in his poem.

3b *Robert:* Because typical farm life is, you know, that's the way that you see yourself, you know, wear jeans, just some old jeans, you know, some old saddle shoes, boots or something, some old kinda shirt, you know, with some weird design on the shoulder pad . . .

3c *Rose:* Uh huh . . .

3d *Robert:* . . . for the guys. And then girls, probably wear some kind of plain cloth skirt, you know, with some weird designs on it and a weird shirt. I couldn't really . . . you really wouldn't know if they're . . . whether they were rich or not. Cause mainly everyone would dress the same way . . .

Now we can turn to the farm fashion scenario. Given that the "small cluster of wooden shacks" doesn't seem to function for Robert as it might for the conventional reader, he is left more to his own devices when asked: "do you think her parents are wealthy or poor?" What begins as a seeming non sequitur — and a concrete one at that — does reveal its purpose as Robert plays it out. Though Robert has a frame of reference to understand the economics of the scene in "And Your Soul Shall Dance" and the longing of its main character, he is, after all, a city boy, born and raised in central Los Angeles. What he does, then, when asked a question about how one determines the economic background of people moving across a farm landscape is to access what knowledge he does have about farm life — things he's read or heard, images he's gleaned from movies and television shows (e.g., *Little House on the Prairie*) — and create a scenario, focusing on one indicator of socioeconomic status: fashion. (And fashion is a sensible criterion to use here, given the poem's emblematic use of clothing.) Classroom-observational and stimulated-recall data suggest that Robert makes particularly good use of visual imagery in his thinking — e.g., he draws pictures and charts to help him comprehend difficult readings; he rehearses sentences by visualizing them before he writes them out — and here we see him reasoning through the use of scenario, concluding that in certain kinds of communities, distinctions by readily discernible indicators like dress might not be all that easy to make.

> 4d   *Robert:*   washes her clothes probably at home somewhere and then walks down to this place where the wind . . . the wind . . . so the eucalyptus trees block this wind, you know, from . . .
>
> 4e   *Rose:*   so that the clothes can dry.
>
> 4f   *Robert:*   Right.

This section also involves the wooden shacks, though the concern here is Robert's assertion that the mother doesn't have to live in the shacks to hang the wash there. Robert's reasoning, again, seems inappropriately legalistic. Yes, the mother could walk down to this place to hang her clothes; the poem doesn't specify "that [the girl] lives with her mother, or that [the mother] just goes to this wooden shack place to *hang* her clothes." But to Rose during the conference this seemed like a jurisprudential rather than a poetic reading. In the follow-up interview, however, Robert elaborated in a way that made Rose realize that Robert might have had a better imagistic case than his teacher first thought — for Rose missed the full visual particulars of the scene, did not see the importance of the "tractors grinding through the alkaline earth." Robert elaborates on "this place where . . . the eucalyptus trees block this wind." He describes this "little shack area where the clothes can dry without being bothered by the wind and dust . . . with all this . . . the tractor grinding through the earth. That brings up dust." Robert had pictured the surrounding landscape — machines stirring up grit and dust — and saw the necessity of trees to break the dust-laden wind so that wash could dry clean in the sun. The conventional reader could point out that such a windbreak would be necessary as well to protect residents, but given Robert's other interpretations, it makes sense, is coherent, to see the shacks — sheds of some kind perhaps or abandoned housing — as part of this eucalyptus-protected place where women hang the wash. What's important to note here is that Robert was able to visualize the scene — animate it, actually — in a way that Rose was not, for Rose was focusing on the dramatic significance of the shacks. Robert's reading may be unconventional and inappropriately jurisprudential, but it is coherent, and it allows us — in these lines — to animate the full landscape in a way that enhances our reading of the poem.

Conclusion

We hope we have demonstrated the logic and coherence of one student's unconventional reading. What we haven't addressed — and it could certainly now be raised — is the pedagogical wisdom of encouraging in a writing classroom the playing out of such unconventional readings. Reviewing the brief stretch of Rose's and Robert's discourse, we see how often teacher talk is qualified, challenged, and interrupted (though not harshly), and how rarely teacher expectations are fulfilled. If the teacher's goals are to run an efficient classroom, cover a set body of material, and convey certain conventional reading and writing strategies to students who are on the margin of the academic community, then all these conversational disjunctions are troubling.

What we would like to suggest, though, is that the laudable goal of facilitating underprepared students' entry into the academic community is actually compromised by a conversational pattern that channels students like Robert into a more "efficient" discourse. The desire for efficiency and coverage can cut short numerous possibilities for students to explore issues, articulate concerns, formulate and revise problems — all necessary for good writing to emerge — and can lead to conversational patterns that socialize students into a mode of interaction that will limit rather than enhance their participation in intellectual work.[3] We would further suggest that streamlined conversational patterns (like the Initiation-Comment-Response pattern described by Mehan) are often reinforced by a set of deficit-oriented assumptions about the linguistic and cognitive abilities of remedial students, assumptions that are much in need of examination (Hull et al.; Rose, *Lives*).

We would pose instead a pedagogical model that places knowledge-making at its center. The conversational techniques attending such a model are not necessarily that demanding — Robert benefits from simple expressions of encouragement, focusing, and reflecting back — but the difference in assumptions is profound: that the real stuff of belonging to an academic community is dynamic involvement in generating and questioning knowledge, that students desperately need immersion and encouragement to involve themselves in such activity, and that underprepared students are capable — given the right conditions — of engaging in such activity. We would also underscore the fact that Robert's reading (a) does bring to light the problem with the Sears catalogue and (b) animates the landscape as his teacher's reading did not do. Finally, we would suggest that engaging in a kind of "social-textual" reading of Robert's reading moves us toward deeper understanding of the social base of literary interpretation (cf. Salvatori, "Pedagogy").

In calling for a richer, more transactive model of classroom discourse, we want to acknowledge that such a model removes some of the control of teacher-centered instruction and can create moments of hesitance and uncertainty (as was the case with Rose through the first half of the transcript). But hesitancy and uncertainty — as we all know from our own intellectual struggles — are central to knowledge-making. Furthermore, we are not asking teachers to abandon structure, goals, and accountability. A good deal of engineering still goes on in the transactive classroom: the teacher focusing discussion, helping students better articulate their ideas, involving others, pointing out connections, keeping an eye on the clock. Even in conference, Rose's interaction with Robert is clearly goal-driven, thus Rose's reliance on focusing and reflecting back. Rose operates with a conventional reading in mind and begins moving toward it in 5a — and does so out loud to reveal to Robert the line of such reasoning. Robert's interpretation, though, will cause his teacher to modify his reading, and the teacher's presentation of his interpretation will help Robert acquire an additional approach to the poem. (In fact, the very tension between academic convention and student experience could then become the focus of discussion.) This, we think, is the way talk and thought should go when a student seems to falter, when readings seem a little off the mark.[4]

Notes

1. In stimulated recall, a student's writing is videotaped and, upon completion, replayed to cue recall of mental processes occurring during composing. For further discussion of the procedure and its advantages and limitations, see Rose, *Writer's Block*.
2. Frankly, we had trouble arriving at a way to designate the readings we're calling conventional and unconventional. And we're not satisfied yet. Certain of Robert's responses seem to be influenced by class (e.g., his reaction to the wooden shacks and Sears), and we note that, but with reluctance. We don't want to imply that class is the primary determiner of Robert's reading (vs., say, socialization into an English department — which, we realize, would correlate with class). We also don't want to imply that middle-class readers would, by virtue of class, automatically see things in a certain way, would have no trouble understanding particular images and allusions. One of the people who read this paper for us, Dennis Lynch, suggested that we use Wayne Booth's notion of "intended audience" — that Robert is simply not a member of the audience for whom the poem was written, thus he offers a reading that differs from the reading we're calling conventional. The notion of intended audience makes sense here, and fits with our discussion of socialization. Hongo, like most younger American poets, honed his craft in an English department and an MFA program, places where one's work is influenced by particular audiences — fellow poets, faculty, journal editors, etc. But, finally, we decided not to use the notion of intended audience, for it carries with it a theoretical framework we're not sure does Robert or Hongo full justice here. We use words like "conventional" and "middle-class," then, with reserve and invite our readers to help us think through this problem.
3. For two different but compatible perspectives on this claim see Shor; Tharp and Gallimore.
4. We would like to thank Linda Flower, Kay Fraser, Marisa Garrett, Jonathan Lovell, Dennis Lynch, Sandra Mano, Cheryl Pfoff, Mariolina Salvatori, Melanie Sperling, and Susan Thompson-Lowry for their comments on this paper. We benefited from a discussion at a meeting of the directors of the California Writing Project, and we would also like to acknowledge three anonymous *CCC* reviewers who gently guided us toward an understanding of the gaps and blunders in the essay. This work has been supported by grants from the McDonnell Foundation Program in Cognitive Studies for Educational Practice and the Research Foundation of the National Council of Teachers of English.

Works Cited

Bartholomae, David, and Anthony Petrosky, eds. *Facts, Counterfacts and Arti-facts: Theory and Method for a Reading and Writing Course.* Upper Montclair: Boynton, 1986.

Hongo, Garrett Kaoru. "And Your Soul Shall Dance." *Yellow Light*. Middletown: Wesleyan UP, 1982. 69.

Hull, Glynda, and Mike Rose. "Rethinking Remediation: Toward a Social-Cognitive Understanding of Problematic Reading and Writing." *Written Communication* 6 (Apr. 1989): 139–154.

Hull, Glynda, Mike Rose, Kay Losey Fraser, and Marisa Garrett. "The Social Construction of Remediation." The Tenth Annual Ethnography in Education Forum. Univ. of Pennsylvania, Feb. 1989.

Mehan, Hugh. *Learning Lessons*. Cambridge: Harvard UP, 1979.

Rose, Mike. *Lives on the Boundary: The Struggles and Achievements of America's Underprepared.* New York: Free Press, 1989.

———. *Writer's Block: The Cognitive Dimension.* Carbondale: Southern Illinois UP, 1984.

Salvatori, Mariolina. "Pedagogy: From the Periphery to the Center." *Reclaiming Pedagogy: The Rhetoric of the Classroom*. Ed. Patricia Donahue and Ellen Quandahl. Carbondale: Southern Illinois UP, 1989. 17–34.

———. "Reading and Writing a Text: Correlations between Reading and Writing Patterns." *College English* 45 (Nov. 1983): 657–666.

Shor, Ira. *Empowering Education: Critical Teaching for Social Change.* Chicago: Chicago UP, 1992.

Tharp, Roland G., and Ronald Gallimore. Rousing Minds to Life. New York: Oxford UP, 1989.

Classroom Activities

Hull and Rose ask readers to think critically about the class and cultural backgrounds of their students. Extend this inquiry by asking students to think critically about the class and cultural backgrounds of their audience for a specific writing task. Focusing on the audience will help them answer such questions as the following: What does my audience already know about this topic? What is the attitude of my audience toward this topic? What background information do I need to supply to help the audience to understand my point of view? Such an activity can help students frame their purposes more concisely; it can also serve as a journal entry or prewriting exercise.

Thinking about Teaching

Hull and Rose discuss how their interpretation of Garrett Hongo's poem is influenced by what they call a "conventional middle-class reading." It might be interesting to spend some time discussing what constitutes a conventional middle-class reader or writer. Such an activity could lead to a better understanding of how class differences may play out in the classroom. Recall, for example, an assignment that you presented in class that elicited a very different response from what you had expected, with varied responses among the students themselves. Perhaps differences in social class conventions or expectations account for the variety of interpretations, as Hull and Rose maintain. Discussing such incidents with other teachers may help you draw connections between classroom experiences and real life and could provide insights into teaching the processes of critical thinking and writing.

Collaborative Learning

M any of us have attempted to use collaborative learning strategies
in our classes and have been discouraged or dissatisfied with the
results. In the revision stage of the writing process, for example, students often seem afraid to critique their peers and are not willing to
trust other students to critique their writing, since they see this task
as belonging strictly to the teacher. Group members may fall off task or
have difficulty communicating with each other because of cultural or
other differences. Yet many teachers continue to revise their strategies
and expectations because they see the potential benefits: increased communication among students, better problem solving, and better critical
thinking skills. The selections in this chapter highlight the use of teamwork as part of a comprehensive plan for the writing classroom and
present two interesting experiments.

Richard Raymond writes about a collaborative learning community he helped create with teachers of Speech Communications and
Anthropology at the University of Arkansas-Little Rock. A class of entering first-year students took linked courses in these disciplines, as
well as Raymond's course in composition. Raymond documents the collaboration that took place as teachers and students came together as a
community of learners. Andrew Fleck provides a step-by-step collaborative learning activity for students faced with challenging reading
assignments. The examples Fleck uses to illustrate his classroom narrative will be helpful to those instructors interested in trying new approaches to collaborative learning.

Building Learning Communities on Nonresidential Campuses

Richard Raymond

Richard Raymond, Chair of the Department of Rhetoric and Writing at the University of Arkansas-Little Rock, won TETYC's nineteenth annual best article award for 1999. Readers will find a clearly written narrative of how three teachers at Raymond's institution created a successful learning community at a primarily nonresidential campus. In addition, Raymond offers pragmatic suggestions and assignments for fostering collaborative learning and critical thinking in the writing classroom — and for drawing connections among a linked, interdisciplinary series of three courses that his entering first-year students were required to take. With help from a university grant and support from the administration and from teachers of composition, speech communication, and anthropology, they all worked together inside and outside of the classroom to create an innovative collaborative learning environment for students. Raymond also includes entries from his teaching journal, comments from a student assessment of the program conducted outside the classroom, and an excerpt from a student paper in order to document the progress that students made throughout the semester.

Introduction

Over the last three decades, I have taught in a rural two-year college and in two urban universities; all three schools have been dormless or nearly so. In each of these institutions, I have worked with writing teachers who shared my dismay when we learned of a first- or second-year student transferring elsewhere, having found no community, no place to live and learn, no core as she accumulated credits in the "core." We grieved, too, over students lost not to other schools but to learning. Sometimes, these students dropped out; others stayed, writing just well enough to pass the state Regents' essay, but not well enough to connect ideas in and among other disciplines.

Over these same years, "learning communities" have emerged, with program designers and administrators hoping that clustered classes would shore up enrollment, the first concern described above. But they have claimed a more high-minded motive as well: to help students form a site where — through writing — they feel connected even as they connect what they learn. According to recent comprehensive studies of learning communities, promises of enduring friendships and enriched learning have been kept (Matthews et al.; Tinto, Goodsell-Love, and Russo). Major universities — including BYU, Wisconsin, Washington, UC Berkeley, and SUNY — have kept these promises with interdisciplinary explorations of a common theme such as "World Hunger." Four-year and two-year colleges, notably Evergreen State in Washington and La Guardia Community College in New York, have done likewise, "clustering" courses in composition, social science, and humanities around topics like "Work, Labor, and Business in American Life" (Matthews et al. 460). Assessment of these programs consistently confirms that students have found not only a place to stay but also a way to learn, constructing knowledge through reading and writing, listening and speaking (Matthews et al. 469).

In fall semester 1997, encouraged by this history of success, I joined two colleagues in starting a learning community at the University of Arkansas at Little Rock (UALR). Our community linked my section of Comp I with Carol Thompson's section of speech communication and Julie Flinn's section of cultural anthropology. Naturally, we hoped to help solve the retention problem at UALR, where fifty-nine percent of the first-year students never see a second year, having dropped out or having transferred to the cheaper Pulaski Technical College, to the residential, less urban University of Central Arkansas thirty miles away, or to the more fashionable University of Arkansas at Fayettville, the state system's flagship institution. We also wanted to help twenty-five students to connect these core courses by exploring themes of acculturation, the role of language in finding one's place.

In addition to the studies mentioned above, we found decades of literature on structuring learning communities to help us set up the thematically linked courses. However, we quickly saw an obstacle faced only by the nonresidential schools mentioned in the literature: lack of student residents. UALR, an urban university of some eleven thousand students, has just one five-story dormitory; most of the nonresident students, averaging twenty-seven years of age, work part- or full-time off campus. Such students — even the traditional eighteen-year-olds — come to campus for back-to-back classes and then leave for work. With this student profile, we could not promise the bonding that would come with living as a community in a dorm, nor could we promise regular student-faculty meals, a selling point in some programs.

Below I describe a solution to this problem, one that roots in demographics but that finds solutions in expressivist, cognitive, and social constructionist pedagogies (White 59). The narrative, I hope, will honestly expose the errors — strategic and pedagogical — as well as ground our feelings of success. I hope, too, that this story will encourage the many four- and two-year colleges whose non-residential campuses make learning communities seem improbable consider developing them.

This story begins with crucial preliminaries: letter-writing, securing the help of administrators and registrars, coordinating schedules, and linking syllabi thematically. Moving then to the teaching of the community, the narrative relates first-day activities, the linking of assignments and communal learning, then discusses assessment.

Preliminaries

Julie, Carol, and I wanted to see if a learning community could help average students connect core curriculum courses and, in so doing, help them find their place as learners. Therefore, in collaboration with the dean, we decided to aim the promotional letter at *all* entering first-year students eligible for Composition 1, that is, those who had scored a quite modest 19 or higher on the ACT, a pool of some seven hundred students. The letter stressed communal learning, even though we had no dormitory and regular meals to offer (see Appendix A).

Stressing connected, communal learning, the letter apparently addressed a need that both students and parents recognized. Within five working days, we had accepted thirty students, begun a waiting list, and mailed a follow-up letter inviting the students to one of the advising and registration sessions.

Prior to mailing the letters, we three teachers met twice with Dr. Thea Hoeft, Director of Undergraduate Advisement, deans, the head registrar, and the vice-chancellor for student activities, all of whom we needed to make the community happen:

- The vice-chancellor, head of UALR's First-Year Experience program, promoted the learning community in his oral and written recruiting efforts.

- The registrar approved listing the three courses as "restricted" to ensure that we would have only volunteers in the community. He also approved cross-listings in the university course schedule, including a "comment line" instructing the students to call any of the three instructors for further information.

- The dean of the College of Arts, Humanities, and Social Sciences, Deborah Baldwin, agreed to pay for mailing the letters and to receive all the response cards. She also has taken every opportunity to promote this and subsequent learning communities before the college faculty.

- Thea Hoeft gave up five hours of her time to conduct the two advisement sessions.

Such collaboration between faculty and administrators builds a professional community that doesn't exist on every campus; more to the point here, this teamwork proved critical to starting and sustaining the learning community.

We also received help from the associate vice-chancellor, whose committee on curriculum development grants approved our proposal for financial support. The grant provided each teacher $1,950 as compensation for developing the courses over the summer. We also happily accepted an additional $400 to pay for assessment materials and for food we would share with the students on the first day and during assessment sessions (see discussion below).

As each teacher developed a syllabus over the summer, we met three times — twice over coffee, once over lunch — to find and synchronize the thematic links, a process made possible by reading each other's texts. Eventually, we settled on the following interrelated anthropological themes, each taken up at approximately the same time in each class:

- Coming into a Culture,
- Making Words and Making a Living,
- Gender and Marriage,
- Social Ranking and Stratification, and
- Government, Religion, and Justice.

Using Jack Selzer's thematic reader *Conversations* in a Comp I class, I easily found selections that would help the students explore the concepts they were learning in anthropology.[1] While they learned about ethnocentrism in anthropology, for example, the students read Alice Walker's "Everyday Use" in Comp I to find distinctions between ethnocentrism and legitimate racial pride. Similarly, the students read and discussed Sizer's "Horace's Compromise" to understand the difference between teaching that produces conformists and teaching that acculturates thinkers. They explored Rodriguez's "Aria" and Darrow's "Address to the Prisoners" to contemplate the causes of exclusion from cultures, Glaspell's "Trifles" to learn what happens when marriage stifles individualism, Orwell's "A Hanging" and Koch's "Death and Justice" to understand the causes and effects of capital punishment, and King's "Birmingham Jail" to see the roles of government and churches in making justice a dream deferred.

Speaking, Reading, and Writing in the Learning Community

With the syllabi thematically linked, we teachers met one more time to plan strategy for the first day of class. Wanting to assess the learning that occurred in the community, we thought of devoting the first session to an in-class essay on a "Doonesbury" cartoon depicting a jaded lecturer and his mindless students (Selzer 95). We would then ask for another essay on this same cartoon on the last day, hoping to see not only better writing but also better understanding of the traditional classroom as a potentially destructive site of acculturation.

The need for assessment data notwithstanding, we quickly realized the deadening effect of such an opener, one that would intimidate most students and do nothing to establish community. We therefore moved the "Doonesbury" essay to a first homework assignment (see discussion of assessment below), focusing instead on community-building activities. First, we decided that all three teachers as well as the assessment expert, Dr. Kathy Franklin, should attend my 8:00 A.M. composition class, where we would reintroduce ourselves as their learning community teachers — we had already met at the advisement sessions mentioned above — and invite the students to enjoy the donuts and coffee provided by the grant budget.

Wanting learning as well as pastries to characterize the first day, we also borrowed a "birth order" workshop from the National Writing Project to stimulate thought on the influence of early discourse communities in shaping the ways we learn and interact. Appendix B displays the guidelines we distributed to move from pleasantries to active learning for all the Older Children, Middle Kids, Babies, and Onlies in the class.

As each student stood by his or her birth order poster and reported the group's findings, predictably celebrating the group's virtues — leadership, flexibility, patience — while playfully demonizing the Other, the Bossy Big Sisters, the Spoiled Little Brothers, we quickly saw the value of this one-hour workshop.

- First, we had broken the ice, with instructors participating in the appropriate birth order group, underscoring implicitly the idea of students and teachers as peers in learning.

- We also moved from conversation to writing (posters), then to public speaking and listening, modeling thereby the interconnectedness of speech and composition.

- We introduced the role of family in acculturating students, a central theme in the anthropology class.

- We bonded with laughter, a far stronger glue than donuts when it comes to holding communities together.

Having bonded on day one, we devoted the next two weeks to readings and writings on families and education to explore further the anthropological theme of "coming into a culture" (header in Comp I syllabus, weekly schedule). To help the students read anthropologically, I first assigned Alice Walker's story "Everyday Use" and asked them to answer the questions in Figure 1 in their journal.

Questions one through six introduced the students to close reading and helped them understand the term "ethnocentrism," the first word they would learn in anthropology; question seven helped them to understand journaling as a reflective process, a way of moving from "what happened?" to "what does the text mean?" At the same time, answering these questions prepared the students for class discussion and for writing their first papers on one of the ethnocentrism topics in Appendix C.

While the essay assignment does restrict students to the "conversation" started by Walker — thereby fostering responsible reading — it also encourages the students to find their own topics (Murray; Graves). In addition, the assignment allows students to interpret Walker's text in anthropological terms or to respond to her story with an anthropological story of their own.

Figure 1. Questions on Walker's "Everyday Use"

Walker, "Everyday Use," pp. 74–82

1. In paragraphs 1–6, what actions and details reveal the narrator's (mother's) view of Dee?

2. How has the fire (2, 10) affected Maggie's personality?

3. How does Dee's education affect her view and her treatment of her mother and her sister Maggie (11, 22, 25–27, 36)? What is the nature of her **ethnocentrism?**

4. Why does Dee want the churn top and the quilts (53, 66)?

5. Why does the mother return the quilts to Maggie?

6. Find five similes (or metaphors) in the narrative and explain what each comparison reveals about the character described.

7. What inference can you draw from this narrative that will answer the question at the top of p. 74, "What's college for?"

Reinforcing the concept of community, I scheduled a writing group day, when each student shared her first draft with two peers, who then responded orally and in writing, using guidelines I provided. After this community-building experience, the students conferred individually with me, then revised their papers and submitted the draft and the revision. Having received my written responses to the second draft, the students revised a second time, then submitted the piece again for further comment and a grade (see discussion below on further revision in portfolio assignment). Then to underscore the *ongoing* nature of dialogue in any learning community, I scheduled a reading day, when four volunteers read their papers to the whole class and invited responses.

During the two-and-a-half-week period devoted to the writing of this paper in response to Walker, the students continued their reading and journaling on the anthropological theme of "coming into a culture." Focusing now on nonfiction pieces — Gardner's "A Nation at Risk," Rich's "Claiming an Education," and others — students examined the roles of schools and teachers in effecting — or stifling — healthy acculturation.

Moving next to a related theme concurrently studied in the anthropology class, "making words and making a living," the students continued these same rhythms of study — reading, journaling, discussing — exploring such pieces as Smitherman's "White English in Blackface, or Who Do I Be?" and Rodriguez's "Aria: a Memoir of a Bilingual Childhood." Such work led to a second essay (Appendix D), one asking students to narrate their experiences being brought into their cultures by teachers.

Having moved through the drafting-responding-revising process on this assignment, I held a second communal reading day, then broke new anthropological ground with the themes "gender and marriage" and "social ranking and stratification," featuring not only Glaspell's "Trifles," as mentioned above, but also Steele's "A Negative Vote on Affirmative Action" and Wilkins's "Racism Has Its Privileges."

To help students probe more deeply into the connection between these readings and the textbook material in anthropology, all three teachers periodically asked students to write in class in their reflective journals (a journal separate from the one they kept for Comp I), noting points of anger, confusion, or enthusiasm as they learned of placement and displacement in cultures, both American and Other. Also, Kathy Franklin, the assessment expert, began meeting with a student focus group. Having lured volunteers with pizza (paid for by the grant) to meet with her outside of class, Kathy asked them to practice the collaborative techniques they learned in speech to examine their experiences — negative as well as positive — learning in a community. They spoke of teachers allowing too little time for journaling, of students having no time to meet as study groups outside of class, of peers who seem unprepared for response sessions, of students and teachers who talk too much; they also admitted — now — to seeing their peers as friends, their teachers as fellow learners, and the classroom far less stratified than those they had experienced in high school or in college.

Having received this midterm assessment from Dr. Franklin, we resolved to allow more writing/reflecting time in class and to draw out the less talkative students by inviting them to read from their journals. We also resolved to bite our lips more often, sharing our views as community members but not dominating any conversation. Though duly chastened by the students' negative remarks, we teachers enjoyed hearing that the students shared our perception of a growing community that had learned how to learn.

Buoyed by a shared sense of community, we continued reading, talking, and writing, focusing now on the themes that would round out the students' course in cultural anthropology: "Government, Religion, and Justice." In addition to the pieces by Orwell, Koch, and Dr. King noted above, we read Weisberg's "This Is Your Death." The students journaled as always to monitor their responses to these controversial texts; in so doing, they also prepared for class, where I asked them to mediate arguments on crime and punishment, on order and justice. These discussions, usually quite lively, generated healthy peer exchanges over drafts and mainly successful essays.

In helping the students find their topics, I did not require them to confront an adversary, to strike the militant Aristotelian stance of one who seeks to vanquish a foe rather than to build community (Lamb). Instead, I asked them to enter an ongoing conversation, using the text — whether the fictional text of Glaspell, the nonfiction texts of Steele, Koch, or King, or the "text" of the learning community — to present readings designed to keep readers talking, encouraging healthy dissensus as well as mediated consensus (Bruffee; Trimbur).

As the end of the semester approached, I wanted to give the students a chance to position themselves as individuals within the community. To facilitate this finding of place, I asked each student to focus on a text(s) and a conversation she or he had found most compelling. Appendix E shows this invitation to critical analysis.

The first topic invited students to respond to an ethnographic text read in anthropology, either the exotic story of Eskimo life recorded in *Never in Anger* or the story of RVing in America, *Over the Next Hill*. The second topic encouraged students to return to a conversation in Comp I, choosing a text worthy of response and of rhetorical analysis; the third offered the same encouragement but took students beyond the texts we had read in the community. Whatever the student's choice, each wrote on the nature of living in communities and the challenge of doing so as an individual, as one voice responding to many voices.

Assessing the Nonresidential Learning Community

Naturally, we will need to accumulate years of data to show conclusively that the learning communities have performed as well as their predecessors on other campuses in achieving the two objectives: to retain students and to improve learning. However, we have been encouraged by the early results, as generated by the following instruments of assessment (Franklin):

- Pretest: The "Doonesbury" essay, given as the first night's homework, showed some understanding of learning theory and the potentially stupefying effect of lecturing. However, nearly all the essays lacked development, offering little or no textual support for the inferences drawn. I returned the papers, with comments but no grade, and asked the students to file them in their journals. They did so and promptly forgot the exercise.

- Posttest: We asked the students to write about the same cartoon again, this time as a final exam, counting ten percent of the grade in Comp I. Many complained loudly, a reaction I anticipated, given their weariness by the end of the semester. Their objections notwithstanding, I stuck with the requirement, not wanting to sabotage the assessment plan. In addition, I saw the analysis of the cartoon as a way to see what they had learned about its imbedded anthropological themes. Of course, in assessing the results, we factored in their low motivation on the pretest (no grade) and the high motivation on the posttest (grade). Nevertheless, we were pleased by the papers: they showed more sophisticated understanding of the cartoon as an example of misacculturation; also, unlike the pretests, all but two of the essays showed facility in using examples to support generalizations.

- Attitude Survey: This lengthy questionnaire, prepared by Dr. Franklin, provided qualitative data suggesting that students generally endorse the idea of learning communities. However, they more frequently praised the linked courses for increasing their number of friends rather than for helping them learn anthropology, failing to see the connection between the "fun, comfortable environment" of the community and the depth and range of their learning. Predictably, too, some said that "learning community" means "more work, less credit."

- Focus Group: This group of eight students echoed the voices in the survey, praising the "comfort," the new friendships, wishing for more time to meet outside of class, objecting to having to do "more work" than other first-year students do in unlinked classes. As mentioned above, they also complained of too little time for journal writing in class and of too much teacher talk. Having purged these complaints, they recognized, too, the connectedness of writing and speaking as ways to learn anthropology; consequently, they hoped to take more linked courses at higher levels in and beyond the core curriculum.

- Portfolio: The students' sense of "belonging" to the learning community — and the learning generated, at least in part, by that sense of connectedness — were born out in most of the portfolios. Determining forty percent of the course grade in Comp I, the portfolio included a piece from Comp I, from speech (an outline or text of a speech), and from cultural anthropology; it also included an artifact symbolizing their work in the learning community (or their life in the family), their reflective journal (not graded, just required), and the metacognitive cover essay.

- Grades on the Portfolio: Seven of the students earned an *A* on the portfolio, twelve a *B*, three a *C*, one a *D*. No one received an *F*. These high grades resulted primarily from cover essays that showed the metacognitive ability to analyze the strengths and weaknesses of a piece of writing and to place each piece in a larger picture of struggle and growth.

- Faculty Reflective Journals: All three faculty kept a reflective journal, as did the students. For both students and teachers, the reflective journal provided a place to complain without fear of penalty of too little time, of annoying or uncooperative peers, of having to meet unrealistic expectations. More important, this journal also invited a healthy looking back, attempting to see where and how learning happened or collapsed.

To provide admittedly selective evidence of these claims of partial success, I share some remarks from my reflective journal, then move to a sample of student writing strong enough — particularly in contrast to writing in recent unlinked writing classes — to motivate me to try the learning community again.

Reflective Journal Entries

September 18

Before class begins each day, the students grow ever more rowdy. I complimented them today for their noise: they seem comfortable with one another, joking as well as talking — quite a contrast to the beginning of the semester.

September 25

Class got off to a rocky start today; sleepy faces, no show of interest. But Heather Rainey read from her thoughtful journal; her remarks challenging Darrow's view of the causes of crime led to some rich discussion, some honest talk about access to the American Dream.

December 9

Just finished reading the portfolios. I'm pleased. After all their stewing about artifacts, they came through with photos of family members, pictures of the tools of our community, ritual necklaces made in anthropology. My favorite portfolio is that of Sarah Martin. Using her photographic skills, she composed a 9"x12" portrait of the ethnographies, The Easy Access Handbook, a CD, and owl candles — all really quite striking. Sarah's cover piece offers sophisticated reflection on her growth as writer and learner. While Sarah's cover piece may be the best, it is not atypical. As far as I'm concerned, these portfolios tell us what we need to know to assess the educational value of learning communities. The case of Zhang Bing-wen confirms this view. In the beginning, Zhang, as Asian student, begged to drop the LC. He just knew he would fail anthropology and lose "face" at school and at home. His older sister phoned me to beg for his release. Instead of granting their request, I urged Zhang to give us three teachers a chance; I also referred him to Carol and Julie, invoking our "talk first" policy. It worked. He stayed, earned a *B* on the first anthro test. With his head no longer bowed in silence, he went on to become one of the most talkative students in the class. He earned a *B* in Comp and *B*s in the other courses as well. In short, he learned and we retained him!

Excerpt from Student Writing

This excerpt comes from a student who early in the course confessed her American ethnocentrism. In this passage, written near the end of the semester, she expresses tolerance, even appreciation, for the Other, suggesting that she has achieved an objective of the community: to value difference:

From a Comp I essay on the anthropological ethnography, *Never In Anger*: [The Utku Eskimos] show a great amount of affection to a child before he or she acquires *ihmuma,* reason. . . . *Ihuma* is developing when a child begins to respond to the social world, to recognize people . . . to understand and talk . . . to participate in useful social games . . . used to tease the child into doing what is right. In America, we have do's and don'ts for our children, but the Utku just wait for the child to conform. One example occurs when Saarak had to quit nursing from her mother because a new baby was born. Saarak screamed and slapped at her mother and sister, but Saarak's mother only said, "Don't hurt her" . . . Many Americans believe the best way to get a child to conform to society is by using strict discipline. The Utku culture has showed, however, that a child without discipline can decide his or her own progress without spoiling society.

— Heather Rainey,
"The Utka Acculturation"

Impressions

While we lack sufficient data to make any conclusive claims about the value of learning communities on a primarily nonresidential campus, I can describe two strong impressions shared by me and my two colleagues, as well as by Dr. Franklin, the assessment chief.

- Having spent hours together in designing and teaching the linked courses, we teachers have transformed ourselves from professional acquaintances to professional friends. Clearly, we should expect our students to experience the hollowness of the curricular core if we work in isolation from our colleagues across campus. A fragmented faculty will almost certainly teach a fragmented curriculum.

- Most first-year students can write and think metacognitively in thematically linked courses.

Two-thirds of the students shared these impressions, valuing their deeper capacities for independent thought as well as their new friends. The following comment from a student's reflective journal speaks for many in the group:

The connections of these courses taught me not only the use of the skills, but also how to use those skills to connect smaller things in my life to form a larger picture, a broader spectrum, of what the world actually looks like. . . . [The teachers have] taught me to take off my ethnocentric lenses and to look at the world in a new light.

Such sentiments bode well for using learning communities not only to facilitate this connected learning but also to retain students. Though five withdrew before the semester began, the result of conflicts with work or family responsibilities, only one student dropped the learning community after it had formed. Typically, core composition classes lose at least five students over the course of the semester.

Teaching in this learning community has also convinced me that we can overcome the inherent obstacles to linked courses on nonresidential campuses. True, we have far less time to meet, eat, and talk outside of class, compared to that time available on residential campuses. But we knit the students together by relying on social constructionist theory in all three classes, using small group work to interpret texts and to respond to writers, collaborating in the making of community knowledge. We also encouraged the students to develop and heed individual voices in the community. We did so by using the reader-response journal as a cognitive prewriting activity; by encouraging expressivist writing — freewrites, narratives — and by holding reading days that celebrate individual voices.

Last fall I taught a Comp I linked to courses in ethics and in personal awareness — the newest learning community. This spring, my colleagues offered communities linking Comp II with ethics and religious world views, Comp I with earth science, and Comp II with Civilization II. As other ideas for linkages percolate across campus, we have begun to see the campus's single dorm as the reason why we must build learning communities, not as the reason why we can't.

Appendix A

Invitation Letter

Dear _____:

Congratulations on your admission to UALR! We're looking forward to your studying here with us. We're also eager to help you make those choices that will shape your life — socially, academically, and professionally — during and after your years at UALR.

With this letter, we invite you to make that first choice: to consider enrolling in our **Learning Community,** a new program for eligible first-year students. And you're eligible!

Here's how the Learning Community works: You will enroll in a "block" of **three core courses: Rhetoric 1311.19, Composition I,** 8:00–9:15, Tuesday and Thursday; **Speech Communication 1300.17,** 9:25–10:40, Tuesday and Thursday; **Cultural Anthropology 2316.02,** 10:50–12:05, Tuesday and Thursday.

Consider the advantages of enrolling in this block of back-to-back courses:

- Preferred Scheduling: You'll be first to register. Also you'll have Tuesday and Thursday afternoons free for study, for part-time work on or off campus, or for other courses.

- Study Groups: You'll be part of a Community of Learners studying and working together in all three courses. Such support from trusted peers will help you do well in these three courses and foster habits of collaborative learning that will carry you far in your academic and professional lives. And study partners often become good friends!

- Making Connections: You will reinforce your learning by connecting each class to the other two. For example, some of your compositions and speeches will ask you to respond to readings from cultural anthropology. In turn, your anthropology class will give you further practice in writing and speaking as means of learning the material.

Please let us know if you're interested in joining our Learning Community by returning the enclosed card. We will select twenty-five students, filling the slots as we receive the cards, so please don't delay!

After we have chosen our Community members, we will invite you to campus to get acquainted and to complete your academic advisement for fall semester. We look forward to hearing from you!

Dr. Juliana Flinn, Professor of Anthropology
Dr. Carol Thompson, Associate Professor of Speech
Dr. Rich Raymond, Professor of Rhetoric and Writing

Appendix B

Collaborative Learning Task: Birth Order

Directions:

1. Pull your chairs together with others of your birth order group.

2. Appoint a person to read through the task before you go any further.

3. Agree on another person to record the views expressed by the group and the decisions the group makes collectively.

4. Choose a person to speak for the group.

5. Read and discuss the following questions:

   a. How did your position in the family affect your behavior in the family?

   b. How might that family history affect your behavior in a group within the learning community?

6. Review the recorder's notes to see that they accurately express the views of the group. List your findings on the poster paper provided; tape your paper to the wall.

Source: Pat Fox and the Coastal Georgia Writing Project; the Little Rock Writing Project.

Appendix C

Essay Assignment on "Ethnocentrism"

First Essay: Ethnocentrism

Please write an essay on one of the following topics. Be sure that your paper presents a **thesis** that addresses your **purpose** and your **audience**. Because you must present **examples and explanations** to support your thesis, your essay will probably be 2–3 pages long (double-spaced, 12 point type). Your final draft, **due Tuesday, September 2,** must be word processed. I will return your essay on Thursday, September 4; the **revision** will be due on **September 9.**

1. Use Wangeroo Leewanike (Dee) in Walker's story: "Everyday Use," to illustrate the meaning of "ethnocentrism." *Audience:* Parents or friends who have heard you use the term "ethnocentrism" but aren't sure what you mean. *Purpose:* to make sure that your audience understands the difference between healthy ethnic pride and ethnocentrism.

2. Describe two or three artifacts cherished by your family. *Audience:* Members of your learning community. *Purpose:* to explain the "everyday use" of each artifact (it need not be valuable in monetary terms) and the reasons for cherishing each object.

3. Devise your own topic in response to Walker's story. You might focus on brother/sister rivalries as students, or on the role of parents as teachers, or on your reasons for attending college. *Audience:* Members of your writing group and, potentially, the whole class. *Purpose:* to introduce yourself as an individual shaped as a learner by your experience as a family member.

Appendix D

Narrative Assignment

Your essay should explore at least three episodes in your life in which a teacher or teachers have shaped your attitudes toward learning, toward formal education, and toward your local, state, or national culture. Your essay should reach a conclusion on what conditions foster — and stifle — your sense of place, of belonging in American culture.

Appendix E

Critical Analysis

For your fourth assignment, please compose a critical essay on a text or texts that have some anthropological significance. The word "critical" does not mean "to find fault"; rather, it means to analyze and interpret your chosen text(s).

Suggested Topics

1. Focusing on *Never in Anger* or on *Over the Next Hill,* discuss one of the author's conclusions about the subculture examined in the ethnography. The possibilities are endless: sources of entertainment, distribution of

work, gender roles, attitudes toward the Other (outsiders, dominant culture), methods of subsistence, language, contributions to dominant culture. Audience: Members of the learning community for spring semester, all of whom dread having to read an ethnography.

2. The title of your reader, *Conversations,* implies that reading and writing involve an **exchange,** a "conversation" between writer and reader. Focusing on one of the essays (five pages or longer) that we have read, discuss the **techniques** the author uses to draw us into the conversation on the anthropological issue at hand (education and acculturation, gender roles, ethnocentricity, capital punishment, social justice, and the roles of church and state). Your essay should explain to what extent the author made you respond, lured you into conversation. Your **audience** doubts that any "freshman reader" is worth the paper it's printed on.

3. Design your own topic. *Guidelines:* Your topic must relate to one of the anthropological themes printed in your Comp I syllabus. Your paper must also respond to a "text" — a book, a novel, an essay, a film. You must aim your paper at a particular audience, people who need to hear what you have to say.

Note

1. For a copy of the Comp I syllabus — and any other pedagogical or assessment tool mentioned in this article — send an e-mail message to rcraymond@ualr.edu.

Works Cited

Bruffee, Kenneth. "Collaborative Learning and the 'Conversation of Mankind.'" Villanueva 393–414.

Franklin, Kathy K. "Making Connections: Evaluation of the 1997 Learning Community Pilot." Univ. of Arkansas at Little Rock, July 10, 1998.

Graves, Richard L. "What I Learned from Verle Barnes: The Exploratory Self in Writing." *Rhetoric and Composition: A Sourcebook for Teachers and Writers.* 3rd ed. Ed. Richard L. Graves. Portsmouth: Heinemann, 1990. 132–136.

Lamb, Catherine E. "Beyond Argument in Feminist Composition." *College Composition and Communication* 42(1991): 11–24.

Matthews, Roberta S., Barbara Leigh Smith, Jean MacGregor, and Faith Babelnick. "Creating Learning Communities." *Handbook of the Undergraduate Curriculum.* Ed. J. G. Gaff and J. L. Ratcliff. San Francisco: Jossey, 1997. 457–475.

Murray, Donald. "Teach Writing as a Process Not Product." Villanueva 3–6.

Selzer, Jack. *Conversations.* 3rd ed. New York: St. Martin's, 1997.

Tinto, Vincent, Anne Goodsell-Love, and Pat Russo. "Freshman Interest Groups and the First-Year Experience: Constructing Student Communities in a Large University." *Journal of the Freshman Year Experience* 6.1 (1994): 7–28.

Trimbur, John. "Consensus and Difference in Collaborative Learning." Villanueva 439–456.

White, Charles R. "Placing Community-Building at the Center of the Curriculum." *Metropolitan Universities:An International Forum*. Baltimore:Towson U, 1998. 55–62.

Villanueva, Victor. ed. *Cross-Talk in Comp Theory:A Reader*. Urbana: NCTE, 1997.

Classroom Activities

In Appendix B, Raymond provides a collaborative learning task on birth order (from Pat Fox and the Georgia Coastal Writing Project and the Little Rock Writing Project) that was used as a first-day icebreaker for students in the composition course and was a key element of the collaborative learning community. An important purpose of this activity was to build community in the classroom from the very beginning as students divided themselves into groups and followed a set of directions based on birth order ("Older Children, Middle Kids, Babies, and Onlies"). Teachers also participated in this activity, "underscoring implicitly the idea of students and teachers as peers in student learning." Consider participating in this collaborative learning task with your own students, either as a first-day exercise or later in the term when the class may need support and continued focus in the benefits of creating a learning community. You may want to give more emphasis to writing by changing steps 5a and 5b to include an in-class writing component that students can then read aloud to other members of their group. Another way to build writing into this task would be to assign students to write a journal entry or short summary that evaluates the success of this collaborative learning task on birth order.

Thinking about Teaching

Although the learning community that Raymond helped to build was designed for students who were eligible for first-year composition, successful learning communities have also been created for students in developmental studies. To find out more about how these collaborative learning groups work at other colleges and universities, consult an Internet search engine such as [www.google.com] and do a search using the term *learning communities*. You will then have access to several web pages that describe learning communities for colleges and universities that serve a variety of populations, including "virtual" learning communities located on the World Wide Web. From this selection, and from the details included in Raymond's article, you can begin to create your own idea of what a learning community for developmental learners might look like at your own institution. Consult with other teachers across disciplines to discern interest, and share your thoughts with administrators.

Instructional Note: "We think he means . . .": Creating Working Definitions through Small-Group Discussion

Andrew Fleck

In a course with an "organizing theme" of "The Arts of the Contact Zone," Andrew Fleck asked students to read difficult essays by such writers as Mary Louise Pratt (whose essay title provides the name for the course theme) and Stephen Greenblatt. What Fleck discovered was that, although students were interested in reading these essays, they had difficulties with reading comprehension. Perhaps the most tangible problem was that students had a hard time defining complex terms presented in the text. Rather than lecturing students on his own interpretations, Fleck set students to work in small groups to figure out the definitions of difficult terms. Collaborating as readers and critical thinkers, the students arrived at working definitions, which were then compared to operational definitions used in the text. Fleck found that this activity worked well for his students, and he believes that "using small-group discussion to develop working definitions should succeed in most discussion-oriented courses" because "in small peer groups, students are more inclined to ask questions and help each other clarify their thinking." Andrew Fleck writes this instructional note as a teacher of composition at Mt. San Antonio College in Walnut, California.

Introduction

Occasionally I switch textbooks, searching for one that will draw the students into discussion about significant issues that interest them. Recently, I began using the composition reader by David Bartholomae and Anthony Petrosky, *Ways of Reading*. I was excited to find a text that would bring together complex essays in new and interesting ways. On the first day of the term, I told the students that they would find the readings challenging but manageable.

After a few weeks of uneven classroom discussion, however, I needed a way to involve more students in the discovery of knowledge that I had hoped would occur in the course. Implementing small-group discussion and what I called "small-group definitions" dramatically changed the classroom dynamic and involved more students in the discovery process. This form of group work should be useful whenever the course objectives are to challenge students to understand complex ideas and to use those concepts in their writing.

The Problem: Fragmented Understanding

The organizing theme for the course was "The Arts of the Contact Zone," and the readings included a series of essays that built on the ideas in Mary Louise Pratt's essay of that name. The students read Pratt's essay and several others that considered issues of cross-cultural contact and composed several essays on subjects related to their readings. I hoped the students in this culturally diverse classroom would find the issues relevant and important enough that a mastery of the ideas would allow them to feel that they had a stake in the larger academic community. As the course began, I explained that the first few discussions would help us understand Pratt's term "contact zone," a term important for reading the essays that would follow.

During discussion, initial student response to Pratt's essay was mixed. Some students enthusiastically embraced the challenges of this complex essay. They seemed energized by the difficulties of interpretation posed by the text. Others, however, were not sure how to understand the essay. They found the structure of the academic writing daunting and did not grasp the author's development of her ideas about the "contact zone." As a result, I had to intervene in the discussion in order to lead students to an understanding of the essay's ideas. Eventually some students appeared to have only partially understood Pratt's concept, around which much of the rest of the course would revolve. In their essays, some students had difficulty making use of Pratt's idea and could not effectively articulate their understanding of it. Frustrated with these initial results and recognizing that I had not helped the students come to an understanding of their own, I sought a way to improve the quality of both classroom discussion and, I hoped, student comprehension.

A Solution: Small Groups and Working Definitions

The solution the students and I implemented relied on work in small groups. The next essay students read for discussion was a chapter from Stephen Greenblatt's *Marvelous Possessions*. Before the students began to read their assignment, I told them that two important terms, "form" and "discourse," would be repeated throughout Greenblatt's essay. I asked them to read the essay twice: once to discover the general sense of the essay, and a second time with careful attention to Greenblatt's use of these two terms as well as related words such as "formalism" and "discursive." I asked them to use their reading-response journals to keep track of the occurrence of these two words: on one page, they were to write out each clause in which Greenblatt used one of the terms and similarly note each use of the second term on another sheet. Some of the students who had had difficulty with the previous essay seemed relieved to have specific suggestions for approaching the upcoming assignment.

When students next came to class for discussion, I asked them to join in a group with three or four other students. With twenty-eight students in the class, we ended up with seven groups of three to five students each. I then asked each group to choose one of the two terms and develop a working definition for it. I explained that although they might wish to start by looking for a definition in their college dictionaries, their definition would not necessarily coincide with those they would find in a dictionary. Instead, the definition they were to establish as a group should explain Greenblatt's meaning when he used the term. With the lists they had made before class, they would be able to identify places where Greenblatt had made frequent use of the term and might begin their group discussions by closely examining those parts of the essay. I also suggested that the term might be used in a number of ways and that their objective should be to provide a definition that would operate in a particular part of the text, rather than a vague definition that might only superficially account for Greenblatt's general meaning. Finally, I reminded the class that this was not a competitive exercise. I suggested that with a clear understanding of Greenblatt's terms they would be able to write better essays, and that they should use this smaller forum as a way to begin clarifying their understanding of these concepts. I asked the groups to write down the definition they agreed upon, and then I left them to their own devices for the rest of the class period.

The Rationale: Establishing Learning Communities

The use of small groups to enhance comprehension and application of concepts has been extensively researched and supported. Wells, Chang, and Maher have recently studied the process of discovering and refining ideas through group discussion which

> can thus provide a forum in which individuals calibrate their representations of events and states of affairs against those of other people, and realign and extend their existing mental models to assimilate or accommodate to new or alternative information. In this way, knowledge, although residing in individuals, can be exposed to social modification and undergo change and revision (97).

In small groups, each student brings his or her ideas into contact with others' understanding and can modify and clarify those ideas through discussion with other students. By working in groups, as Cohen has shown, students can assist each other to reach "concept attainment" (10) by reacting to each other and explaining themselves, allowing teachers to offer more challenging concepts rather than having to oversimplify ideas to reach students who are having the most difficulty (19). If the teacher and students succeed in creating a nonthreatening, noncompetitive environment, a "community of discourse" (Brown and Campione 236), students will feel more comfortable trying out new ideas. I hoped that by giving the students a direction for their discussion while allowing them to decide how to define their objectives — what Wells, Chang, and Maher might call "goal-oriented engagement with new information" (118) — would help them to read academic texts with more engagement and confidence and relate their understanding to the central themes of the course.

Results: Comprehension, Application, and Involvement

As the groups began their discussions, I sat near the classroom's white board and skimmed through the text so that students would be free to discuss their ideas without worrying that I was judging their performance. Nevertheless, I could still discretely observe events in the groups. Whereas about a quarter of the students had never spoken up in class before, most students participated in their group's definition process. Several students asked others for clarification of Greenblatt's text and received helpful explanation from their peers. In the end, only a few students remained quiet during the class period.

Near the end of the class meeting, I asked each group to report to the class on their working definitions. Five groups had defined "discourse," and two had grappled with "form." As a spokesperson for each group read the new definition aloud, I wrote it on the white board without commenting, and then I asked the student to identify page numbers or passages where that meaning appeared to operate. I noticed that several students wrote down other groups' definitions, and I encouraged everyone to consider the differences between the provisional meanings the groups had given to the terms. I then asked the students to reread Greenblatt's essay, keeping these definitions in mind, before the next class meeting.

The results of this exercise were generally positive. At the beginning of the next class, I again wrote on the white board the "working definitions" and the page numbers where each one was supposed to have meaning. I began the day's discussion by asking the class to consider one group's definition of "discourse" in relation to the text: did it appear to operate in other parts of the essay? Both students from the group that had offered the definition and many students from outside that group participated in the discussion. Without my prompting, many students from other groups directed questions to those who had developed the definition, furthering the process of group discovery as the members of the first group began to explain, defend, and clarify their meaning. Students were generally more engaged in the discussion than previously, and by moving through each of the group definitions, first of "discourse" and then of "form," the discussion continued over several class periods. When students wrote their next essays, many students made sophisticated use of Greenblatt's terms and appeared to be able to articulate their own grasp of Greenblatt's concepts. They appeared to be pleased with their success and eagerly participated in similar activities with the rest of the quarter's reading assignments.

Using small-group discussion to develop working definitions should succeed in most discussion-oriented courses. Asking students to work in small, nonthreatening groups to arrive at a provisional understanding of an important concept liberates them from the anxiety of speaking out in front of a class or directly to the instructor. In small peer groups, students are more inclined to ask questions and help each other clarify their thinking. After working in small groups, students are prepared to engage in more complex discussion of texts. Perhaps because students are responsible for creating their definitions, they retain and can apply their understanding of these concepts in more sophisticated ways.

Works Cited

Bartholomae, David, and Anthony Petrosky, eds. *Ways of Reading: An Anthology for Writers*. 4th ed. Boston: Bedford, 1996.

Brown, Ann L., and Joseph C. Campione. "Guided Discovery in a Community of Learners." *Classroom Lessons: Integrating Cognitive Theory and Classroom Practice*. Ed. Kate McGilly. Cambridge: MIT, 1994. 229–270.

Cohen, Elizabeth G. *Designing Groupwork: Strategies for the Heterogeneous Classroom*. New York: Teachers College, 1986.

Wells, Gordon, Gen Ling M. Chang, and Ann Maher. "Creating Classroom Communities of Literate Thinkers." *Cooperative Learning: Theory and Research*. Ed. Shlomo Sharan. New York: Praeger, 1990. 95–121.

Classroom Activities

You can use Fleck's process for generating small-group discussion as an aid to reading comprehension in your own classroom. When you preview the day's reading for class, make a list of complicated terms (or symbols or metaphors in short stories, poetry, or novels), and have students divide into groups to arrive at working definitions. Even better, suggest that students come up with the list of difficult terms or concepts themselves. Make sure that each group works through the same terms, and leave sufficient time in the class period for discussing these definitions as a whole group. You should then compare the working definitions with the operational definitions presented in the text. This activity should work especially well for students who seem most challenged by complex readings, since the text is broken down into manageable chunks and terms can be clearly defined in students' own words. Moreover, learning is often best facilitated when students must teach difficult concepts to each other. This collaborative learning exercise presents just such an opportunity for developing readers and writers.

Thinking about Teaching

Consider creating a small-group discussion with fellow instructors for working on your own reading and writing projects, or creating a small e-mail group for the same purposes. A collaborative reading group would give members an opportunity to read and discuss critical essays in your field (including the articles in this ancillary) and would allow you to draw connections between the essays and "teacher talk": What are the practical implications of these essays for your work with students in the classroom? The purpose of a collaborative writing group would be quite similar. Distribute electronic or "hard" copies of the work of several interested peers, and meet together (or over e-mail) to discuss ideas for revision and possible audiences for publication. This activity will give you an interesting sense of your students' own experiences with collaborative learning and will provide you with useful feedback as well. Share your experiences with students and compare notes on the effectiveness (and potential problems and solutions to those problems) of collaborative learning.

10

Technology

Teachers of composition help students become better communicators, more skillful problem solvers, and more engaged members of their community. Many now recognize the advantages of electronic technology in teaching and developing these skills. However, access to technology for the composition classroom can be a volatile political issue, stirring up problems of institutional privilege and financial solvency. Moreover, whereas some students arrive in our classrooms already acquainted with the Internet and have access to computers at home or at work, others can barely afford the bus fare to campus. Limited access to computers at educational institutions may seem an inconvenience to the first group of students; to the second, it is a serious liability.

In this chapter, Susan Stan, Terence G. Collins, and Smokey Wilson provide important insights for this discussion. Stan and Collins report the results of a nationwide survey on technology, documenting the successes and difficulties that teachers experience with the new technologies. "Again and again, instructors noted that working on computers had positively altered attitudes in their writing classes." Wilson concurs, documenting the changes that she sees in students' commitments to the course and to their writing as they familiarize themselves with computer-mediated instruction. "We are most fortunate to be here to observe the unfolding of different kinds of literacy," writes Wilson. "It will come with or without us, and I don't want to miss it." Whether or not we and our students have access to technology now, we can begin to consider the benefits of and issues surrounding computer-assisted instruction in our classrooms.

Basic Writing: Curricular Interactions with New Technology

Susan Stan and Terence G. Collins

In the following excerpt from a longer article, Susan Stan and Terence Collins focus on a nationwide survey, Curricular Transformation and Technology in Developmental Education, *that they conducted for their cross-disciplinary collaboration at the University of Minnesota. The purpose of this survey, and of their research, was "to assess the extent to which composition teachers are using technology in their developmental writing courses — and to uncover some of the reasons others aren't using technology in the classroom. . . ." As might be expected, Stan and Collins found that lack of funding and lack of access to technology were often given as reasons for not implementing some of the newer technologies. Yet these researchers do more than merely lament such inequitable circumstances: they provide concrete suggestions for learning about and gaining access to technology. Stan, a former basic writing teacher at the University of Minnesota–Twin Cities' General College, is now Assistant Professor of composition and children's literature at Central Michigan University in Mount Pleasant. Terence Collins is Director of Academic Affairs, Director of the Center for Research on Developmental Education and Urban Literacy, and Morse-Alumni Distinguished Teaching Professor of Writing and Literature at General College at the University of Minnesota–Twin Cities.*

Nationwide Survey

To assess the extent to which composition teachers are using technology in their developmental writing courses — and to uncover some of the reasons others aren't using technology in the classroom — we conducted a nationwide survey of developmental writing teachers.[1] These surveys were directed at instructors whose names had been supplied by administrators belonging to either the National Association of Developmental Education or to the League for Innovation. All of the respondents taught at community colleges or in developmental programs within universities or four-year colleges. Viewed as a whole, their responses indicate great disparity in use of technology, a disparity that does not always correlate to the type of institution. In the main, however, their responses reinforce the findings of the empirical studies cited above. The comments of respondents quoted in the sections to follow can all be found at the Curricular Transformation website at <www.gen.umn.edu/research/currtran>.

Kinds of Technology in Use

For some of the writing teachers in this survey, the presence of a lab on campus where students are able to word-process their papers was the closest connection they could make between computers and writing.

Having access to a computer lab in which to hold class periodically was a high priority on their wish lists. Other respondents taught in networked computer classrooms with an Internet connection, enabling them to make use of e-mail and the World Wide Web in their pedagogies. To these seasoned users, the idea of computers as word-processing tools was such a given that it was not even worthy of mention. They were already looking forward to technology that is beginning to emerge from the development stage, such as CUCME (see you, see me) video conferencing.

The most prevalent kind of technology identified on the surveys was the computer, whether part of a fully equipped writing classroom or off somewhere — usually in inadequate numbers — in a learning lab, department lab, or campus lab. The software available on these computers ranged from the minimal word processing package (several respondents mentioned world-ware programs such as PFS Write, WordPerfect, and MS Word) to grammar and mechanics checking programs (e.g., Grammatik) to tutorial programs such as SkillsBank or Invest. Diagnostic and placement software was also mentioned frequently. Two respondents specifically mentioned software packages (MS Office, WordPerfect Works, and Microsoft Works) that enable students to integrate graphics into their writing assignments and oral presentations.

Three software packages developed specifically to support the workshop approach to writing instruction were also mentioned. The Daedalus Integrated Writing Environment features Interchange, and electronic discussion forum, along with a series of invent and respond prompts, a word processing program, and a bibliography preparation tool. CommonSpace supports peer editing by enabling students to comment on each other's papers in separate columns that run alongside the text column. Norton Connect is a system in which students can share their work electronically with others, turn it into the instructor electronically, and follow links to sections of a grammar or style manual that can be imbedded in the instructor's feedback.

Relative to the number of responses that named hardware and resident software as instructional tools, significantly fewer respondents mentioned Internet-related technologies as items in their pedagogical bookbags. This figure, under ten percent, most likely reflects the proportion of developmental education programs with equipment that provides Internet access. Of those who did mention the Internet connection, e-mail was cited most often, both in terms of its ability to facilitate communication among students and between student and instructor. In a few cases, students hand in their papers via e-mail. Larry Silverman at Seattle Central Community College uses e-mail to match his students up with students in other states and even countries: "I've had my developmental writing class correspond with students in Hawaii, and next quarter they will correspond with a group of students in Japan." To find these classes, he advertises on a listserv designed to make these connections.

Some writing teachers on campuses with access to the World Wide Web use it as a way to teach research techniques and a place to conduct research and gather information. One respondent makes full use of the Internet and World Wide Web technologies, posting his syllabus to the web and using an e-mail distribution list to assign homework. He has students post their comments about reading assignments to a class listserv and initiates them in the use of a MOO (a virtual meeting place) so he can hold class even on those days when he can't be in the room.

Two respondents listed CD-ROMs among the technologies available to their students. A teacher in adult education uses *Grolier's Encyclopedia* on CD as a text for writing: "The database set-up allows students to access all kinds of information. They then write anything from research papers to outlines to summaries."

Devices for projecting images onto large screens for all students to view are a staple of instruction in the writing classroom. The overhead projector enabled teachers to create transparencies for use in lecture situations or as a means of displaying examples and supplanted the need to laboriously write out such information ahead of time on the chalkboard or reproduce multiple copies for students. The development of liquid crystal display panels (LCDs) and computer projectors that plug directly into a computer's central processing unit has added a dynamic quality to this instructional tool. A handful of respondents reported having access to LCDs or computer projectors, either as part of the basic classroom equipment or available on a cart for checkout.

Jack Sexton of Paradise Valley Community College, part of the Maricopa Community College District, puts the LCD to multiple uses in his writing classroom. To teach editing skills, he might put a student paper on the screen and ask students as a group to discuss possible revisions, keying in changes as the students agree on them. For a lesson on thesis statements, he will ask students to type their thesis statements into a common file at the beginning of the class period and then work through them, one by one, so that everyone has access to all of the examples.

In short, the use of computers in instruction ranged from computer-aided instruction (CAI), exemplified by tutorial programs, to computer-assisted composition (CAC), where students did much of their composing at the keyboard, to computer-mediated communication (CMC), where the emphasis was on electronic communication using software packages such as Daedalus InterChange and Norton Connect and technologies such as computerized projectors, e-mail, and the World Wide Web.

Impact of Technology on Teaching and Learning

Basic Writing instructors who have introduced elements of technology into their courses are mixed in their evaluation of its impact on student learning. While one instructor states that he has not found technology to improve student writing ("I believe computers are basically a gimmick"), another asserts that technology has made his an entirely different course that has resulted in more literate students.

Responses tend, not surprisingly, to cluster around other factors, such as the level of commitment a department or institution has made in hardware, software, and training. The instructor who stated he saw no improvement in writing, for instance, teaches in a department with access to a "room with computers," no training, and little technical support, while the instructor who felt that teaching with technology was producing more literate students teaches at an institution that provides workshops to train faculty in new forms of technology and has access to the Internet and the World Wide Web, as do his students. Cause and effect is difficult to sort out in these situations.

Whether they were making use of the computer to deliver computer-aided instruction in a venue outside the classroom, such as a writing or academic resource center, or using the computer as a writing tool, holding class sessions in the computer lab or a computer classroom, instructors reported largely similar results. The positive evaluations of using technology overwhelmingly outweighed the neutral or negative ones, and the rewards noted by instructors fall naturally into four groups: positive impact on students' attitudes toward writing; improved appearance of papers; improved student writing, in terms of both quantity and quality; and an increase in efficiency on the part of the instructor.

Again and again, instructors noted that working on computers has positively altered students' attitudes in their writing classes. "Using technology has made the basic English requirements more interesting and relevant for vo-tech students," observed one respondent. In related observations, other instructors stated that students see the computer as a useful tool and feel they are learning the technology of the future when they work on a computer. Instructors variously reported that students have more confidence in their writing when using the lab and develop self-esteem by working at their own pace to accomplish writing tasks. Among other reasons cited: students respond well to computer-based instruction; working on a computer provides variety and adds interest; computer-related assignments increase student involvement in their own educations.

Simply turning in word-processed papers, instead of the often illegibly handwritten ones, was noted by some instructors as a positive change brought about by technology. Most often, however, instructors saw this "improvement" as benefiting themselves as much as the student. Yes, word-processed papers are a "neat end product," as one teacher put it, presumably offering satisfaction to the student upon completion, but even more to the point, they are easier to read and make writing teachers' time more productive.

By far the most frequently cited examples of ways in which using technology had had an impact on developmental writing courses were outcome-based and revolved around both the process and products of student writing. The ease with which documents can be changed has significantly affected the amount of revision that is taking place. Teachers can insist on revision and editing if they choose; students are more likely to exercise some editing and revision strategies on their own work with or without pressure from their instructor. Spelling checkers not only help to eliminate surface errors in final drafts, but their mere existence encourages some writers to try words they aren't sure they can spell, knowing they'll be able to correct them in a later draft. Students just plain write more — more words, more pages, more drafts. And teachers say they are able to fit more writing assignments into a term because computers speed up the editing and revision processes.

There were some contradictions in what writing instructors had to say. One asserted that meeting in a computer lab changed the structure of the class so that more time was spent writing and less on grammar lectures or demonstration. For another, meeting in a computer lab required the instructor to spend more time teaching word-processing and computer skills and less time on writing instruction. No doubt both are true.

Whereas most of the successes cited were student-related, the majority of the problems mentioned by instructors were institutional in nature. Lack of funding for adequate equipment was the biggest issue: not enough computers to serve all students in a class, outdated hardware that doesn't support new software, hardware and software that doesn't perform as promised. Insufficient faculty training (or none at all) and not enough technical support were also seen as roadblocks to increased use of computers in developmental writing courses. Instructors reported problems with specific software as well as general system malfunctions and breakdowns. One respondent specifically mentioned that the administration is supportive of technology in the classroom — for the engineering and science departments. Convincing them that the writing program should receive the same level of funding has been a greater effort.

The fact that students arrive in writing classes with minimal or no computer skills is perceived by almost all instructors as a problem, as they are required to show students how to use the machines before they can ask them to work on writing assignments. Most agreed that while this lack of computer experience does create a problem in the beginning, it disappears as students become more familiar with the hardware and software. Almost all instructors surveyed agreed that students offer little if any resistance to technology. Several noted that anxiety seems to be age-related and that returning students, who are usually older, are most prone to it. Even their fears, however, dissipate quickly.

Some students, however, lack keyboarding, or typing, skills, which is a decided disadvantage. "A small handful of students," noted one instructor, "refuse to even hunt and peck on the keyboard, get frustrated, and fall way behind." Should knowledge of word-processing be a requirement for entry into a basic writing course? At one college, the instructor who teaches word-processing thinks it should and wants students to take his class first. Only one instructor reported that students use technology as an excuse for not completing assignments on time, saying, for instance, that they couldn't get to the lab.

Perhaps because these surveys were sent to people who had been recommended by administrators at their institutions as teachers who were using technology as part of their developmental writing courses, many of the instructors who responded to the survey complained of not having colleagues who were similarly involved. These people became the sole instructors taking students into the computer lab or lobbying for more equipment; their colleagues were often reluctant to get their feet wet, for any number of reasons, including technophobia.

Faculty Training

In cases in which the instructor is the department technology expert or the only teacher to be using computers in writing instruction, he or she has usually been propelled by a personal interest in computers and has been self-taught. One person wrote of "sitting in the basement computer lab until 4 A.M. until I figured this stuff out." These people consulted manuals, called helplines, and learned by trial and error. Many of them credited other people — colleagues, computer science department staff members, patient friends, and others, such as secretarial staff members, who were already using the particular hardware or software.

Some teachers were first introduced to ways that computers could enhance writing instruction in graduate school or at conferences or workshops put on by professional organizations such as the Conference on College Composition and Communication (CCCC) and the National Association for Developmental Education (NADE), and by federally funded or privately funded organizations such as the National Endowment for the Humanities and the Epiphany Project. Epiphany, a project funded for two years by Annenberg/CPB in collaboration with the American Association for Higher Education and the Alliance for Computers and Writing and now continuing as a non-profit organization, conducts three-day intensive institutes around the country to introduce teachers to pedagogies involved in using computers in writing instruction. Interestingly, among its recommendations is that schools send people in teams of two or more, a strategy that provides synergy when participants return to their own institution and helps to eliminate the sense of isolation reflected in many of the completed surveys received.

As evidenced in the responses, some colleges are providing training for their writing faculty. It is often the early adopters — those instructors who discovered technology on their own — who end up organizing workshops to teach others in their departments or institutions. Some instructors reported attending workshops offered at the institutional or district level, and a few reported that their institutions have instructional technology committees. Still, the profile is uneven. Many instructors who have integrated some technology into their courses report that they do not even have computers in their offices, and many more report that their institutions have not yet geared up to provide access to e-mail for faculty members, much less students.

Visions of the Future

The great disparity among the levels of technology currently in place across the country in colleges and universities with developmental education programs means that individual and departmental goals for the implementation of technology in writing instruction also vary widely. One teacher's dream is in effect another teacher's reality. Some instructors long for more equipment, better computer classrooms, or networking capabilities, while others have all that and simply want more time in which to explore these tools or develop assignments around them. Still others envision kinds of technology or software programs that have yet to be developed. A lone voice expressed the sentiment that "we would be satisfied if the student just came every day with paper, pencils and pen, and textbook."

No matter what may be the vision of implementing technology, pervasive in the responses are indications of writing pedagogies that these technologies support. At either end of the spectrum are teachers who believe that a collaborative environment leads to learning. The instructor who reports that her college encourages its faculty members to get training in multimedia still forthrightly states, "I don't see much use for multimedia in basic writing. . . . I rely heavily on the photocopier and chalkboard. I type worksheets based on students' writing and duplicate them for class members to discuss. We do a great deal of collaborative work." Her counterpart in another college has a different way of facilitating collaboration — by using the computer projector to display samples of student text to be discussed. These two technologies, the former far more labor-intensive for the instructor, fulfill the same purpose in the writing classroom, allowing students to see writing as a dynamic process and one in which the effective communication of ideas is paramount.

Another principle underlying the workshop approach to writing is that of writing for an audience other than the teacher, whether that means one's classmates or the portion of the world funneled through the World Wide Web. Those respondents whose students use e-mail to conduct a text-based conversation with students elsewhere or who post their papers to the Web quickly develop, in the words of one respondent, "a sense of what their readers need to understand the texts they produce."

The approach to developmental writing instruction that emphasizes the mastery of discrete skills is also very much in evidence in these responses. Despite the existence of research that suggests that grammar tutorials, style analyzers, and other tutorial programs are detrimental to developmental writers, many writing instructors continue to rely on them. Without polarizing writing instruction pedagogies as either product or process, repeated comments that focus on appearance of text (e.g., "a neat end product") or promote excessive dependence on style checkers nonetheless suggest that technology is sometimes being used to reinforce, perhaps unwittingly, a product-oriented view of writing.

When instructors were asked to comment on what their writing courses will be like in the future, most conceived of courses along the lines of current models but enhanced by more and better hardware and software. Only a few people considered that future writing instruction might undergo a total transformation in form while still grounded in the same theory. Several respondents suggested that their classes might be offered in an electronic format — over the web or Internet — and one envisioned an interactive CD-ROM teaching module, but then noted that "the institutional pedagogy is moving away from any individualized learning, so whatever it is, it better be communal!"

Issues and Policies

Whether in their capacity to foster collaborative learning, enrich opportunities for student research, encourage students to write longer papers of a higher quality, or simply modify students' negative attitudes toward writing, computers have already made an incalculable impact on the field of writing instruction. As the results of our survey have shown, however, only a fraction of developmental writing teachers are in a position to incorporate technology into their courses to the extent that they would like. They are stopped by factors both economical and political: lack of support for technology at the department or institutional level (as manifested in funds for equipment, space that has been retrofitted with the appropriate wiring, and technical support), and lack of clout within the department for access to the computer facilities that do exist.

Faculty training has emerged as another roadblock, since many of the people who teach developmental or Basic Writing courses carry heavy courseloads that cannot accommodate time-outs for training without compensatory release time. To compound the problem, many departments employ adjunct or part-time faculty to teach their developmental writing courses; even if training sessions are offered, these instructors cannot always be available to attend them. To ensure that access to technology does not become a factor dividing institution from institution, department from department, and ultimately student from student, those of us *with* access must find ways to eliminate the impediments in the paths of those *without* access.

These obstacles, which occur not just in Basic Writing sites but also in Composition departments (which in turn are often situated in English departments), are topics of frequent discussion on listserv groups devoted to issues of writing pedagogy or technology in higher education. Such discussion groups have created virtual communities of teachers and administrators with like interests and goals who often pool their experiences and expertise to address problems presented to them. Need recommendations from users to bolster your request to purchase a new kind of writing instruction software? Go online. Need suggestions for the most effective layout for a computer classroom? Go online. Need data to convince a hesitant chair that the expense of a computer classroom is warranted? Go online. Many of the respondents to our survey remarked that, as the resident "expert," they felt isolated at their institutions; listservs provide them with the chance to develop virtual colleagues.

While listserv discussion groups represent informal sites for sharing information, websites (including the website developed by this project and the many web resources linked to it) are more formal sites for the sharing of information about writing pedagogy and technology. Such websites can be productive as entry-level places to learn about everything from terminology to available technologies; they can also act as information exchange sites and clearinghouses to put inexperienced technology users in touch with experienced teachers at nearby institutions.

Sending a group of Basic Writing faculty members to conferences and workshops to learn about new uses of technology is an expense beyond the budget of most departments. The trend toward cyber-conferences and satellite conferences responds to this situation by bringing the workshop or the conference to faculty members who may have neither the time nor the financial support to travel. Electronic conferences, or cyber-conferences, can either occur asynchronously (a highly regulated form of listserv discussion), or they can take place synchronously in a MOO. Satellite conferences, in which presenters are projected live onscreen in an auditorium setting, can be particularly affordable if the conference costs are being shared by several institutions simultaneously.

In addition to providing a place for new users to learn about technology, cyber sites (e.g., listservs, websites, electronic conferences) provide a way to capture what we earlier termed fugitive information: classroom practices that do not appear in traditional print sources. The innovative work of so many instructors with part-time status and heavy courseloads goes unpublished and thus remains hidden to all but their immediate colleagues. Searchable websites such as ours, where these teachers can post lessons developed around specific technologies, will augment the amount of information available and provide a more realistic picture of how technology is being used to enhance Basic Writing pedagogy. Taken together, all of these efforts — emerging communities of support, online collection and dissemination of information, and electronic venues for training — represent an initial step in lessening the disparity between the kinds of technology available to basic writers in learning institutions throughout the nation.

Note

1. The authors gratefully acknowledge the support of the Annenberg/CPB Projects Initiative II and the General College Center for Research of Developmental Education and Urban Literacy, which funded *Curricular Transformation and Technology in Developmental Education,* a cross-disciplinary collaboration at the University of Minnesota.

Classroom Activities

If you have access to an e-mail account, consider following the strategy of Larry Silverman at Seattle Central Community College, who uses e-mail to find penpals for his students in places like Hawaii and Japan. As Stan and Collins note, to find classes in faraway places, Silverman advertises on a listserv designed to facilitate such connections between students. Two listservs that specialize in exchanges among teachers are the Conference on Basic Writing <http://www.asu.edu/clas/english/composition/cbw/>, affiliated with Arizona State University, and the NCTE-Talk <http://www.ncte.org/lists/ncte-talk>, affiliated with the National Council of Teachers of English. By corresponding via e-mail (or surface mail, if e-mail access is not available) with students at other institutions, your students can discuss important issues with peers in other, perhaps quite dissimilar cultural environments and geographic locations. (See the Bedford/St. Martin's developmental English web site at <http://www.bedfordstmartins.com/development/> for further suggestions regarding electronic resources. If you have trouble accessing the developmental English web page directly, try accessing it from Bedford/St. Martin's home page instead.

Thinking about Teaching

Stan and Collins offer the results of their nationwide survey at the Curricular Transformation web site <www.gen.umn.edu/research/currtran> affiliated with the General College of the University of Minnesota–Twin Cities. This web site also includes a searchable database on curriculum practice in basic writing education throughout the United States. Visitors to the site can find information and suggestions for classroom practice based on a variety of teaching styles in such subject areas as English as a Second Language, writing, reading, and learning centers. Furthermore, in the longer version of this essay, Stan and Collins state that "dozens of site-specific innovations and transformative practices in basic writing courses are in place in a range of institutions around the country. (We invite your submissions to further this work.)"

Consider submitting ideas to the web site yourself, or contributing with colleagues. Perhaps a most critical means to technological empowerment for basic writing teachers and their students is communication with other practitioners around the country. This means of communication allows teachers to find out what colleagues at other institutions are doing; it may also enable us to make contributions of our own from which others can gain inspiration and support. See the Curricular Transformation web site for further details.

When Computers Come to English Class

Smokey Wilson

Smokey Wilson is a composition instructor at Laney College in Oakland, California. She leads a teacher-researcher group for the Bay Area Writing Project and serves on the English Advisory Board for Academic Systems Corporation. In 1997, she was the winner of TETYC's Best Article of the Year Award for her article "Acts of Defiance (and Other Mixed Messages): Taking Up Space in a Nontransfer Course." Building on observations made in that article, Wilson now "outline[s]. . .some of the major changes in the computer-intensive classroom that may have some bearing on improved student performance." Among the many benefits that Wilson includes are "new instructional strategies," "increased time on task," and "raised expectations." Working with "Interactive English," Wilson continues to observe the implications of computer-mediated instruction for students and teachers alike, both in her own classrooms and in discussions and e-mail exchanges with other instructors.

Accounting for Change: Some Qualitative Notes

What is teaching in an electronic classroom like, and why should this writing environment have positive effects on students' retention and pass rates? I can say something about what the electronic classroom was like for me and provide speculations as to why students in computer sections did better than students in the discussion/workshop classes.

The long rows of tables covered with computers, the daunting tasks of getting students logged on and used to learning routine course content on the computer was not easy. Some had no idea how to use a mouse or what a double click meant. That first month tossed me, along with the students, into more than we had bargained for.

I wondered if I had made a terrible mistake. That first week, nostalgia for dusty chalkboards and familiar desks in rows or circles hit me hard. These concerns were not lessened by missteps in the first days — like saying "just play around with the program"; they did not know where to begin. As I came out of my first shock about the changes in the class, I wrote daily journals about what I noticed. I got a grip and began to learn a new kind of teaching. Here, in outline, are some of the major changes in the computer-intensive classroom that may have some bearing on improved student performance.

- *Stability.* Although instructors have been concerned that technology would lead to larger classes, I have found the opposite is true. The number of computers limits the number of students to thirty. I don't begin these days with thirty-seven students. In addition, sporadic attendance has decreased. Students select a spot, a favorite machine, and they make sure they are there regularly to claim it. The importance of stable attendance is probably not such an issue in institutions where the number of students in "remedial" classes is kept to fifteen or where there are dormitories, but in this urban commuter college, where attendance is often irregular, it's a big deal.

- *New Instructional Strategies.* Some of my old standbys in workshop/discussion classes, such as whole-class recitations, became impractical. I learned this lesson the hard way by trying to lead class discussion of readings while many students kept on working at their computers. I reminded myself that these whole-group sessions were not necessarily the most productive anyway: one of my main complaints in "Acts of Defiance" had been the unproductiveness of this format.

   Other strategies that had been peripheral in the discussion/workshop classes expanded. Many days became writing workshop days. Individual communications via dialog journals became important for me to maintain teacher-student connections: small group reading/discussion sessions took on new importance, as did peer-review partners and the end-of-year class publication.

- *Explicit Instruction.* The instructions and commentaries that I rarely successfully put into words in the classrooms I had known were actually in the texts inscribed online. After a few weeks of practice, I stopped trying to get everyone on the same page. I learned to manage a small reading group in one part of the room, to check on partners doing peer review in another part of the room, to field individual questions from everywhere. Yet with all that, I still had time to sit down with a deaf student and compare English word order with the topic-comment syntax of American Sign Language — a luxury I'd rarely had.

   While I wrote in a journal about how busy I was in class, it was only after I viewed a videotape of my classroom that I could see just how busy. And students adjusted (more quickly than I): they learned that "the teacher is in the box," as someone said; students told me more than once that they could not talk to me right then, as they were listening to the online writing coach.

- *Increased Time on Task.* The fifty-minute hour was over. Students came before class and stayed late. Students came in at different times, got their folders, went to work. Everyone, however, was due to be in class at the hour we were supposed to begin; to mark this "class-has-started" boundary, I always gave a short "orienting" lecture to set up the day's agenda. I used this time to emphasize where everyone should be working and make group assignments.

  But for some, class work had begun an hour before class officially opened, and for others it would continue after its official end. I found myself teaching much more in the tradition of vocational instructors at my campus: practicing what I taught with teams of two or three, or working with a single student. As vocational teachers know, such teaching requires more hours and a different kind of time than does the typical discussion-based instructional approach.

- *Raised Expectations.* Because I knew that students had access through the computer program to the knowledge I demanded, my expectations became higher.

  Students might or might not pay attention to the activities, but since I sat with them and showed them what needed to be done, tasks were tangible; concepts were explained in two or three different ways. Some of the things I had always hoped to do but never really did, like refusing to accept a draft until I'd seen the prewriting "plans" or insisting that students actually mastered sentence structure, were finally standards I could make stick. For example, in one essay I assigned, students working in the invention phase of composing had to list language experiences, select one, and freewrite on that experience to decide whether or not to use it as the basis for an essay. When they got on the wrong track, I could intervene at the right time; the numbers of essays that failed because they were not on topic dropped almost to zero.

  Or again, with errors in conventions, I could actually hold students responsible for specific errors. Once they passed the "quizzes" on fragments or comma splices, they were responsible for correcting those errors in their essays.

For Further Study

Within the last two years, instructors at a number of institutions across the country began using *Interactive English*. If the notion of the isolated "close-the-door-and-let-me-teach" teachers has ever applied, teaching in this new computer writing environment would have made it impossible. Although we had not properly anticipated it, electronic technology changes one's instructional habits — changes everything from the nailed-down seating arrangement to the absence of the semicircle of faces that surrounded the big desk.

In fact, the familiar image of the computer as a desktop with files arrayed on it loses its utility as an explanatory metaphor. In this guided writing environment, teachers are clearly beyond (or behind) the desktop as we watch students maneuvering among online instructional text, audio, "hard copy" readings, journals, library links, and an array of video characters.

For this, instructors found we needed each other. On e-mail, through the *Interactive English* Roundtable, or by telephone, we asked, "What's it like for you? Do you find so and so? What about the other and such?" It was those contacts that helped us begin to regularize the novelty, that gave us sea legs in this sometimes watery new place to teach, a place where we could no longer stand — or sit, for that matter — and deliver. By the time the program had been in use for two years, a group of nine instructors using the program began to work together on an "English Evaluation" team. As we study the use of this program across institutions, we will learn more about underprepared students at various campuses, different teaching expectations, and the underlying assumptions we share about what constitutes "good" composing practices and products.

What I've found beyond the desktop has been sufficiently intriguing to keep me teaching. But at my college, not everyone has been as excited as I. It seems that wherever computer-assisted instruction appears at a campus, some cry "foul!" on grounds of mechanized instruction; others, because it smacks of the corporate world (although no more, certainly, than textbooks these days).

There has been hand-to-hand combat between faculty and administrators over academic freedom, fueled by the bottom line, or by nostalgia, or — in the best scenarios — by a passionate instructor's wisdom about what can happen when an inspiring teacher lectures.

Sometimes these skirmishes between teachers and administrators get pretty bloody: as if heroes and heroines from two different Greek plays have wandered onto the same stage and are threatening mayhem if technology is (or is not) allowed, and all in the name of student good. Meanwhile, the students are standing stage left, trying to figure out who the players are and how to get what they need since the other actors in the drama have taken leave of their senses.

It's not just fancy, either, that brings images of Greece to mind. Technology wars are not new. It was Socrates, I think, who wanted to outlaw writing; he wanted to maintain the spoken memory, the living exchange, between instructor and student; written words would break this link. The rhetoricians, too, wanted to maintain spoken language, the kinds of argumentation and memorization strategies that made them so effective.

Predating these debates, however, the commercial shippers in the Fertile Crescent were coming up with a new technology by bundling sticks so that they could count their cargo as they sent it down the Nile. I am sure that these shippers would not have been interested in Plato's dialogues, and if some Grecian dean had told Socrates to write his lectures down so that he could improve his FTE's, there would have been a somewhat earlier hemlock scene. I hope somewhere there is a teacher who is documenting this current debate over whether or not to use technology — between teachers and teachers, and between administrators and teachers; it's going to be vital history for the twenty-first century.

We are most fortunate to be here to observe the unfolding of different kinds of literacy. It will come with or without us, and I don't want to miss it. Programs like *Interactive English* will change what it is underprepared students will do when they write and read for college. Visualize the long journey one of my students is taking. This student's mother could neither read nor write. This 24-year-old woman entered the classroom with fingernails so long that they were the equivalent of Chinese women's bound feet; she had never used a computer. In a couple of weeks, she had trimmed her nails so she could put her composition on the computer. By the end of the semester, she was composing online.

I did not remember to check back to see if she had shortened her fingernails even more by the end of the semester. Since I was handling awkwardly a classroom filled with these technologies myself, I had too little time in my first semesters with *Interactive English* to watch any one student's behaviors closely. With my own desktop a bit clearer about how to operate in this new teaching situation, I have begun to examine students' drafts in light of the Student Performance Reports which the program provides. How much instruction are students actually taking in? If they don't look at the screens, they receive little more instruction than if they had slept through class.

Like me, the other eight instructors in the English Evaluation project are pursuing their own classroom questions. But since we all are using comparable coursework with students who are in most cases in developmental courses, we can also — for the first time — compare students' writing performance across institutions. Through this collaboration, we intend to report about the writing behaviors of those who are considered underprepared at various types of colleges and what these students learn when computers come to English class.

Note

Special thanks are due to Jo Ann Phillips in the Research and Development Department of Peralta College District for her work on readying the data for this study and to Ronald G. Downey of Kansas State University who kindly ran appropriate statistical tests for me.

Works Cited

Boyle, Frank T. "IBM, Talking Heads, and Our Classrooms." *College English* 55 (1993): 618–26.

Hawisher, Gail, and Cynthia Selfe. "The Rhetoric of Technology and the Electronic Writing Class." *College Composition and Communication* 42 (1991): 55–64.

Interactive English. CD-ROM. Ten discs. Twelve Readers. Versions 1.0, 1.1. Mountain View: Academic Systems, 1997–99.

Lu, Min-Zhan. "Professing Multiculturalism: The Politics of Style in the Contact Zone." *College Composition and Communication* 45 (1994): 442–58.

"Perspectives: Understanding the Changes Affecting the Peralta Colleges, An Environmental Scan." Prepared for the Peralta Community College District by Moore, Iacofano, Goltsman, Inc. Berkeley: 1998.

Selfe, Cynthia, and Dickie Selfe. "The Politics of the Interface: Power and Its Exercise in Electronic Contact Zones. *College Composition and Communication* 45 (1994): 480–504.

Spellmeyer, Kurt. "Travels to the Heart of the Forest: Dilettantes, Professionals, and Knowledge." *College English* 56 (1994): 699–809.

Wilson, Smokey. "Acts of Defiance and Other Mixed Messages: Taking Up Space in a Non-Transfer English Class." *Teaching English in the Two-Year College* 24 (1997): 291–303.

———. "Other Stories." *Teaching English in the Two-Year College* 27 (1999): 78–82.

Classroom Activities

Although many commentators on the "information age" assume that access to computers is universal, those of us who teach developing writers and readers at struggling institutions may have had different experiences. Wilson clearly reminds us that not all students will enter our classrooms with computer literacy and that what many regular computer users take for granted will be brand new and not a little daunting for many students. (See Kay Thurston's article "Mitigating Barriers to Navajo Students' Success in English Courses" in Chapter 11, "Writing and Race, Class, and Gender," for one example of students with limited access to phone lines, much less to computers.) Even as we grow accustomed to teaching in computer-mediated environments, Wilson reminds us to review what might seem to us to be the simplest skills, such as "how to use a mouse or what a double click mean[s]." You might assign students to keep a journal of how technology has an impact on their lives both inside and outside the composition classroom. These essays could be compiled into a course book or the "end-of-year class publication" that Wilson refers to in her article.

Thinking about Teaching

Wilson writes: "I hope somewhere there is a teacher who is documenting this current debate over whether or not to use technology — between teachers and teachers, and between teachers and administrators; it's going to be vital history for the twenty-first century." In your teaching journal, write down your response to Wilson's statement. Have you been a participant in or witness to any aspect of this debate? If so, what seem to be the compelling reasons given by teachers and administrators at your institution for their positions on technology? Does everyone have equal access to computer use and to computer-mediated instruction? If not, what barriers to access seem to be in place? How can those barriers be changed, or at least ameliorated? Compare notes with other teachers to broaden your perspective. You may also wish to initiate a discussion, such as Wilson describes, on such teaching tools as Interactive English. Are such approaches to computer-mediated instruction appropriate for your student population? Have your colleagues tried other approaches that have been successful (or not)? How has the Internet changed the ways in which writing is taught at your institution?

11

Writing and Race, Class, and Gender

How do we meet the challenges of a culturally diverse classroom? Often the classroom is a microcosm of the community outside its doors — where race, social class, gender, sexual orientation, age, ethnicity, and language differences create fear and conflict rather than understanding and harmony among our students. Moreover, based on past experiences with those who openly displayed prejudices or held inappropriate stereotypes, students may perceive teachers as representatives of alien cultures. How can we facilitate a classroom in which differences are not denied but mediated? The challenge is to create a learning environment in which all students feel valued and appreciated for who they are and who they are becoming.

The writers in this chapter deal with these issues by personal, political, philosophical, and practical means. Feminist cultural critics Gloria Anzaldúa and bell hooks discuss how they have responded to racism in their own lives as writers and teachers, and how childhood experiences with language and education have affected their adult perceptions of cross-cultural relations. Confronting the reader with real-life situations, Anzaldúa and hooks provide thoughtful explorations of potentially transforming cultural practices that have powerful implications for our students and ourselves. Kay Thurston writes about challenges facing students at Navajo Community College. In describing the cultural background of her students, she also challenges white composition teachers to confront their own Western ethnocentrism and to begin to envision a more inclusive course design. The purpose of such a redesign would be to "mitigate barriers" between Euro-centric ideas of education and a Navajo approach.

How to Tame a Wild Tongue

Gloria Anzaldúa

Gloria Anzaldúa writes, "So, if you really want to hurt me, talk badly about my language. Ethnic identity is twin skin to linguistic identity — I am my language. Until I take pride in my language, I cannot take pride in myself." As a Chicana, tejana lesbian feminist poet, fiction writer, and teacher, she explores the implications of growing up on the "borderlands" of the Mexican and American cultures in Texas. In her preface to Border-lands/La Frontera, *Anzaldúa clarifies her terms: "[B]orderlands are not particular to the Southwest. In fact, borderlands are physically present when two or more cultures edge each other, where people of different races occupy the same territory, where under, lower, middle, and upper classes touch, where the space between two individuals shrinks with intimacy." Such cultural space sounds not unlike many of our classrooms.*

In this selection, a chapter from Borderlands/La Frontera, *Anzaldúa recounts how growing up Chicana continues to shape her life, especially in terms of language. She writes in "Spanglish," a combination of Spanish and English, both to help the reader understand the rich cultural conditions of the borderlands and to demonstrate to Anglo and non-Spanish-speaking readers what it means to be the "other" — outside of so-called mainstream language and culture. Certainly, many ESL students may have shared Anzaldúa's childhood experience of the teacher who did not care to understand how Anzaldúa pronounced her name. "If you want to be American, speak 'American,'" her teacher tells her. In this essay, Anzaldúa reminds us that there are many ways of speaking American.*

"We're going to have to control your tongue," the dentist says, pulling out all the metal from my mouth. Silver bits plop and tinkle into the basin. My mouth is a motherlode.

The dentist is cleaning out my roots. I get a whiff of the stench when I gasp. "I can't cap that tooth yet, you're still draining," he says.

"We're going to have to do something about your tongue," I hear the anger rising in his voice. My tongue keeps pushing out the wads of cotton, pushing back the drills, the long thin needles. "I've never seen anything as strong or as stubborn," he says. And I think, how do you tame a wild tongue, train it to be quiet, how do you bridle and saddle it? How do you make it lie down?

"Who is to say that robbing a people of its language is less violent than war?"

— Ray Gywn Smith[1]

I remember being caught speaking Spanish at recess — that was good for three licks on the knuckles with a sharp ruler. I remember being sent to the corner of the classroom for "talking back" to the Anglo teacher when all I was trying to do was tell her how to pronounce my name. "If you want to be American, speak 'American.' If you don't like it, go back to Mexico where you belong."

"I want you to speak English. *Pa'hallar buen trabajo tienes que saber hablar el inglés bien. Qué vale toda tu educación si todavía hablas inglés con un* 'accent,'" my mother would say, mortified that I spoke English like a Mexican. At Pan American University, I, and all Chicano students were required to take two speech classes. Their purpose: to get rid of our accents.

Attacks on one's form of expression with the intent to censor are a violation of the First Amendment. *El Anglo con cara de inocente nos arrancó la lengua.* Wild tongues can't be tamed, they can only be cut out.

Overcoming the Tradition of Silence

> *Abogadas, escupimos el oscuro,*
> *Peleando con nuestra propia sombra*
> *el silencio nos sepulta.*

En boca cerrada no entran moscas. "Flies don't enter a closed mouth" is a saying I kept hearing when I was a child. *Ser habladora* was to be a gossip and a liar, to talk too much. *Muchachitas bien criadas,* well-bred girls don't answer back. *Es una falta de respeto* to talk back to one's mother or father. I remember one of the sins I'd recite to the priest in the confession box the few times I went to confession: talking back to my mother, *hablar pa' 'tras, repelar. Hocicona, repelona, chismosa,* having a big mouth, questioning, carrying tales are all signs of being *mal criada.* In my culture they are all words that are derogatory if applied to women — I've never heard them applied to men.

The first time I heard two women, a Puerto Rican and a Cuban, say the word *"nosotras,"* I was shocked. I had not known the word existed. Chicanas use *nosotros* whether we're male or female. We are robbed of our female being by the masculine plural. Language is a male discourse.

> And our tongues have become
> dry the wilderness has
> dried out our tongues and
> we have forgotten speech.

> — Irena Klepfisz[2]

Even our own people, other Spanish speakers *nos quieren poner candados en la boca.* They would hold us back with their bag of *reglas de academia.*

Oyé como ladra: el lenguaje de la frontera

Quien tiene boca se equivoca.

— Mexican saying

"*Pocho,* cultural traitor, you're speaking the oppressor's language by speaking English, you're ruining the Spanish language," I have been accused by various Latinos and Latinas. Chicano Spanish is considered by the purist and by most Latinos deficient, a mutilation of Spanish.

But Chicano Spanish is a border tongue which developed naturally. Change, *evolución, enriquecimiento de palabras nuevas por invención o adopción* have created variants of Chicano Spanish, *un nuevo lenguaje. Un lenguaje que corresponde a un modo de vivir.* Chicano Spanish is not incorrect, it is a living language.

For a people who are neither Spanish nor live in a country in which Spanish is the first language; for a people who live in a country in which English is the reigning tongue but who are not Anglo; for a people who cannot entirely identify with either standard (formal, Castillian) Spanish nor standard English, what recourse is left to them but to create their own language? A language which they can connect their identity to, one capable of communicating the realities and values true to themselves — a language with terms that are neither *español ni inglés,* but both. We speak a patois, a forked tongue, a variation of two languages.

Chicano Spanish sprang out of the Chicanos' need to identify ourselves as a distinct people. We needed a language with which we could communicate with ourselves, a secret language. For some of us, language is a homeland closer than the Southwest — for many Chicanos today live in the Midwest and the East. And because we are a complex, heterogeneous people, we speak many languages. Some of the languages we speak are:

1. Standard English

2. Working class and slang English

3. Standard Spanish

4. Standard Mexican Spanish

5. North Mexican Spanish dialect

6. Chicano Spanish (Texas, New Mexico, Arizona and California have regional variations)

7. Tex-Mex

8. *Pachuco* (called *caló*)

My "home" tongues are the languages I speak with my sister and brothers, with my friends. They are the last five listed, with 6 and 7 being closest to my heart. From school, the media and job situations, I've picked up standard and working class English. From Mamagrande Locha and from reading Spanish and Mexican literature, I've picked up Standard Spanish and Standard Mexican Spanish. From *los recién llegados,* Mexican immigrants, and *braceros,* I learned the North Mexican dialect. With Mexicans I'll try to speak either Standard Mexican Spanish or the North Mexican dialect. From my parents and Chicanos living in the Valley, I picked up Chicano Texas Spanish, and I speak it with my mom, younger brother (who married a Mexican and who rarely mixes Spanish with English), aunts and older relatives.

With Chicanas from *Nuevo México* or *Arizona* I will speak Chicano Spanish a little, but often they don't understand what I'm saying. With most California Chicanas I speak entirely in English (unless I forget). When I first moved to San Francisco, I'd rattle off something in Spanish, unintentionally embarrassing them. Often it is only with another Chicana *tejana* that I can talk freely.

Words distorted by English are known as anglicisms or *pochismos.* The *pocho* is an anglicized Mexican or American of Mexican origin who speaks Spanish with an accent characteristic of North Americans and who distorts and reconstructs the language according to the influence of English.[3] Tex-Mex, or Spanglish, comes most naturally to me. I may switch back and forth from English to Spanish in the same sentence or in the same word. With my sister and my brother Nune and with Chicano *tejano* contemporaries I speak in Tex-Mex.

From kids and people my own age I picked up *Pachuco. Pachuco* (the language of the zoot suiters) is a language of rebellion, both against Standard Spanish and Standard English. It is a secret language. Adults of the culture and outsiders cannot understand it. It is made up of slang words from both English and Spanish. *Ruca* means girl or woman, *vato* means guy or dude, *chale* means no, *simón* means yes, *churro* is sure, talk is *periquiar, pigionear* means petting, *que gacho* means how nerdy, *ponte águila* means watch out, death is called *la pelona.* Through lack of practice and not having others who can speak it, I've lost most of the *Pachuco* tongue.

Chicano Spanish

Chicanos, after 250 years of Spanish/Anglo colonization have developed significant differences in the Spanish we speak. We collapse two adjacent vowels into a single syllable and sometimes shift the stress in certain words such as *maíz/maiz, cohete/cuete.* We leave out certain consonants when they appear between vowels: *lado/lao, mojado/mojao.* Chicanos from South Texas pronounce *f* as *j* as in *jue (fue).* Chicanos use "archaisms," words that are no longer in the Spanish language, words that have been evolved out. We say *semos, truje, haiga, ansina,* and *naiden.* We retain the "archaic" *j,* as in *jalar,* that derives from an earlier *h* (the French *halar* or the Germanic *halon* which was lost to standard Spanish in the sixteenth century), but which is still found in several regional dialects such as the one spoken in South Texas. (Due to geography, Chicanos from the Valley of South Texas were cut off linguistically from other Spanish speakers. We tend to use words that the Spaniards brought over from Medieval Spain. The majority of the Spanish colonizers in Mexico and the Southwest came from Extremadura — Hernán Cortés was one of them — and Andalucía. Andalucians pronounce *ll* like a *y,* and their *d*'s tend to be absorbed by adjacent vowels: *tirado* becomes *tirao.* They brought *el lenguaje popular, dialectos y regionalismos.*[4])

Chicanos and other Spanish speakers also shift *ll* to *y* and *z* to *s.*[5] We leave out initial syllables, saying *tar* for *estar, toy* for *estoy, hora* for *ahora* (*cubanos* and *puertorriqueños* also leave out initial letters of some words). We also leave out the final syllable such as *pa* for *para.* The intervocalic *y,* the *ll* as in *tortilla, ella, botella,* gets replaced by *tortia* or *tortiya, ea, botea.* We add an additional syllable at the beginning of certain words: *atocar* for *tocar, agastar* for *gastar.* Sometimes we'll say *lavaste las vacijas,* other times *lavates* (substituting the *ates* verb endings for the *aste*).

We use anglicisms, words borrowed from English: *bola* from ball, *carpeta* from carpet, *máchina de lavar* (instead of *lavadora*) from washing machine. Tex-Mex argot, created by adding a Spanish sound at the beginning or end of an English word such as *cookiar* for cook, *watchar* for watch, *parkiar* for park, and *rapiar* for rape, is the result of the pressures on Spanish speakers to adapt to English.

We don't use the word *vosotros/as* or its accompanying verb form. We don't say *claro* (to mean yes), *imagínate,* or *me emociona,* unless we picked up Spanish from Latinas, out of a book, or in a classroom. Other Spanish-speaking groups are going through the same, or similar, development in their Spanish.

Linguistic Terrorism

> *Deslenguadas. Somos los del español deficiente.* We are your linguistic nightmare, your linguistic aberration, your linguistic *mestisaje,* the subject of your *burla.* Because we speak with tongues of fire we are culturally crucified. Racially, culturally, and linguistically *somos huérfanos* — we speak an orphan tongue.

Chicanas who grew up speaking Chicano Spanish have internalized the belief that we speak poor Spanish. It is illegitimate, a bastard language. And because we internalize how our language has been used against us by the dominant culture, we use our language differences against each other.

Chicana feminists often skirt around each other with suspicion and hesitation. For the longest time I couldn't figure it out. Then it dawned on me. To be close to another Chicana is like looking into the mirror. We are afraid of what we'll see there. *Pena.* Shame. Low estimation of self. In childhood we are told that our language is wrong. Repeated attacks on our native tongue diminish our sense of self. The attacks continue throughout our lives.

Chicanas feel uncomfortable talking in Spanish to Latinas, afraid of their censure. Their language was not outlawed in their countries. They had a whole lifetime of being immersed in their native tongue; generations, centuries in which Spanish was a first language, taught in school, heard on radio and TV, and read in the newspaper.

If a person, Chicana or Latina, has a low estimation of my native tongue, she also has a low estimation of me. Often with *mexicanas y latinas* we'll speak English as a neutral language. Even among Chicanas we tend to speak English at parties or conferences. Yet, at the same time, we're afraid the other will think we're *agringadas* because we don't speak Chicano Spanish. We oppress each other trying to out-Chicano each other, vying to be the "real" Chicanas, to speak like Chicanos. There is no one Chicano language just as there is no one Chicano experience. A monolingual Chicana whose first language is English or Spanish is just as much a Chicana as one who speaks several variants of Spanish. A Chicana from Michigan or Chicago or Detroit is just as much a Chicana as one from the Southwest. Chicano Spanish is as diverse linguistically as it is regionally.

By the end of this century, Spanish speakers will comprise the biggest minority group in the U.S., a country where students in high schools and colleges are encouraged to take French classes because French is considered more "cultured." But for a language to remain alive it must be used.[6] By the end of this century English, and not Spanish, will be the mother tongue of most Chicanos and Latinos.

So, if you want to really hurt me, talk badly about my language. Ethnic identity is twin skin to linguistic identity — I am my language. Until I can take pride in my language, I cannot take pride in myself. Until I can accept as legitimate Chicano Texas Spanish, Tex-Mex, and all the other languages I speak, I cannot accept the legitimacy of myself. Until I am free to write bilingually and to switch codes without having always to translate, while I still have to speak English or Spanish when I would rather speak Spanglish, and as long as I have to accommodate the English speakers rather than having them accommodate me, my tongue will be illegitimate.

I will no longer be made to feel ashamed of existing. I will have my voice: Indian, Spanish, white. I will have my serpent's tongue — my woman's voice, my sexual voice, my poet's voice. I will overcome the tradition of silence.

> My fingers
> move sly against your palm
> Like women everywhere, we speak in code . . .
> — Melanie Kaye/Kantrowitz[7]

"Vistas," corridos, y comida: My Native Tongue

In the 1960s, I read my first Chicano novel. It was *City of Night* by John Rechy, a gay Texan, son of a Scottish father and a Mexican mother. For days I walked around in stunned amazement that a Chicano could write and could get published. When I read *I Am Joaquín,*[8] I was surprised to see a bilingual book by a Chicano in print. When I saw poetry written in Tex-Mex for the first time, a feeling of pure joy flashed through me. I felt like we really existed as a people. In 1971, when I started teaching High School English to Chicano students, I tried to supplement the required texts with works by Chicanos, only to be reprimanded and forbidden to do so by the principal. He claimed that I was supposed to teach "American" and English literature. At the risk of being fired, I swore my students to secrecy and slipped in Chicano short stories, poems, a play. In graduate school, while working toward a Ph.D., I had to "argue" with one advisor after the other, semester after semester, before I was allowed to make Chicano literature an area of focus.

Even before I read books by Chicanos or Mexicans, it was the Mexican movies I saw at the drive-in — the Thursday night special of $1.00 a carload — that gave me a sense of belonging. *"Vámonos a las vistas,"* my mother would call out and we'd all — grandmother, brothers, sister, and cousins — squeeze into the car. We'd wolf down cheese and bologna white bread sandwiches while watching Pedro Infante in melodramatic tearjerkers like *Nosotros los pobres,* the first "real" Mexican movie (that was not an imitation of European movies). I remember seeing *Cuando los hijos se van* and surmising that all Mexican movies played up the love a mother has for her children and what ungrateful sons and daughters suffer when they are not devoted to their mothers. I remember the singing-type "westerns" of Jorge Negrete and Miquel Aceves Mejía. When watching Mexican movies, I felt a sense of homecoming as well as alienation. People who were to amount to something didn't go to Mexican movies, or *bailes* or tune their radios to *bolero, rancherita,* and *corrido* music.

The whole time I was growing up, there was *norteño* music sometimes called North Mexican border music, or Tex-Mex music, or Chicano music, or *cantina* (bar) music. I grew up listening to *conjuntos,* three- or four-piece bands made up of folk musicians playing guitar, *bajo sexto,* drums and button accordion, which Chicanos had borrowed from the German immigrants who had come to Central Texas and Mexico to farm and build breweries. In the Rio Grande Valley, Steve Jordan and Little Joe Hernández were popular, and Flaco Jiménez was the accordian king. The rhythms of Tex-Mex music are those of the polka, also adapted from the Germans, who in turn had borrowed the polka from the Czechs and Bohemians.

I remember the hot, sultry evenings when *corridos* — songs of love and death on the Texas-Mexican borderlands — reverberated out of cheap amplifiers from the local *cantinas* and wafted in through my bedroom window.

Corridos first became widely used along the South Texas/Mexican border during the early conflict between Chicanos and Anglos. The *corridos* are usually about Mexican heroes who do valiant deeds against the Anglo oppressors. Pancho Villa's song, *"La cucaracha,"* is the most famous one. *Corridos* of John F. Kennedy and his death are still very popular in the Valley. Older Chicanos remember Lydia Mendoza, one of the great border *corrido* singers who was called *la Gloria de Tejas.* Her *"El tango negro,"* sung during the Great Depression, made her a singer of the people. The everpresent *corridos* narrated one hundred years of border history, bringing news of events as well as entertaining. These folk musicians and folk songs are our chief cultural mythmakers, and they made our hard lives seem bearable.

I grew up feeling ambivalent about our music. Country-western and rock-and-roll had more status. In the fifties and sixties, for the slightly educated and *agringado* Chicanos, there existed a sense of shame at being caught listening to our music. Yet I couldn't stop my feet from thumping to the music, could not stop humming the words, nor hide from myself the exhilaration I felt when I heard it.

There are more subtle ways that we internalize identification, especially in the forms of images and emotions. For me food and certain smells are tied to my identity, to my homeland. Woodsmoke curling up to an immense blue sky; woodsmoke perfuming my grandmother's clothes, her skin. The stench of cow manure and the yellow patches on the ground; the crack of a .22 rifle and the reek of cordite. Homemade white cheese sizzling in a pan, melting inside a folded *tortilla.* My sister Hilda's hot, spicy *menudo, chile colorado* making it deep red, pieces of *panza* and hominy floating on top. My brother Carito barbequing *fajitas* in the backyard. Even now and three thousand miles away, I can see my mother spicing the ground beef, pork, and venison with *chile.* My mouth salivates at the thought of the hot steaming *tamales* I would be eating if I were home.

Si le preguntas a mi mamá, "¿Qué eres?"

> "Identity is the essential core of who
> we are as individuals, the conscious
> experience of the self inside."
>
> — Kaufman[9]

Nosotros los Chicanos straddle the borderlands. On one side of us, we are constantly exposed to the Spanish of the Mexicans, on the other side we hear the Anglos' incessant clamoring so that we forget our language. Among ourselves we don't say *nosotros los americanos, o nosotros los españoles, o nosotros los hispanos.* We say *nosotros los mexicanos* (by *mexicanos* we do not mean citizens of Mexico; we do not mean a national identity, but a racial one). We distinguish between *mexicanos del otro lado* and *mexicanos de este lado.* Deep in our hearts we believe that being Mexican has nothing to do with which country one lives in. Being Mexican is a state of soul — not one of mind, not one of citizenship. Neither eagle nor serpent, but both. And like the ocean, neither animal respects borders.

> *Dime con quien andas y te diré quien eres.*
> (Tell me who your friends are and I'll tell you who you are.)
> — Mexican saying

Si le preguntas a mi mamá, "¿Qué eres?" te dirá, "Soy mexicana." My brothers and sister say the same. I sometimes will answer *"soy mexicana"* and at others will say *"soy Chicana" o "soy tejana."* But I identified as *"Raza"* before I ever identified as *"mexicana"* or "Chicana."

As a culture, we call ourselves Spanish when referring to ourselves as a linguistic group and when copping out. It is then that we forget our predominant Indian genes. We are seventy to eighty percent Indian.[10] We call ourselves Hispanic[11] or Spanish-American or Latin American or Latin when linking ourselves to other Spanish-speaking peoples of the Western hemisphere and when copping out. We call ourselves Mexican-American[12] to signify we are neither Mexican nor American, but more the noun "American" than the adjective "Mexican" (and when copping out).

Chicanos and other people of color suffer economically for not acculturating. This voluntary (yet forced) alienation makes for psychological conflict, a kind of dual identity — we don't identify with the Anglo-American cultural values and we don't totally identify with the Mexican cultural values. We are a synergy of two cultures with various degrees of Mexicanness or Angloness. I have so internalized the borderland conflict that sometimes I feel like one cancels out the other and we are zero, nothing, no one. *A veces no soy nada ni nadie. Pero hasta cuando no lo soy, lo soy.*

When not copping out, when we know we are more than nothing, we call ourselves Mexican, referring to race and ancestry; *mestizo* when affirming both our Indian and Spanish (but we hardly ever own our black ancestry); Chicano when referring to a politically aware people born and/or raised in the U.S.; *Raza* when referring to Chicanos; *tejanos* when we are Chicanos from Texas.

Chicanos did not know we were a people until 1965 when Cesar Chavez and the farmworkers united and *I Am Joaquín* was published and *la Raza Unida* party was formed in Texas. With that recognition, we became a distinct people. Something momentous happened to the Chicano soul — we became aware of our reality and acquired a name and a language (Chicano Spanish) that reflected that reality. Now that we had a name, some of the fragmented pieces began to fall together — who we were, what we were, how we had evolved. We began to get glimpses of what we might eventually become.

Yet the struggle of identities continues, the struggle of borders is our reality still. One day the inner struggle will cease and a true integration take place. In the meantime, *tenémos que hacer la lucha. ¿Quién está protegiendo los ranchos de mi gente? ¿Quién está tratando de cerrar la fisura entre la india y el blanco en nuestra sangre? El Chicano, si, el Chicano que anda como un ladrón en su propia casa.*

Los Chicanos, how patient we seem, how very patient. There is the quiet of the Indian about us.[13] We know how to survive. When other races have given up their tongue, we've kept ours. We know what it is to live under the hammer blow of the dominant *norteamericano* culture. But more than we count the blows, we count the days the weeks the years the centuries the eons until the white laws and commerce and customs will rot in the deserts they've created, lie bleached. *Humildes* yet proud, *quietos* yet wild, *nosotros los mexicanos-Chicanos* will walk by the crumbling ashes as we go about our business. Stubborn, persevering, impenetrable as stone, yet possessing a malleability that renders us unbreakable, we, the *mestizas* and *mestizos,* will remain.

Notes

1. Ray Gwyn Smith, *Moorland Is Cold Country,* unpublished book.
2. Irene Klepfisz, "*Di rayze aheym*/The Journey Home," in *The Tribe of Dina: A Jewish Women's Anthology.* Melanie Kaye/Kantrowitz and Irena Klepfisz, eds. (Montpelier, VT: Sinister Wisdom Books, 1986), 49.
3. R. C. Ortega, *Dialectologia Del Barrio,* trans. Hortencia S. Alwan (Los Angeles, CA: R. C. Ortega Publisher & Bookseller, 1977), 132.
4. Eduardo Hernandéz-Chávez, Andrew D. Cohen, and Anthony F. Beltramo, *El Lenguaje de los Chicanos: Regional and Social Characteristics of Language Used by Mexican Americans* (Arlington, VA: Center for Applied Linguistics, 1975), 39.
5. Hernandéz-Chávez, xvii.
6. Irena Klepfisz, "Secular Jewish Identity: Yidishkayt in America," in *The Tribe of Dina,* Kaye/Kantrowitz and Klepfisz, eds., 43.
7. Melanie Kaye/Kantrowitz, "Sign," in *We Speak in Code: Poems and Other Writings* (Pittsburgh, PA: Motheroot Publications, Inc., 1980), 85.
8. Rodolfo Gonzales, *I Am Joaquin / Yo Soy Joaquin* (New York, NY: Bantam Books, 1972). It was first published in 1967.
9. Gershen Kaufman, *Shame: The Power of Caring* (Cambridge, MA: Schenkman Books, Inc., 1980), 68.
10. John R. Chávez, *The Lost Land: The Chicano Images of the Southwest* (Albuquerque, NM: University of New Mexico Press, 1984), 88–90.
11. "Hispanic" is derived from *Hispanis (España,* a name given to the Iberian Peninsula in ancient times when it was a part of the Roman Empire) and is a term designated by the U.S. government to make it easier to handle us on paper.
12. The Treaty of Guadalupe Hidalgo created the Mexican-American in 1848.
13. Anglos, in order to alleviate their guilt for dispossessing the Chicano, stressed the Spanish part of us and perpetrated the myth of the Spanish Southwest. We have accepted the fiction that we are Hispanic, that is Spanish, in order to accommodate ourselves to the dominant culture and its abhorrence of Indians. Chávez, 88–91.

Classroom Activities

Anzaldúa suggests that there are many languages that Chicanos speak; she lists them as follows:

1. Standard English

2. Working class and slang English

3. Standard Spanish

4. Standard Mexican Spanish

5. North Mexican Spanish dialect

6. Chicano Spanish (Texas, New Mexico, Arizona, and California have regional variations)

7. Tex-Mex

8. *Pachuco* (called *caló*)

Like Anzaldúa, students can also list the languages they speak and write as well as discuss how language usage may change depending on such variables as audience, purpose, and occasion. We as teachers might use Anzaldúa's work to help us think about what it means to "speak American"; furthermore, what does it mean for our students? Do these definitions continue to change in relation to cultural shifts?

Thinking about Teaching

The cultural conflicts between students, and between teachers and students, often mirror the actual problems in our communities — and sometimes the difficulties seem insurmountable. Yet Anzaldúa's work offers a vision of how change might be enacted. With other teachers, you may wish to read and discuss the issues Anzaldúa presents in *Borderlands / La Frontera,* including how language is implicated in the formation of identity and culture. How do Anzaldúa's ideas figure in your teaching? What are the social and political implications for basic writing and ESL courses, at your school and across the country?

Embracing Change:
Teaching in a Multicultural World

bell hooks

Distinguished Professor of English at City College in New York, bell hooks is a feminist cultural critic, insurgent black intellectual, and the author of several books of cultural criticism. The following essay is taken from her 1994 book Teaching to Transgress: Education as the Practice of Freedom, *in which hooks addresses issues of race, social class, and gender as they pertain to multicultural education. "When we, as educators, allow our pedagogy to be radically changed by our recognition of a multicultural world," she suggests, "we can give students the education they desire and deserve." In her work, hooks offers strategies for classroom teachers working with a diverse student body; moreover, the author provides insights for faculty members willing to question their assumptions about teaching in multicultural environments. She remains inspired by the work of the Brazilian educator* Paulo Freire, *who influenced hooks to interrogate her notions of critical pedagogy, liberatory education, and student-centered learning.*

Despite the contemporary focus on multiculturalism in our society, particularly in education, there is not nearly enough practical discussion of ways classroom settings can be transformed so that the learning experience is inclusive. If the effort to respect and honor the social reality and experiences of groups in this society who are nonwhite is to be reflected in a pedagogical process, then as teachers — on all levels, from elementary to university settings — we must acknowledge that our styles of teaching may need to change. Let's face it: most of us were taught in classrooms where styles of teaching reflected the notion of a single norm of thought and experience, which we were encouraged to believe was universal. This has been just as true for nonwhite teachers as for white teachers. Most of us learned to teach emulating this model. As a consequence, many teachers are disturbed by the political implications of a multicultural education because they fear losing control in a classroom where there is no one way to approach a subject — only multiple ways and multiple references.

Among educators there has to be an acknowledgment that any effort to transform institutions so that they reflect a multicultural standpoint must take into consideration the fears teachers have when asked to shift their paradigms. There must be training sites where teachers have the opportunity to express those concerns while also learning to create ways to approach the multicultural classroom and curriculum. When I first went to Oberlin College, I was disturbed by what I felt was a lack of understanding on the part of many professors as to what the multicultural classroom might be like. Chandra Mohanty, my colleague in Women's Studies, shared these concerns. Though we were both untenured, our strong belief that the Oberlin campus was not fully facing the issue of changing curriculum and teaching practices in ways that were progressive and promoting of inclusion led us to consider how we might intervene in this process. We proceeded from the standpoint that the vast majority of Oberlin professors, who are overwhelmingly white, were basically well-meaning, concerned about the quality of education students receive on our campus, and therefore likely to be supportive of any effort at education for critical consciousness. Together, we decided to have a group of seminars focusing on transformative pedagogy that would be open to all professors. Initially, students were also welcome, but we found that their presence inhibited honest discussion. On the first night, for example, several white professors made comments that could be viewed as horribly racist and the students left the group to share what was said around the college. Since our intent was to educate for critical consciousness, we did not want the seminar setting to be a space where anyone would feel attacked or their reputation as a teacher sullied. We did, however, want it to be a space for constructive confrontation and critical interrogation. To ensure that this could happen, we had to exclude students.

At the first meeting, Chandra (whose background is in education) and I talked about the factors that had influenced our pedagogical practices. I emphasized the impact of Freire's work on my thinking. Since my formative education took place in racially segregated schools, I spoke about the experience of learning when one's experience is recognized as central and significant and then how that changed with desegregation, when black children were forced to attend schools where we were regarded as objects and not subjects. Many of the professors present at the first meeting were disturbed by our overt discussion of political standpoints. Again and again, it was necessary to remind everyone that no education is politically neutral. Emphasizing that a white male professor in an English department who teaches only work by "great white men" is making a political decision, we had to work consistently against and through the overwhelming will on the part of folks to deny the politics of racism, sexism, heterosexism, and so forth that inform how and what we teach. We found again and again that almost everyone, especially the old guard, were more disturbed by the overt recognition of the role our political perspectives play in shaping pedagogy than by their passive acceptance of ways of teaching and learning that reflect biases, particularly a white supremacist standpoint.

To share in our efforts at intervention we invited professors from universities around the country to come and talk — both formally and informally — about the kind of work they were doing aimed at transforming teaching and learning so that a multicultural education would be possible. We invited then-Princeton professor of religion and philosophy Cornel West to give a talk on "decentering Western civilization." It was our hope that his very traditional training and his progressive practice as a scholar would give everyone a sense of optimism about our ability to change. In the informal session, a few white male professors were courageously outspoken in their efforts to say that they could accept the need for change, but were uncertain about the implications of the changes. This reminded us that it is difficult for individuals to shift paradigms and that there must be a setting for folks to voice fears, to talk about what they are doing, how they are doing it, and why. One of our most useful meetings was one in which we asked professors from different disciplines (including math and science) to talk informally about how their teaching had been changed by a desire to be more inclusive. Hearing individuals describe concrete strategies was an approach that helped dispel fears. It was crucial that more traditional or conservative professors who had been willing to make changes talk about motivations and strategies.

When the meetings concluded, Chandra and I initially felt a tremendous sense of disappointment. We had not realized how much faculty would need to unlearn racism to learn about colonization and decolonization and to fully appreciate the necessity for creating a democratic liberal arts learning experience.

All too often we found a will to include those considered "marginal" without a willingness to accord their work the same respect and consideration given other work. In Women's Studies, for example, individuals will often focus on women of color at the very end of the semester or lump everything about race and difference together in one section. This kind of tokenism is not multicultural transformation, but it is familiar to us as the change individuals are most likely to make. Let me give another example. What does it mean when a white female English professor is eager to include a work by Toni Morrison on the syllabus of her course but then teaches that work without ever making reference to race or ethnicity? I have heard individual white women "boast" about how they have shown students that black writers are "as good" as the white male canon when they do not call attention to race. Clearly, such pedagogy is not an interrogation of the biases conventional canons (if not all canons) establish, but yet another form of tokenism.

The unwillingness to approach teaching from a standpoint that includes awareness of race, sex, and class is often rooted in the fear that classrooms will be uncontrollable, that emotions and passions will not be contained. To some extent, we all know that whenever we address in the classroom subjects that students are passionate about there is always a possibility of confrontation, forceful expression of ideas, or even conflict. In much of my writing about pedagogy, particularly in classroom settings with great diversity, I have talked about the need to examine critically the way we as teachers conceptualize what the space for learning should be like. Many professors have conveyed to me their feeling that the classroom should be a "safe" place; that usually translates to mean that the professor lectures to a group of quiet students who respond only when they are called on. The experience of professors who educate for critical consciousness indicates that many students, especially students of color, may not feel at all "safe" in what appears to be a neutral setting. It is the absence of a feeling of safety that often promotes prolonged silence or lack of student engagement.

Making the classroom a democratic setting where everyone feels a responsibility to contribute is a central goal of transformative pedagogy. Throughout my teaching career, white professors have often voiced concern to me about nonwhite students who do not talk. As the classroom becomes more diverse, teachers are faced with the way the politics of domination are often reproduced in the educational setting. For example, white male students continue to be the most vocal in our classes. Students of color and some white women express fear that they will be judged as intellectually inadequate by these peers. I have taught brilliant students of color, many of them seniors, who have skillfully managed never to speak in classroom settings. Some express the feeling that they are less likely to suffer any kind of assault if they simply do not assert their subjectivity. They have told me that many professors never showed any interest in hearing their voices. Accepting the decentering of the West globally, embracing multiculturalism, compels educators to focus attention on the issue of voice. Who speaks? Who listens? And why? Caring about whether all students fulfill their responsibility to contribute to learning in the classroom is not a common approach in what Freire has called the "banking system of education" where students are regarded merely as passive consumers. Since so many professors teach from that standpoint, it is difficult to create the kind of learning community that can fully embrace multiculturalism. Students are much more willing to surrender their dependency on the banking system of education than are their teachers. They are also much more willing to face the challenge of multiculturalism.

It has been as a teacher in the classroom setting that I have witnessed the power of a transformative pedagogy rooted in a respect for multiculturalism. Working with a critical pedagogy based on my understanding of Freire's teaching, I enter the classroom with the assumption that we must build "community" in order to create a climate of openness and intellectual rigor. Rather than focusing on issues of safety, I think that a feeling of community creates a sense that there is shared commitment and a common good that binds us. What we all ideally share is the desire to learn — to receive actively knowledge that enhances our intellectual development and our capacity to live more fully in the world. It has been my experience that one way to build community in the classroom is to recognize the value of each individual voice. In my classes, students keep journals and often write paragraphs during class which they read to one another. This happens at least once irrespective of class size. Most of the classes I teach are not small. They range anywhere from thirty to sixty students, and at times I have taught more than one hundred. To hear each other (the sound of different voices), to listen to one another, is an exercise in recognition. It also ensures that no student remains invisible in the classroom. Some students resent having to make a verbal contribution, and so I have had to make it clear from the outset that this is a requirement in my classes.

Even if there is a student present whose voice cannot be heard in spoken words, by "signing" (even if we cannot read the signs) they make their presence felt.

When I first entered the multicultural, multi-ethnic classroom setting I was unprepared. I did not know how to cope effectively with so much "difference." Despite progressive politics, and my deep engagement with the feminist movement, I had never before been compelled to work within a truly diverse setting and I lacked the necessary skills. This is the case with most educators. It is difficult for many educators in the United States to conceptualize how the classroom will look when they are confronted with the demographics which indicate that "whiteness" may cease to be the norm ethnicity in classroom settings on all levels. Hence, educators are poorly prepared when we actually confront diversity. This is why so many of us stubbornly cling to old patterns. As I worked to create teaching strategies that would make a space for multicultural learning, I found it necessary to recognize what I have called in other writing on pedagogy different "cultural codes." To teach effectively a diverse student body, I have to learn these codes. And so do students. This act alone transforms the classroom. The sharing of ideas and information does not always progress as quickly as it may in more homogeneous settings. Often, professors and students have to learn to accept different ways of knowing, new epistemologies, in the multicultural setting.

Just as it may be difficult for professors to shift their paradigms, it is equally difficult for students. I have always believed that students should enjoy learning. Yet I found that there was much more tension in the diverse classroom setting where the philosophy of teaching is rooted in critical pedagogy and (in my case) in feminist critical pedagogy. The presence of tension — and at times even conflict — often meant that students did not enjoy my classes or love me, their professor, as I secretly wanted them to do. Teaching in a traditional discipline from the perspective of critical pedagogy means that I often encounter students who make complaints like, "I thought this was supposed to be an English class, why are we talking so much about feminism?" (Or, they might add, race or class.) In the transformed classroom there is often a much greater need to explain philosophy, strategy, intent than in the "norm" setting. I have found through the years that many of my students who bitch endlessly while they are taking my classes contact me at a later date to talk about how much that experience meant to them, how much they learned. In my professorial role I had to surrender my need for immediate affirmation of successful teaching (even though some reward is immediate) and accept that students may not appreciate the value of a certain standpoint or process straightaway. The exciting aspect of creating a classroom community where there is respect for individual voices is that there is infinitely more feedback because students do feel free to talk — and talk back. And, yes, often this feedback is critical. Moving away from the need for immediate affirmation was crucial to my growth as a teacher. I learned to respect that shifting paradigms or sharing knowledge in new ways challenges; it takes time for students to experience that challenge as positive.

Students taught me, too, that it is necessary to practice compassion in these new learning settings. I have not forgotten the day a student came to class and told me: "We take your class. We learn to look at the world from a critical standpoint, one that considers race, sex, and class. And we can't enjoy life anymore." Looking out over the class, across race, sexual preference, and ethnicity, I saw students nodding their heads. And I saw for the first time that there can be, and usually is, some degree of pain involved in giving up old ways of thinking and knowing and learning new approaches. I respect that pain. And I include recognition of it now when I teach, that is to say, I teach about shifting paradigms and talk about the discomfort it can cause. White students learning to think more critically about questions of race and racism may go home for the holidays and suddenly see their parents in a different light. They may recognize nonprogressive thinking, racism, and so on, and it may hurt them that new ways of knowing may create estrangement where there was none. Often when students return from breaks I ask them to share with us how ideas that they have learned or worked on in the classroom impacted on their experience outside. This gives them both the opportunity to know that difficult experiences may be common and practice at integrating theory and practice: ways of knowing with habits of being. We practice interrogating habits of being as well as ideas. Through this process we build community.

Despite the focus on diversity, our desires for inclusion, many professors still teach in classrooms that are predominantly white. Often a spirit of tokenism prevails in those settings. This is why it is so crucial that "whiteness" be studied, understood, discussed — so that everyone learns that affirmation of multiculturalism, and an unbiased inclusive perspective, can and should be present whether or not people of color are present. Transforming these classrooms is as great a challenge as learning how to teach well in the setting of diversity. Often, if there is one lone person of color in the classroom she or he is objectified by others and forced to assume the role of "native informant." For example, a novel is read by a Korean American author. White students turn to the one student from a Korean background to explain what they do not understand. This places an unfair responsibility onto that student. Professors can intervene in this process by making it clear from the outset that experience does not make one an expert, and perhaps even by explaining what it means to place someone in the role of "native informant." It must be stated that professors cannot intervene if they also see students as "native informants." Often, students have come to my office complaining about the lack of inclusion in another professor's class. For example, a course on social and political thought in the United States includes no work by women. When students complain to the teacher about this lack of inclusion, they are told to make suggestions of material that can be used. This often places an unfair burden on a student. It also makes it seem that it is only important to address a bias if there is someone complaining. Increasingly, students are making complaints because they want a democratic unbiased liberal arts education.

Multiculturalism compels educators to recognize the narrow boundaries that have shaped the way knowledge is shared in the classroom. It forces us all to recognize our complicity in accepting and perpetuating biases of any kind. Students are eager to break through barriers to knowing. They are willing to surrender to the wonder of relearning and learning ways of knowing that go against the grain. When we, as educators, allow our pedagogy to be radically changed by our recognition of a multicultural world, we can give students the education they desire and deserve. We can teach in ways that transform consciousness, creating a climate of free expression that is the essence of a truly liberatory liberal arts education.

Classroom Activities

Before starting class discussions, have students arrange their chairs in a circle. This arrangement fosters an equitable classroom environment and facilitates communication and collaboration. Invite students to respond in writing to their reading of an essay or an important issue presented in class discussion. The response could be an informal journal entry or brief paragraph written in class. Each student then reads his or her response aloud, without comments and without interruptions, until the class has progressed around the entire circle. This gives you a chance to hear your students and students a chance to hear each other. As hooks suggests, such an exercise allows every student to have a voice in the discussion and provides an opportunity for sharing diverse "cultural codes" and "ways of knowing."

Thinking about Teaching

Since multicultural education represents a paradigm shift for many teachers and remains a controversial notion, hooks suggests that "there must be training sites where teachers have the opportunity to express those concerns while also learning to create ways to approach the multicultural classroom and curriculum." She notes that teachers need space away from students to confront their own and one another's attitudes toward racism and resistance to multicultural education. Some of the most successful sessions at Oberlin, where hooks facilitated seminars on transformative pedagogy, included teachers from different disciplines and guest speakers from other universities discussing how they had made their classes more inclusive.

Discussions like these might well prove useful in considering the implications of multicultural education as it pertains to basic writing programs at the local, regional, or national level. Faculty may have questions or suggestions about how or whether to include multicultural content in a writing course. Moreover, a forum for sharing ideas may lead to curricular and institutional changes. Faculty across the curriculum may want to share syllabi and assignments; guest speakers could also be arranged. Structuring these sessions as a discussion among colleagues may be a first step in listening nonjudgmentally for the sake of facilitating.

Mitigating Barriers to Navajo Students' Success in English Courses

Kay Thurston

Kay Thurston, a teacher of writing and literature at Navajo Community College, won TETYC's 1998 Best Article Award for this description of "the tremendous barriers to success in colleges and universities" that Navajo students face. Navajo Community College is a two-year tribal college in the center of the Navajo or Diné nation. Ninety-six percent of the students are Navajo, the majority of whom live in poverty. Thurston does a thorough job of describing the geographic isolation of her students and the rich cultural heritage with which they arrive in the composition classroom. Rather than blaming the victim or the culture for "the high failure rate" experienced by her students, Thurston suggests that we look at more global factors, which she sees as applicable to "students from radically different cultures." Thurston describes in detail five major barriers that her students encounter: "financial difficulty, family obligations, prescriptive attitudes toward Standard American English, instructor/faculty ethnocentrism, and ambivalence toward Western education." Thurston also presents thoughtful solutions that challenge the reader to examine his or her own values and prejudices.

Introduction

Navajos, or the Diné, are one of four hundred Native American tribes currently recognized by the U.S. government. Of the 150,000 people living on the Navajo reservation despite its isolation and intense poverty, many are struggling to retain their traditional ways — their language, spiritual beliefs and ceremonies, and a culture completely unlike that of white, middle-class Americans.

Navajo Community College (NCC), the first tribally controlled college, was built in 1968 by tribal leaders and medicine men on a sacred site between the Chuska Mountains, Tsaile Lake, and Canyon de Chelly in northeastern Arizona. NCC is located in the center of the Navajo Nation which is, in many ways, like a third-world country, about the size of West Virginia. To buy groceries, NCC staff, faculty, and students make a 60-mile round trip to Chinle, Arizona, a town of seven thousand. To shop at K-Mart, a hardware store, or to see a movie, they make a 180-mile round trip past pine-covered mountains, red-orange Navajo sandstone towering above rugged piñon and juniper, and sheep, cows, and horses scattered among clumps of sage to Gallup, New Mexico.

Of the 550 students who attend NCC's main campus annually, 96 percent are Navajo. NCC's mission is to take these Navajo students, most of whom grew up on the reservation (some in very traditional families, and others in families that have been influenced, to varying degrees, by dominant society), and make them bicultural so that they can function effectively in both the Western and Navajo worlds. NCC succeeds because it focuses on Navajo culture, tradition, and beliefs; it addresses Navajo students' unique needs; and its faculty, knowing that most Navajo dropouts are not academic failures, accept part of the blame for the high Navajo failure and attrition rate. Still, these students face tremendous barriers to success in colleges and universities, and it seems to me that the barriers take five major forms: financial difficulty, family obligations, prescriptive attitudes toward Standard American English, instructor/faculty ethnocentrism, and ambivalence toward Western education.

Financial Difficulty

Probably the number one reason for the high attrition rate of Navajo students is financial. While it would, of course, be incorrect to suggest that every Navajo student struggles financially, the fact is that poverty on the Navajo reservation is so widespread it's the norm. According to the Navajo Nation's 1990 Census Report, only 44.8 percent of those over sixteen are employed in the labor force — for males sixteen and over, the unemployment rate is 30.3 percent. In 1989, the Navajo Nation's median household income was $10,433, and per capita income was $4,106, putting 56.1 percent of the Navajos living on the reservation below the poverty level. Half the homes are without water and electricity — it is disconcerting to see hogans (traditional round dwellings made of wood and earth) without power standing beneath massive systems of power lines strung from the reservation's coal-generating plants to meet energy consumption needs in distant cities in California. Many commuting students live in traditional hogans with earthen floors and can't make it to class after heavy rains that turn their roads into slippery mud. Most cannot call for a missed assignment, either, as 77.5 percent of the homes on the Navajo Nation are without telephone service.

For me, the reality of the students' extreme level of poverty was hammered home recently when I required students to use the college's computers to type their writing assignments. Two weeks later, two students were still turning in handwritten assignments because they had been unable to find one dollar for a disk. To ameliorate students' financial burdens, I allowed some class time each semester for a student services or financial aid representative to counsel students. I also considered the cost of the textbooks I selected, put texts and articles on reserve in the library, and remained flexible about requiring typed assignments. I learned to ask questions and then to make exceptions, for example, for the single parent who has returned to school and is trying to feed four children on food stamps. Though computer and typewriter use may be free, child care is not. To middle-class faculty, this level of poverty may seem inconceivable, but I assure you it is real, and it is a factor with which many, if not most, Navajo students struggle continuously.

Family Obligations

A second serious obstacle the Navajo student faces is the faculty member who doesn't understand or won't acknowledge the importance and time-consuming nature of family responsibilities. Many of us, probably, would raise an eyebrow at a student who tells us that she missed a week of classes because her grandfather had a stroke, but to a traditional Navajo's way of thinking, this problem is not only legitimate but imperative. The student and her family would first take the stroke victim to a diagnostician to determine what healing ceremony (or ceremonies) needed to be performed. If the diagnostician calls for a Lightning Way or Wind Way ceremony, the student's presence will be required for four or five days; if the grandfather should pass on, then for four days, her presence would be required to help her grandfather's spirit travel on to the fifth world. Since most reservations are located far from urban centers and universities, and since most ceremonies last from two to nine days, the student is likely to be out of town for seven to ten days. If her English teacher's absence policy drops students after three or four absences, but the student's family requires her presence for a ceremony that will enable her grandfather to walk again, chances are high that the student will drop the class, especially if the family needs the grandfather out of the nursing home as quickly as possible to care for the livestock that constitute the economic base for the entire extended family.

The family ties of Native American students are usually strong and can never be underestimated. Navajo students, for example, introduce themselves not by telling what they do for work, but by naming their four clans. When, in developmental writing courses, I ask students to write a paragraph describing their best friend, most describe a parent, grandparent, uncle, aunt, brother, sister, or cousin. In the Navajo kinship system, cousins are more akin to brothers and sisters, and aunts and uncles more like mothers and fathers. The Navajo word for paternal uncle, in fact, means "little father," and for maternal aunt, "little mother": these terms reflect the Navajo relatives' assumption of far more responsibility than Anglos for the welfare of their nieces and nephews. Such relationships lend an urgency that an Anglo instructor may not understand to a student's attendance at his niece's Kinaaldá a female puberty ceremony lasting four days, held when a niece begins menstruation — a family duty that cannot be put off, for example, until spring break. A traditional Navajo student with strong family ties, when forced to choose between honoring a teacher's absence policy and his "little daughter's" entrance into womanhood, will probably choose the latter. Other ceremonies require the participation of the entire community: the Jemez Pueblo people of New Mexico, for example, have feast days and dances, most lasting about a week. For instance, late in November, Jemez Pueblo students attending the University of New Mexico return home for three to five days to pray and fast, clean the Pueblo village, replaster houses, prepare food for the guests, and perform ceremonial dances.

The holidays scheduled at mainstream institutions — Columbus Day, the Fourth of July, President's Day, and Christmas — do not hold special significance for Navajos. Therefore, Anglo instructors follow the lead of Native American instructors who, because they are more likely to understand and respect Native American students' need for family contact and involvement, are generally more flexible with absence policies and more willing to accommodate students with family responsibilities.

Prescriptive Attitude toward Standard American English

A third problem that Navajo students encounter in the English classroom is that an Anglo instructor often has little or no knowledge of Native American language conventions. Such instructors (1) assume in students a level of familiarity with Standard American English (SAE) that a middle class Euro-American would have; (2) are untrained and unaware of dialect or second language difficulties, regarding conventional Indian English as "wrong," and expecting students to "clean up" the English they have spoken and heard their entire lives; and (3) expect students to replace their Navajo English dialect with SAE in fifteen to sixteen weeks.

When 82 percent of the adults on the Navajo reservation speak Navajo, and only 21 percent of the 131,229 Navajos five years and older speak English only, it's unreasonable to expect Navajo students to be as familiar with SAE as Anglo students.[1] Navajo English is quite different from SAE. Let me illustrate with three examples. Navajo students, in general, have difficulty with plural formation, verb tenses, and rhetorical style. In Navajo, animate nouns are made plural not by adding an "-s" but by adding a variety of other endings. "Boy," in Navajo, is *ashkii;* "boys" is *ashiike.* No affix is attached to inanimate nouns; instead, the plural is indicated by changes in the verb associated with the noun in question. As a result, Navajo students will write that they have one ball, "two ball," and "many ball scattered about the field." Or

"Many of my relative live in Shiprock." Navajo English forms plurals by adding "-s," but also contains words such as "elderlies," "sheeps," "cattles," "firewoods," "mens," "womens," and "childrens." Another example illustrates the special difficulties of bilingual or nonstandard dialect. In Navajo, verb tense is shown by the position of the verb in a sentence, not by a change in its ending. In Navajo English, although the position of the verb does not change, past tense endings are often omitted, as in "I hear him sing yesterday." Irregular verbs pose problems as well — often, after learning to form the regular past tense, students create words like "hurted" and "eated."

Recognition that Native American students are often bilingual and speak a nonstandard American English dialect has led to two strategies at NCC[2]: first, ESL, bilingual, and nonstandard American English speakers, as well as students from historically oral cultural backgrounds require more than one or two semesters to establish and refine college-level writing skills. For this reason, NCC instructors offer three developmental English courses. About 96 percent of the students complete at least one of them before moving on to first-year composition, and many work their way through all three. In the first level are students who cannot write a complete, coherent sentence. The second and third levels of developmental English deal not only with the nuts and bolts of English usage and Western rhetorical styles, but also with problems specific to Navajo and Navajo English speakers. NCC faculty members are in the process of designing a textbook for these classes — an English textbook specifically for Navajo students, one that uses Navajo themes in its sample writings and exercises and that addresses the kinds of errors bilingual Navajo students are most likely to make.

In addition, maximum enrollment in developmental English courses at NCC is limited to 15 so that students can receive the individual attention and the specific instruction they require to become proficient in written SAE. Finally, composition instructors at NCC approach SAE as one dialect, not superior to Navajo English, but the one required for success in the world beyond the Navajo Nation's four sacred mountains.

Instructor/Faculty Ethnocentrism

Anglo instructors' (often unconscious) ethnocentrism and almost total ignorance about Native American cultures constitute a fourth barrier to Navajo students' success in English courses. I believe this ethnocentrism is caused primarily by gaps in our education: even though we understand that to be effective teachers, in Hap Gilliland's words, we "must understand and accept as equally valid, values and ways of life different from our own," we know little about others' cultures, histories, and educational philosophies. Gilliland adds that when "the teacher does not know, understand, and respect the culture of the students, then the students are at a disadvantage *in that teacher's class*" (4).

Such ethnocentrism or ignorance causes us to lose far more Native American students than we realize. During the second week of teaching a composition course at the University of New Mexico, I used an essay by Jessica Mitford on embalming; the next day, the three Navajos enrolled in the class dropped it. Later, I discovered that in Navajo culture, talking or writing about death is taboo. By requiring the students to discuss death and then write about it, I had offended and alienated them. Patricia Clark Smith had a similar experience teaching on the Navajo reservation. When she once brought an owl she'd fashioned out of scrap cloth to a class, the students "literally recoiled." "I learned too late," she writes, "that owls and images of owls are just something you do not mess with if you are Navajo" (287). Owls, in Navajo culture, are messengers warning a person to be alert and careful, especially for the next four days.

But instructor ethnocentrism does more than cause instructors inadvertently to alienate Native American students; it also leads to failure to acknowledge and validate different rhetorical styles. The Navajo rhetorical style differs considerably from the European linear style. In an unpublished paper, Navajo English instructor Della Toadlena writes that "Navajo is an oral language in which much story telling takes place," and that this tradition explains why Navajo students do better with narrative essays that follow chronological order than with expository essays (5). "An English speaker wastes no time in stating his argument right off and then brings in details to support his idea. Unlike his Anglo counterpart, a Navajo brings out detail after detail and eventually arrives at the point he wants to make" (Toadlena 13). For Navajos, it is important not to offend the audience they are addressing by coming right to the point. To illustrate the more indirect communication style of Navajo people, Toadlena discusses a typical visit from relatives. First, greetings are exchanged, and then the welfare of each family and its members is discussed. Next, food is served while weather, livestock, and crops are discussed. Only after all this exchange is the real reason for the visit brought out by the visitors — the relatives, in this case, were sponsoring an Enemy Way Ceremony and needed some help (13–14).

Use of the Western rhetorical style is, therefore, awkward and difficult for some Navajo students. When Anglo instructors ask students to state their thesis at the beginning of an essay, they're asking students to go against their cultural conventions — and asking them to be bad storytellers. Most composition instructors fail "thesis-less" papers, or papers that make their point in a roundabout or indirect way near the conclusion; when instead, we should be learning, promoting, and assigning equal value and legitimacy to the various rhetorical styles of all cultures. Here in the Southwest, then, effective instructors would teach both the Western and the Navajo rhetorical styles, privileging neither, and would explain the necessity of taking audience and purpose into account when choosing a particular rhetorical strategy.

Instructor ethnocentrism also manifests itself in the tendency to gear courses and methods toward the Anglo student, with little or no consideration for others. Navajo educators criticize Western education for its lack of relevance, saying that it fails to tie schoolwork to anything real; that course content is not connected to everyday life — to family, community, and nation. This criticism is legitimate. Too often, the texts in the composition classroom speak only to the experiences and cultural backgrounds of Anglo students. Textbook publishers' efforts to include multicultural readings in texts have not gone unnoticed at tribal colleges. Still, instructors must supplement those texts with others and explore issues impacting students' lives today, such as the Navajo/Hopi land dispute, Anglo appropriation of Native American rituals and spirituality, the American Indian Religious Freedom Act, the use of peyote in the Native American Church, and autobiographical narratives. And here at NCC, some instructors are successfully experimenting with portfolios that include community projects like writing letters for illiterate community members, making videos, recording oral histories, and so forth.

Although the traditional Navajo way of life is based on sharing and cooperation, and not on acquiring and competing, English instructors often expect work to be performed individually, with little (if any) collaboration. Those teaching Navajos need to place less focus on the individual and more on community — to lecture less, plan more collaborative and small group work, and try to build "learning communities."

Finally, I've noticed that the discussion styles of Navajo and Anglo students are a bit different. Navajo students typically take more time to consider a response to a question — a few seconds longer than most Anglo instructors are willing to wait. The Navajo method of discussion takes more time, is more thorough, and more in depth. I expect students to be open and expressive — and some are — but, as Toadlena writes, "that is not the proper way Navajos are taught to deal with strangers" (8). I like the way Northern Cheyenne elder Grover Wolf Voice explains the "delay" in responding. He says, "Even if I had a quick answer to your question, I would never answer immediately. That would be saying that your question was not worth thinking about" (Gilliland 32).

Patricia Clark Smith's experience teaching on the reservation illustrates the Navajo discussion style. She writes:

> I had to get used to the fact that when I asked a question, I would not see several hands waving competitively in the air. Instead, there'd usually be a silence — sometimes a long silence. Then someone might say something. And after a while, someone else. And then another person. It wasn't that there were never heated exchanges and wild laughter; there were, especially as the class came to trust me and one another more. But for the most part the class felt not so much like a tennis match with questions and answers volleyed back and forth from the teacher's side to the students' side as like a circle slowly drawing

together in consensus. The actual result was that a larger percentage of
the people in that class eventually spoke up than during an average
class on campus, where the most persistent handwavers often shut
down other students. (286)

In order to eradicate ethnocentrism and ignorance about Navajo
cultures, Navajo Community College formally educates its instructors
so that they become familiar with Navajo students' cultural backgrounds and the historical context within which they teach. In two
mandatory semester-long courses, faculty learn about the Navajo creation stories — or at least the first of twelve levels of understanding
the stories. The first level seems like a fairy tale, myth, or religion,
with Holy People and insect people, Father Sky and Mother Earth, monsters, and the Twins who slay the monsters. Instructors learn that the
stories represent a historical charter between the Holy People and the
Diné and that relating course material to traditional creation stories
will inspire and motivate traditional Navajo students. Instructors also
learn about Navajo history, for example, that the United States government paid fifty dollars for each scalp (or, sometimes, an ear) of a
dead Navajo. They learn that the Diné — as well as Native Americans
of almost every tribe — were "relocated" or forced from their homelands
and contained within reservations on less desirable land. They learn
that Kit Carson, who is portrayed as an American hero in Anglo school
books, led the United States Army in hunting down resisting Navajos
and forcing their surrender by destroying their shelters, livestock, and
crops. After four years' incarceration in Ft. Sumner, New Mexico, a location so barren that self-sufficiency was impossible, the Diné were
allowed to return to their traditional homeland, only to find that 90
percent had been taken by settlers, ranchers, and mining interests. In
return for the loss of land, and for agreeing to accept reservations, tribes
were offered annuities and education. Navajo leaders thought they were
agreeing to an education that would combine the best of both the Navajo and Western worlds — one that would allow the Diné to keep their
own traditional ways and values. What they got was something very
different.

Often well-meaning educators (both Anglo and Navajo) saw Native
Americans' cultural customs as "stumbling blocks" and set out to de-
stroy them. They tried to eradicate Navajos' language, dress, and traditions, including their complex healing ceremonies. Educators went
to reservations also determined to negate Navajo ways of knowing, such
as crystal-gazing and hand trembling; and to negate Navajo ways of
doing — it is said, for example, that before white people came and the
knowledge was lost, Navajos could travel from one place to another by
means of prayer. Navajos had, too, an advanced judicial system in which
perpetrators of crimes, rather than being locked up or banished, were
brought back into balance through participation in certain ceremonies
and by making restitution to the victim or victim's family. White educators tried to eradicate the Navajos' completely different way of view-

ing the world, one that, rather than being based on separation and difference, is circular and cyclic, one that sees things in terms of patterns in nature.

To "civilize" Indians, the United States government created off-reservation boarding schools designed not to provide a real education, but to assimilate Native Americans into the dominant culture and to train them for menial positions in the labor force. A 1950s Bureau of Indian Affairs (BIA) program report from Riverside, California, for example, describes in glowing terms the successful training of four bus boys. Anglo educators considered that a laudable achievement. Navajo leaders did not agree and were also deeply troubled that Navajo children placed in BIA boarding schools were separated from their parents for three to five years, even throughout the summers, when they were placed with area families; were paddled or forced to clean toilets for speaking Navajo instead of English; were punished for refusing to worship a Christian god or for participating in traditional Navajo religious practices like praying with corn pollen to the Holy People at dawn; and were one hundred times more likely to commit suicide than white teenagers. Most Navajo students at any institution have either attended BIA boarding schools or have close relatives who did, and today, many traditional Navajos blame the rise in domestic violence and alcoholism on the trauma experienced by students at BIA boarding schools. Knowing the history of Navajo experience of Western education helps NCC faculty understand why some students' grandparents discourage them from attending college (among traditional people, some students tell me, education still has a "bad, bad name").

Ambivalence toward Western Education

Often what instructors interpret as poor or lackluster performance, lack of ability, or lack of motivation by Navajo students is actually ambivalence toward Western education. Historical, philosophical, and practical reasons for this ambivalence toward Western education exist that have far more to do with failure and attrition rates than have been acknowledged. In teaching English, we deny or negate the students' own tribal languages. Toadlena writes that for Navajo students, "English often represents more than the usual freshman irritant. It is a symbol of oppression and, as such, is a formidable stumbling block" (1). "Even today," she adds,

> there is no choice about learning English. While for most Americans learning a second language is not a requirement for economic survival, for the Navajo student, it is a must. It is not a cultural imposition suggesting that the individual give up something of who he is in order to survive. For the Navajo students, surviving has to do with being able to operate adequately within a different value system foreign to them. (1)

The goals of Navajo education are actually broader than our own: they include a deeper understanding of and appreciation for Western as well as Navajo history, culture, language, and literacy; an understanding of the importance of the Navajo values of equality, balance, sharing, cooperation, kinship, and high ethical standards; and the building of students' self-confidence and inner strength. Self-confidence and inner strength are important to Navajo people because they believe that before individuals can go out and build or contribute to their community, they must build their own centers. Only after building a strong personal foundation can they focus on livelihood, and only then on building community or nation. Also considered absolutely essential to a quality education is the application of knowledge. Clearly, Navajos raised to believe that this is the nature of a quality education will be disillusioned when they enter institutions of higher education that negate, deny, or exclude their native values and beliefs.

Navajo students may be ambivalent about Western education for practical reasons, too. Success in college can cost the student a great deal in terms of family and culture, and it is not hard to understand why they might not be especially eager to pay the price. Success in a Western institution, too often, means leaving home and traditional ways behind. It means assimilation into a dominant culture that values materialism, and that, to many Navajos' way of thinking, focuses on technological development at the expense of other equally or more important ends.

How should educators address students' ambivalence toward Western education? I'm not sure, but it is my opinion that as long as the ambivalence remains hidden or unstated, it constitutes an obstacle to students' success. It helps when the instructor understands his or her place in the larger historical context and when the instructor understands the reasons for his or her students' ambivalence. Perhaps if we acknowledge up front that the United States education system has been used as a tool for all-out assimilation and affirm that that is not our purpose, emphasize that SAE can be used as a tool to resist assimilation and preserve Navajo tradition, and show students how writing skills can help students meet the needs of their families, communities, and nations, we can make a difference. On a practical level, this might mean having Navajo students use reading skills to analyze and interpret government documents for community members at Chapter Houses and then use their Navajo literacy skills to translate government documents from English into Navajo. Students could also be taught to use their English skills to write letters to newspaper editors, members of Congress, and other public officials to express their views. If we can make English writing skills relevant, perhaps we can retain more Navajo students.

Conclusion

Navajos and other Native Americans have a great deal to contribute to their own communities and to the larger society.[3] But are we doing enough to mitigate the barriers between Navajos and a college degree? Statistics indicate that we are not: five years ago, the Native American high school student dropout rate, at 35.5 percent, was over twice that of Euro-American students and higher than that of any other United States ethnic or racial group; and according to the Navajo Nation's 1990 Census Report, 56.5 percent of the adults living on the reservation do not have high school degrees, and only 5.5 percent have a bachelor's degree or higher. In 1993, an unpublished study of composition courses at the University of New Mexico conducted by the Orality/ Literacy Committees[4] found that Native Americans are two and a half times more likely to drop or fail those courses than their Anglo counterparts — and because it is the only course required of all college graduates at many institutions, failure to pass composition means failure to attain a degree.

It is time for English instructors, when faced with students from radically different cultural backgrounds and whose needs differ from those of mainstream students, to stop blaming the high failure and attrition rates solely on bilingualism, substandard schooling, low self-esteem, lack of familiarity with SAE, and/or lack of motivation — it is time to look beyond these factors and work to mitigate all the barriers that all minority culture students face.

Notes

1. This situation is not unique to the Navajo people: 221 different Indian languages are known today, and before European colonization, the number was as high as 2,000 (Snipp 41).
2. Mainstream institutions in the Southwest (including the University of New Mexico, Northern Arizona University, and Arizona State University, where the Native American student populations are relatively high), have established composition sections specifically for Native American students. Typically taught by instructors familiar with Native American students' cultures and their dialects, most of these sections use readings and create assignments geared toward Indians and issues that affect them. Problems associated with this strategy include first the assumption of the existence of the "Native American," when the term actually refers to four hundred different Native American peoples in the United States alone, each with different customs, beliefs, languages, and English dialects. Second, each student comes to college with different levels of traditionalism and assimilation into dominant culture, and the more assimilated often don't need or want to enroll in a special section of composition.
3. What impact, for example, would the Native American belief that before a decision is made, its impact on the next seven generations must be considered have on, say, the development of use of nuclear power? The federal deficit? The stockpiling of nuclear weapons?

4. An interdisciplinary group of interested University of New Mexico faculty and graduate students organized the Orality/Literacy Committee in 1992 to explore the causes and to devise appropriate responses to a perceived high failure rate for Native Americans in UNM composition courses.

Works Cited

Gilliland, Hap. *Teaching the Native American*. 2nd ed. Dubuque: Kendall, 1992.

Navajo Nation Government. 1990 Census: Population and Housing Characteristics of the Navajo Nation. Scottsdale: Printing, 1993.

Smith, Patricia Clark. "Icons in the Canyon." *The New Criticism and Contemporary Literary Theory: Connections and Continuities.* Ed. William J. Spurlin and Michael Fischer. New York: Garland, 1995. 275–95.

Snipp, C. Matthew. *American Indians: The First of This Land*. New York: Sage, 1989.

Toadlena, Della. "Why Navajo Students Have Problems with Writing." Unpublished manuscript, 1989.

Classroom Activities

Many developing writers from a variety of cultural backgrounds have had to deal with cultural issues and concerns about assimilation in regard to learning Standard American English. Thurston suggests that instructors "acknowledge up front that the United States education system has been used as a tool for all-out assimilation." In this way, instructors can begin to recognize their students' concerns and "ambivalence toward Western education." However, Thurston advises, we need to go even further, to "show students how writing skills can help students meet the needs of their families, communities, and nations. . . ." Classroom activities that inspired Thurston's pedagogy include translating government documents for those who cannot read or write in English (which uses both Navajo and English literacy skills) and writing "letters to newspaper editors, members of Congress, and other public officials to express their views." Most communities have immediate, if often hidden needs, for those with literacy skills, and opportunities exist for developing writers to intervene in purposeful ways. Ask students to research what kinds of literacy issues exist in their home communities. Students can work together to make lists and brainstorm ideas for service learning projects. If your college or university also has a service learning or volunteer services office, invite a representative from that office to speak to your class on the literacy needs in your community — and on how students can help. Students can keep journals of their service learning work and can complete research-oriented tasks related to their service learning projects. Thurston's letter-writing project would also work well in conjunction with this activity.

Thinking about Teaching

Thurston suggests that teachers need to confront their own "often unconscious" ethnocentrism, which may include the privileged Eurocentric and Western notions of the teaching of writing and reading. One means of doing this work is to learn as much as you can about your students' cultural backgrounds. Students should not be expected to do this work for their teachers (especially since many students are still engaged in the lifelong process of learning more about their own cultural heritage); rather, teachers can take on this task themselves, either individually or in groups. In addition, you and your colleagues may wish to examine your views concerning stereotypes. What can be done to help us face our fears, intolerance, impatience, or lack of understanding of students from cultural, racial, religious, or class backgrounds different from our own — and to create an environment in which we internalize and then model tolerance, cultural appreciation, and community?[1] All of these goals, Thurston offers, go a long way toward promoting a positive learning climate for students and for increasing retention. Reflect on these issues in your teaching journal, and share your ideas with other instructors and students.

---

[1] I am indebted to Susan Peterson and Lynne Shivers, English department faculty at the Community College of Philadelphia, who ran workshops on confronting stereotypes for students and instructors when I was a junior faculty member at the College in the mid-1990s. Participating in forums that gave people of many backgrounds the opportunity to speak and listen openly with each other is an experience that has inspired my teaching ever since.

12

Teaching ESL

E SL students come from a great diversity of backgrounds — from international students choosing to study abroad, to refugees who are forced to flee for their lives from their countries of origin. This chapter accounts for this diversity by focusing on pedagogies that value this wide range of student voices and experiences. Readers will have encountered many of the concerns in this chapter when they read about combining reading and writing, collaborative learning and peer review, and writing and race, class, and gender elsewhere in this ancillary. The writers in this chapter are aware of the need to understand their students' cultural differences. Clearly, the focus here is not on the "grammatical correctness" of ESL students' writing. Instead, readers will encounter a pedagogy that emphasizes student-centered learning and writing as a means of gaining fluency in English. Although such a pedagogy may now be a commonplace in courses for developing writers who learned English as their first language, traditional approaches to ESL have focused on teacher-centered classrooms, with an emphasis on the "basics" of English. In contrast, the articles in this section emphasize a student-centered approach in which understanding the writing process (including peer review and small-group discussion) is a primary goal. Loretta Frances Kasper examines her work with ESL students in a process-based classroom. Yu Ren Dong asks students to write literacy narratives about their experiences with writing and reading in their first language so that they can understand the continuum of the writing process. Together, these essays demonstrate a pedagogy that focuses on English language fluency and that values the whole student. The student voices represented in these selections help to tell an important part of the story.

ESL Writing and the Principle of Nonjudgmental Awareness: Rationale and Implementation

Loretta Frances Kasper

In the following article, Loretta Frances Kasper clearly articulates the differences between emerging basic writing pedagogy and traditional ESL pedagogy: "Basic writing programs generally apply a process approach to writing, emphasizing development of ideas and gradually placing a greater responsibility on the students as they go through the writing process. . . . In contrast, many ESL programs still maintain a product approach to writing in which grammar is explicitly taught and in which the final product becomes more important than the process which it was created by." Kasper suggests that the emphasis on product creates anxiety for ESL students, especially in placement examination situations. She found that when she switched to a process-based pedagogical model, her students not only improved their fluency but also achieved better results on their final writing examination, which "was cross-graded by two other ESL instructors." Loretta Frances Kasper is Associate Professor of English at Kingsborough Community College/CUNY and the author of Teaching English through the Disciplines: Psychology.

R ecent statistics show that ESL students enrolled in community colleges are steadily increasing. In fact, Crandall reports that ESL is the fastest growing area of study in community colleges in the United States. In community colleges within the City University of New York system (CUNY), dubbed by Crandall, a "microcosm of the United States as a whole," (4) 25 percent of entering students now need instruction in English as a Second Language (Nunez-Wormack). By 2000, estimates are that more than 50 percent of full-time first-year students in the CUNY system will be ESL students (Professional Staff Congress). College ESL students must demonstrate writing proficiency for full entry into the mainstream curriculum. However, developing this proficiency presents an especially difficult problem for such students.

Studies of both basic and ESL writers have shown that instructor feedback plays a significant role in students' progress as writers (Bass; Zak) and that the priorities of the instructor become the priorities of the student. Therefore, when responding to ESL students' writing, instructors must be aware of the priorities they communicate to their students and should provide evaluative feedback that decreases writing anxiety as it increases writing satisfaction. I have found that implementing Gallwey's principle of nonjudgmental awareness with a process approach that emphasizes fluency and clarity of expression and deemphasizes correctness has improved the performance of intermediate-level (TOFEL score of approximately 350) ESL students.

The Principle of Nonjudgmental Awareness

The principle of nonjudgmental awareness was first advanced by W. Timothy Gallwey in his book, *The Inner Game of Tennis*. Gallwey believes that learning proceeds most effectively and effortlessly when the learners allow themselves to move naturally through the learning process, aware of relevant aspects of performance without making excessive critical judgments about that performance.

Although initially advanced as a means of learning a physical skill such as tennis, the principle of nonjudgmental awareness has been applied to learning skills in academic domains. For example, Ploger and Carlock successfully used this principle to teach students to construct computer programs designed to represent ideas from biology. They found that implementation of the principle of nonjudgmental awareness made it easier for students to learn how to write programs that were both meaningful and accurate, and then, to revise those programs to explain the problem-solving strategy step-by-step. Ploger and Carlock believe that the nonjudgmental instructional technique lessened the anxiety students felt about the task of writing a computer program and ultimately enabled these students to gain a deeper overall understanding of the principles of biology.

Task anxiety and insufficient understanding of the writing process also plague and inhibit the writing performance of ESL students. For this reason, I decided to adopt a nonjudgmental instructional approach in an attempt to lessen my intermediate-level ESL students' writing anxiety and to improve their writing performance. As I use the term, "nonjudgmental instructional approach" refers to an approach to writing instruction that is process- rather than product-oriented, is student-centered, and one in which the chief goal of instruction is to help students attain fluency and clarity of expression. I do not explicitly teach grammar in the ESL writing class; rather, students acquire and improve their use of the grammatical structures they need to express ideas most effectively through a series of progressive attempts to refine and clarify those ideas. Thus, mechanical accuracy is not the means to achieving fluency and clarity of expression; rather, mechanical accuracy is the result of having worked to express ideas most fluently and clearly.

To evaluate the effectiveness of this approach, I conducted an informal three-semester study. My students come from a number of diverse linguistic, ethnic, and cultural backgrounds, including Russian, Hispanic, Haitian, and Asian. Over a period of three semesters, I gradually adopted a less error- and more expression-oriented response approach in which I moved from correcting virtually all student errors to simply identifying those errors and requiring that the students themselves correct them. The results of my informal analyses indicated that over the course of the three semesters a progressively greater percentage (61 percent, 82 percent, 89 percent) of the students passed the final writing examination. This writing final required students to plan, write, and revise a persuasive essay on their choice of three assigned topics based on the work done during the semester and was cross-graded by two other ESL instructors in the department.

Rationale for the Nonjudgmental Approach

Although basic writing instructors may find nonjudgmental response not a radical departure from traditional pedagogy, the approach to teaching writing in many ESL programs is quite different from that in most basic writing programs. Basic writing programs generally apply a process approach to writing, emphasizing the development of ideas and gradually placing greater responsibility on the students as they go through the writing process. In this approach, writing becomes a process of discovery in which "ideas are generated and not just transcribed" (Susser 35).

In contrast, many ESL programs still maintain a product approach to writing in which grammar is explicitly taught and in which the final product becomes more important than the process by which it was created. In product-driven ESL writing programs, instructors continually provide students with accurate models of language, the assumption being that, with more grammar and more correction, students will be able to produce fluent and clear compositions.

One of the rationales offered for product-driven ESL writing programs is that ESL students are required to pass college assessment examinations that often judge writing on the basis of grammatical accuracy. In one study, Sweedler-Brown found that "sentence-level error was . . . the crucial factor in pass/fail decisions in ESL essays" (12), and she concludes that "we may be doing our ESL students a disservice if we are not willing to become language teachers as well as writing teachers" (15). The problem with this approach is that too often the priority becomes teaching students sufficient language rules so they can write accurately enough to pass an examination, rather than helping them develop their potential to discover and express their ideas.

Furthermore, a study conducted by MacGowan-Gilhooly demonstrated that when the ESL writing course focused on producing grammatical correctness for the purpose of preparing students to pass a college writing assessment test, they did not progress as well, and some actually regressed from former performance levels. Of course, this regression may have been the result of students' attempts to produce more sophisticated linguistic structures: however, MacGowan-Gilhooly attributes it to the pressure produced by writing for evaluation where that evaluation depends upon correctness of language rather than upon quality of content. Like MacGowan-Gilhooly, Bass has also found that, in general, students' progress is often inhibited when they anticipate that their writing will be evaluated for its correctness.

Implementing the Principle of Nonjudgmental Awareness

On the very first day of classes, I describe the nonjudgmental instructional approach to my ESL student writers. I explain that I want them to focus on expressing ideas in their essays, and we discuss the purpose of writing as the communication of those ideas to another person. I tell students not to worry about correctness in their initial drafts, to allow their ideas to flow freely onto the paper. I explain that they will receive both instructor and peer feedback on each essay. I then announce that when I respond to their essays, I will not be correcting errors in grammar. Instead, I will point out where the errors are, but that they will be responsible for correcting those errors. I tell them that if they have any problems, they should discuss those problems with me, and we will solve them together.

Some students do express anxiety when they first hear about this approach; however, after only a few assignments, they discover that as they work through several drafts of each essay, increasing the fluency and clarity of each subsequent draft, they gradually become aware of the mechanical errors and rhetorical features which obscure meaning in their writing. With their continued practice, my support, and the suggestions of their peer partners, the students learn how to reduce their errors. Successfully assuming this responsibility not only gives ESL students the confidence they need to continue to improve their writing skills, but also helps them to view good writing as clear communication rather than merely as accurate grammar.

Because priorities communicated through instructor feedback have such a great impact on the progress of student writers, it is important to adopt response styles that will be most facilitative to this progress and which will lessen students' anxiety and increase their confidence. We can help students gain confidence in their writing abilities by asking them to gradually assume more responsibility for their growth as writers, while at the same time providing them with the instructional support they need to achieve their writing goals. Implementing a nonjudgmental approach in an ESL writing class does just that by creating a climate in which students are acknowledged for their successes and, at the same time, are taught specific strategies for dealing with their deficiencies in writing. Moreover, a nonjudgmental instructional approach asks students to assume a more active role in their own learning as they critique both their own and their classmates' work. Feedback from both the instructor and their peers encourages students to express ideas more clearly and more fluently. As Connors and Lunsford's research demonstrates, the more student writers focus on clarifying meaning, the fewer the number of errors they make.

Nonjudgmental Techniques

The pedagogical techniques used in a nonjudgmental writing class are, for the most part, student — rather than instructor — centered. Students assume greater responsibility for their progress and learn instructional techniques to help them assume this responsibility. Below I describe some of the nonjudgmental techniques that I have found effective. These techniques include providing instructor feedback via task-oriented questions, guiding students in providing peer evaluation, teaching students to vocalize thoughts when they have trouble writing, and obtaining student feedback through writing evaluation questionnaires and writing autobiographies.

Providing Instructor Feedback via Task-Oriented Questions

While error correction is instructor-centered, task-oriented questions are student-centered. Task-oriented questions direct students' attention to ways they may improve the content and the clarity of their ideas. Task-oriented questions may request more information, reflect on students' thoughts, and/or share experiences similar to those expressed by the student (Beaven). These are some of the task-oriented questions I have used: "Could you be more specific, provide more details, about this point?" "Could you open up the essay with a more general statement?" "How does this example relate to the main point of your essay?" These task-oriented questions have helped ESL students improve and expand the content of their essays and increase the clarity of their ideas.

Using Peer Evaluation

According to Stanley, "peer evaluation can provide student writers with a wide range of benefits, including reduced writing anxiety, increased sense of audience, and increased fluency" (217). Moreover, Stanley asserts that peer evaluation "facilitates the transition from what Flower and Hayes term 'writer-based prose' to 'reader-based prose'" (218). In the process of critiquing their classmates' writings, students take the stance of the reader; they learn what works and what does not work and develop an increased awareness of the elements of fluent and clear writing. However, Stanley has found that for peer evaluation to be effective, students need to be coached "to be specific in their responses, . . . to point to problematic portions of text, to alert writers to lapses in coherence, to offer specific advice for solving these problems, and to collaborate with the writer on more suitable phrases" (226–227).

Following Stanley's recommendations, I offered ESL students such coaching. Then I divided the class into several groups of two or three students each, with the only restriction that, whenever possible, students within the same group not speak the same native language because they might tend to use (and so not recognize) the same inaccurate English language structures which would obscure the clarity of their writing. I then asked the students to exchange and read the drafts of the others in their group and to fill out a peer evaluation questionnaire for each paper they read. This peer evaluation questionnaire asked the students to evaluate how clearly ideas were expressed as they answered the following eight questions: (1) What was the topic of the essay? (2) What was the writer's opinion about this topic? (3) Where in the essay was this opinion stated? (4) What did you like best about this essay? (5) List any places where you did not understand the writer's meaning. He/she will need to clarify these things in the next draft. (6) What would you like to know more about when the writer revises this essay? (7) Reread the first paragraph of the essay. Do you think this is a good beginning? Does it make you feel like reading on? Explain; and (8) How could the writer improve this paper when he/she revises it? Make only one suggestion.

Some researchers have reported that ESL students are often recalcitrant when asked to evaluate the writing of their peers (Nelson and Murphy); however, I found that, after some initial hesitation, students enjoyed the peer evaluation process and said that it was very helpful. This activity made writing "a task of communicating" (Stanley 217), and in their interactions with peers, students developed increased confidence and were more willing to take risks in their writing. In addition, these partnerships helped to promote interpersonal relationships among students, leading them to an increased understanding and tolerance of cultural differences.

Teaching Students to Vocalize Thoughts

Another effective nonjudgmental technique is teaching students to vocalize thoughts to help them get past writing blocks. Students can do this alone or within the context of their peer evaluation group. Peter Elbow has pointed out the value of vocalizing thoughts: "If you are stuck writing . . . , there is nothing better than finding one person, or more, to talk to. . . . I write a paper; it's not very good; I discuss it with someone: after fifteen minutes of back-and-forth I say something in response to a question . . . of his and he says, 'But why didn't you say that? That's good. That's clear'"(49).

When my ESL students are doing in-class writing or interacting in their peer evaluation groups, I circulate around the room to check work or offer assistance. If I notice an inaccuracy or a confusion in writing, I ask the student, "What did you want to say here?" I then suggest that the student write down what he or she has just told me. I also tell students that if they get stuck in the writing process, they should think of how they would express the idea if they were speaking to someone. More often than not, my intermediate level ESL students, even those with somewhat limited fluency in the spoken language, are able to tell me or their writing partners in relatively correct English what they wanted to say: On those occasions when students are not able to vocalize their ideas completely, they usually can communicate enough of the idea so that either I or their peer partners can provide assistance. Thus, asking students to vocalize thoughts can help them to improve both written and spoken English.

If we can get students to think of how they would communicate their ideas orally and then transfer that oral communication to the written form, we may be able to demystify the writing process and help students to improve their writing. I have found that when ESL students vocalize their thoughts when writing, the result is a decrease in the number of structural and grammatical errors and an increase in the clarity of expression.

Student Feedback: Writing Evaluation Questionnaires

This questionnaire, designed to elucidate the kinds of teacher responses that students perceived as helpful, asked them to identify the specific instructor feedback techniques they found most useful when revising their writing. A majority of the students found instructor feedback in the form of task-oriented questions useful in revision, stating that these questions directed attention to exactly what needed to be improved in the essay. Some of the other responses indicated that feedback on how to organize the essay and on how to write a good introduction and conclusion was helpful. Many of the students also said that although at first they were uncomfortable about correcting their own grammatical errors, as the semester went on, they were able to find and correct many of their errors. This discovery went a long way toward helping students become better writers. As many of them indicated in their feedback questionnaires, being able to find and correct their own errors gave them confidence in their ability to write English.

Student Feedback: Writing Autobiographies

The writing autobiography was the last essay students wrote before taking their writing final. The writing autobiography question sheet was adapted from one used by Sandman and Weiser (19) and asked students to describe positive and negative experiences in writing English and their strengths and weaknesses as writers. In addition to the three questions suggested by Sandman and Weiser, I also asked students the following question, "What have you learned this semester about your ability as a writer? How, specifically, do *you* think your writing has improved? What areas of your writing do you think still need work?" This writing autobiography had several objectives — to elucidate students' attitudes toward writing, to help them monitor their development as writers, and to assist them in developing sound criteria for assessing their writing performance. Moreover, by increasing students' awareness of their own writing experiences and knowledge, the writing autobiography encouraged them to think of themselves as writers.

Their responses to the writing autobiography activity indicated that students had developed a clearer understanding of their personal involvement in the writing task. The students all said that writing was a positive experience when they were writing about something that they enjoyed because then they were able to express their ideas on a subject of interest. They each noted that a negative experience was when they had to write an essay for the writing assessment test upon entrance to the college. Many of them said that they lost confidence and felt unable to write because of the pressure. They knew that they had to write correctly to pass the test and that the result of the test would determine which courses they would be required or allowed to take in college. As a result, some said that the pressure of the test "had made their minds go blank." These responses support the claims of both MacGowan-Gilhooly and Bass that writing for evaluation can inhibit students' progress.

Their responses to the writing autobiographies indicated that when these ESL students focused on expressing their ideas, they found writing to be a positive experience. In contrast, when students focused on producing correct language, they concentrated on their perceived weaknesses, their ideas were stifled, and writing became a negative experience.

After being exposed to the nonjudgmental approach, when asked to describe their strengths and weaknesses, students generally focused on their strengths. A common response was, "I have good ideas, and it's interesting to tell other people about those ideas." Furthermore, few of these students cited grammar as a weakness; in fact, their responses illustrated that they had come to view mistakes as a means to improving writing. Rather than weaknesses in grammar, their responses now focused on weaknesses in conveying meaning, such as difficulty organizing their thoughts or writing an effective introduction or conclusion.

For a nonjudgmental approach to enhance writing proficiency, it must result in students' experiencing increased confidence and decreased anxiety when writing English. The students' feedback on the question of what they had learned that semester about their ability as writers demonstrated that the nonjudgmental approach had achieved this goal. One response predominated in each of the essays; the students had learned that they were able to communicate their ideas in written English. They expressed an increased confidence in their ability to write, so that they were more willing to take risks in their writing. Moreover, they had learned that if they made mistakes, they were not only able to find and correct those mistakes, but they were able to learn from them.

Here are some students' responses: "I learned I could make my writing better if I tried areas that I still need work in"; "I saw that after every writing task, I could express my ideas better and fully"; "I learned how to check my work by myself. I was really surprised when I saw that I could find a lot of mistakes without any help"; "I realized that I can break down a subject in my own words without much difficulty"; "I learned that I have the ability to write more than I used to"; and "I got more confidence in my writing. It is my firm belief that in the future I will know how to write English better if I practice it every day."

The focus on fluency and clarity of expression in the nonjudgmental, process-oriented approach also helped ESL students to learn the value of revision. I encouraged students to refine ideas, not just to correct language in their revisions, and many commented that writing an essay several times had taught them how to clarify meaning by adding new information and by rearranging sections of the essay.

In his research on second language writing, Krashen (19) has found that developmental writers usually do not understand that revision can help them generate new ideas. In fact, they usually think that their first draft contains all their ideas, and they believe that revising an essay simply means making the first draft neater by correcting language errors. In the process of revision for clarity of expression, my students discovered not only that they could write English, but also that writing itself became easier and more satisfying with each subsequent revision.

Conclusion and Implications for Instruction

Bernard Susser has noted the concern of some ESL researchers that process-based approaches emphasize fluency at the expense of accuracy. However, my experience indicates that a process-based, nonjudgmental instructional approach can help intermediate-level ESL students improve both the fluency and the accuracy with which they express their ideas in written English. Like the students in Sweedler-Brown's study, my students had to improve grammatical accuracy to pass the writing final. Nevertheless, in contrast to Sweedler-Brown's contention that we should become "language teachers as well as writing teachers" (15), I found that the number of students who passed the final rose as I provided less grammatical feedback. In fact, the students made the greatest progress in expressing themselves fluently, clearly, and correctly when they themselves assumed the most responsibility for their own learning.

As my ESL students shifted their focus from correctness of form to fluency and clarity of expression, they discovered that they had something to say and that they were able to say it fluently, clearly, and, for the most part, correctly. Writing became a more positive experience as they gained confidence in their ability to express themselves in written English. The students became aware of their strengths and weaknesses as writers, and when given the time and the opportunity to develop their strengths, they were able to minimize their weaknesses.

Most importantly, they got their priorities straight as they came to realize that the primary goal of writing is the communication of ideas and that through the process of writing we discover and refine those ideas. They also learned that in the process of clarifying ideas, they could minimize language errors. As a result, they became less intimidated by their mistakes.

For years, basic writing programs have focused on refining writing skills through a step-by-step process in which the writer is encouraged to develop and expand upon ideas, and is ultimately responsible for his or her own progress. It is time for ESL writing programs to follow suit. If the goal of ESL composition instruction is to help students become proficient writers of English, it must provide a learning environment which both allows students to gain confidence in their ability as writers and transfers the ultimate responsibility for their development as writers from teachers to students. Implementing the principle of nonjudgmental awareness in the ESL writing class achieves this goal by making communicative competence, rather than grammatical accuracy, the primary focus of instruction.

Note

I thank Dr. Don Ploger for sharing his ideas and insights on learning and awareness during my research.

Works Cited

Bass, Barbara Kaplan. "The Mathematics of Writing: Shaping Attitude in Composition Classes." *Teaching English in the Two-Year College* 20(1993): 109–14.

Beaven, Mary. "Individualized Goal Setting, Self-Evaluation, and Peer Evaluation." *Evaluating Writing*. Ed. Charles R. Copper and Lee Odell. Urbana: NCTE. 135–56.

Connors, Robert J., and Andrea A. Lunsford. "Frequency of Formal Errors in Current Writing, or Ma and Pa Kettle Do Research." *College Composition and Communication* 39 (1988): 395–409.

Crandall, JoAnn. "Diversity as Challenge and Resource." *Conference Proceedings ESL Students in the CUNY Classroom: Faculty Strategies for Success.* 5 Feb. 1993. Manhattan Community College/CUNY. 1–2.

Elbow, Peter. *Writing without Teachers*. New York: Oxford UP, 1973.

Flower, Linda S., and John R. Hayes. "A Cognitive Process Theory of Writing." *College Composition and Communication* 32 (1981): 365–88.

Gallwey, W. Timothy. *The Inner Game of Tennis*. New York: Random, 1974.

Krashen, Stephen. *Fundamentals of Language Education*. Torrence: Laredo, 1992.

MacGowan-Gilhooly, Adele. "Fluency before Correctness: A Whole-Language Experiment in College ESL." *College ESL* 1.1 (1991): 37–47.

Nelson, Gayle L., and John M. Murphy. "An L2 Writing Group: Task and Social Dimensions. *Journal of Second Language Writing* 1.3 (1992): 171–93.

Nunez-Wormack, Elsa. "Remarks." *Conference Proceedings ESL Students in the CUNY Classroom: Faculty Strategies for Success*. 5 Feb. 1993. Manhattan Community College/CUNY. 1–2.

Ploger, Don, and Margaret Carlock. "Programming and Problem Solving: Implications for Biology Education." *Journal of Artificial Intelligence in Education* 2.4 (1991): 15–31.

Professional Staff Congress/City University of New York. "CUNY Plans Language Immersion Institute." *Clairon* 24.4 (1994): 1–3.

Sandman, John, and Michael Weiser. "The Writing Autobiography: How to Begin a Two-Year College Writing Course." *Teaching English in the Two-Year College* 20 (1993): 18–22.

Stanley, Jane. "Coaching Student Writers to Be Effective Peer Evaluators." *Journal of Second Language Writing* 1.3 (1992): 217–33.

Susser, Bernard. "Process Approaches in ESL/EFL Writing Instruction." *Journal of Second Language Writing* 3.1 (1994): 31–47.

Sweedler-Brown, Carol O. "ESL Essay Evaluation: The Influence of Sentence-Level and Rhetorical Features." *Journal of Second Language Writing* 2.1 (1993): 3–17.

Zak, Frances. "Exclusively Positive Responses to Student Writing." *Journal of Basic Writing* 9.2 (1990): 40–53.

Classroom Activities

Kasper provides a list of eight questions from a peer review questionnaire that she distributes during rough draft workshops. The questions range from descriptive ("What was the topic of the essay?") to evaluative ("How could the writer improve this paper when he/she revises it? Make only one suggestion.") Give a copy of this questionnaire to your students, and work together with students to make the questionnaire more specific to their own paper assignments. Questions can be revised based on concepts that the students are learning. For example, students could ask: "Does this paper have a thesis statement? If so, what is it? If not, where would the reader expect to see the thesis statement?" and so forth. In addition, when considering how students are to be divided into peer groups, Kasper suggests only one restriction: "whenever possible, students within the same group must not speak the same native language because they might tend to use (and so not recognize) the same inaccurate English structures which would obscure the clarity of their writing." Notice again that the emphasis for Kasper is not on grammatical correctness but on the fluency and clarity of student writing.

Thinking about Teaching

Kasper bases her definition of nonjudgmental awareness on the principles presented in W. Timothy Gallwey's book *The Inner Game of Tennis*. Gallwey believes that learners are most effective when they "allow themselves to move through the learning process, aware of relevant aspects of performance without making excessive critical judgments about that performance." In your teaching journal, reflect on your own response to Gallwey's principles. How might these principles be related to second language learning? Reflect on Noguchi's idea about how "grammatical incorrectness" often seems to violate "socially approved" norms. Is there a connection between such social approval and approaches to grammatical correctness in traditional ESL pedagogy? What might social class or race have to do with how "correctness" is determined? Are some errors made by ESL students traditionally considered to be less acceptable than others? What has usually been the criteria for determining which errors are more or less acceptable? Discuss your findings with other teachers and students, as appropriate.

The Need to Understand ESL Students' Native Language Writing Experiences

Yu Ren Dong

"Teachers are quick to recognize ESL students' grammatical errors in their writing," writes Yu Ren Dong, " but often they are slow to get to know these students, who differ widely in their expectations of schooling, their views of the roles of teacher and student, their reading and writing experiences back home, their learning preferences, and how all of these impact their learning to read and write in English." To ameliorate this situation in her own classroom, Dong invites students to write about "how they learned to write in their native language . . . and about the differences they perceived when comparing writing in their native language to writing in English." Her article documents her study of twenty-six first-year students at a four-year university who had come from a wide variety of backgrounds, had had extensive training in reading and writing in their first language, and had also attended New York City public high schools. Throughout the article, the voices of Dong's students speak clearly and poignantly about their experiences with literacy in their native countries. For instance, a student from Russia writes: "I had one great teacher. . . . She gave us such nice topics to write about that everyone wanted to write. The teacher told us: 'You think you are students? No! You are writers!'" An Assistant Professor of English in the Department of Secondary Education and Youth Services at Queens College, CUNY, Yu Ren Dong has published articles in Research in the Teaching of English, TESOL Journal, *and* English for Specific Purposes.

Introduction

I remember a high school assignment that I dreaded. I had to write about my experiences in life and how they influenced my life. I thought to myself "What real experience did I have in my life?" I sat down for days without anything. But a week later I started to write a list of things that I did when I was young back in my home country, and soon I began to see that there were a lot of things on the list. I began to write my paper and was surprised to see how wonderfully it turned out. This was the most satisfying assignment that I had ever done. This was because I found out something about myself that influenced me tremendously in my life. From that I learned that when writing you can find out more about yourself.

Like the above first-year ESL student, many non-English-speaking students come to college composition with rich home cultural, educational, language, and literacy backgrounds. In particular, some have acquired sophisticated literacy skills in their native languages. Research on second language acquisition in academic settings done by Cummins and Collier has shown that students with native literacy skills often acquire English language skills faster than those without native literacy skills. Unfortunately, these students' native language and literacy learning experiences are often not considered when planning instruction.

Teachers are quick to recognize ESL students' grammatical errors in their writing, but often they are slow to get to know these students, who differ widely in their expectations of schooling, their views of the roles of teacher and students, their prior schooling, their reading and writing experiences back home, their learning style preferences, and how all of these impact their learning to read and write in English. As composition instructors encounter more and more linguistically and culturally diverse students in their classrooms, they must attempt to learn about these students' literacy backgrounds and to develop strategies to make good use of what the students learned back home in order to accelerate their learning of English reading and writing skills. Such knowledge is particularly important not only for these students to succeed in American schools, but also for building a classroom environment where diverse educational, cultural, and literacy backgrounds are valued and become resources rather than problems.

Method

In order to investigate ESL students' native literacy learning experiences, I invited twenty-six first-year college students at a four-year college in New York City to write autobiographies describing how they learned to write in their native language. I wanted to find out how these students learned to read and write in their native countries, what writing assignments they liked, and what the differences in writing were between their native language and English. The twenty-six students who participated in the research project had all had extensive schooling in their home countries before coming to America. Most of them had acquired a high level of native language literacy skills and, therefore, were competent readers and writers in their native languages, which included Chinese, Korean, French/Creole, Hebrew, Italian, Russian, Polish, and Spanish. The majority of them also attended and graduated from New York City public high schools. Their average American educational experience was about two and half years. Therefore, they were able to compare two educational systems and two sets of language and literacy learning experiences, native and United States.

In order to elicit students' responses, I wrote a letter to these students with a series of probing questions (see Appendix). I asked them specifically about how they learned to write in their native language, about the first things they remember writing, about the most satisfying piece of writing in their native language, and about the differences they perceived when comparing writing in their native language to writing in English.

Students were more responsive about their learning experiences with writing in the following three major areas:

- writing instruction in their native languages,
- most satisfying writing assignments in their native languages,
- differences between writing in their native language and in English.

Writing Instruction in Native Languages

Despite a wide range of native literacy learning experiences noted by these twenty-six students, a common theme emerged: students all had had some kind of native language writing instruction before coming to the United States. Very often this instruction began in the elementary school, as one student wrote:

> I was only four year old when I started to go to school in my country, Peru. When I went to the first grade, my teacher began to teach us the vowels and then the consonants of the alphabet. Then the teacher proceeded to teach the class how to form simple words like: mama and papa and then Mi mama me mima, which means my mother cares for me. In the second grade, I was taught to read simple stories and later my teacher taught the class components of a sentence. We learned about the verb, the subject, and the predicate. It was a bit hard for most seven year old, including me to learn these grammar rules. . . . By the time I finished the third grade, I knew how to form complicated sentences and how to construct paragraphs that made sense. I was also able to read books that were more complex, the newspapers and signs in the street that once I wondered what they meant. In my fourth grade, my teacher taught the class words that were similar in meanings and I learned a variety of words quickly and also learned how to use them in sentences too.

Reflecting on their native literacy learning experiences, many students revealed the distinctive ways that their teachers back home used to teach them how to write in their native languages. For example, the student from Haiti recalled writing instruction in his schooling like this:

> I learned speak Creole first, but went to school learning French. Some of the first things that I remember writing were about my family. I was about five year old then. The teacher asked us to describe my family and the games that I played. . . . The teachers in my country (Haiti) would have me recite what I had written for homework. Haitian teachers are also very strict. Some would have me rewrite word-for-word what I had to read the previous day. If I could not write and remember, I would be beaten or be sent to detention. Sometimes a teacher would sent a student to stand in the corner on one foot for fifteen minutes in order to get students to do their work.

Several Russian students revealed a strong focus on language and structure in native writing instruction, for example:

> Usually teachers in Russia paid more attention to the grammar mistakes. Therefore they helped us how to use correct words. We had some special orthographic rules. Teachers helped us to combine sentences and spelling. . . . At school back in Russia, we had a lot of homework and sometimes the teachers gave us the permission so that we could stay behind and study in the afternoon. The classmates who had excellent marks helped us to do better work by tutoring. . . . Some of the teachers who didn't have families stayed with us and gave extra help.

One Russian student noted the excitement of learning to write in Russian and the high expectations that her teacher maintained for the students:

> In Russia, students write a lot. In my middle school years, we used to write compositions for ten to fifteen pages. I had one great teacher. She did not give us any unusual techniques, but she explained to each and every student any mistakes he or she made, and told us how to write better. She gave us such nice topics that everyone wanted to write. The teacher told us: "You think you are students? No! You are writers!"

Students also described a range of writing tasks assigned by their teachers back home. These assignments included: diary/journal, literature responses, research papers, aesthetic prose, and essays. A Korean student recalled a progression from diary writing to writing a book report in her schooling back in Korea and how the teacher motivated the students to write:

> I began to write in Korean when I was about nine year old. I had to write my diary as homework. I wrote almost everyday, and my teacher looked over and gave me some comments. When I was a middle school student, I used to write about my impression of certain books that we read. There were two or three contests about this type of writing on

certain books every month. The teacher gave a prize to a student who was the best writer of the month.

A Polish student wrote about a variety of writing assignments given by her teachers and the expectation of how to write a literary analysis in her high school:

> I started to learn how to write in Polish, my native language, during the last few years in the elementary school. The teacher gave us a lot of freedom in our writing. Our assignments could be a letter, a dialogue, a monologue, or defending a position. Later we had to write what the authors point in the writing the book was and what the main characters and ideas in the book were and how we could compare it to our lives and our experiences and what our personal opinion was about the book.

A Russian student described a kind of research-oriented essay assignment in his high school experience:

> In my high school days back home, we were assigned to write essays. The essays in Russian were usually much longer and complicated. For example, we wrote a book about the life of Tolstoy, a famous Russian writer. It was about twenty-one pages long and very complicated. I had to say a lot of different information from different sources like encyclopedias.

A Chinese student confirmed the similar writing assignments that she had back home and in the United States. However, she mentioned a different type of writing that she was taught to write:

> Back in China at middle school and high school, we learned how to write a kind of prose, we called san wen, an interpretation of a natural scenery using your own voice. This was a literary genre created by classical Chinese writer Zhu Zi Qing. Reading his writing, for example his masterpiece "The moonlight over the lotus pond," I had this (transactional) feeling with the writer and enjoyed the way the writer put the words on the paper. It was beautiful.

Several students noted a close connection between reading and writing when talking about their progression in learning how to write in their native language. These students said that they were taught to use literature for vocabulary development and imitating certain styles of writing. A strong emphasis on reading to write was shown in these students' reflections as shown in the following Chinese student's autobiography:

> Reading is important because it lets you know how a nice piece should be like. You can't write down something nice without knowing what is nice. It's easy to read some stories as entertainment, but it's not easy to catch the ways that how these good writers wrote. My teachers back in

China helped us know how these writers wrote by explaining their ideas and how they chose words with similar meanings.

Reading was closely related to writing. Several students noted the importance of reading to write and imitating the style of the writers:

> When I was more proficient in Spanish, my native language, I was taught to read the famous authors' works like Miguel de Cervantes and other famous Spanish novelists works. They influenced me a lot in my style of writing. I fell in love with the way they used the words in their novels. Since then, I started to use complex sentence structures in Spanish with a great many fancy words. Thanks to them I gained a vast knowledge of the Spanish vocabulary.

A Bangladesh student recalled how he took trouble to bring books to America to use reading to refresh his reading and writing skills:

> Now I write letters to my friends back home and I also read novels in my native language. The best writing practice of my language is to read novels. When I came over here, I brought about two hundred books with me and now I am rereading them again and again since I don't have more books to read. By doing that, I can still feel about my country and keep up with my writing.

Most Satisfying Writing Assignments in Their Native Languages

Reading through these students' writing autobiographies, I noticed a consistency. Though many of these students might not be verbal in class or perform well in English, they were already successful writers in their native languages. Many of them continued writing in their native languages after coming to the United States. Students told stories of how the most satisfying piece of writing that they wrote made a difference in their perception of writing and motivated them to become successful writers. For example, a Polish student recalled:

> I still remember my first favorite book on love and the assignment based on that book back home in Poland. It was an old Celtic myth "Tristan and Tholdo" and "Tristan 1964". My writing was read in front of the class, that made me feel like a really good writer. When I finished elementary school, I already knew that I liked to write and my papers were pretty good. According to that I chose a high school with a special writing program. I wrote a lot, especially poetry. One of my poems "Angel" got the first award in school poetry contest.

A Russian student wrote about competing in a writing contest:

> When I was twelve, I read a story and I hated the end of it. So, I rewrote the end of the story and made it a happy one. There was a writing

contest among all the school students of the Soviet Union. I sent in my story. I was not among the first winners, but I still got a prize of one hundred rubles. It was big money for me, a small girl who have never had more than a ruble.

A Chinese student revealed how he used writing to express his feelings and passion to win his girlfriend back:

I love to write a lyric prose. My most satisfying school assignment came when I was in the secondary school back in Hong Kong. I had a girl-friend back then and we had wonderful days together. But we broke up after a while. I was so hurt. One day, my Chinese teacher asked us to write a letter to someone we love. I wrote about my ex-girlfriend and I didn't know how to stop or did not even want to stop. I said all the words that I wanted to say to her and I listened to my feelings from my heart. Finally this composition was marked a highest grade in class and my teacher encouraged me to send it to the newspaper and I did. A few weeks later, my writing was printed on the prose section of the newspaper. My girlfriend was so touched by all this that we went back together. From writing that piece I learned how powerful writing is and I liked to express myself in writing.

The most satisfying writing assignment was also remembered by many students as the most challenging assignment. The challenge stimulated their interest and motivated them to achieve, as shown in the following:

The most satisfying school assignment that I can remember was when I had to do a research project in my high school back home. The project was about some of the pre-Inca cultures in my country. In the field research I had to go to some ruins in the mountains with my fellow students. The trip was fun and the ruins were a nice place to visit with lots of tourists around. In my group I had to be the leader because I was the one with more background about the subject. At the end our re-search paper was about forty pages long, full of graphs and pictures.

Differences between Writing in a Native Language and Writing in English

Home literacy stories told by these students also revealed their struggles with writing in English. Besides learning a different language and writing system, students indicated that often the differences between their native language and English baffled them and created more barriers in learning to write in English. For example, comparing her writing in Korean and writing in English, Kim talked about her struggle with the whole process of writing in English:

It is quite different to write in Korean and in English. When I write in Korean, I do not worry about my grammar or vocabularies. I just write in papers what I think in my head. Some grammar makes me confused, but I don't think it twice because I know that I can express my thought anyway. However, writing in English takes long time because I have to think about grammar and vocabulary. Every time I write, I have trouble with some sentences because I can't express my thoughts in well organized sentences. So I rewrite three or four times. Also grammar in Korea and in English is different. For example, in Korea, a verb comes after an object. There isn't a subject-verb agreement.

In addition to language differences and rhetorical and stylistic differences in writing, especially the impact of writing instruction on students' perceptions of what was judged as a piece of good writing, teacher expectations varied from culture to culture. For example, a Polish student wrote:

There are a lot of things similar but there are a lot of things different too between the two languages. Sometimes when I write, I like to write it in general not specific. . . . In Polish, we wrote papers, we didn't have to give statistics or write sentences specific, what happened first and then the next, and examples. We were supposed to just give clues rather than being specific in Polish. A lot of times we had to write about our own opinions in Polish. So our own opinions should be counted as good too. But here I had to write about in more specific ways, especially when I don't know how to pick examples from a lot of things. I didn't think of it when I first came to America, because I thought Americans should write the same way as Polish people do. What can be different? But right now I am really seeing the difference.

A Chinese student recalled something considered in American schools as taboo but in her culture a common practice for developing writing skills:

In my high school years, my Chinese teacher used to talking about three parts of essay writing, my opinion, proving it and the conclusion. It looked like writing in English, but it doesn't require a lot of examples or details and we can use other's words without stating where they come from because they are something everyone knows.

Another Chinese student further commented on writing instruction she received in China and how that influenced her learning to write in Chinese:

My Chinese teachers back in high school asked us to use strong supporting details from old times. For example, if you want to write: The soldiers who are not ambitious are not good soldiers. This topic demands you give historical examples to show your point, such as Napoleon and many Chinese historical figures to illustrate that those who did not have high goals in their lives, cannot succeed anything. Very often you don't remember the exact words such as what Napoleon said, but the teacher did not look for those details. In Chinese, good writing often begins with a historical background information from the past to the present. Then the writer leads the reader into the thesis.

Conclusion/Implications

Even though the scale of this native literacy investigation was small, the findings reveal something worth noticing and exploring. Stories coming from students' own voices were telling. They offered a glimpse into the educational systems and cultural values from these students' perspectives. The findings, especially in cross-cultural writing differences, confirmed some results obtained from second language writing research done by Ballard and Clanchy, Carson, and Matalene. The students' insights into their native writing instruction, such as the use of sources for learning to write, the methods used in teaching students how to write, and the ways of motivating students to write, give composition teachers information about different ways of learning and viewing literacy in different cultures. Instead of treating these different ways of knowing as deficient or ignoring the impact of these ways of knowing on students' learning to write in English, we need to, as Matalene suggests, "try to understand and appreciate, to admit the relativity of our own rhetoric, and to realize that logics different from our own are not necessarily illogical" (806). It is only by doing so that we can begin to understand ESL students and to design instruction that is responsive to their needs.

First, in dealing with nonnative students, composition instructors need information about students' native literacy learning in order to tailor their instruction. In getting to know the students and their home literacy backgrounds, teachers send the message that ESL students' home literacy backgrounds are acknowledged and valued rather than dismissed or ignored. This sharing can be used as an activity of cross-cultural literacy awareness for both the teacher and the students in the classroom. Such sharing is crucial in building a community of learners so that students who are outsiders can play the roles of insiders whose native literacy and native cultural backgrounds are considered rich resources and not obstacles.

Second, differences in writing and in writing instruction across languages and cultures challenge teachers to expand their teaching repertoire and to diversify teaching strategies when dealing with diverse students. Composition instructors can pinpoint areas for more focused and individualized instruction according to each individual student's needs and background. For example, the Polish student's native literacy instruction is different from the Chinese student's. As Matalene argues, composition teachers need to be aware of not only students' ways of knowing, but also the social, cultural, historical, and educational contexts where students' schooling has been situated. In doing so, teachers can gain deeper understanding of the students' worlds of learning to write, such as their perceptions of the role of memory, the nature of writing, and the issues of authenticity and ownership of the text. Teachers need to incorporate such knowledge into their teaching, helping students to be consciously aware of the differences in writing between their native language and English and to understand the need to adapt to a new discourse in the new culture.

Third, students from different educational and cultural systems often bring with them a whole set of expectations, including anticipated teacher behaviors and preferences for literacy learning in the new culture. Therefore, teachers need to find ways to accommodate students' needs and make good use of students' strengths. For example, giving students choices in reading and writing assignments and allowing students to use their native language in writing at the initial stage can ease the transition and build confidence on the part of learners.

Fourth, one difficulty identified by these ESL students in their autobiographies was their lack of basic working vocabulary and knowledge about the English language. This points to the need for providing ESL students the time and the opportunity to learn new English vocabulary and to use it in their writing. Effective ways of teaching vocabulary might be keeping a reading vocabulary journal, teaching reading for contextual clues, designing language awareness activities focusing on major language points in reading and writing, and training in dictionary and thesaurus skills. All these provide the language assistance which ESL students desperately need.

Fifth, in the reading and literature oriented curriculum, the purposes and functions of reading need to be expanded to address a wide range of demands and needs, such as reading for pleasure, reading for aesthetic appreciation, reading for comprehension, reading for learning and critical thinking, and reading for writing. Writing needs to be brought into the reading curriculum. Teachers need to make explicit connections between reading and writing.

As indicated by the majority of these ESL students' autobiographies, the students would like their American teachers to understand their struggle with learning the new language, literacy skills, and academic content at the same time. One way of building the understanding is for teachers to learn about the students' native language and literacy backgrounds. The more teachers know, the better they can serve ESL students.[1]

Appendix

Writing Prompt for Native Writing Experience

Dear Student,

Thank you very much for having written a composition on your journey to become a writer in English at the beginning of this semester. I was impressed by your achievement in English, especially in learning to write in a language that is not your native language. Your writing makes me want to know more about your writing, specifically, about your native language writing. In your writing, please try to answer the following questions:

What is your native language?

How did you learn to write in your native language?

What writing assignments did your teacher back home assign to you?

How did your teacher go about teaching you how to write in your native language?

What are the differences in writing in English and in your native language?

Do you write in your native language now? If so, what do you write about and to whom?

Note

1. I would like to thank Kevin Birth, Sue L. Goldhaber, and Norman Lewis for their help with this project, and the students who participated in the study. I am also grateful for valuable input from Judith Summerfield in the course of the research process and to Myra Zarnowski in the course of writing this article.

Works Cited

Ballard, Brigid, and John Clanchy. "Assessment by Misconception: Cultural Influences and Intellectual Traditions." *Assessing Second Language Writing in Academic Contexts*. Ed. Liz Hamp-Lyons. Norwood: Ablex, 1990. 19–36.

Carson, Joan G. "Becoming Biliterate: First Language Influences." *Second Language Writing* 1 (1992): 37–60.

Collier, Virginia Patricia. "Age and Rate of Acquisition of Second Language for Academic Purposes." *TESOL Quarterly* 21 (1987): 617–41.

Cummins, James. "The Role of Primary Language Development in Promoting Education Success for Language Minority Students." *Schooling and Language Minority Students: A Theoretical Framework*. Ed. California State Department of Education. Los Angeles: California State University, Evaluation, Dissemination, and Assessment Center. 1981. 3–49.

Matalene, Carolyn. "Contrastive Rhetoric: An American Writing Teacher in China." *College English* 47 (1985): 789–808.

Classroom Activities

Have students write a narrative on "their native learning literacy experiences." First they can brainstorm a list of important features of their first language (Does their first language include articles? How many letters does the alphabet have? Are there masculine and feminine forms of words?) and of their cultural background (political situations in their homelands, celebration of holidays and rites of passage, favorite foods and activities). In discussing these lists, ask students to describe the relationships they see between language and culture and to explain how language is a medium of expression for culture. After reflecting on these ideas, students can begin to draw connections between language as a form of identity and how they learned to write in their native language.

Thinking about Teaching

Not all ESL students have attained written fluency in their language of origin. This concern may be especially important for students who have experienced interruptions in their education, for a variety of reasons. Students in this situation may share a great deal with native speakers of English who have not attained written fluency in English and who are often enrolled in classes for developing writers. If you already teach native speakers of English, note in your teaching journal the similarities and differences that you see as these students grapple with written fluency in English. If you teach exclusively in an ESL program, consider initiating discussions with teachers in a basic writing program. Similarly, basic writing teachers may want to begin speaking on a regular basis with teachers of ESL students. Work together to create shared conversations on issues of common concern. Keep track of similarities and differences in approaches to pedagogy. Make sure to hold the literacy narratives of your students clearly in mind as you work together to discuss solutions. Share the results of these conversations with students so that you can have their input as well.

13

Placement and Assessment

"M ore than many issues within the field of composition," write the
authors of the Conference on College Composition and Communication position statement, "writing assessment evokes strong passions." Most likely you have struggled at some point to define and refine your own assessment strategies. As a discipline, we continue to
search for the most effective ways of assessing — that is, measuring,
judging, evaluating — our students' writing proficiency. Too often *effective* becomes confused with *efficient*. The three articles in this chapter revisit many of the issues that evoke debate, including placement
and exit testing, proficiency criteria, the writing process, and portfolio
review. The CCCC document presents assessment in hypothetical (if
not utopian) terms. The two other selections, by Daniel Royer and Roger
Gilles, and by Kay Harley and Sally I. Cannon, document actual institutional practice in placing and assessing basic writing students and
in defining the parameters of the basic writing course. In addition to
practical suggestions, these articles offer teachers an opportunity to
contemplate their own individual notions about and definitions of assessment.

CCCC Position Statement

*For several years, the Conference on College Composition and Communi-
cation Committee on Assessment worked to create "an official position
statement . . . that would help [writing teachers] explain writing assessment to colleagues and administrators and secure the best assessment
options for students." Because teachers and administrators often seem to
be at cross-purposes in defining the means and ends of writing assessment, the CCCC position statement attempts to help all parties involved*

reach some sort of consensus. The statement lists ten assumptions regarding writing assessment that should be considered when creating new policies and implementing new classroom practices. The rest of the document illustrates these assumptions, as the writers list how assessment implicates students, faculty, administrators, and legislators. The CCCC Committee on Assessment is forceful in its argument that institutional assessment measures should involve neither an exploitation of students and faculty nor a compromise of pedagogical integrity.

In 1993, the CCCC Executive Committee charged the CCCC Committee on Assessment with developing an official position statement on assessment. Prior to that time, members of CCCC had expressed keen interest in having a document available that would help them explain writing assessment to colleagues and administrators and secure the best assessment options for students.

Beginning in 1990 at NCTE in Atlanta, Georgia, open forums were held at both NCTE and CCCC conventions to discuss the possibility of a position statement: its nature, forms, and the philosophies and practices it might espouse. At these forums, at regular meetings, and through correspondence, over one hundred people helped develop the current document.

An initial draft of the statement was submitted to the CCCC Executive Committee at its March 1994 meeting, where it was approved in substance. The Executive Committee also reviewed a revised statement at its November 1994 meeting. An announcement in the February 1995 issue of CCC invited all CCCC members to obtain a draft of the statement and to submit their responses to the Assessment Committee. Copies of the draft statement were mailed to all 1995 CCCC Convention preregistrants, and the final draft was presented in a forum at the 1995 CCCC Convention in Washington, DC. Changes based on discussions at that session, and at a later workshop, were incorporated into the position statement, which was subsequently approved for publication by the CCCC Executive Committee.

The CCCC Committee on Assessment acknowledges the contributions of the cochairs of the previous [1994] CCCC Committee on Assessment, Edward Nolte and Sandra Murphy. In addition, Donald Daiker provided substantial assistance as a former member of the committee.

Members of the [1995] CCCC Committee on Assessment [were]: Kathleen Blake Yancey, Chair; Arnetha Ball, Pat Belanoff, Kathleen Bell, Renee Betz, Emily Decker, Christine Farris, Thomas Hilgers, Audrey Roth, Lew Sayers, and Fred Thomas.

More than many issues within the field of composition studies, writing assessment evokes strong passions. It can be used for a variety of appropriate purposes, both inside the classroom and outside: providing assistance to students; awarding a grade; placing students in appropriate courses; allowing them to exit a course or sequence of courses;

and certifying proficiency, to name some of the more obvious. But writing assessment can be abused as well: used to exploit graduate students, for instance, or to reward or punish faculty members. We begin our position statement, therefore, with a foundational claim upon which all else is built; it is axiomatic that in all situations calling for writing assessment in both two-year and four-year institutions, the primary purpose of the specific assessment should govern its design, its implementation, and the generation and dissemination of its results.

It is also axiomatic that in spite of the diverse uses to which writing assessment is put, the general principles undergirding writing assessment are similar:

> Assessments of written literacy should be designed and evaluated by well-informed current or future teachers of the students being assessed, for purposes clearly understood by all the participants; should elicit from student writers a variety of pieces, preferably over a period of time; should encourage and reinforce good teaching practices; and should be solidly grounded in the latest research on language learning.

These assumptions are explained fully in the first section below; after that, we list the rights and responsibilities generated by these assumptions; and in the third section we provide selected references that furnish a point of departure for literature in the discipline.

Assumptions

All writing assessments — and thus all policy statements about writing assessment — make assumptions about the nature of what is being assessed. Our assumptions include the following.

First, *language is always learned and used most effectively in environments where it accomplishes something the user wants to accomplish for particular listeners or readers within that environment.* The assessment of written literacy must strive to set up writing tasks, therefore, that identify purposes appropriate to and appealing to the particular students being tested. Additionally, assessment must be contextualized in terms of why, where, and for what purpose it is being undertaken; this context must also be clear to the students being assessed and to all others (i.e., stakeholders/participants) involved.

Accordingly, there is no test which can be used in all environments for all purposes, and the best "test" for any group of students may well be locally designed. The definition of "local" is also contextual; schools with common goals and similar student populations and teaching philosophies and outcomes might well form consortia for the design, implementation, and evaluation of assessment instruments even though the schools themselves are geographically separated from each other.

Second, *language by definition is social.* Assessment which isolates students and forbids discussion and feedback from others conflicts with current cognitive and psychological research about language use and the benefits of social interaction during the writing process; it also is out of step with much classroom practice.

Third, *reading — and thus, evaluation, since it is a variety of reading — is as socially contextualized as all other forms of language use.* What any reader draws out of a particular text and uses as a basis of evaluation is dependent upon how that reader's own language use has been shaped and what his or her specific purpose for reading is. It seems appropriate, therefore, to recognize the individual writing program, institution, consortium, and so forth as a community of interpreters who can function fairly — that is, assess fairly — with knowledge of that community.

Fourth, *any individual's writing "ability" is a sum of a variety of skills employed in a diversity of contexts, and individual ability fluctuates unevenly among these varieties.* Consequently, one piece of writing — even if it is generated under the most desirable conditions — can never serve as an indicator of overall literacy, particularly for high stakes decisions. Ideally, such literacy must be assessed by more than one piece of writing, in more than one genre, written on different occasions, for different audiences, and evaluated by multiple readers. This realization has led many institutions and programs across the country to use portfolio assessment.

Fifth, *writing assessment is useful primarily as a means of improving learning.* Both teachers and students must have access to the results in order to be able to use them to revise existing curricula and/or plan programs for individual students. And, obviously, if results are to be used to improve the teaching-learning environment, human and financial resources for the implementation of improvements must be in place in advance of the assessment. If resources are not available, institutions should postpone these types of assessment until they are. Furthermore, when assessment is being conducted solely for program evaluation, all students should not be tested, since a representative group can provide the desired results. Neither should faculty merit increases hinge on their students' performance on any test.

Sixth, *assessment tends to drive pedagogy.* Assessment thus must demonstrate "systemic validity"; it must encourage classroom practices that harmonize with what practice and research have demonstrated to be effective ways of teaching writing and of becoming a writer. What is easiest to measure — often by means of a multiple choice test — may correspond least to good writing, and that in part is an important point: *choosing a correct response from a set of possible answers is not composing.* As important, just because students are asked to write does not mean that the "assessment instrument" is a "good" one. Essay tests that ask students to form and articulate opinions about some important issue, for instance, without time to reflect, to talk to others, to read on the subject, to revise and so forth — that is, without taking into account through either appropriate classroom practice or the assessment process itself — encourage distorted notions of what writing is. They also encourage poor teaching and little learning. Even teachers who recognize and employ the methods used by real writers in working with students can find their best efforts undercut by assessments such as these.

Seventh, *standardized tests, usually developed by large testing organizations, tend to be for accountability purposes, and when used to make statements about student learning, misrepresent disproportionately the skills and abilities of students of color.* This imbalance tends to decrease when tests are directly related to specific contexts and purposes, in contrast to tests that purport to differentiate between "good" and "bad" writing in a general sense. Furthermore, standardized tests tend to focus on readily accessed features of the language — on grammatical correctness and stylistic choice — and on error, on what is wrong rather than on the appropriate rhetorical choices that have been made. Consequently, the outcome of such assessments is negative: students are said to demonstrate what they do "wrong" with language rather than what they do well.

Eighth, *the means used to test students' writing ability shapes what they, too, consider writing to be.* If students are asked to produce "good" writing within a given period of time, they often conclude that all good writing is generated within those constraints. If students are asked to select — in a multiple choice format — the best grammatical and stylistic choices, they will conclude that good writing is "correct" writing. They will see writing erroneously, as the avoidance of error; they will think that grammar and style exist apart from overall purpose and discourse design.

Ninth, *financial resources available for designing and implementing assessment instruments should be used for that purpose and not to pay for assessment instruments outside the context within which they are used.* Large amounts of money are currently spent on assessments that have little pedagogical value for students or teachers. However, money spent to compensate teachers for involvement in assessment is also money spent on faculty development and curriculum reform since inevitably both occur when teachers begin to discuss assessment which relates directly to their classrooms and to their students.

Tenth, and finally, *there is a large and growing body of research on language learning, language use, and language assessment that must be used to improve assessment on a systematic and regular basis.* Our assumptions are based on this scholarship. Anyone charged with the responsibility of designing an assessment program must be cognizant of this body of research and must stay abreast of developments in the field. Thus, assessment programs must always be under review and subject to change by well-informed faculty, administrators, and legislators.

Assessment of writing is a legitimate undertaking. But by its very nature it is a complex task, involving two competing tendencies: first, the impulse to measure writing as a general construct; and second, the impulse to measure writing as a contextualized, site and genre-specific ability. There are times when re-creating or simulating a context (as in the case of assessment for placement, for instance) is limited. Even in this case, however, assessment — when conducted sensitively and purposefully — can have a positive impact on teaching, learning, curricular design, and student attitudes. Writing assessment can serve to inform both the individual and the public about the achievements of students and the effectiveness of teaching. On the other hand, poorly designed assessments, and poorly implemented assessments, can be enormously harmful because of the power of language: personally, for our students as human beings; and academically, for our students as learners, since learning is mediated through language.

Students who take pleasure and pride in using written language effectively are increasingly valuable in a world in which communication across space and a variety of cultures has become routine. Writing assessment that alienates students from writing is counterproductive, and writing assessment that fails to take an accurate and valid measure of their writing even more so. But writing assessment that encourages students to improve their facility with the written word, to appreciate their power with that word and the responsibilities that accompany such power, and that salutes students' achievements as well as guides them, should serve as a crucially important educational force.

Students should:

1. demonstrate their accomplishments and/or development in writing by means of composing, preferably in more than one sample written on more than one occasion, with sufficient time to plan, draft, rewrite, and edit each product or performance.

2. write on prompts developed from the curriculum and grounded in "real-world" practice.

3. be informed about the purposes of the assessment they are writing for, the ways the results will be used, and avenues of appeal.

4. have their writing evaluated by more than one reader, particularly in "high stakes" situations (e.g., involving major institutional consequences such as getting credit for a course, moving from one context to another, or graduating from college).

5. receive response, from readers, intended to help them improve as writers attempting to reach multiple kinds of audiences.

Faculty should:

1. play key roles in the design of writing assessments, including creating writing tasks and scoring guides, for which they should receive support in honoraria and/or release time; and should appreciate and be responsive to the idea that assessment tasks

and procedures must be sensitive to cultural, racial, class, and gender differences, and to disabilities, and must be valid for and not penalize any group of students.

2. participate in the readings and evaluations of student work, supported by honoraria and/or release time.

3. assure that assessment measures and supports what is taught in the classroom.

4. make themselves aware of the difficulty of constructing fair and motivating prompts for writing, the need for field testing and revising of prompts, the range of appropriate and inappropriate uses of various kinds of writing assessments, and the norming, reliability, and validity standards employed by internal and external test-makers, as well as share their understanding of these issues with administrators and legislators.

5. help students to prepare for writing assessments and to interpret assessment results in ways that are meaningful to students.

6. use results from writing assessments to review and (when necessary) to revise curriculum.

7. encourage policy makers to take a more qualitative view toward assessment, encouraging the use of multiple measures, infrequent large-scale assessment, and large-scale assessment by sampling of a population rather than by individual work whenever appropriate.

8. continue conducting research on writing assessment, particularly as it is used to help students learn and to understand what they have achieved.

Administrators and higher education governing boards should:

1. educate themselves and consult with rhetoricians and composition specialists teaching at their own institutions, about the most recent research on teaching and assessing writing and how they relate to their particular environment and to already established programs and procedures, understanding that generally student learning is best demonstrated by performances assessed over time and sponsored by all faculty members, not just those in English.

2. announce to stakeholders the purposes of all assessments, the results to be obtained, and the ways that results will be used.

3. assure that the assessments serve the needs of students, not just the needs of an institution, and that resources for necessary courses linked to the assessments are therefore available before the assessments are mandated.

4. assure opportunities for teachers to come together to discuss all aspects of assessments; the design of the instruments; the standards to be employed; the interpretation of the results; possible changes in curriculum suggested by the process and results.

5. assure that all decisions are made by more than one reader.

6. not use any assessment results as the primary basis for evaluating the performance of or rewards due a teacher; they should recognize that student learning is influenced by many factors such as cognitive development, personality type, personal motivation, physical and psychological health, emotional upheavals, socio-economic background, family successes and difficulties which are neither taught in the classroom nor appropriately measured by writing assessment.

Legislators should:

1. not mandate a specific instrument (test) for use in any assessment; although they may choose to answer their responsibility to the public by mandating assessment in general or at specific points in student careers, they should allow professional educators to choose the types and ranges of assessments that reflect the educational goals of their curricula and the nature of the student populations they serve.

2. understand that mandating assessments also means providing funding to underwrite those assessments, including resources to assist students and to bring teachers together to design and implement assessments, to review curriculum, and to amend the assessment and/or curriculum when necessary.

3. become knowledgeable about writing assessment issues, particularly by consulting with rhetoricians and composition specialists engaged in teaching, on the most recent research on the teaching of writing and assessment.

4. understand that different purposes require different assessments and that qualitative forms of assessment can be more powerful and meaningful for some purposes than quantitative measures are, and that assessment is a means to help students learn better, not a way of unfairly comparing student populations, teachers or schools.

5. include teachers in the drafting of legislation concerning assessments.

6. recognize that legislation needs to be reviewed continually for possible improvement in light of actual results and ongoing developments in writing assessment theory and research.

Selected References

Belanoff, Pat, and Marcia Dickson, eds. *Portfolios: Process and Product.* Portsmouth: Boynton, 1991.

Black, Laurel, Donald Daiker, Jeffrey Sommers, and Gail Stygall, eds. *New Directions in Portfolio Assessment: Reflective Practice, Critical Theory, and Large Scale Scoring.* Portsmouth: Boynton, 1994.

Cooper, Charles, and Lee Odell, eds. *Evaluating Writing: Describing, Measuring, Judging.* Urbana: NCTE, 1977.

CCCC Committee on Assessment. "A Selected Bibliography on Postsecondary Writing Assessment, 1979–91." *College Composition and Communication* 43 (1992): 244–55.

Elbow, Peter. "Ranking, Evaluating, and Liking: Sorting Out Three Forms of Judgment." *College English* 55 (1993): 187–206.

Gordon, Barbara. "Another Look: Standardized Tests for Placement in College Composition Courses." *WPA: Writing Program Administration* 10 (1987): 29–38.

Greenberg, Karen. "Validity and Reliability: Issues in the Direct Assessment of Writing." *WPA: Writing Program Administration* 16.1–2 (1992): 7–22.

Greenberg, Karen, Harvey Wiener, and Richard Donovan, eds. *Writing Assessment: Issues and Strategies.* New York: Longman, 1986.

Huot, Brian. "Reliability, Validity, and Holistic Scoring: What We Know and What We Need to Know." *College Composition and Communication* 41 (1990): 201–13.

Moss, Pamela. "Can There Be Validity without Reliability?" *Educational Researcher* 23.2 (1994): 5–12.

———. "Validity in High Stakes Writing Assessment: Problems and Possibilities." *Assessing Writing* 1.1 (1994): 109–28.

Odell, Lee. "Defining and Assessing Competence in Writing." *The Nature and Measurement of Competency in English.* Ed. Charles Cooper. Urbana: NCTE, 1981: 95–139.

White, Edward. "Issues and Problems in Writing Assessment." *Assessing Writing* 1.1 (1994): 11–29.

———. *Teaching and Assessing Writing.* 2nd ed. San Francisco: Jossey, 1994.

Wiggins, Grant. *Assessing Student Performance: Exploring the Purpose and Limits of Testing.* San Francisco: Jossey, 1993.

———. "Assessment: Authenticity, Context, and Validity." *Phi Delta Kappan* 75.3 (1993): 200–14.

Williamson, Michael, and Brian Huot, eds. *Validating Holistic Scoring for Writing Assessment.* Cresskill: Hampton, 1993.

Yancey, Kathleen Blake, ed. *Portfolios in the Writing Classroom: An Introduction.* Urbana: NCTE, 1992.

Classroom Activities

The writers of the CCCC document argue that "the means used to test students' writing ability shape what they, too, consider writing to be." Consider this assumption in the context of your basic writing curriculum. Near the beginning of the course, ask students to reflect in their journals about how their placement test seems to define writing ability. Then, near the end of the course (and especially if the writing program includes an end-of-course assessment measure), have students reflect on what they have learned about writing ability. How do students define *good writing?* Have their assumptions changed or remained the same? Why? How are these ideas implicated in the end-of-term assessment? Asking students to reflect on the content of the course, the assessment process, and their own success as learners further encourages them to use their critical thinking skills.

Thinking about Teaching

The sixth assumption of the CCCC document states: "assessment tends to drive pedagogy." With this statement in mind, examine the assessments used in your writing program; what is driving your pedagogy? With other teachers, consider evaluating your institution's assessment strategy in light of the CCCC recommendations. Determine which guidelines your program already includes and which aspects of your program are in need of reevaluation and revision. Also consider how the assessment of basic writing students may be driven by institutional or legislative goals. Are such goals congruent with your goals for the course? With students' goals?

You may wish to suggest faculty review of assessment tools and processes, if such a review does not already exist. The CCCC position statement suggests that faculty affected by (but not responsible for designing) an assessment should demand an explication of its theoretical base.

Directed Self-Placement: An Attitude of Orientation

Daniel Royer and Roger Gilles

Daniel J. Royer, the former director of the writing program at Grand Valley State University, and Roger Gilles, the current director of the same program, offer a solution to the dilemmas of placement testing which they call "directed self-placement," a system that enables students to choose the writing course that they think is most appropriate for them. Although students make this decision independently, they are given input from the director of composition as well as from their academic advisers. As students choose their courses, they examine course descriptions for both basic writing and college writing and are asked to assess their own experiences with reading and writing. Such a system, Royer and Gilles suggest, allows students to focus on those aspects of their education that need the most attention and creates an environment conducive to student-centered, self-directed learning. It also opens up possibilities for course design.

Daniel J. Royer serves as Managing Editor for Process Papers, *a journal of process philosophy and education; he has published articles on Dewey's pragmatism, A.N. Whitehead, and the phenomenology of writing. Roger Gilles's areas of publication include the rhetoric of news, political rhetoric, and Richard Weaver's theory of argument. Consistent with their scholarly interests, in this article Royer and Gilles examine how Dewey's theories of education help to support their argument.*

> No particular results then, so far, but only an attitude of orientation, is what the pragmatic method means. *The attitude of looking away from first things, principles, "categories," supposed necessities; and of looking towards last things, fruits, consequences, facts.*
>
> — William James (27)

D an stands at the front of a buzzing lecture hall, a yellow trifold brochure in hand, watching about a sixth of next year's 2400 "seats" find a seat. New students are seats; that's the kind of talk one hears as director of composition at a university that breaks its own enrollment record every year, doubling in size to nearly 16,000 students over the last decade. What Dan has to say to these 400 new seats invites an interesting irony: the administrators love what he's about to say precisely because they think of students as "seats," while Dan is eager to talk because, in Deweyan fashion, he is eager to upset the prevailing student/teacher power relations by presenting the students with an authentic educative choice.

The buzzing subsides, and after brief speeches by the Dean of Students and a counselor from the Financial Aid office, Dan steps forward, holding up the yellow brochure, and introduces himself as the director of composition. "In the next few minutes I'm going to ask you to make the first of many important choices you'll make as a student at this university — so please listen carefully.

"The Admissions people have placed a yellow trifold brochure, like this one, in your folder. Let's take a look at it. It says on the front, *English 098 or 150: Which Course is Right for You?* Before you register for classes this afternoon, you'll need to select one of these two courses to begin with as you begin your freshman year.

"Before I get to the specifics, let me explain why it is we want you to make this decision and why we aren't going to make it for you. At many schools, in fact at this school until very recently, people like me 'place' you into a writing course by looking at your ACT or SAT score, your high-school GPA, and perhaps by having you step into another room and return to us two hours later with a 'sample' of your writing. But it turns out that this is not a very valid or reliable way to find out which first-year writing course is best for you. Writing ability, at least as we conceive of it, is far too complex to measure so quickly and easily.

"The fact is, we just don't know very much about you as writers. Perhaps the *best* way to measure your writing ability would be for us to sit down with each one of you for an hour or so and talk with you about writing. If I had an hour with each of you, I'd ask you to show me samples of your best writing from high school. I'd ask you to describe your strengths and weaknesses as a writer. I'd ask you to tell me how much you read, and how well you read. If your GPA or standardized test-score didn't look too impressive, I'd ask you if anything much has changed in your image of yourself or in your habits as a student since you started your last year of high school. I know that many students arrive as college freshmen very different people — and become very different students — from what they were just a few months earlier. Some of you here today must know what I mean.

"I'd ask you how motivated you are. I'd ask you how much you like to write. I'd ask you how well you type. I'd ask you many things. I think you get my point: to find out which first-year writing course is really right for you, I would need to know more than a single test score, and I'd need to see more than a single sample of how you write under pressure or even a portfolio of your high school writing — which has probably gotten pretty stale over the summer.

"Instead, I'm going to ask you to make a responsible choice about which course to take. The question you face is: Should I take English 098 or English 150? Let me explain the difference. English 098 is a preparatory course that helps you write more confidently and purposefully, and it helps you develop ways to clarify and edit your writing for a college-level audience. You will get a letter grade in English 098, and it figures into your GPA, but it doesn't count as one of the 120 credits you need to graduate. English 150, on the other hand, is a four-credit course that prepares you for the variety of writing experiences you will have as a university student in the coming years. The focus is on source-based writing in a variety of genres. All students must eventually get a C or better in English 150 in order to satisfy the freshman composition requirement. The decision you face is whether to go ahead and begin with English 150, or to take a two-semester sequence by starting with English 098 in the first semester and taking English 150 the second.

"Before you make up your mind too quickly, hear me out. Many schools offer a two-semester sequence of first-year writing anyway, so don't feel that you are going to get behind if you begin with 098. You don't want to enroll in 098 if 150 is best for you, and you don't want to enroll in 150 if 098 is best for you. The university has no interest in making you start with either course — that's why *you* are deciding. What we do have an interest in is your success as a student. There is no advantage to beginning with English 150 if you fail or struggle in the course because it's not the right course for you. People do fail that course, and you don't want that to happen to you.

"Generally speaking, you are well prepared for English 150 if you have done quite a bit of reading and writing in high school. English 150 instructors will assume that you can summarize and analyze published material from magazines, newspapers, books, and scholarly journals. They will also assume that you have written a variety of essays in a variety of forms, including narrative, descriptive, and persuasive writing. Look at the checklist on the center panel inside the brochure. These are some of the characteristics that we faculty look for in solid writing students. Do any of these statements describe you?

I read newspapers and magazines regularly.

In the past year, I have read books for my own enjoyment.

In high school, I wrote several essays per year.

My high school GPA placed me in the top third of my class.

I have used computers for drafting and revising essays.

My ACT-English score was above 20.

I consider myself a good reader and writer.

"Perhaps you do see yourself in at least some of those statements. If many of the statements don't describe you or if you just don't consider yourself a strong reader or writer, you might consider taking English 098. In 098 you will focus on writing in specific ways to reach specific audiences. You will write a lot in order to develop comfort and fluency. You will get lots of practice, including many hours with our Writing Center tutors, and you will work on understanding the conventions of standard written English — spelling, grammar, punctuation, and usage. Let's look at the list of general characteristics that may indicate that English 098 is best for you.

Generally I don't read when I don't have to.

In high school, I did not do much writing.

My high school GPA was about average.

I'm unsure about the rules of writing — commas, apostrophes, and so forth.

I've used computers, but not often for writing and revising.

My ACT-English score was below 20.

I don't think of myself as a strong writer.

"In English 098 you will read successful samples of essays written by professionals and by other students. In a typical class, you will complete five or six short essays — two or three pages each. You may cite some of the essays you have read or people you have interviewed, but generally you will not write research-based essays. Indeed, the purpose of English 098 is to give you the confidence, organization, and command necessary to write the research-based essays demanded in

English 150 and beyond. English 098 will get you ready to do well in English 150 the next semester.

"Many of you will see statements that describe you in both lists. Others may clearly see that one or the other course is the right one to begin with. If after thinking about it you still can't decide, I'll be glad to talk with you — even to spend an hour and look at some of your writing as I talked about a minute ago — but I think most of you can make the right choice on your own. You all have advisers, and they can help you as well. You'll be meeting with them later today.

"I said before that we don't know much about you. About all I *do* know is that before you earn a 'C' or better in English 150, you'll become a pretty solid college writer. Today you simply have to decide if that will take you one semester or two.

"You may be wondering if you can squeeze your way through English 150 if you aren't really ready for it. Probably not. We use a portfolio-based grading system that requires each student to submit a folder of final work that is graded by a total of three faculty members from a larger group of English 150 teachers who have met all semester to discuss their own and our university's expectations about college writing. Your final portfolio accounts for the majority of your final course grade, and because we 'team grade,' we're confident that an 'A' in one class matches up pretty well with an 'A' in another. Our grading system is described in more detail in the brochure. For now, I just want you to realize that your decision today should not be taken lightly. You really do have to write well in order to move beyond English 150.

"There's other important information in this brochure. Look at the back page under the heading, 'What to Expect the First Day.' Go ahead and read those paragraphs while you listen to me talk for another minute or so. Notice that in both 098 and 150, on the first day of class your teacher will ask you to write a brief essay. Your teacher will read the essay as a simple indication of your writing abilities and let you know what he or she thinks. During this first week of class, you will have the opportunity to switch from one class to the other if you wish. But remember, the decision is yours, not your teacher's. Note too that the brochure includes information about the Writing Center, the Library Skills program, our junior-level writing requirement, and our Writing Across the Curriculum program. We value writing a lot, and in your time as a student here you'll be doing quite a bit of it, so we want you to be as ready as you can be.

"English 098 and 150 are both very good courses. English 150 is a course you will share in common with every freshman. You will all take it. And many of our very best instructors teach English 098. Believe me, we will have many full sections of 098 and every student in that class with you, if that's the one you take, will be there because he or she chose to take it. Nobody will be in 098 against their will, and for this reason many students find the atmosphere there encouraging and helpful. For many, it is a way to brush up, get some practice, and prepare themselves for the challenge of English 150.

"Finally, before I leave, I'd like to see a show of hands, not to indicate which course you will take, but to indicate whether or not you have made a choice. OK. If you're still not sure which course you should enroll in, please talk with me or your adviser later today. Thanks for your time, and I wish you all the best of luck."

Why Directed Self-Placement?

During the summer of 1996, either Dan or Roger, the previous composition director, gave a version of this ten-minute speech to five other groups — and in the end over 22 percent of the students placed themselves into ENG 098. What compels 500 students to place themselves in a course that doesn't count as college credit? Are these the same students that we would have placed in ENG 098 had we used our old method of ACT-English score plus writing sample? We don't yet fully know the answers to these questions, but after our second full year of using what we're calling "directed self-placement," we feel that we've found a placement method that works very well for all of us — teachers, students, and administrators alike.

Our decision to give directed self-placement a try originated with widespread frustration over our traditional placement method. We knew of the well-documented limitations of placement tests — the artificiality of direct writing and the questionable reliability and validity of traditional direct assessment (see, for instance, Elbow). And we'd never liked using ACT-English scores, but we'd resorted to them as a preliminary screen when our freshman-orientation groups got so big we had trouble scoring all the essays in the brief turnaround time available to us. The Admissions people who ran orientation didn't like our method much, either; they had to schedule an hour for writing, then wait for the results before they could help the students register.

Our ENG 098 students weren't very fond of the system, either. They started the class with a chip on their shoulder after having been told during orientation that, despite their "B" average in high school, they were *required* to take a no-credit English class. We surveyed our students in the Fall of 1995 and found that only 38 percent of the ENG 098 students felt they were properly placed in the course. There were quite a few negative comments about both the placement procedure and the course itself.

Finally, the teachers themselves were frustrated. Not only did they have to deal with unhappy students, but they also had to replicate the placement essay during the first week of classes and shift students to the appropriate course, often against the students' will. By January of 1996, it became clear that we were kidding ourselves if we believed that these "supposed necessities" were fair to anyone involved. We decided to rethink our approach.

We first considered trying to improve traditional placement-test procedures. Schools such as the University of Pittsburgh and Washington State have "contextualized" placement decisions by shifting their focus from how student writing matches up against general and fixed criteria to how it fits with the actual curriculum (Huot 553–54). In other words, they place students into *courses* rather than into categories. This alternative does involve some looking away from what William James would call "first things, principles, and 'categories,'" but it seemed to us not to make the full pragmatic turn toward "last things, fruits, consequences, facts." Indeed, we had already been using a version of this method to place our students. But we realized that no matter how site-specific and contextualized we made our reading of placement essays, we might side-step some reliability concerns and finesse our notion of validity, but we would inevitably wind up making decisions based on the inadequate data of a single writing sample. We were beginning to feel that our old placement engine could not, once again, be retuned or rebuilt.

We toyed with the idea of entrance portfolios — which would move us beyond the single piece of writing — but the Admissions directors balked. "This isn't Stanford," they told us. "If we make students put together an entrance portfolio and the next school doesn't, the students will simply pick the next school." Besides, we knew that asking for entrance portfolios would place quite a burden on our already overburdened summer faculty. How would we read over two thousand portfolios? And even if we could do this, we would still be mired in the interrater-reliability fix, even if it was transformed into a question of reliability among those rater/teachers who would be teaching the course. The only real way around this last problem would be to insure that raters taught just those students whose portfolios they assessed, and this would be impossible in the context we faced.

We were stuck. In the meantime, at our administration's prompting, our "institutional analyst" evaluated the placement data and composition grades over the past several years. His conclusion was bleak: statistically speaking, neither of our two placement devices bore much relationship to student success in composition classes, if "success" could be defined as earning credit for the course (earning a "C" or better). High ACT scores did correlate somewhat with *high* grades in our ENG 150 course, but students on all levels of the ACT appeared to have about the same chance of getting a "C" or better. From an administrative point of view, we couldn't very well keep students out of a course they could earn a "B–" or "C+" in.

Of more concern to us within the writing program was the fact that fully one-fifth of our ENG 150 students were either withdrawing or earning below a "C" — that is, failing to earn credit for the course — but according to our analyst these students did not show any particular ACT-score tendencies. That is, ACT scores alone could not predict who would fail or struggle in ENG 150.

Our placement-essay system didn't fare much better, according to the analyst. Over the past few years, enough students had either not taken a placement test or simply ignored our placement decision that he could conclude again that not much relationship existed between "placement" and "success" in composition classes. Students who'd been placed into ENG 150, students who'd skipped the placement test, and even students who'd been placed into ENG 098 but taken ENG 150 instead all had about the same chance of earning credit in our ENG 150 course.

From the students' point of view, they had little to lose in giving ENG 150 a try, for ACT score or placement-essay results had very little predictive value. Statistically, about 80 percent of them — regardless of test scores — would get a "C" or better. Finally, at a meeting between upper-administration and writing-program administrators, the statistician remarked that, given all the time, effort, and money we put into placing students in composition courses, a random placement would make as much sense and that we might just as well let the students place themselves. At first we chuckled. Then we looked again at our options. In the end, we decided to take the man seriously.

Our statistician had lifted a veil from before our eyes: all of our efforts had been directed toward finding a better way for *us* to place our students — for us to assess our students' writing abilities quickly and effectively, preferably in an hour or two. Before this nudge from the statistician, we lacked what Peter Elbow calls the "utopian or visionary impulse," which kept us "blinded by what seems normal" (83). Normally, the placement universe revolves around teachers; we choose the methods, we score the essays, we tell students what courses to take. Now we began to envision students at the center, and for the first time we turned our attention to the people who knew our students best: the students themselves.

We have not regretted our decision. Our ENG 098 "placement rate" has dropped from 33 percent to 22 percent, but for the first time we feel the right students are taking our developmental writing class. All in all, we believe there are several good reasons to adopt directed self-placement.

Directed Self-Placement Feels Right

Directed self-placement possesses what computer programmers call elegance, what philosophers might call the shine of Ockham's razor. It has a pleasing feel about it with influence stretching in every direction: from a simple brochure at the hub, its vectors point to students, local high schools, teachers, and administrators. Its simplicity recommends it over the unreliability of test scores. Its honesty calls out to students and lures them in the right direction. Its focus is on the future and each student's self-determined advance. This alternative placement strategy is a consummate movement toward what Patricia Mann terms "familial unmooring," a concept that Grego and Thompson use to urge compositionists and their academic institutions to break nostalgia's hold on students and their writing and enable students to "remember themselves as whole people (not just a number or a grade)" (74). In this manner, directed self-placement involves the restoration of interpersonal agency — but not without some cost. Grego and Thompson remind us:

> Nostalgic views of student writing would rather hold on to ways of assessing and teaching students writing which make the institution's job predictable and containable, neat and tidy. To do otherwise is to get pretty messy, to engage in the struggle to make sense of the complexities of student writing not "organized" by the traditional assessments and curriculum of a particular academic site. (75)

And it's not just students who are encouraged to change. Directed self-placement is an attitude, James's pragmatic attitude. We feel very differently about our jobs, about students, and about writing after our ten-minute speech, much differently from the way we felt after several hours of reading placement essays. Our old concerns about validity and reliability are now replaced with something akin to "rightness." And the rightness of the choice now lies with the student, where we feel it belongs.

We surveyed our Fall 1996 students, and they told an altogether different story from the previous group. Their written comments repeatedly stressed that when the two courses were explained to them at orientation, the students who chose ENG 098 simply felt that it was the course for them. Because of their past experiences with writing, they felt they needed to "brush up" before tackling ENG 150. Interestingly, the reasons students cited most frequently for choosing ENG 098 centered on behavior and self-image — not test scores or grades. Our ENG 098 students saw *themselves* as poor readers and writers. In the past, we had done the seeing for them.

We asked students to tell us which of the seven potential indicators most strongly influenced them to take ENG 098. These were the indicators that we faculty had designed as we thought about our own composition classes. The indicators reveal what we saw, and continue to see, as the main prerequisites for success in our first-year composition program: solid reading habits, writing confidence, familiarity with the mechanical aspects of writing, and experience with computers. They are analogous to the "contextualized" placement practices that Huot cites (553–54), but instead of measuring sample student writing against our contextualized expectations, we have asked the students to measure their own perceptions of themselves against our expectations. We added ACT scores and high-school grades to our list primarily as a possible anchor for students not used to assessing their abilities qualitatively.

We were pleasantly surprised by what we found. Of the 230 responses, barely a quarter cited test scores and grades:

1. 24 percent said "Generally I don't read when I don't have to."

2. 23 percent said "I don't think of myself as a strong writer."

3. 15 percent said "My ACT-English score was below 20."

4. 12 percent said "My high school GPA was about average."

5. 12 percent said "I'm unsure about the rules of writing."

6. 9 percent said "In high school, I did not do much writing."

7. 6 percent said "I've used computers, but not often for writing and revising."

Notice that items 1, 2, and 5 (59 percent) reflect self-image and self-assessment, items 3 and 4 (27 percent) reflect external judgments, and items 6 and 7 (15 percent) reflect high-school or other past educational experience. It seems right to us that our students are selecting ENG 098 because of their own view of themselves. And indeed, we hope that the course will help them change that view and give them confidence as they move on in the curriculum.

In retrospect, we believe that our discomfort with traditional placement methods arose from an uneasy feeling of impropriety. In the space of an hour or two, we had been trying to make a major decision for hundreds of students. At ten o'clock we didn't know their names, but by noon we "knew" what first-semester course they should take. No matter how careful we tried to be, we felt that any decision would be hasty. The "emergent" placement procedures cited by Huot, which view placement either as "a teaching decision" or as "a screening process," share an assumption that simply doesn't sit well with us — that whatever decision made is to be made by teachers, not students (556).

But what of reliability? Obviously two of the items listed in our brochure, ACT-English scores and high-school GPA, are extremely "reliable" data, even if they are problematic measures of writing ability per se. But we have come to view the other indicators as very reliable as well. First, there is no "interrater-reliability" problem since there is only one rater. More importantly, a student is unlikely to respond to a statement like "I don't read when I don't have to" differently from one week to the next. Leaving aside for a moment the question of validity, we are convinced that student responses to our brochure prompts are very reliable — more reliable, we believe, than summer faculty's holistic responses to anonymous and impromptu student writing.

Directed Self-Placement Works

What does it mean to say that directed self-placement works? First, we might admit failure if *no one* chose our developmental writing course, although even then we might chalk it up as a victory for mainstreaming first-year writing students. Along with those who, with some important cautions, advocate mainstreaming (Elbow and Soliday), we agree that students should not be marginalized, but we think the most practical reconception of remediation does not involve eliminating basic writing courses, but rather thinking very differently about placement.

Indeed, conventional notions of "remediation" may not apply to students who in effect *ask* for the extra course. Elbow anticipates this development when he concedes that some students may *"want* to be held apart in a separate and protected situation . . . , so perhaps it would make sense to have a conventional basic writing course for those who want it. But let us ask them and give them a choice instead of deciding for them" (93).

In practice, we observe that many students decide for themselves that they need a basic or conventional writing course, "a sheltered educational pocket" (Soliday 85). For us, reconceiving remediation begins by taking student choice seriously — that is, to heed Elbow's wise concession. Our 22 percent placement rate has held steady for two years, so we feel that we are reaching a significant population of students. In a sense, our new placement method "works" no matter how many students choose ENG 098; we simply want to make the course available to those who want or need it.

We also might say that self-placement works if it manages to locate the same group of ENG 098 students that our more traditional (and labor-intensive) methods located. In 1995, our method was to screen with ACT-English scores and then to look at a timed writing sample. In 1996 and 1997 we used directed self-placement. We compared two of the most easily measured characteristics of the two populations and found that the groups shared very similar high-school GPAs (just under 3.0, compared to our freshman class's overall average of just over 3.2) and ACT-English scores (17.8 in 1995, 18.6 in 1996 and 1997, compared to our overall average of 22). This suggests that the students took their high-school GPAs and ACT-English scores into account: we didn't need to do it for them. So as a "replacement" of the old system, directed self-placement worked, though as we have begun to discover, there may be good reasons to dismiss these general indicators of academic ability as unable to predict success in writing courses.

We also looked at grades in ENG 098 and ENG 150. The overall GPA in ENG 098 was significantly lower in 1996 (2.56) than it was in 1995 (2.90), but then it jumped back up to 2.82 in 1997. We hesitate to conclude too much from these three years, but one possible explanation for the general drop in GPA in ENG 098 is that directed self-placement did a better job of locating genuinely struggling writers — that is, the very writers we hope to assist in ENG 098 — within the larger group with below-average ACT scores and high-school GPAs. On the other hand, perhaps our grading has simply fluctuated.

If our overall goal is to help students succeed in ENG 150 (so that they can go on and succeed in other classes and in their careers), then perhaps it's too early to say whether our directed self-placement system really works. We do know that about 66 percent of our 1995 ENG 098 students went on to earn credit for ENG 150 by the end of the next semester, while just 55 percent of the 1996 group did the same. The difference seemed to be that while in 1995 about 87 percent of the ENG 098 students went on to take ENG 150 the next semester, in 1996 only

75 percent of our ENG 098 students took ENG 150 the next semester. There could be several reasons for this, and we're still looking into it. Did they drop out of school? Did they feel overwhelmed by writing and choose to stay away from the next course? Or did they feel well-prepared for their other classes and simply decide to delay ENG 150 until a more convenient time?

Even with questions like these unanswered, we are convinced that directed self-placement is working at our school. We continue to locate hundreds of students each year that feel they need additional help with their writing, and we do it very efficiently and on terms the students understand and appreciate.

Directed Self-Placement Pleases Everyone Involved

To analyze numbers is, to some extent, to fall back into the thinking that what's most important about placing students in developmental or regular first-year writing courses is a quantifiable assessment of their writing ability. Teachers assess students' ability at the end of every term, but placement ought to be a student's own choice. Traditional placement procedures, as well as those procedures that Huot calls "emergent writing assessment" (556), assume that students don't know enough about what lies before them to make an intelligent choice. Or perhaps they cynically hold that students don't want to make wise choices and that they want to take as few writing courses as possible. We are careful to address the former assumption with our talk and our brochure. We address the latter concern by assuming ourselves that students will live, for better or for worse, with the choices they make, and by teaching each class at the level described in our brochure and course catalog.

Huot indicates that notions of assessment validity are evolving. Beyond measuring what they purport to measure, valid assessment procedures "must have positive impact and consequences for the teaching and learning of writing" (551). We tell students that their education — and this first decision about ENG 098 or ENG 150 — is their responsibility. We can offer direction, we can outline the purposes and expectations of each course, but we simply can't make the decision as intelligently as they can. It pleases students to know that they are in charge of their learning. It may be the most important message they receive at freshman orientation. It also puts some pressure on them — pressure that rightly belongs to them. When we place students, we take away from them a critical component in their educational lives. If we choose for them, they may think that the right thing is being done, but it is understandable that many take our choosing for them as an excuse to become either angry or defeated. The sense of rightness comes to students who make their own decisions in a matter like this and when they vow to affirm through hard work that the right decision has been made.

Students who appraise their ability too highly have a challenge before them. On the other hand, students who believe that ENG 098 is the best course for them are happy to have the opportunity to improve themselves and pleased to possess the dignity of making such a choice for themselves.

To illustrate this, we'll describe the experiences of two students — not to prove that directed self-placement works in the same way for everyone, but to show how it *can* work for individual students.

Kristen and Jacob were both traditional freshmen, a month or two past their 1997 high-school graduation ceremonies, when they attended summer orientation and selected their first composition courses. Based on sheer numbers (3.68 high-school GPA, ranked in the top 12 percent of her class, ACT-English score of 19), we might have expected Kristen to place herself into ENG 150, but she selected ENG 098. And we might have expected Jacob (3.16 high-school GPA, ranked in the top 46 percent of his class, ACT-English score of 15) to place himself into ENG 098, but he selected ENG 150.

What went into their decisions? Kristen, who made her decision while looking over the two lists of "characteristics" in the brochure, felt unsure of her ability to step right into college-level writing. "I was just being cautious," she says now. "I was just starting college and didn't know what to expect. I figured that English 098 would get me back into the writing mode. I'd been out of school all summer." Kristen's parents supported her decision, but she told them about it afterwards, after she'd already registered. "I made the decision during orientation," she recalls. "I was on my own."

Jacob, on the other hand, sought advice from others before making his final decision. He registered for ENG 150 during orientation, but then he spoke with his parents and high-school English teacher over the next several days. "When I was back home after orientation, I gave my advanced-comp teacher a call and read the class description of both classes, and both she and I decided that 150 was a good choice." His parents, though, disagreed. "My parents wanted me to take 098 because they didn't want me to screw up my first semester. But I wanted to take 150 to show them I wouldn't screw up."

Both Kristen's caution and Jacob's determination seem to us excellent reasons for selecting the courses they chose. Kristen did well in ENG 098 (she earned a B+) and enjoyed the class. "It was flexible, and everyone wrote at their own pace. It was not very stressful. We mostly wrote on things that interested us." She also says that she improved her writing: "We went to a tutor once a week. During the semester, I learned that there are different ways to write a paper. There are different emotions and audiences that a person must consider. You must also deal with many drafts before a final draft. You have to make enough time to get everything done."

Now that she is in ENG 150, Kristen feels well-prepared and well-situated as a college writer. "ENG 150 is more of an 'on-your-own' class.

We use computers, and we do a lot of reading and research. Overall, I think I'm doing pretty well."

Jacob also looks back on his decision as a good one. He says that he took the decision very seriously — more seriously than he might have back in high school: "In high school you're just taking classes, but in college you've got money involved." Like Kristen, he feels that he learned a lot in the course. "My final paper was a work of art compared to my high-school papers. The most important thing I gained from the class was to simply make my paper flow much better than I could before, not jumping from thought to thought."

Jacob earned a "C" in ENG 150, and he feels content with the experience. "Now I feel like I'm writing at a proficient college level. In my opinion, that's the goal of a freshman course."

In the responses of these students, we see a welcome shift in attitude, a merging of our goals and theirs. Where there might have been conflict, there is now cooperation. And we can say that as teachers, we adopt a very different attitude toward students who place themselves in ENG 098 or ENG 150. Teachers in ENG 098 know that the students, by their own admission, are asking for some help to get ready for college writing. No developmental writing teacher begins class with the view that the first order of business is to prove to the student that he or she was indeed placed correctly. Our best students are the ones that ask us to help them learn, and now in no other class on campus can a teacher assume with as much confidence that this is precisely what every student in the ENG 098 class wants. In fact, the ENG 098 class is becoming a favorite choice among writing faculty because of this positive attitude of orientation. This class fulfills no college requirement and doesn't count as credit toward graduation, yet the students are there and this pleases anyone with teaching instincts.

Those of us teaching ENG 150 know that each student has accepted the challenge of the course. The students have another option, but they feel ready to begin the required first-year writing course. Although occasionally the first-day writing sample indicates there is a student or two that might be better off in ENG 098, the teacher now faces a student, not an ACT score or the evidence of a one-shot writing sample. If the student knows what is expected and accepts the challenge, who are we to tell them they can't take this course? If a student fails ENG 150, that student must recur to his or her own self-placement, not a writing sample or the inflated high-school transcript. Teachers are pleased when the placement responsibility lies with the student, for the relationship is thus cleaner, less muddied with the interference of test scores and with predictions for success or failure from everyone *except* the student.

Finally, we have discovered that administrators are also pleased with directed self-placement. Admissions directors don't have to help organize placement exams or explain to students why they need to begin their college career with a not-for-college-credit course. They are pleased to invite potential students to compare the way we and other schools treat their incoming students: we provide options, while other schools take them away. And of course, unlike placement exams, directed self-placement costs nothing.

Like Huot, we want a placement procedure that focuses "inward toward the needs of students, teachers, and programs rather than outward toward standardized norms or generalizable criteria" (555). With directed self-placement we've found a way to place the focus first and foremost on students and their own self-understanding, capabilities, and purposes. Our teachers have been freed from an uncomfortably hasty kind of assessment so that they can focus entirely on the more authentic kinds of assessment that go on over the course of an entire semester. And the integrity of our program has benefited from the honest challenge presented by our promise to stick to our advertised course standards and objectives and to offer help and preparation to those who believe they need it.

A Pragmatist Theory of Writing Assessment

As we've indicated above, we believe that the assumptions and practices that Huot describes as "new, emergent writing assessment" are not yet deeply enough contextualized in the students' own personal and educational lives. The placement method we are advocating has its theoretical roots in John Dewey's democratic and pragmatist philosophy of education. Pragmatist understanding of experience, particularly Dewey's instrumentalism, supplies the soundest theory in support of directed self-placement. Dewey supplies us with these principles of learning: educational growth should be directed; inquiry begins in uncertainty and moves toward transformation; instrumental intelligence requires the freedom and power to choose.

Dewey says that "it is the office of the social medium," which includes schools, "to direct growth through putting powers to the best possible use" (*Democracy* 114). We direct our students' growth in part by establishing and communicating the goals of ENG 150 and the abilities required to succeed in the course. The *power* that directed self-placement taps is the desire among new college students to get started on the right foot and to finally make some personal choices about their education. Freshmen come to the university hyper-aware of their educational background, their capabilities, and the promise of success. They generally have a good sense of where they stack up in comparison to their peers. Where there is indetermination and uncertainty — uncertainty about preparation, about writing, and about one's ability to fit in to the new discourse community — there is a need for what Dewey calls transformation.

The *instrumental* function involves the way inquiry is used as a tool to intelligently direct one's experience. For Dewey, inquiry "is the controlled or directed transformation of an indeterminate situation into one that is so determinate in its constituent distinctions and relations as to convert the elements of the original situation into a unified whole"

("Pattern" 320). Instrumentalism replaces static understanding ("you are a basic writer") with an emphasis on the dynamic relation between the student and the possibilities waiting in his or her environment ("perhaps I should take a developmental writing course").

Our placement program thus relies on honest student inquiry and interactive participation. Our orientation talk offers direction: it is a critical first moment in four years of communication. We tell students where they need to end up, and they tell us how they want to get there. Dewey writes in *Democracy and Education:* "The communication which insures participation in a common understanding is one which secures similar emotional and intellectual dispositions — like ways of responding to expectations and requirements" (4). Our invitation to satisfy the first-year writing requirement in two semesters or one, by beginning with either ENG 098 or ENG 150, fosters the disposition characteristic of genuine learning and offers an invitation to academic community as opposed to establishing from the get-go that teachers are going to take over control of student learning.

Other theories of assessment define too narrowly what placement is all about. Edward White maintains that essay tests are "perfectly appropriate" if all we seek is "information that will help students enroll in courses for which they are ready" (33). But placement is not about *our* discovery of information; it is about getting a student's higher education started in the best possible way. If we want to communicate to students the dispositions characteristic of all inquirers, then most decidedly an essay test is *not* perfectly appropriate. To think so is to take on the mindset of administrators, who often view students merely as "seats" in a classroom. Finding the right "seat" for a student is not enough.

A pragmatist theory of assessment situates placement with regard to each student's aims and dispositions. The power relations that are violated by taking away choices are not repaired by mainstreaming, which simply eliminates options, or by updating methods of administering and scoring placement-essays, which continues to tell students that they are not ready to make their own decisions. Dewey remarks that "aims, beliefs, aspirations, knowledge — a common understanding — . . . cannot be passed physically from one to another like bricks" (4). What is required is communication — and every placement method communicates something important to students. Perhaps this is why traditional placement into remedial courses has not proven to equip students to succeed in the regular writing course. Perhaps those students are still waiting for someone to fix what ails them. We hope that we are encouraging in our new students, in pragmatist fashion, an intelligent way of responding to expectations and requirements.

If proper placement is a matter of guiding students into the course that is best suited to their educational background and current writing ability, directed self-placement may be the most *valid* procedure we can use. If the clarity of criteria and their consistent application is the standard of *reliability*, directed self-placement ranks high as long as we use current course goals and standards for success to inform and guide students in their choice.

Directed self-placement is no panacea. It does not address the problem of how to teach, how to bring students in from the margins, or how to deal with all of the politics of institutional change. Soliday, Grego and Thompson, Bartholomae and others address many of these concerns that would take us far beyond the limited scope of placement alternatives. But our placement alternative does lay the ground work for much that these authors recommend.

And so to conclude this essay, we return finally to a practical concern we confronted when we turned an important choice over to students — the risk. The "risk" of directed self-placement is peculiar. We imagined, for example, that, left to make the final decision on their own, no students would enroll in ENG 098. There we would be with twenty empty sections. If this were to happen, who would we blame? How bad would it really be? Who would be hurt? The peculiar feature of directed self-placement is that, in one sense, it can't really fail. If nobody took our developmental writing class, it could be a choice that each student made with his or her eyes open; our brochure and our orientation talk would make sure of that much. And if ill-prepared students take ENG 150, the teacher's complaint about unprepared students would have to be directed back toward the students. If they pass the course, who can blame them for taking the chance? If they fail, they will, we hope, learn that a college education is a serious endeavor and that success often begins with a proper estimation of one's abilities.

Acknowledgments

We would like to thank Peter Elbow for his generous encouragement and for his thoughtful comments on the early drafts of this article. We also want to acknowledge our indebtedness to Thomas Newkirk's "Roots of the Writing Process" for its clear exposition of several key concepts in Dewey's philosophy as they relate to writing instruction.

Works Cited

Bartholomae, David. "Inventing the University." *Perspectives on Literacy*. Ed. Eugene R. Kintgen, Barry M. Kroll, and Mike Rose. Carbondale: Southern Illinois UP, 1988. 273–85.

Dewey, John. *Democracy and Education*. 1916. New York: Free P, 1966.

———. "The Pattern of Inquiry." *Logic: The Theory of Inquiry*. New York: Holt, 1938. 101–19. Rpt. in *Pragmatism: The Classic Writings*. Ed. H. S. Thayer. Indianapolis: Hacket, 1982. 316–34.

Elbow, Peter. "Writing Assessment in the Twenty-First Century: A Utopian View." *Composition in the Twenty-First Century: Crisis and Change*. Ed. Lynn Bloom, Donald Daiker, and Edward White. Carbondale: Southern Illinois UP, 1996.

Grego, Rhonda, and Nancy Thompson. "Repositioning Remediation: Renegotiating Composition's Work in the Academy." *CCC* 47 (1996): 62–84.

Huot, Brian. "Toward a New Theory of Writing Assessment." *CCC* 47 (1996): 549–66.

James, William. "What Pragmatism Means." *Pragmatism*. 1907. Cleveland: World, 1955.

Newkirk, Thomas. "Roots of the Writing Process." *More than Stories: The Range of Children's Writing*. Portsmouth: Heinemann, 1989. 177–208.

Soliday, Mary. "From the Margins to the Mainstream: Reconceiving Remediation." *CCC* 47 (1996): 85–100.

White, Edward M. "An Apologia for the Timed Impromptu Essay Test." *CCC* 46 (1995): 30–45.

Classroom Activities

Royer and Gilles in "Directed Self-Placement" present educational issues of interest to students who may be questioning the goals and purposes of a basic writing course. Students may be interested in reading and discussing this article and may find it useful as a writing prompt. Of particular concern to students may be the criteria used for directed self-placement into basic writing and college writing. Students may also be interested in the description of how first-year orientation works at Grand Valley State University and in the profiles of the two students who selected different first-year writing courses for very different reasons. Students could compare and contrast their own experiences with the events described in the article. What are some of the assumptions made about students and writing courses in the Royer and Gilles article? How is placement in writing courses at your own institution different from or similar to the approach at Grand Valley State University? Do students have access to academic advisers before classes begin? What do they say about their experiences of new-student orientation? What aspects of orientation work well? What would students like to see changed or improved? Students may then wish to work in small groups to create a description of the basic writing course(s) at their own institution; based on this description, they could develop a set of criteria for directed self-placement. What are the unstated assumptions behind placement in a basic writing course? How could students' descriptions and criteria address those assumptions and help future students understand the goals and purposes of the course?

Thinking about Teaching

To create a more student-centered environment, take notes on your students' discussions of basic writing course descriptions and placement issues. Which of their ideas can be readily implemented? Which ideas seem unfeasible or would require a great deal of institutional change? To test out your ideas, share the Royer and Gilles article, and your students' responses, with other teachers of developing writers — and pose questions similar to those asked by your students. What are Royer and Gilles's unstated assumptions about placement systems and writing courses? Do those assumptions apply to the realities of your institution? How would a system of directed self-placement work at your institution? What conditions would have to be present to make such a system feasible? Moreover, what implications does the notion of directed self-placement hold for ideas of student agency? What does it mean to ask a student to place himself or herself in a course, as opposed to the skills-based model of placement tests described in the article? Finally, how are placement systems linked to course design? Examine the pragmatic aspects of Royer and Gilles's argument to determine how placement criteria can be applied to the practical issues of syllabus construction and course content.

Failure: The Student's or the Assessment's?

Kay Harley and Sally I. Cannon

The following article by Kay Harley, Chair of the Saginaw Valley State University English Department and Director of the Saginaw Valley National Writing Project, and Sally I. Cannon, Writing Coordinator of the Saginaw Valley State University English Department, is powerful and poignant. Both a "good read" and pedagogically provocative, the article presents a case study of Mica, a student in a pilot program at Saginaw Valley State University that combined basic and first-year English courses. Harley and Cannon use this study to explore the notion of assessment.

The writers acknowledge the ongoing struggle to define and redefine academic discourse related to assessment. For instance, most assessment instruments look at a sample as an isolated text instead of reading a piece of writing contextually and intertextually. That is, much assessment deals with what a writer doesn't do, how his or her writing doesn't measure up. Such criteria often fail to recognize current controversies in composition studies, such as the role of personal voice in academic writing. After considering these and other controversial issues, Harley and Cannon conclude that assessment practices need further evolution. Moreover, Mica's voice resonates throughout this article, arguing for a reconsideration of what it means to be a basic writing student.

> The issue, then, is not who misses the mark but whose misses matter and why.
>
> — Bartholomae ("Margins" 68)

> Being in an college english class I felt I was final going to learn some-
> thing about this word call english. . . . I knew I was going to learn
> everything I always want to learn it made me feel good.
>
> — Mica

Overview

In some ways, Mica was like other underprepared, basic writers who
enrolled in the pilot program for developmental writers at our
midwestern state university. Acknowledging her checkered academic
past and resolved to start afresh, Mica was attracted to our pilot program. Instead of taking the traditional sequence of a three-hour, noncredit, basic writing course followed by a two-semester freshman writing course, students like Mica, whose placement essay exam indicated
the need for developmental work in writing, could enroll in our program, which combined the developmental and the first semester freshman English courses. The pilot provided intensive support through increased contact time with faculty, collaboration with peers, and tutoring
from upper class students who focused on improving students' writing
and on assisting the freshmen in negotiating their ways into the university community. We used Mike Rose's *Lives on the Boundary* as a
focal text to foreground issues of language and learning, access and
denial, power and education, supplemented by brief articles from local
and national sources.

The pilot program gave another option to students like Mica, a young
African American, nineteen years old, and a single mother of a young
child. Her high school performance garnered a 2.7 GPA but was interrupted by the emotional and physical demands of a pregnancy during
her junior year. She scored in the fourth percentile on the Nelson-Denny
reading test (equivalent to an upper elementary student) which placed
her in the university's developmental reading course. She felt unsure
about herself and her writing, and, in her own words, went through
high school worried that "someone knew my secret and they were calling me dumb behind my back." She was a student "at risk" whose success at the university was a gamble. In addition, Mica found herself at
a preponderantly white university, where 300 African American students often feel isolated in a university population of about 7,000. The
university's demographics were mirrored in our pilot population; Mica
was one of three African Americans out of a total of 45 enrolled in the
Fall 1992 pilot.

However, Mica stood apart from her peers because she was a student whom our best teaching and assessment strategies did not serve.
She forced us to rethink just about everything we did. Her writing continually challenged our expectations and ways of reading. Mica was
also often vocal and forthright, letting us know what she was thinking,
and not afraid of challenging us: "Why are you teaching us this?"; "What
do you mean?"; "You said this yesterday and today you're telling us

this!" Then, increasingly as the semester wore on, she became sullen and silent, defensive about our response to her writing. We had often praised her writing for its strong content and lively voice. At the same time, however, we would note the structural and grammatical problems that plagued every draft. She seemed confused about what she perceived as our ambivalence toward her writing.[1]

At the end of the semester, Mica failed the pilot program. We, however, asked ourselves how we had failed Mica, specifically in our assessment of her work. With over 80 percent of the students passing the combined course with a "C" or better, it became particularly important to analyze reasons for Mica's failure.

The assessment practice we used is widely considered one of the best to date in the discipline: a holistically scored portfolio, judged pass/fail by English faculty both within and external to the pilot. Nonetheless, as we've reflected upon our assessment of Mica, we have come to believe that a mismatch exists between our portfolio criteria and the texts Mica produced, even texts that had been revised over the semester with our criteria in mind. We now doubt that current assessment criteria and practices can "read" Mica's work adequately, or the work of other culturally diverse students whom our institutions are publicly committed to educating. Jay Robinson and Patti Stock in "The Politics of Literacy" have written, "if we would be literate, and help others to become so, it is time for thoughtful listening to those voices that come from the margins; it is time for reflective reading of texts that inscribe those voices as centrally human ones" (313). While many of us have made progress in learning to listen to others' voices, this progress is not embodied adequately in our assessments.

While the profession discusses writing as embedded in a context, we represent writing in our assessments as uniform and monolithic. We may call for multiple samples by which to evaluate performance, but during the portfolio evaluation itself, we read each paper largely as an isolated text, not contextually or intertextually. And while we may specify different genres, the criteria we use for evaluation fail to acknowledge the blurring of genres that is evident in much writing both within and outside the academy today. Further, our criteria fail to recognize the current controversies over the role of personal voice in academic writing and argument. They also privilege linear forms of organization. In short, our assessments penalize students for "missing the mark" in ways that may be incompatible with our profession's evolving notions of the socially contextualized nature of writing and discourse.

This paper, then, explores what we now see as our failure in assessing Mica's work and speculates on how we might reconceptualize the assessment of writing, particularly the writing of culturally diverse students.

Assessment and the Pilot Program

Briefly, our assessment required the students to submit a portfolio of four pieces selected from writing they had done during the course. While we urged students to incorporate ideas or examples from early papers in later ones or revise versions of early ones as their thinking on issues was deepened by the reading, writing, and discussions in the course, the requirements for the portfolio didn't describe or reflect this. Rather they read quite conventionally:

a. Personal Reflective piece: This essay should demonstrate your ability to use details effectively to narrate/describe; it should have a focus, a point.

b. Expository piece: This essay should demonstrate your ability to create a thesis and support it with evidence — personal examples, examples of others, material from the coursepack or Rose.

c. Synthesis paper: This essay should demonstrate your ability to synthesize (make connections between) ideas from the coursepack, Rose, and your own thinking about education and work, to focus them in a thesis, and to present them in an organized and coherent fashion.

d. In-class/Impromptu paper: This essay should demonstrate your ability to write a clear and organized essay under timed conditions and without the opportunity to revise.

The criteria we shared with students and used as a department in the pass/fail evaluations of student portfolios also reflected traditional rubrics.

A Pass portfolio should demonstrate the ability to:

a. write fluently

b. grapple with a topic; develop and explore the implications of ideas and insights

c. provide a focus, generally through an explicit thesis statement

d. support ideas with reasons and/or examples from personal experience and/or outside sources

e. organize ideas into clear paragraphs

f. avoid multiple grammatical mistakes, particularly sentence boundary problems.

Challenges of Reading and Assessing Mica's Writing

The following essay, Mica's first of the semester, illustrates the difficulty we had in assessing her writing. The assignment asked the students to describe an experience or moment in their lives in which they learned something. By establishing a clear focus and drawing upon sensory details, they were to narrate the experience so that their readers could relive the moment with them and reflect upon what that experience taught them. Mica decided to write about the birth of her child. The first two paragraphs of her essay, entitled "Ready or Not," are reprinted below:

> Waking up saying good-bye to everyone "Bye Mama, Beebee, and Chris". Oh well I'm left here in this empty house again no one to talk to. Don't anybody care that I'm 9-1/2 months pregnant and my stomach is as big as a beach ball, and that I wobble like a weeble when I walk.
> I remember whimpering as if I was a two years old. Mica get a whole to yourself stop whimpering for your eyes get puffy. Baby, why don't you come out. All my friend have had their babies. What are you waiting on to come out of there; sweetie your mama is tired of being pregnant. I can remember being so angry that if anybody would have came over here I would have chewed them up alive. Oh! I got to get out of here before I go crazy. Running up and down the stairs, I figure if I jiggle you up then maybe you will come out. Doing this for five minutes and nothing happen. Just huffing and puffing like a dog sitting in the hot summer sun. Well, I guess I'll take me a shower. Getting undress and guess what the telephone rang, Oh, Oh, somebody cares about me. The Mrs. Know-it-all-mother-in-law, the bat. Hello, "Mica what are you doing?" "I replied," nothing, I was about to get into the shower, can you call me back?" Yeah, bye bye. Wicked witch I never thought she cared. Oh well back to the shower. In the shower the water running on my stomach I can feel you in there come out of there my stomach began making the gesture like the baby was trying to really come out.

For most readers of freshman English essays, this paper misses the mark. It isn't "correct." Yet, we want to argue, these notions of "correctness" — correctness not only in terms of surface features but also of acceptable styles, genres and organization — though deeply embedded in our thinking and assessment criteria are often unstated and not fully examined. Mica's paper jars and challenges, yet it handles language in complex ways. It shifts from direct to indirect discourse; from Mica as narrator, to Mica as a character thinking aloud, to Mica speaking directly to other characters or her unborn child. But we dismiss this complexity and judge through the lens of "error." The direct discourse is often unmarked. Sentences are sometimes fragmented or fused. Tense shifts occur seemingly at random. The missing tense markers, particularly "d" or "ed," and copula ("to be") deletions reflect Black English Vernacular (BEV). Further, her organization contains nothing explicit.

Mica's writing did not include any of the distancing and reflecting that were part of our expectations for a personal reflective essay. In "Reflections on Academic Discourse: How It Relates to Freshmen and Colleagues," Peter Elbow explores how academic discourse assumes "that we can separate the ideas and reasons and arguments from the person who holds them" (140).[2] Mica was unable or refused to squelch the personal — to separate the message from the messenger — to adopt a disinterested, objective stance. Her preference for situating her ideas in personal terms is seen in several other essays discussed later in this paper.

Rather than reading Mica's text for what it doesn't do, it can be read for what it is achieving. Robert Yagelski, for example, suggested in his 1994 CCCC presentation that we might evaluate a student text like this as personal testimony. Mica's writing does render the immediacy of her experience of labor with her first child. It is filled with strong details. The storying patterns, oral resonances, and rich rhythm give the piece its poignancy and power. These reflect a mode of discourse prevalent in Black English that Geneva Smitherman in *Talkin and Testifyin: The Language of Black America* defines as tonal semantics. One feature of tonal semantics, Smitherman notes, is the use of repetition, alliterative word play, and a striking and sustained use of metaphor, something seen throughout Mica's work (134). Mica writes about a jumbled, chaotic, and intensely personal time that demands a strong emotive voice. That Mica has achieved such a voice is a mark, not of a basic writer, but of an accomplished one.

Features similar to those in Mica's personal essay appeared in all of her subsequent writing in the course, including her summaries and explanatory essays. More clearly in those papers did we see how personal anecdotes are acceptable in academic discourse only when framed by generalizations. It is the framing that appears indispensable, for if a student like Mica offers a personal example without a corresponding generalization, the personal doesn't qualify as support.

David Bartholomae has noted that all errors are not created equal.

> The errors that count in the work of basic writers have no clear and absolute value but gain value only in the ways that they put pressure on what we take to be correct, in the ways that these errors are different from acceptable errors. The work that remains for the profession is to determine the place of those unacceptable styles within an institutional setting, within an institution with its own styles of being right, its own habitual ways of thinking and writing ("Margins" 68–69).

Mica's paper challenged our habitual ways of assessing writing and left us questioning whether the "unacceptable" in Mica's writing might have a rightful place in a freshman writing course and in academic discourse more generally. Can the boundaries of academic discourse be broadened so that "personal testimony" or an "emotive voice" or "tonal semantics" might find a place? In suggesting this, we are not suggesting that a student like Mica cannot or should not learn the dominant academic discourse, including what some describe as the "superficial features" of grammar, style, and mechanics. Nor are we suggesting that our job as teachers is not to help all students to do so, giving them access to many voices and styles. Nonetheless, we are suggesting that the writing of students like Mica may also call us to transform academic discourse and the assessment practices which support it.

Unpacking Metaphors of Exclusion: Deficiency, Foreignness, and Monogeneric Papers

Bartholomae demonstrates that we sort out and label "on the assumption that basic writers are defined by what they don't do (rather than by what they do), by the absence of whatever is present in literate discourse: cognitive maturity, reason, orderliness, conscious strategy, correctness" ("Margins" 67). While we immediately recognized a power and immediacy in Mica's writing, our early diagnoses of her work focused on deficits — the lack of reason, orderliness, conscious strategy, and correctness that Bartholomae (and our assessment guides) enumerate. These quick notes made for ourselves, for example, focus on what Mica failed to do in an expository essay exploring the distinction between child abuse and discipline, a paper that drew upon a time when she was accused of abusing a toddler at a day care center at which she worked:

> — problems framing the experience and/or moving between her frames/ generalizations and her examples — movement is a key problem, transitions — abruptly inserts dictionary definitions of discipline and child abuse — moves directly into 1st person narrative example with no lead in and a complete shift in style — ends with question posed to reader rather than restatement (or even direct statement) of main point of paper — multiple tense marker errors and other BEV features —

While these notes exemplify error analysis and try to move beyond a simple recording of errors ("her moves show an awareness of what is needed"), they nonetheless show that we read Mica's essay primarily in terms of its deficits: it lacks conventional features of academic prose.

Here is the opening of the essay:

> Ten years ago if you told your child "don't do that," and they did it any way you would spank them for not listening to you. Back then the way you discipline your child was your business. Now days its everybodys business the way you discipline your child.

> *Child Abuse vs. Discipline*

> When do you know its child abuse? And when do you know it simply discipline.

> DISCIPLINE is defined as training especially training of the mind.

CHILD ABUSE is defined as mistreatment of a child by parents or guardians.

It's Thursday, I said to myself, I have one more day before I can rest, rest, rest. Dealing with 20-5 kids a day really takes a lot out of you. . . .

It was 10:05 and all the kids had arrived. We sang good morning to each other then split up in groups. We had a full load and that was about 25 kids so that made us have five kids a piece. As the day went along it was time for coloring. I caught one of my kids putting crayons in his mouth. "David get the crayons out of your mouth. They're not to eat, but to color," I said. He didn't have anything to say back. But as soon as I turned my head he had them back in his mouth. We went through this about four times. The fourth time I got up and tapped him on his hand — Not hit, or smack but tapped him on his hand. He didn't cry, he just took the crayons out of his mouth and continued coloring.

If, instead of assessing Mica's essay in terms of its deficits, we set it alongside some of the reading we were doing and asked students to do, Mica's style does not look so foreign or lacking. Her abrupt shifts and lack of transitions are not altogether dissimilar to those of Mike Rose in his opening of *Lives on the Boundary,* the book used in our course.

Rose moves from description of students and of the university campus, to a carefully recorded observation of a teacher drawing out students' knowledge about the renaissance, to a pictorial image of the medieval goddess Grammatica which then functions metaphorically, to statistics about changing enrollment patterns in American universities — all of which create a rich and multifaceted collage. No explicit transitions mark the movements, only white space on the page.

Rose's style is quite different from directly stated thesis and support pattern that guides much of our instruction and assessment of basic writers. He interweaves precise objective description, vivid image, significant anecdote, personal experience, quotes from official documents, general statement, and reflection. Mica's child abuse paper parallels Rose in significant ways. Her essay is full of ideas and passion as she explores the damaging consequences of mistaking discipline for child abuse and the difficulties of clearing your name, particularly if you are a single mother from a minority group, when charges of abuse have been leveled. She offers personal testimony, clearly conveys the events/examples, includes detail and dialogue to place the reader in the scene, and writes with a strong sense of conviction. While not using many of the devices of academic argument, she is nonetheless making a claim: that discipline should not be mistaken for child abuse. She elaborates upon her points and shows the harm that mistaking discipline for child abuse can cause. She writes to effect change.[3]

To take another example, David Bartholomae has demonstrated how a careful look at the writing of Patricia Williams, an African American legal scholar and author of *The Alchemy of Race and Rights,* can cause us to question the way we read the prose of basic writers. Williams, like Rose, upsets our conventional expectations of academic prose.

"Williams' writing is disunified: it mixes genres; it willfully forgets the distinctions between formal and colloquial, public and private; it makes unseemly comparisons. In many ways, her prose has the features we associate with basic writing, although here those features mark her achievement as a writer, not her failure" ("Tidy House" 11). We do not, Bartholomae suggests,

> read "basic writing" the way we read Patricia Williams' prose, where the surprising texture of the prose stands as evidence of an attempt to negotiate the problems of language . . . She is trying to do something that can't be conventionally done. To say that our basic writers are less intentional, less skilled, is to say the obvious . . . It is possible . . . that when we define Williams-like student writing as less developed or less finished . . . we are letting metaphors of development or process hide value-laden assumptions about thought, form, the writer, and the social world ("Tidy House" 19).

Errors in Our Expectations

Two papers Mica wrote later in the course again show her defying our expectations about the appropriate form and content. In one, we had asked students to select an article, summarize it, and respond. Mica chose a collection of brief interviews concerning women and work entitled "Is Success Dangerous to Your Health?" She opens as follows:

> In reading the interview article, "Is Success Dangerous to your Health," none of the three interviewees in their interview explain or answer the question ask in the title of the interview, Is Success Dangerous to your Health? I couldn't grasp what the author was try to do however, what I did find in the article is "RESPECT". All of the three interviewees felt they were not respect. The title of the article pull me right into the paper. However, I was very disapointed not to find what I was looking for. Will my career affect my health in anyway.

Mica had written guidelines, model opening sentences, and class assistance on how to write a summary and response. However, she sets these aside (perhaps largely unconsciously) to pursue her own frustration with the title, a point she returns to in her conclusion where she unabashedly makes suggestions to the author about how to answer the question the title posed. Her "back talk" to the author is a significant rhetorical move, yet it and her use of first person belie the expectations for an objective summary. Again, our immediate response to Mica's summary/response is to dismiss it as not meeting the terms of the assignment. And, indeed, it does not. However, her gutsy move in challenging the author surely demonstrates critical thinking as well as a critical engagement with the text, something our assessment practices sometimes overlook in favor of acceptable genre features. Consider, for example, the "safe" and predictable but totally unengaged five paragraph theme that passes without question. The paper passes, no doubt, because it can demonstrate the surface features and stylistic conventions of academic discourse: the clear structure, the explicit signposting, etc. But content — which we continually maintain is the most important feature when assessing any kind of prose — is often overlooked. Is this a "fair" and accurate assessment of either writer?

The last assignment of the semester was a synthesis paper which asked students to bring together their thinking about education or work, the two themes of the class. Students were to create a fresh look at the topic by making connections among the different readings from the course and integrating those with their views, experience, and writing done in earlier papers and in their journal.

Mica chose to write about education, specifically her experience in the pilot project. Our initial assessment of Mica's paper was that it failed to do what was expected. In our minds it did not "read" as a synthesis. The paper never established a focus in the form of a thesis statement, it failed to smoothly link specific examples and personal experience to generalizations, and it made little use of quotations from the reading as support. Instead, Mica recounted her experience from the beginning of the semester to the end with no immediately apparent synthesis or reflection, as these first two paragraphs suggest:

> It's first day in college, and I'm excited I drove around the hold campus to find a policeman so, I can get direction to my class. Finally I found one he and looked like he was hiding behind the trees waiting to give someone a ticket. I drove over to him, and rolled down my window. "Can I help you?," He said, Yes you can I need help trying to find my class the room number z204. "O.K. young lady you keep straight on this street we one and turn right, Then you see this building a lot of people will be coming in and out of it." Thank you very much sir. I seen this big building about as half big as a major hotel like the Marriot Hotel. I entered the building, Everyone was walking so fast like they were in a marathon.
>
> Finally, I found room z204 I walk in; it was pretty full. I sat by the window so I could look out of it since no one was talking. Being in a college English class I felt I was final going to learn something about this word call english. All through high school I felt so insure about writing, I always felt someone knew my secret and they were calling me dumb behind my back. I felt a little dumb but, I knew someday I will learn were to put a period, comma, and a semicolon without feel unsure about it. So, in college I felt this is when every thing is going to change. I knew I was going to learn everything I always want to learn it made me feel good.

The paper adopts a narrative stance from which it never departs, thus defying our expectations for a synthesis paper. However, if we temporarily put aside those expectations to read differently, the paper does synthesize Mica's experience in the pilot course. She captures the confusion and anxiety of a new student coming to a college campus for the first time, likening the campus buildings and the policeman's behavior to the closest thing she knows: the city. She compares our modern buildings to a Marriot hotel. That comparison, coupled with her admission of her "secret" about feeling "dumb," suggests how much strength it actually took to walk in the doors of our institution.

The paper shows Mica as a beginning writer, new to the university and its expectations, negotiating her way into academic discourse, just as she seeks to find her way physically into the academic campus. She explores issues of anxiety about writing, the pitfalls of peer response groups, and power relations in the classroom. This reading acknowledges a focus, which our initial reading could not because, limited by predetermined portfolio requirements and paper features, it linked focus with thesis. Now we realize that the focus was there: it was Mica's — her story of her first semester college English experience. The narrative mode was her way of shaping her experience, of telling her story.

Carolyn Heilbrun in *Writing a Woman's Life* discusses the ways female literary figures write to organize and make sense of their lives. While Heilbrun is discussing works of fiction, not academic discourse, Jane Tompkins and other scholars writing academic discourse do directly call upon their personal experience to enrich and organize their understanding of professional concepts. If Tompkins, why not Mica? Certainly the profession is expanding its notion of what is acceptable in its own academic discourse. And while Mica's writing is far from model prose, and she does not have conscious control over the strategies she uses, her writing has made us realize that the time is ripe for a reconsideration of what is "acceptable" in student discourse as well.

Locating Oneself in the Privileged Discourse of the Academic World

Clearly, Mica is a student whose style betrays her and sets her apart from the mainstream at our — and most — college campuses. Perhaps, then, we need to assess Mica's work as her attempt to locate herself in the privileged discourse of the academic community. This would lead us to view her writing problems not as internal or cognitive, but rather as ones of appropriation. Mica's work throughout the course was marked by styles that clashed with our deeply embedded notions of academic discourse represented in our assignment and evaluation constructs. In assessing her, we judged these as deficits. Consistently rich in details, we said, but she could not control them. Our assignments called for the person, the details, yet our assessments demanded that these be "controlled," that specifics be framed, that thesis and generalization be tied to example. If her status in coming to the university is deeply divided, fragmentary, how can we expect a central point, a main idea?

David Bartholomae suggests

> if we take the problem of writing to be the problem of appropriating the power and authority of a particular way of speaking, then the relationship of the writer to the institutions within which he writes becomes

central (the key feature in the stylistic struggle on the page) rather than peripheral (a social or political problem external to writing and therefore something to be politely ignored) ("Margins" 70).

Our assessment criteria didn't allow us to read Mica's prose as an attempt to negotiate the problems of language. Rather, the assessment criteria were presented as objective and uniform. Such criteria may protect us and the university community at large from looking critically at the mismatch between the rhetoric of our policies and programs for ethnically underrepresented and academically underprepared students and the realities of their struggles to make sense of an unfamiliar social dialect.[4]

Grammar Is Not Neutral

Mica describes quite poignantly her purpose in voluntarily enrolling in our pilot program: "I was final going to learn something about this word call english." She suggests an academic history fraught with insecurity, afraid that someone would find out her "secret." Interestingly, Mica views that secret and the solution to her problem as a mechanical one: "I knew someday I will learn were to put a period, comma, and a semicolon." This characterization of writing in terms of grammar, of course, is not unusual. Many writers (and teachers) conflate the two. (Consider the numbers of people who, when told that you are an English teacher, respond with a comment about "watching their grammar.") As we continued to study Mica's writing and reflect upon our work with her long after the semester ended, we began to understand how strongly Mica held to her belief in the power of punctuation. We realized that learning correct grammar *was* Mica's agenda. As Mina Shaughnessy noted, "grammar still symbolizes for some students one last chance to understand what is going on with written language so that they can control it rather than be controlled by it" (11).

Carolyn Hill discusses how grammar is a political issue to basic writers: "Grammar is not a neutral 'thing' to them, rather a completely socialized representative of those authorities who *seem* to students to be outside themselves" (250). Later in her synthesis paper, Mica constructs her instructors' point of view and appears suspicious of our motives in not focusing dominantly upon grammatical issues. She writes:

I enjoy every bit of writing I did in the class but, I felt disappoint cause I didn't learn what I want to learn in the class. . . . I really felt that we should have discuss more of what I believe she saw going on in the class. Since, she mentioned it herself that she was having a problem with grammer, fused sentence, tense sentences, and fragments. We did work on this for a couple of days but i felt it wasn't enough.

In saying "we should have discuss more of what *I believe she saw going on in the class*" Mica seems to feel that we were unjustly withholding information that she believes could solve her writing problems and eliminate her "secret." That intensive one-on-one tutoring from peers and instructors, diagnostic analyses of her patterns of error, comparisons of her own patterns to typical nonstandard patterns of Black English Vernacular, and extensive opportunities for revision did not help Mica gain greater power over spelling, punctuation, and syntax remains one of our greatest puzzles.

Mica's sentence points to power relations in the classroom. Mica frames the teacher/student relationship as a struggle between two people with two competing solutions to her writing problems. She is indignant (perhaps rightfully so) that her solution, more grammar instruction, is being ignored. In retrospect, we suspect that our actions are well described by Hill: "Ostensibly I wanted to give up authority, help students to be self-starters. Covertly, the institution and I collaborated to see to it that students be quickly notified if that start did not place them in the proper arms of Standard English, focused and controlled" (78).

Mica wanted to gain control over her writing and her errors; she wanted access to the social power identified with academic discourse. Yet neither she nor her instructors confronted this agenda centrally. Her relationship to the institution within which she wrote, her very placement in a basic writing course, the value placed by the university and those exercising influence in the society on copy editing, correctness and conventional styles were peripheral concerns. Correctness was thought of as context-free. That is something the English profession can no longer afford to assume. Perhaps that is why we saw such little change in these areas of Mica's writing.

Rethinking Assessment

Reexamining and questioning our assessment of Mica's portfolio has left us with more questions than answers. As we now critique our portfolio assessment we see that we inadvertently worked to keep intact the boundaries and borders by which basic writing is institutionally defined, ironically the very boundaries our pilot project meant to collapse.

Thus, while we endorse and encourage more courses like ours, courses which collapse borders and work to eliminate notions of basic writers as "foreigners,"[5] we realize that our assessment practices must evolve significantly as well.

First, we need to understand that assessment is complexly situated, and different audiences may require different evaluations. In reviewing our guidelines for a passing portfolio we would now ask, "For whom are we evaluating Mica's work?" During the portfolio reading, who is the primary audience? Is it Mica? Is our purpose to reveal to her where she has succeeded or failed in meeting the standards set for an introductory university writing course? Is the primary audience her future college instructors? If so, what do they need to learn about writing as a deeply embedded cultural and social act, about the time needed to acquire new discourse practices, and about current challenges to hierarchical patterns of organization if they are to determine what should constitute "passing" work in an introductory writing course which enrolls culturally diverse students? Or is the audience the local, state, or national community? The needs and interests of these groups differ; our assessments need to reflect this.

In addition, we need to devise ways to read student texts contextually and intertextually not only in the classroom setting but in evaluation sessions. Our prespecified portfolio requirements pressured us into reading each paper as an individual entity. What we now want to strive for is a more intertextual reading of the portfolios, an assessment practice that views the essays in a portfolio as interrelated and recursive. Read as a whole, Mica's papers have a surprising unity, both in content and approach. We wonder what would happen if during the portfolio evaluation we actively read Mica's work as her ongoing exploration of the issues that were central to her views of education, work, and mastery of written English. All of them contain strong narrative elements; all have a directness in confronting the issues she's chosen as her topics; all fail to clearly and explicitly link example to generalization, provide direct transitions, or follow a linear order; and all demonstrate a lack of control of surface features including spelling, word ending, person and tense inflections, and punctuation.

We need to resist (or read against) our unconscious notions of academic discourse as monolithic and standard. It's a myth that all synthesis papers will look like some imagined prototype of a synthesis paper. Yet, when evaluating portfolios holistically, we often operate under this myth. Papers that contain the expected features of a particular assignment pass without question, while quirky papers that don't easily correspond to a genre or mode — even if particularly rich in content — are often failed. Narrative strategies are undervalued, even when they are deeply reflective. In professional conferences and articles, we repeatedly remind ourselves to avoid false dichotomies, yet too often we fall back into simplistic either/or formulations in evaluation. Our assessment criteria suggest an essay is either personal reflection or exposition, either narrative or argument. The language is either academic discourse or not. The thesis/generalization is either directly stated or it cannot be credited. We need to immerse students in a variety of discourses, being careful not to limit students like Mica to only one voice. We do well to remember the frustration of feminist writer, bell hooks, with teachers who "did not recognize the need for African American students to have access to many voices" (qtd. in Delpit 291).

Finally, we need to understand errors, not as deficits, but as attempts at appropriating the discourses of other communities. This shift would allow us to recognize and extend rather than automatically penalize these attempts at appropriation. Matters of syntax and usage are not neutral as our portfolio criteria imply. We need to become sensitive to the power relationships implicit in all language use and to the political implications of judgments of error as "nonstandard," particularly as higher education opens itself to an increasingly diverse student body.

We have no clear answer to the question raised in our title. Was the failure Mica's or that of our assessment procedures? We suspect the failure rests on both sides. We did fail Mica: we failed to read her texts contextually; we failed to assess her portfolio in light of her attempts to appropriate a new discourse; we failed by oversimplifying the nature of academic discourse; we failed by setting her work against some constructed "mythical" portfolio demonstrating competence; we failed by not seeing the power relations involved in any attempts to work on nonstandard usages. The answer, however, is also complex — as complex, perhaps, as Mica's writing and as Mica herself. At times she appeared evasive and angry; at times bewildered; at times fiercely proud and determined.

Would we pass Mica's portfolio today? No. However, Mica's writing has challenged our notions of what is good and acceptable written discourse in introductory academic settings, and we think it should challenge others in the English profession, the university, and society.

Mica did not meet our expectations. Her writing continues to intrigue and frustrate us. Yet it may be the Micas — those students who do not meet our expectations — who shed the strongest light on our practices.

Notes

1. Some ambivalence was undoubtedly present, both on our part and on Mica's. In working with Mica, we probably at times exemplified "a certain sense of powerlessness and paralysis" that Lisa Delpit has described "among many sensitive and well-meaning literacy educators who appear to be caught in the throes of a dilemma. Although their job is to teach literate discourse styles to all of their students, they question whether that is a task they can actually accomplish for poor students and students of color. Furthermore, they question whether they are acting as agents of oppression by insisting that students who are not already a part of the 'mainstream' learn that discourse" (285). Mica also may have been deeply ambivalent, caught in the conflicts between her home discourses and the discourses of the university, and feeling torn between institutions and value systems in ways that Keith Gilyard documents. Thus, she may have been choosing to resist or "not learn" as Herb Kohl describes it, rather than learn that which she perceived as denying her a sense of who she was. While issues such as these are important to our thinking, this paper looks more specifically to the implications of current assessment practices.

2. Elbow makes the good point that "it's crazy to talk about academic discourse as one thing" (140). However, we often teach and assess academic discourse as if it were. We believe that many teachers of writing (perhaps unconsciously) hold a collective, monolithic view of academic discourse, which

poses problems to assessment, particularly the assessment of students at risk. This monolithic view of academic discourse is defined primarily by its stylistic and mechanical surface features, features such as mapping or signposting, explicitness, objectivity, and formal language (Elbow 144–46).

3. Smitherman discusses a characteristic use of narrative as a persuasive tool in black English: "The relating of events (real or hypothetical) becomes a black rhetorical strategy to explain a point, to persuade holders of opposing views to one's own point of view, and in general, to 'win friends and influence people'" (147–48).

4. Anne DiPardo explores this issue in *A Kind of Passport* when she examines the "patterns of tension" in an institution's commitment to educational equity, looking particularly at the "good intentions and enduring ambivalence" embedded in the language of the basic writing curricula.

5. See Bruce Horner for a recent discussion of this and other metaphors used to characterize basic writers.

Works Cited

Bartholomae, David. "The Tidy House: Basic Writing in the American Curriculum." *Journal of Basic Writing* 12.1 (1993): 4–21.

———. "Writing on the Margins: The Concept of Literacy in Higher Education." *A Sourcebook for Basic Writers.* Ed. Theresa Enos. New York: Random House, 1987. 66–83.

Delpit, Lisa D. "The Politics of Teaching Literate Discourse." *Freedom's Plow: Teaching in the Multicultural Classroom.* Ed. T. Perry and J. W. Fraser. New York: Routledge, 1995. 285–95.

DiPardo, Anne. *A Kind of Passport: A Basic Writing Adjunct Program and the Challenge of Student Diversity.* Urbana: National Council of Teachers of English, 1993.

Elbow, Peter. "Reflections on Academic Discourse: How It Relates to Freshmen and Colleagues." *College English* 53.2 (1991): 135–55.

Gilyard, Keith. *Voices of the Self.* Detroit: Wayne State UP, 1991.

Heilbrun, Carolyn. *Writing a Woman's Life.* New York: Ballantine Books, 1988.

Hill, Carolyn Ericksen. *Writing from the Margins: Power and Pedagogy for Teachers of Composition.* New York: Oxford UP, 1990.

Horner, Bruce. "Mapping Errors and Expectations for Basic Writing: From the 'Frontier Field' to 'Border Country.'" *English Education* 26.1 (Feb. 1994): 29–51.

Kohl, Herb. *I Won't Learn From You! The Role of Assent in Education.* Minneapolis, MN: Milkweed Editions, 1991.

Robinson, Jay and Patti Stock. "The Politics of Literacy." *Conversations on the Written Word: Essays on Language and Literacy.* Ed. Jay Robinson. Portsmouth: Boynton/Cook, 1990. 271–317.

Rose, Mike. *Lives on the Boundary.* New York: Free Press, 1989.

Shaughnessy, Mina. *Errors and Expectations.* New York: Oxford UP, 1977.

Smitherman, Geneva. *Talkin and Testifyin: The Language of Black America.* Boston: Houghton Mifflin, 1977.

Williams, Patricia. *The Alchemy of Race and Rights.* Cambridge: Harvard UP, 1991.

Yagelski, Robert P. Speech. "Writing Assessment and the Challenges of Cultural Diversity." Conference on College Composition and Communication. Nashville, March 1994.

Classroom Activities

Mica writes: "I enjoy every bit of writing I did in the class but, I felt disappoint cause I didn't learn what I want to learn in the class." Harley and Cannon identify Mica's concern as wanting "to gain control over her writing and her errors; she wanted access to the social power identified with academic discourse. Yet neither she nor her instructors confronted this agenda centrally." Such an agenda seems difficult to confront; nonetheless, it may be worthwhile to stage such a confrontation with students to allow them "to gain control" over their progress in the course. The goals and reasons for institutional assessment can be presented not only to discuss these tools but also to challenge them.

Moreover, students can learn to chart their own improvement when you replicate the conditions of institutional writing assessment on a small scale. At the beginning of the semester, have students write a timed essay in response to a question or prompt. Collect the essay, but do not mark or grade it. Instead, put this writing away until the end of the semester, at which time students can complete a timed in-class essay based on a prompt or question similar to the initial assignment. Have students compare and contrast their writing from the beginning and the end of the semester. What has changed? Where do students see improvements? If you use writing portfolios in your course, this reflective response can be a valuable addition to each student's portfolio.

Thinking about Teaching

If our pedagogy continues to change to include more diverse student voices, Harley and Cannon affirm, so also must our assessment procedures and policies "evolve significantly." Harley and Cannon urge us to consider that assessment is "complexly situated" and that we need to look not only at the texts we are assessing but also at the multiple audiences for whom the assessment is intended.

Such reflection introduces the notion of standards as a political issue. Assessment practices tend to privilege correctness, orderliness, reason, distance, and formula, mirroring the value placed on these categories by administrators and employers, if not by ourselves and our students, as markers of good writing. Yet at the same time, we emphasize in our classes that rhetorical maturity, risk taking, and critical engagement are also important goals in a basic writing course. If these practices and emphases need not contradict each other in the classroom, then perhaps they also need not be at cross-purposes in assessment. Such issues may be critical starting points for an important discussion among teachers and administrators evaluating the assessment needs of their students in writing courses.

14

Basic Writing and the Writing Center

In this final section, Ellen Mohr and Gregory Shafer discuss how the writing center works to supplement the education of developing writers. Mohr provides an overview of what writing centers can accomplish with such special needs populations as ESL students and students with learning disabilities; at the same time, she demonstrates how a writing center can support writing instruction at all levels of composition instruction, as well as in courses that feature writing across the curriculum. In this section, both Ellen Mohr and Gregory Shafer refer to the work of Brazilian educator Paulo Freire as they articulate purposes of the writing center as a site of democratic education and of critical pedagogy.

The Writing Center: An Opportunity in Democracy

Ellen Mohr

Ellen Mohr has been the Director of the Johnson County Community College Writing Center since 1983. She has also chaired the Midwest Writing Center Association (and hosted several of its conferences), in addition to being an executive board member at the National Writing Center Association and a regular presenter at its annual conferences.

In this article, Mohr describes the many functions and pedagogical imperatives of the Writing Center she directs. Inspired by the work of Paulo Freire on democratizing education and also by Howard Gardner on multiple intelligences, Mohr details the services that her community college writing center provides. She sees it not only as a support system for developmental students, but also as a place that has "served the needs of all writers." Listing the qualities of a successful writing center, Mohr details how learning theory can be implemented to respond to the needs of all student writers while providing personal attention to those writers with special needs, such as ESL students or writers diagnosed with learning disabilities. Mohr emphasizes in particular the need to make the writing center available to all those on campus, everyone from peer tutors, to students writing across the curriculum, to faculty in all disciplines. She writes: "Probably the most important factor needed for success is the approval of the campus at large."

Few settings offer a richer diversity of voices than the community college writing center. If functionally healthy, the writing center provides a dynamic setting where diverse voices can be heard, varied perspectives explored, and myths about discourse and writing dispelled.

Theoretically, writing center pedagogy can be explained. Students have a problem with a writing assignment, with a product they have already written, or with clearly expressing their ideas. Students see the writing center as a step to writing better prose. However, the student tutors who work there provide more than feedback or static instruction; they provide a connection to the affective learning domain as they question ideas, reveal motives, and build confidence. To achieve an understanding of learning and discourage labeling, tutor training has to be part of the writing center's modus operandi. A portion of the tutor training should include some study of varied learning styles and brain compatible learning theory. Trained tutors should become sensitive to each student's different struggle, each student's unique experiences, and each student's varying view on any subject.

Paulo Freire criticizes higher education when he writes about the superiority reflected in how teachers presume to provide education for all yet do not think about their students' experiences or, worse yet, allow their students to reflect on those personal experiences within the context of the course. Freire's view of education presented in his banking metaphor sees the instructor as the "depositor" and the student as the "depository" to be filled with the treasures of knowledge (59). Knowledge is then bestowed by those who have it upon those who do not. In this metaphor, the writing center might be the receptacle through which the treasure is poured or considered just another depositor.

However, we who work in writing centers believe that the centers do much more than pass on knowledge; they provide a haven for the disenfranchised, the disenchanted, and the oppressed. The writing center can and, in many cases, does restructure that metaphoric assumption. Paulo Freire would have loved the ideal of a writing center: its democratic emphasis, its nonpolitical stance, and its revolutionary treatment of writers and their writing. During its twenty-year history, the Johnson County Community College (JCCC) Writing Center has continually worked toward that ideal. It has been successful because it has been steadfast in its philosophy that all students can learn to write effectively, because it has received consistent financial support, and because it has been judged important by all in the institution.

The JCCC Writing Center is democratic: those who work in the center attempt not to distinguish between instructors and student tutors; they never rank, label, or belittle students with "levels"; they treat each student equally — as an individual and as a writer. Even though the center has both full-time instructors and student tutors on staff, student drop-ins receive help from any available staff member, emphasizing that all the staff members are well qualified and valued equally.

An ongoing discussion on the National Writing Center listserv is the issue of staffing policies in writing centers. Members debate the pros and cons of hiring instructors, graduate students, and student (peer) tutors. Each of these groups represents a different approach to the instruction in a center. All new, full-time composition instructors at JCCC are assigned to do some work in the writing center, helping orient them to the composition program and to the general campus. Adjunct instructors who teach in the college's composition program are selected to work six hours in the writing center in lieu of a three-credit-hour composition class. These instructors work mostly with the students who enroll in one-credit modules that offer study and practice in writing improvement. The modules vary in focus from basic grammar rules and terminology to writing style and revision. They may be taken for institutional credit (nontransfer) or noncredit, for a grade or pass/fail, and as an interim class between courses, a basic review, or as a lab to a traditional class where extensive writing takes place. Students enroll in a module; the writing center instructors assess the students' skills, and then the instructor for the individual student modifies the module. The writing center instructors monitor the students enrolled in the module while the student tutors often give the feedback on the papers written for these modules. Similarly, the instructors give feedback on papers for drop-in students. Thus, both peer tutor and instructor provide (without distinction) the primary service of the writing center — dialoguing with students about writing assignments.

Both faculty and students at some colleges believe that peer tutors are not qualified to help their classmates. The misconception, however, that student (undergraduate) tutors do not have the knowledge or skills to give adequate assistance is unfounded. With careful selection criteria, formal training, and on-going evaluation, student tutors are an excellent resource in a community college writing center. Well-worded interview questions and instructor recommendations guide the tutor selection at JCCC, and extensive training assures tutor excellence. The tutor training sessions at JCCC begin with a full-day workshop, which covers not only the center's procedural policies but also its philosophical foundation. Weekly two-hour meetings provide problem-solving strategies and practice in meeting the diverse writing challenges of the center's clients. Topics for discussion include training in learning styles, questioning strategies, listening skills, and computerized instruction applications. The tutors also produce a newsletter which features articles written by the tutors for the students they serve.

Generally, the student tutors work with the numerous drop-in students who come into the center to get feedback on a draft, to get help with documentation or the format of a paper, to work on a review module, or to better understand an assignment. The peer tutors respond as readers, not as instructors. They listen empathetically to the student stories and interact well with other students. Highly adaptable because of their willingness to learn, the tutors refine their ability to respond to a variety of writing situations and writing levels.

Most drop-in students bring rough drafts to be "proofread," not knowing exactly what it is that the writing center does. Student writers tend to limit themselves, writing to a specific instructor or tutor rather than for themselves or for a larger audience. They make assumptions about writing, writing instructors, and writing center tutors. Thus, the role of the writing center tutor is to free the writer's voice, to get the student writers to think about what they know, not what they think others want to hear. Once students write for themselves, they begin the process of digesting their own experiences which leads to a better understanding of themselves and the world in which they live. The tutors help writers make connections between what they are thinking and what they want to write about. They help writers connect their problems as writers to their problems as students. Without judging, the tutors encourage students to reveal their unique perspectives. Eventually, writing becomes the vehicle to self-awareness and the unlocking of student potential.

Writing center tutors then can help students move beyond the superficial goal of grade seeking. In the usual writing center paradigm, students hold certain assumptions about the center and the kind of help they will receive. When asked why they come to the center, they often answer, "I just want someone to read my paper and see if it flows all right." The trained tutor probes to find out what is meant:

> *Tutor:* "Are you concerned about the support and development of your thesis?"
>
> *Student:* "Yes, tell me if it flows right."
>
> *Tutor:* "Are you concerned about transitions?"
>
> *Student:* "Yes, and could you tell me if I have any errors?"

A writing center has its own language, too. As a discourse community — one where language is at the very root of what occurs — tutors seek a common or universal language which will set their students at ease rather than marginalize them. In many instances, student tutors use the same language as their peers. They learn to listen so that students bring in/out their own language to "tell their stories." They seek clarification and probe for meaning. They have writers define words and seek to understand an assignment's expectations. An example of the importance of language is shown in a Russian student who works diligently in the writing center day after day in spite of a hearing deficit and health problems. She is highly motivated to speak and understand English because her grandchildren speak and understand only English. She wants to be able to tell them their family history. Language can be a barrier when social and political cultures clash. Tutors learn ways to understand the diversity of the writers and their many voices and styles. Realizing that teachable moments often arise out of conflict or a moment of "need to know," tutors quickly recognize that if they just wait, the teaching opportunity will come; the students will often solve their own problems. Tutors know that an angry student is not mad at them but unhappy with a grade earned, and they help that student to understand what may have happened in the writing (the rhetorical problem). Tutors learn to appreciate both the commonality of human experience and the vast differences in theirs and their students' worlds.

As noted earlier, first-time student writers in the center seem to be most concerned with errors. In later visits, after they have learned what the tutors will do, they begin to ask more direct questions or to better understand the hierarchy of concerns. Returning adults (students who have been out of school for five or more years) generally lack confidence about their skills, when in actuality, they are able writers. They are intimidated by the classroom and the younger students who seem at ease in the academic setting. Tutors, who often times are returning adults themselves, help these students to gain confidence and a sense of belonging, to learn the academic dialogue, and better understand the assignment. Muriel Harris cites student comments about writing center tutors and how the tutors give the writers encouragement while offering suggestions on how they can better assess their own writing and whether they have or have not fulfilled the assignment. Writers comment afterwards on "feel[ing] better about their writing" (35).

Another possibly "oppressed" group of students visiting the writing center is the learning disabled. These students also come seeking confidence and acceptance in the academic setting, an environment that often isolates through labeling these students as "not college material." At JCCC, specialized tutor training sessions focus on strategies to help tutors work with various learning styles and learning disabilities. Assessments of student writing skills are used to provide resources for students' individual needs. Trained tutors view these students as individuals with valid experiences and histories. The tutors' nonjudgmental, nonauthoritative stance enables these student writers to express their ideas freely. Carolyn O'Hearn notes that, "Composition teachers are uniquely placed to hear the silent cries of the learning disabled; we should listen for them" (302). Tutors also listen and respond providing these students with an opportunity to move beyond their disabilities and realize that well-written prose gives power to their views. A writing center should not specialize or work with a single group — underprepared or developmental, writing from other disciplines, English composition courses, English as a second language, or continuing adults. It should be an open center providing services in a holistic yet individualized way. It should not label, categorize, or judge. It should be a place where all voices are heard, encouraged, and validated. Michael Holzman writes,

> . . . the truth of education is to be found in a rejection of specialization and outside authority . . . an education which is holistic and democratic is not only desirable, it is the only education practical for the oppressed. Upon reflection, one also asks why should anyone, anywhere be given an education that is not holistic, not democratic? (188)

Where better for such an education than a writing center?

Nowhere in academia is a setting more open for honest discourse than in a writing center. Student problems with abuse, violence, romance, racism, sexism, ageism often surface in this friendly, non-threatening discourse of the writing center community. Tutors are listeners, observers, and participants in the discourse, having learned how to ask questions which get to the heart of a rhetorical problem. Those who may feel disenfranchised in the classroom, which can tend to be a closed community with its own set of values, should find openness and acceptance in a writing center environment.

Writing center staff encourage students to question, to think, to see other viewpoints, yet to validate their own viewpoints. They practice this strategy by focusing on a hierarchy of writing: first, the purpose or aim of the assignment, then the focus, next organization and development, followed by paragraphing, sentence construction, word choice, and style. They practice a Socratic method of questioning and critical thinking; they apply knowledge of body language, multiple intelligence, and listening skills. They role play using various dialogic strategies for responding, clarifying, probing, rewording, and summarizing. Students who only want the errors corrected on their papers learn quickly that tutors will discuss the students' papers with them, give advice on what rules the student needs to learn and apply to the paper, and provide resources, such as handouts or computer programs for practice in correcting writing errors. This unswerving focus on process and commonality of purpose makes the writing center successful and unifies the institution's attitude toward the need for writing practice in all classes.

The writing center tutors attempt to socialize the language misfits — the ones whose writing has made them feel less than adequate in the classroom or in the community. I think of the many Russian, Chinese, Iranian and other immigrants who through the years have found refuge in the JCCC center, not only learning the language to better express themselves, but also learning more about American culture and, in turn, teaching their culture, until the blended cultures become a new community rich with words, understanding, and respect.

Understanding learning styles can be helpful in working with a writing center's diverse population. Tutors must become aware of the variety of student learning styles and preferences. Tutors can then be provided with a wide range of activities and testing methods to allow for all styles. The Kolb, McCarthy, and Myers-Briggs inventories all help determine a learning style preference. Although preferences may overlap, generally one style will be dominant. Tutors learn that instruction must, therefore, be delivered in many forms. Some students may work better with a small group. Others want a quiet space to reflect. Still others need the repetitious rote learning of computer tutorials.

Intelligence theory has allowed educators to better understand the brain and how students learn and remember facts. Howard Gardner's multiple intelligence (MI) theory translates the cognitive and affective domains of the brain into seven ways of knowing: verbal/linguistic, logical/mathematical, visual/spatial, body/kinesthetic, musical/rhythmic, intrapersonal, and interpersonal. Each has its own explicit developmental pattern which needs to be nurtured. Brain research tells us that when brain cells are stimulated, their structure actually changes. We also know that activities like writing on a regular basis can actually train the neurons to trigger automatically and make writing easier.

Gardner argues that in the traditional classroom, where primarily verbal and logical intelligences are nurtured, students are missing out on rich learning experiences. Freire would say that this practice in the traditional classroom exacerbates the pedagogy of the oppressor. Training tutors in learning theory provides them with nontraditional strategies to help nontraditional students. For instance, a hearing impaired student who is having difficulty with sentence structure can learn in the writing center to correct syntax in his/her own writing by adding phrases and clauses to simple sentences, by sentence combining, and by modeling sentence structures which the tutor provides.

To be successful, a community college writing center must be valued by the whole academic community. Freire says that some students (the oppressed) are marginalized by their inability to connect to the academic world, to fit-in, to "talk the talk" of academia. One of the great failings of academia has been its inability to help these students to feel that their past has some meaning or significance. The very nature of a community college is democratic. Sometimes community colleges recruit and accept students but then either do not adequately assess student needs or have nowhere to place them according to their needs. Thus, the open door policy of the community college becomes for some a revolving door. The very students for whom the community college concept was initiated fail to succeed.

Learning theory tells us that writing is a necessary component of all classes, and businesses complain that their employees do not write coherently. Writing is and must remain an integral part of every requirement in general education, a philosophy which commands the presence of a writing center. If a community college supports a writing center, its open door policy is not only preserved but also reinforced.

The democratic nature of a writing center can only be achieved if certain pieces are in place. One piece already discussed is the peer tutor program including the formal tutor training. Another equally important piece is financial support from the college.

I have colleagues in other community colleges who never know from year to year what their budget will be. Every year they must justify their writing centers. Some colleges have assigned the writing center to a corner in a library or in a learning center; some have no permanent home, quartering in those spaces which nobody wants at the moment. Most community college writing centers do not have full-time directors. The director is required to be super human, teaching a full load of classes and supervising all of the activities of the center. Some colleges have a part-time director, only on campus 20–30 hours a week. Needless to say, the turnover of directors in these colleges is counterproductive to achieving the ideal center, especially when other staff members are temporary. In a community college, tutors rarely stay longer than two years and adjunct instructors are assigned as needed when their regularly assigned classes are canceled or reassigned. A full-time director position demonstrates the administration's commitment to finance the program. The growth and continuity of a successful writing center depends on both consistent financial and administrative support. The JCCC Writing Center has never had to justify its existence or hire a new director. The allocated space has changed as growth warranted it, just as resources were added as needs were assessed.

The third significant piece needed for the ideal writing center is college-wide support. Most instructors and administrators know the value of writing in all classes. However, not all of these people believe that a writing center can help their students achieve success in their classes where writing is assigned. Many of my colleagues in other institutions tell how instructors actually direct their students not to use the writing center. They cite as reasons fears that the tutors will not give good advice, that the tutors will do the work for the students, and that instructors do not want to lose their classroom autonomy. Several factors have helped the JCCC Writing Center to get beyond those fears. One factor is that the center operates as a drop-in system. If it were appointment only, we could not serve the number of students that visit us (over a hundred students a day). No students are ever turned away. A second factor is that we are not developmental only.

From the beginning, we have served the needs of all writers. John Paul Tassoni notes that teachers who acknowledge the writing center as supplemental or remedial to their classes are missing a great opportunity to reinforce their students' writing opportunities through the "democratic and dialogic capacity of the writing center." He goes on to say that instructors who promote "learning as an act of negotiation" (34) in their classes should certainly explain to their students that the writing center provides an opportunity for dialogue and does not merely give practice on grammar rules. He also advises that to keep a writing center open to all writers, the college must support a staff large enough to handle those writers (42).

Probably the most important factor needed for success is the approval of the campus at large. The JCCC Writing Center has evolved from a single-purpose center intended only to enhance composition classes to a role of serving the writing needs of the entire college and its community. Even though the center's budget is through the English Department, the director is an English instructor, and most of the writing center teachers are composition instructors, who seek advice from colleagues across the campus. Instructors have confidence in the writing center because they recommend the students who become tutors, suggest the materials (computer software and written resources) which will best help the students in their disciplines on specific assignments, post assignments and good student samples in the center, give feedback on handouts developed for the center, and come to the tutor training sessions to talk about writing assignments in their courses. Thus, campus-wide, instructors feel an ownership of the center. This semester we have an instructor from the humanities program and one from business communications tutoring in the center.

The shared interest in the writing center by faculty across the campus ensures its continued success. When tutors are trained in strategies which enhance the dialogic sessions, when the tutor-writer and the student-writer discover their commonality in both language and historiography, and when the uniqueness of the individual is valued, a comfortable environment for learning is created.

Freire would see the writing center environment as an opportunity to remove the barriers often imposed by educators. In a writing center where information is shared equally, not "deposited," democracy endures. In fact, it is the democratic ideal that makes the best writing centers possible and the open door community college a reality.

Works Cited

Freire, Paulo. *Pedagogy of the Oppressed.* Trans. Myra Bergman Ramos. New York: Continuum, 1970.

Gardner, Howard. *Multiple Frames of Mind.* New York: Basic, 1985.

———. *Multiple Intelligences: The Theory in Practice.* New York: Basic, 1991.

Harris, Muriel. "Talking in the Middle: Why Writers Need Writing Tutors." *College English* 57 (1995): 27–42.

Holzman, Michael. "A Post-Freirean Model for Adult Literacy Education." *College English* 50 (1988): 177–89.

O'Hearn, Carolyn. "Recognizing the Learning Disabled College Writer." *College English* 51 (1989): 294–302.

Tassoni, John Paul. "The Liberatory Composition Teacher's Obligation to Writing Centers at Two-Year Colleges." *Teaching English in the Two-Year College* 25 (1998): 34–43.

Classroom Activities

If your campus has a writing center, take your students on a tour or have a peer tutor or other personnel representative visit your class to talk about the services that the writing center offers. As Mohr suggests, it is important to emphasize that the writing center does not exist to teach grammar and mechanics, or to "correct" student papers. Rather, writing center peer tutors "provide a connection to the affective learning domain, as they question ideas, reveal motives, and build confidence." Find out how your writing center recruits peer tutors, and make sure to recommend that interested students have an opportunity to apply for those positions. If your campus does not have a writing center, have your students do research on other support systems that are available for developing writers and readers both on and off campus. For instance, what kinds of tutoring services are available at public libraries or community centers? If you or your students are interested in finding more information about resources offered by writing centers at other campuses, visit the National Writing Centers Association home page on the Internet at [http://departments.colgate.edu/diw/NWCA.html]. This site includes resources for writers, tutor stories, e-mail discussion groups, a writing center start-up kit, and more.

Thinking about Teaching

If your campus doesn't have a writing center, find out what is needed to create out-of-class support services for student writing. See the above section on Classroom Activities for appropriate Internet resources. If your campus has a learning center, rather than a writing center, ask what services are available specifically for students who need support with writing — whether there is "remedial" help or general feedback for more "advanced" students. If your campus does have a writing center, it may be possible for you to work there yourself. Some writing centers encourage faculty to hold office hours in the writing center or to work as tutors in the center themselves. As Mohr states, such participation accounts for the fact that "campus-wide, instructors feel an ownership of the center." Meet with the director of your writing center to find out what his or her policy is on instructors working in the writing center. If either arrangement is viable given writing center policies and your own schedule, try spending time working in the writing center over the course of a semester. This opportunity will enable you to experience firsthand what Mohr calls "the democratic ideal that makes the best writing centers possible and the open door community college a reality."

Negotiating Audience and Voice in the Writing Center

Gregory Shafer

"Back in the writing center," writes Gregory Shafer, "composition is too often about imposed power, about learning to write for one's teacher, about learning a prefabricated, immutable form. It is too often about following orders." In the following article, Shafer attempts to negotiate basic writing students' struggles with voice, with instructors' emphases on teaching five-paragraph themes and other "basic skills" in a typical developmental writing curriculum. Included in this selection are the inspired voices of four developing writers, whose compelling stories could not be confined to the strictures of the five-paragraph essay. Using the ideas of Freire and hooks, as well as those of Elbow and Shaughnessy, Shafer attempts to evolve a pedagogy that values both audience and voice as he and students work together in the writing center at Mott Community College. Gregory Shafer is a Professor of English at Mott Community College in Flint, Michigan. His publications include articles in English Journal *and* The Humanist. *He is the Regional Coordinator for the Michigan Council for the Arts and has received four Excellence in Education awards from the Kellogg Foundation. He is also the author of "Using Letters for Process and Change in the Basic Writing Class," included in Chapter 3 of this ancillary.*

Introduction

Each day they trudge into the writing center with the same familiar look of consternation and anger. Sometimes it's because their instructor has failed to address the content of their essays, but more often it's simply about voice and control. Within their classes, a kind of power struggle ensues as each writer attempts to transcend the mechanical and prescribed prose that has become a staple of the five-paragraph theme. They are developmental writers, but they want to use elements of their dialect, include their culture and diction, and pepper their narratives with the occasional obscenity when it accurately captures the heart of their story.

Marcus, a husky African American student, slides into the seat next to me and gingerly lays his paper in front of my eyes. "She says I can't use the word 'thug-ass' to describe my cousin," he says as he wipes the sweat from his forehead and lowers his backpack to the floor. Marcus's essay is a character paper about his cousin, a man who has comic aspirations to be a big-time criminal. Thus, Marcus, in his smartly sarcastic style, has given the appellation of "My Thug-Ass Cousin" to his paper. Quickly, I read it over again, only I already know the content and style. Marcus is a wonderfully fluid writer. His style is unrestrained and honest. His detailed description of his cousin chronicles both the humor and pathos in a young man who has romanticized the "gangster" image. Marcus's approach to his paper is both personal and racial. He wants to make his audience laugh while helping them to see the continuing blight of racism and the concrete way it affects real people. And yet, through all of the raw honesty and pathetic humor, he is being told to "eliminate the obscenities" because they are "inappropriate in an academic setting." "So what am I supposed to do?" he asks me with his big, undaunted smile. "She's not gonna let me use 'ass' in my paper."

Silence. I sit and contemplate the things I'd like to say to his instructor. The way she is blunting and effacing the voice of a talented young writer seems unethical, unconscionable, but I can't sacrifice his grade so I can make a statement. "Let me talk to her," I say. "Leave the paper as it is," I add with reassurance. "It's beautiful and thoughtful. It makes your audience think. I like it a lot!" Marcus smiles and shakes his head. Now the hard work begins as I think about talking to his instructor about voice and a very special talent.

Each week, my work in the writing center presents me with at least a couple of the dilemmas that I describe with Marcus. I have come to call them questions of autonomy and voice, since their implications go well beyond issues of "appropriateness" or academic format. Indeed, they touch upon the basic freedom we are willing to extend to basic and minority writers. With all of the talk about empowerment and hegemony in our profession, are we really willing to elevate genuine expression above petty, egocentric worries about academic protocol? In the same way, is our hesitance about "obscenities" more about academics or culture? Are we jittery about "nasty language" because it symbolizes an unharnessed and angry political voice? And finally, are we truly doing our job, if we censor the uninhibited writer simply because he doesn't fit into the narrow parameters of what has come to be called safe "academic discourse"? Who, in the end, are we serving when we shape and limit unconventional students? In this essay, I hope to answer some of these questions.

Another Example

Polly is twenty-five, but her experience and wisdom make her seem much older. As she strolls confidently into the writing center, she personifies bell hooks's description of the student who is adamant about receiving a "liberatory education" while feeling "terribly wounded" (19) by the dearth of true freedom she receives from her instructors. As with Marcus, Polly is engaged in a very riveting, flesh-and-blood experience concerning her ex-husband. As I read over her paper, I'm shocked and moved by her vivid description of the beatings, the verbal abuse, the cavalier use of intimidation. "This is real — right?" I ask her with an incredulous look. Quickly, she smiles and shakes her head, yes. Polly is reliving her marriage and the emotional scars it left. As I read more, the dialogue, the detail of the beatings seem more and more authentic and dramatic. I stop and take a deep breath.

It is, put simply, a paper that exposes the brutality that is lamentably a part of too many marriages. Its style is unreserved, unbridled. Polly isn't holding back: "He scratched me with his long nails. He was doing more than hurting me now. He wanted to leave a scar, to leave his mark on my face."

Finally I reach her instructor's comments and recognize the focus of Polly's frustration. The evaluation seems detached and unrelated to the paper. Somehow, the instructor has washed away the emotion and violence that oozes from the writing and has limited her observations to questions of form and usage. Her comments are professional, surgical. She has taken a personal drama and reduced it to insipid comments on rules and form: "Your form is good, but you sometimes deviate from the thesis. Remember, you're writing a comparison/contrast paper. Don't lose that focus. You might consider a review of fragments too. They pop up quite frequently. Well done!"

"What do you think of my paper?" asks Polly. "Because this doesn't tell me nothing!" she fumes with obvious anger. Again, as with Marcus's work earlier, I see what seems to be a stripping away of the meat and blood of a paper. Each instructor seems unsure or unwilling to deal with the topics that transcend the "academic community." Lost in both of their evaluations is the need for writers to be heard, to bring a piece of their lives, culture, and social context into the writing they do. The struggle, while simmering beneath the surface, is very real and raises serious questions about the role of college writing instruction. Is it our job to assist students in becoming models of academic discourse, replete with properly placed commas and standard white English, or rather, is it our job to help them unleash the clamor and discord that rumbles inside their heads, a cacophony that can enliven their papers if it is allowed to become part of their discourse?

The Practice of Academic English

Most scholarship I have read seems to suggest that we should be guardians of civilized English, that we should quiet writers by molding them into "academic scholars," into people like us. David Bartholomae's "Inventing the University" talks candidly about the cumbersome but necessary task a college student faces in trying to approximate the jargon and style of the academic community. His message is that the academy's first job is to prescribe a style that mirrors itself. Forget about individualism, our role is to make students more like us. "I am continually impressed with the patience and good will of our students," writes Bartholomae in describing the daunting task of learning academic prose. The students are "appropriated by a specialized discourse," which requires them to "speak our language," or "carry the bluff" (273). In short, then, the most difficult but important role of the college composition instructor is to help writers become more like the university, to shed their cultural personas and learn to embrace a foreign and rather stiff language, one that serves them in few ways beyond the context in which they use it.

Little is said about self-actualization, expression, or fulfillment. Indeed, it is an ironic aspect of our profession that we extol the democratic and strive for student autonomy while forcing students to write in a contrived discourse that serves to exult the academic community over the students it is supposed to empower. Is this what students would call a paradox if they were in Literature 101?

Marcus and Polly are certainly left empty and alienated by the practice. Neither have aspirations of being scholars or academics, but that doesn't prevent their instructors from compelling them to learn the specific style and expectations that academic discourse entails. Should we then wonder why students feel that college composition is less about them and their lives than the foreign register of their instructor, who stands at the front of the class loaded with answers? In the same way, should we feel surprised or upset when our students crank out the plastic, apocryphal prose that is too often a part of first-year composition? We cry for voice and power. We preach liberation. And then we require the fabricated prescriptions that embody nothing of the person behind the words.

Working with students like Marcus and Polly helps highlight the importance of a curriculum that transcends this egocentric, self-aggrandizing approach. Both demonstrate an extremely deft and vivid eye for their world and the significance of their experiences. Marcus writes about his "Thug-Ass Cousin" as both a parody on the romanticism some youths have toward a violent world and a dramatic statement on the limitations placed on African Americans:

> He sits in front of this bank, getting himself up for a big-time bank robbery that's ain't ever gonna happen. He could have and probably should have gone to work that day. But minimum wage doesn't get him out of bed the way it should. And it probably never will.

The writing is poetic, almost song-like. The wisdom and message are profound. Marcus doesn't write like any university or college professors I know, and this is perhaps one of the reasons his prose is so dramatic and riveting. The challenge for us as a scholarly community is what to do with this forever emerging and organic voice. Do we define a liberatory education as shaping our students to be like us, or do we celebrate a mosaic of new styles and voices radiating from our classrooms — voices and styles that are troubling and difficult because they are not part of our formal education? There is a kind of arrogance in Bartholomae's message, and it hasn't been lost on the academic community that enforces it. Instead of reaching out to the dialects and cultures outside the ivy-covered walls of the college, it defines success as a labor of mimicry.

Support from Freire and bell hooks

I have often felt that the sentiments of Paulo Freire and bell hooks better reflect the ideas of a truly emancipatory education. Rather than advocating an experience that exults the power and inherent goodness of the academic world, it seems clearly revolutionary and rebellious. Marcus and Polly, I am virtually certain, would be better served by their inclusive political pedagogy. In particular, bell hooks seems in touch with the power of "transgressing" and the implications of such an education. "I have been most inspired," writes hooks, "by those teachers who have had the courage to transgress those boundaries that would confine each pupil to a rote, assembly-line approach to learning" (13). She writes about the dichotomy between an education of "active participation" and one that embraces the "passive consumer" (14). In other words, students become most alive and empowered when they are personally creating, actively evaluating their world in a style that reflects and changes that world. Marcus tells his story through not only the content but the style as well. The pathos and violence of his life is reflected in his use of double negatives, in his deviations from standard English.

To eliminate this component from his essay is to rip out its viscera and leave it as little more than an assembly line replica of what too many first-year students think is effective writing. How often have I heard college instructors lament such spiritless writing? And yet, how often have I seen these same instructors practice a prescription that takes the pen out of their students' hands?

Many professors should ask themselves if they are afraid or threatened by a truly emancipatory education, one that begins with students and transcends the safe haven of the college theme. Many, I believe, are intimidated by the idea that their students might force them to think, that prose like that of Marcus's might compel them to redefine and broaden the concept of acceptable writing — forcing them into unknown territory. Indeed, when I asked Marcus's instructor why it was "wrong" or "inappropriate" to use "gonna" or a double negative, she fell safely back on the assertion that it is not part of "academic writing." Really? Would this instructor, I silently wondered, be surprised to read some of the work of Geneva Smitherman or bell hooks? Is the premise that such writing is "inappropriate" an arbitrary way of precluding new voices, as many attempt to do in the field of canonical literature? Clearly, this instructor, while seeming to want the best for Marcus, was acting as an oppressor.

Such instructors hooks calls "benevolent dictators," those who are more interested in maintaining their authority "within their mini-kingdom, the classroom" (17) than in self-actualization. Within such a system, few people grow, learn, or change, as a static and immutable form of discourse is inculcated to its passive subjects. The key, add hooks, is to promote risk-taking and to embrace it as a part of learning for both teacher and student. "Professors must practice being vulnerable in the classroom, being wholly present in mind, body, and spirit," she contends (21). The alternative, she later adds, is a curriculum that "reinforces systems of domination," that perpetuates a smug and lifeless status quo. "Empowerment cannot happen if we refuse to be vulnerable while encouraging students to take risks" (21), she reminds us.

For Paulo Freire, such risks are key to humanistic education. In his classic *Pedagogy of the Oppressed,* he labels passive, top-down approaches to learning as a "banking system of education," one that relegates students to the role of receptacle. For Freire, true, humanistic education emanates from a pedagogy that promotes problem-posing and dialogue over transferals of information and "domestication" (71). In considering the plight of both Marcus and Polly, we can quickly see his point. In a composition class that seeks to deposit information in a linear, static way, there is simply no room for thought, dialogue, or growth. In such a scenario, students become little more than robots who obediently learn and memorize the single, instructor-endorsed way to success. Without dialogue or debate, the instruction is narrative in form, flowing from teacher to student and devoid of action and reflection. The task becomes one of pursuit, chasing the instructor and trying to unlock the keys to success.

For Polly and Marcus, the process is also demoralizing because it leaves them as something less than human. Indeed, how can we consider ourselves thinking and vital individuals when our culture and language is being expunged without critical discussion? Again Freire speaks to this in his distinction between animal and human. For Freire, the animal is primarily a being that lives without reflection, a being that adapts without considering implications or meaning. "Animals," writes Freire, "are beings in themselves" (87). They do not, in other words, step away from their lives to contemplate the significance of why and how they exist. It is not, in short, a critical, introspective life.

In contrast, truly human beings are able to step back and analyze their lives and values. They can ascribe meaning to actions and synthesize events to make conclusions about their feelings and ethics. In short, they construct reality rather than simply respond to it. They, to use Freire's words, "infuse the world with their creative presence" (88). They become active partners in their education.

Polly and Marcus both find themselves being treated as passive beings that are expected to learn the routine in much the same way a dog learns tricks. With the context being bereft of dialogue or active problem-posing, the learning is more akin to rote memorization. The students are irrelevant, voiceless. Again, Freire addresses this with eloquent prose: "Animal activity, which occurs without praxis, is not creative; man's transforming activity is" (91).

In the end, then, we must ask ourselves who is really being served in a pedagogy that elevates prescription over critical dialogue. Is it the developmental writer, who, according to many of my colleagues, needs close instruction because of a lack of experience? Or is it really the instructor, who finds it both easier and safer to disseminate rules and forms over an organic process of learning? My experience in the writing center would clearly indicate that the instructor is the main beneficiary of a top-down education. While such a pedagogy instills students with a formula for organization and usage, it negates the fundamental act of thinking, of learning through a heuristic, personal process.

After our second meeting, Marcus is ready to change his essay to "what will ever make my instructor happy," while Polly is resigned to the limited comments she receives. Both, lamentably, have come to see the context as being despotic and impersonal. "I'm just worried about my grade in the end," says Marcus later in the semester. "I'll do what makes her happy. It's her class."

Solutions and Alternatives

Writing Is Social

On Tuesday, Sally wheels herself into the writing center, surveying the room as she maneuvers her wheelchair to the computer and timidly touches the keys. She is a fifty-eight-year-old student who has returned to school to take writing classes and get out of the house.

"Think you could take a look at this?" she asks me in a deferential tone. Her essay is titled "My Old Brown Coat," and as I read it over, I'm immediately touched by the quaint voice as well as the short, simple sentences. Her paper is nostalgic and filled with a curious affection for a piece of apparel:

> The old brown coat I owned was not like any coat I owned. After it was torn, it became a disaster. It lost its shape and style. It was tattered. The coat was ten years old. It was so special.

"This is nice," I say with a smile. However, as I continue to reread, I become increasingly aware of the jerky sentences, and I wonder how her audience will respond to the lack of fluidity. I begin to think of strategies to help her connect sentences and assist her audience in reading and enjoying her paper. "You know," I say to her as I look away from the computer screen, "we could work on the flow of your prose. I like your paper, but as I read it, I want you to combine some of your sentences — so I don't have to work so hard as a reader."

My work with Sally begins to provide me with ideas for how to empower other students, students like Marcus and Polly who are struggling with demands of audience. All three, it seems to me, highlight the social character of writing. When we sit down to write a paper, we are not simply writing for ourselves but for a group of subjective people. The content and style, then, must reflect a cooperative effort to express our views without alienating readers.

In the case of Marcus and Polly, decisions must be made as a negotiation. Teachers must ask themselves what is essential in terms of diction, organization, and style, while writers must consider both their readers and the goals of their writing. For Polly and Marcus, the value of their cultural lexicon must be weighed along side audience expectations. For Sally, integrity of voice must be weighed against the demand for more melodic sentences.

Similar questions, it seems to me, must be asked in response to nonstandard dialects. Both writers and instructors must consider the transaction between reader and writer (Rosenblatt) — the social dynamic of communication — and come to a collaborative decision as to what is acceptable in a certain context. Such a democratic approach includes students and helps illuminate the realities of writing for an audience. At the same time, it eliminates a linear caveat from teacher to student, resulting in a class that stresses obedience over construction.

This vision is especially important as I begin to work with Kathy. Her essay on how she contracted a socially transmitted disease is poignant and moving. However, it is rife with the most offensive array of gratuitous obscenities I have ever read in a student paper. And then, there is the request from her teacher to place the thesis statement at the end of the introduction.

Kathy is the consummate example of why it is important to protect the integrity of the writer's voice while fulfilling the demands of one's audience. Indeed, as I read over her writing, I am plunged into the chaos of the doctor's examination table. And yet, the obscenities seem to intrude more than enhance:

> I winced as the assistant rolled in a tray of metal gadgets. There was no little speculum this time. This man was wielding what looked like a fucking shoehorn. I cried out when he shoved it between my legs. He then chided me, telling me it didn't hurt. Like he had a god damn clue [. . .].

I finish reading, take a deep breath, and smile. "This is wonderful," I assure her. "I'm wondering, however, if we could respond to your teacher's concerns about language and thesis. Do the obscene words contribute to your message or divert attention from it?"

Later, as we begin to reconsider the essay, we work together to capture the essence of this personal experience while respecting the concerns of readers. It is always a collaborative experience, a negotiation. There are ways, we find, to respect the visions of author and teacher. Writing is about more than either a monolithic model of the university essay or a personal vision of what the author has planned.

Writing Is a Process

Much has been written about alternatives to the traditional composition class. Many of these suggestions have centered on the importance of process, development, and autonomy as integral parts of learning as one writes. Little debate exists as to the need for time as one constructs and designs a piece of writing. We know, for instance, that composition is not a clean, linear act but one that is recursive, messy, social, and cooperative. While more and more instructors allow for this freedom and process in the college composition class, fewer are willing to extend this same autonomy to basic writers, who are often perceived as unable to generate prose without careful and direct instruction. This, I believe, gives rise to the benevolent despot, the instructor, who, in his/her attempt to help the basic writer, actually stymies any generative process. "These students come from deprived backgrounds," an instructor once told me. "They simply need more help from us."

That help, I would contend, begins with process and the journey of discovery that every writer experiences as he/she begins to write. It does not begin with a prescriptive, emasculating set of caveats but enough freedom so that the student has the opportunity to "cook and grow" as Peter Elbow would say. Basic writers, argued Mina Shaughnessy, must "learn by making mistakes" (5). The process, as with other writers, is one of gradual, evolutionary construction. While it is filled with errors, it is also a time of learning through direct experience. "The writer understands that writing is a process, not a rigid procedure. He continually rediscovers his subject," says Donald Murray. It is "discovery of meaning, discovery of form — and the writer works back and forth [. . .]" (7).

Conclusion

All of this would suggest that the best way to teach basic writers is through both process and a respect for the social discovery that ensues as one composes. To negate or trivialize the context in which they write is to alienate students and relegate them to a passive process of imitating others rather than learning to create and synthesize information from their own world. "Bartholomae's pedagogy," writes Richard Boyd, "sets up a kind of master/slave relationship where the student-as-mimic is relegated to a perpetually subordinate role" (41). Indeed, to reduce writing to a series of "skills" and prescriptions does not teach empowered, creative thought. Rather, it marginalizes writers, telling them their experiences are not important, that composition is not about social critique but rules and obedience. It is the antithesis of Freire's vision for a liberated, problem-posing community.

Back in the writing center, composition is too often about imposed power, about learning to write for one's teacher, about learning a prefabricated, immutable form. It is too often about following orders. For Polly and Marcus, two basic writers who show incredible insight, ideas and experiences become submerged as they are coerced into joining this "university of writers." It is a practice that needs to be changed if we are ever to be truly democratic and inclusive in the way we teach college composition.

Works Cited

Bartholomae, David. "Inventing the University." *Perspectives on Literacy*. Ed. Eugene Kintgen, Barry Kroll, and Mike Rose. Carbondale: Southern Illinois UP, 1988. 273–85.

Boyd, Richard. "Imitate Me; Don't Imitate Me: Mimeticism in David Bartholomae's 'Inventing the University.'" *Journal of Advanced Composition* 11(1991):335–45.

Elbow, Peter. *Writing without Teachers*. New York: Oxford UP, 1973.

Freire, Paulo. *Pedagogy of the Oppressed*. New York: Continuum, 1990.

hooks, bell. *Teaching to Transgress*. New York: Routledge, 1994.

Murray, Donald. *A Writer Teaches Writing*. Boston: Houghton, 1968.

Rosenblatt, Louise. *The Reader, the Text, the Poem*. Carbondale: Southern Illinois UP, 1978.

Shaughnessy, Mina. *Errors and Expectations*. New York: Oxford UP, 1977.

Classroom Activities

What happens when a student has a particular story to tell and needs to tell it in his or her own voice, a voice that mirrors the streets or the rural back roads, a voice with much to say, but in language often not easy to hear? Shafer poses this important problem as he describes his work as a tutor in the writing center and his discussions with teachers and students. One way to approach this issue is to discuss it directly with students. Where do students find topics for "narrative" writing assignments? What happens if their story doesn't fit the conventional five-paragraph essay format? How do students "negotiate" the need to find their own voices and tell their own stories with the need to write in "audience-appropriate" language that their instructors and tutors will accept as "correct"? This activity can be an opportunity to empower students, as Freire would have it, to begin to claim their own education. Students can learn what kinds of questions to ask of their teachers and of their writing center tutors in order to learn and grow in their writing — and to not merely produce "what the teacher wants." Moreover, teachers can see this discussion as an opportunity to examine their own views about what "counts" as acceptable prose in the basic writing course. Should the basic writing course concern itself only with survival skills, such as writing five-paragraph essays in academic discourse? Or should students new to process-based writing (as many basic writing students often are) have the opportunity to experiment with prose style and storytelling as a way to learn the variety of rhetorical choices available to writers?

Thinking about Teaching

In your teaching journal, reflect on the questions presented above and work out some of the difficult issues presented in Shafer's article. Have you or a colleague ever received a paper similar to Marcus's "My Thug-Ass Cousin"? What was the response to this writing — and on what criteria was the response based? How were those criteria constructed in relation to the course requirements of basic writing and in relation to facilitating an opportunity for students to grow as writers? Shafer frames the question as follows: "Is it our job to assist students in becoming models of academic discourse, replete with commas and standard white English or rather, is it our job to help them unleash the clamor and discord that rumbles inside their heads, a cacophony that can enliven their papers if it is allowed to become part of their discourse?" Perhaps this problem need not be posed as two diametrically opposing sides. Moreover, as Shafer suggests, "Writing is about more than either a monolithic model of the university essay or a personal vision of what the author has planned." There is, in fact, room for negotiation and for honoring process, which Shafer contends is often taken for granted more in composition courses than in the basic writing course. Consider other essays in this ancillary that refer to the problematic nature of the purpose of the basic writing course, such as Laurie Grobman's "Building Bridges to Academic Discourse: The Peer Group Leader in Basic Writing" in Chapter 9, and to the purposes of developmental reading and writing education, such as Marilyn S. Sternglass's "The Changing Perception of the Role of Writing: From Basic Writing to Discipline Courses" in Chapter 4. Also take a look at Paulo Freire's germinal work, *Pedagogy of the Oppressed*, which provides an important perspective on student-centered learning. Consider facilitating an open discussion on this issue among teachers, students, and tutors. Perhaps such a discussion could be sponsored by the writing center and could involve a wide range of participants across the curriculum. Finally, consider writing an article on your own perspective on this issue, based on your ideas and experiences as a teacher in the basic writing classroom.

Bibliography

Readers may wish to consult the "Basic Writing Reading List" at <http://www.gen.umn.edu/research/cbw/reading_list.html>. Many of the following works were located via this excellent source for texts on basic writing pedagogy.

1 Basic Writing: Teacher's Perspectives

Adams, Peter D. "Basic Writing Reconsidered." Journal of Basic Writing 12.2 (1993): 22–26.

Bartholomae, David. "Inventing the University." *When a Writer Can't Write: Studies in Writer's Block and Other Composing Problems.* Ed. Mike Rose. New York: Guilford, 1985. 134–65.

———. "The Tidy House: Basic Writing and the American Curriculum." *Journal of Basic Writing* 12.1 (1993): 4–21.

Collins, Terence G. "A Response to Ira Shor's 'Our Apartheid: Writing Instruction and Inequality.'" *Journal of Basic Writing* 16.2 (1997): 95–100.

David, Denise, Barbara Gordon, and Rita Pollard. "Seeking Common Ground: Guiding Assumptions for Writing Courses." *College Composition and Communication* 46 (1995): 522–32.

Dwinnel, Patricia L., and Jeanne L. Higbee, eds. *Developmental Education: Enhancing Student Retention.* Carol Stream, IL: National Association for Developmental Education, 1997.

Enos, Theresa, ed. *A Sourcebook for Basic Writing Teachers.* New York: Random, 1987.

Freire, Paolo. *Pedagogy of the Oppressed.* Rev. ed. New York: Continuum, 1994.

Gay, Pamela. "Rereading Shaughnessy from a Postcolonial Perspective." *Journal of Basic Writing* 12.2 (1993): 29–40.

Glau, Gregory R. "The 'Stretch' Program': Arizona State University's New Model of University-Level Basic Writing Instruction." *Writing Program Administration* 20 (1996): 79–91.

Higbee, Jeanne L., and Patricia Dwinell, eds. *Defining Developmental Education: Theory, Research, and Pedagogy.* Carol Stream, IL: National Association for Developmental Education, 1996.

Hindman, Jane E. "Re-inventing the University: Finding the Place for Basic Writers." *Journal of Basic Writing* 12.2 (1993): 55–77.

Horner, Bruce. "Discoursing Basic Writing." *College Composition and Communication* 47 (1996): 199–222.

Rich, Adrienne. "Teaching Language in Open Admissions." *On Lies, Secrets, and Silence: Selected Prose, 1966–1978.* Ed. Adrienne Rich. New York: Norton, 1979. 51–68.

Shaughnessy, Mina P. Introduction. *Errors and Expectations: A Guide for the Teachers of Basic Writing.* New York: Oxford UP, 1997. 1–13.

Shor, Ira. "The First Day of Class: Passing the Text" from *Empowering Education: Critical Teaching for Social Change.* U of Chicago P 1992.

——. "Inequality (Still Rules): Reply to Collins and Greenberg." *Journal of Basic Writing* 17.1 (1998): 104–08.

Soliday, Mary. "From the Margins to the Mainstream: Reconceiving a Remediation." *College Composition and Communication* 47 (1996): 85–100.

2   Basic Writing: Student's Perspectives

Berlin, James. *Rhetoric and Reality.* Carbondale: Southern Illinois UP, 1987.

Connors, Robert. *Composition-Rhetoric.* Pittsburgh: U of Pittsburgh P, 1997.

De Beaugrande, Robert, and Marjean Olson. "Using a 'Write-Speak-Write' Approach for Basic Writers." *Journal of Basic Writing* 10.2 (1991): 4–32.

Gary-Rosendale, Laura. "Revising the Political in Basic Writing Scholarship." *Journal of Basic Writing* 15.2 (1996): 24–49.

Harrington, Susanmarie and Linda Adler-Kassner. "The Dilemma that Still Counts: Basic Writing at a Political Crossroads." *Journal of Basic Writing* 17.2 (1999): 1–24.

Hull, Glynda and Mike Rose. "This Wooden Shack Place": The Logic of an Unconventional Reading. *College Composition and Communication* 41.3 (1990): 299–329.

Mortensen, Peter. "Going Public." *College Composition and Communication* 50 (1998): 182–205.

Mutnick, Deborah. *Writing in an Alien World.* Portsmouth, NH: Boynton/Cook, 1996.

Perl, Sondra. "A Look at Basic Writers in the Process of Composing." *Basic Writing: Essays for Teachers and Administrators.* Ed. Lawrence N. Kasden and Daniel R. Hoeber. Urbana, IL: NCTE, 1980: 13–32.

Rose, Mike. "Narrowing the Mind: Cognitive Reductionism and Remedial Writers." *Cross-Talk in Comp Theory.* Ed. Victor Villanueva. Urbana, IL: NCTE, 1997.

——. *Lives on the Boundary: The Struggles and Achievements of America's Underprepared.* New York: Penguin, 1989.

3   Adapting the Writing Process

Anokye, Aku Duku. "Oral Connections to Literacy: The Narrative." *Journal of Basic Writing* 13.2 (1994).

Boese, Peggy, Mary Ellen Byrne, and Louise Silverman. "The Rewards of a Publication of Student Writings." *Teaching English in the Two-Year College* 24 (1997): 42–46.

Collins, James L. "Basic Writing and the Process Paradigm." *Journal of Basic Writing* 14.2 (1995): 3–18.

Davis, Mary Beth Lindley. "Revisioning the Basic Writer as Seeker and Quester: A Preparatory Course Design." *Teaching English in the Two-Year College* 17 (1990): 24–29.

Elbow, Peter. "Freewriting." *Writing with Power: Techniques for Mastering the Writing Process.* New York: Oxford UP, 1981. 13–19.

Elliot, Norbert. "Narrative Discourse and the Basic Writer." *Journal of Basic Writing* 14.2 (1995): 19–30.

Fleckenstein, Kristie S. "Writing and the Strategic Use of Metaphor." *Teaching English in the Two-Year College* 22 (1995): 110–15.

Flower, Linda, and John Hays. "Cognitive Process Theory of Writing." *College Composition and Communication* 32 (1981): 365–87.

Fulwiler, Toby. Introduction. *The Journal Book*. Ed. Toby Fulwiler. Portsmouth, NH: Boynton, 1987. 1–8.

Keithley, Zoe. "'My Own Voice': Students Say It Unlocks the Writing Process." *Journal of Basic Writing* 11.2 (1992): 82–102.

Lay, Nancy Duke S. "Response Journals in the ESL Classroom: Windows to the World." *Teaching English in the Two Year College* 22 (1995): 38–44.

Parisi, Hope A. "Involvement and Self-Awareness for the Basic Writer: Graphically Conceptualizing the Writing Process." *Journal of Basic Writing* 13.2 (1994): 33–45.

Perl, Sondra. "The Composing Processes of Unskilled College Writers." *Research in the Teaching of English* 13 (1979): 317–36.

Rico, Gabrielle. "General Principles of Clustering." *Writing the Natural Way*. Boston: Houghton, 1983. 35–39.

Robinson, William S. "On Teaching Organization: Patterns, Process, and the Nature of Writing." *Teaching English in the Two-Year College* 21 (1994): 191–98.

Schor, Sandra. "The Short Happy Life of Ms. Mystery." *Journal of Basic Writing* 10.1 (1991): 16–25.

Sills, Caryl Klein. "Arguing from First-Hand Evidence." *Journal of Basic Writing* 11.2 (1992).

Sommers, Nancy. "Revision Strategies of Student Writers." *College Composition and Communication* 31 (1980): 378–88.

Wells, Neil R. "Imitate This: Modeling Essays for Students." *Journal of Developmental Education* 3.3 (1998) 31 July 1999 <http://inet.ccp.cc.pa.us/vpacaff/divess/jde/model.htm>.

Wiener, Harvey. "Basic Writing: First Day's Thoughts on Process and Detail." *Eight Approaches to Teaching Composition*. Ed. Timothy R. Donovan and Ben W. McClelland. Urbana, IL: NCTE, 1980. 87–99

4 Writing and Reading

Chase, Nancy, Sandra U. Gibson, and Joan G. Carson. "An Examination of Reading Demands Across Four College Courses." *Journal of Basic Writing* 18 (1994): 10–16.

Daniels, Harvey. *Literature Circles: Voice and Choice in the Student-Centered Classroom*. York, ME: Stenhouse, 1994.

Palmer, James C. "Do College Courses Improve Basic Reading and Writing Skills?" *Community College Review* 12.2 (1984): 20–28.

Smith, Frank. *Understanding Reading: A Psycholinguistic Analysis of Reading and Learning to Read*. 5th ed. Hillsdale, NJ: Erlbaum, 1994.

Sternglass, Marilyn S. *Time to Know Them: A Longitudinal Study of Writing and Learning at the College Level*. Mahwah, NJ: Erlbaum, 1997.

Wiener, Harvey S. "The Attack on Basic Writing—And After." *Journal of Basic Writing* 17 (1998): 96–103.

5 Approaches to Grammar Instruction

Chafe, Wallace. "What Is Good Punctuation?" *Center for the Study of Writing Occasional Paper No. 2* Berkeley: Center for the Study of Writing, 1985. ERIC ED 292 120.

Dawkins, John. "Teaching Punctuation as a Rhetorical Tool." *College Composition and Communication* 46 (1995): 533–48.

Devet, Bonnie. "Errors as Discoveries: An Assignment for Prospective English Teachers." *Journal of Teaching Writing* 15.1 (1996): 129–39.

Hartwell, Patrick. "Grammar, Grammars, and the Teaching of Grammar." *College English* 47 (1985): 105–27.

Haussamen, Brock. *Revising the Rules: Traditional Grammar and Modern Linguistics.* Dubuque, IA: Kendall, 1993.

Meyer, Charles. "Functional Grammar and Its Application in the Composition Classroom." *Journal of Teaching Writing* 8 (1989): 147–67.

Newman, Michael. "Correctness and Its Conceptions: The Meaning of Language Form for Basic Writers." *Journal of Basic Writing* 15.1 (1996): 23–38.

Noguchi, Rei R. "Transformational-Generative Syntax and the Teaching of Sentence Mechanics." *Journal of Basic Writing* 6.2 (1987): 26–36.

Weaver, Constance. *Grammar for Teachers.* Urbana, IL: NCTE, 1979.

———, ed. *Lessons to Share: On Teaching Grammar in Context.* Portsmouth, NH: Boynton, 1998.

———. *Teaching Grammar in Context.* Portsmouth, NH: Boynton, 1996.

6 Students' Learning Styles

Dunn, Patricia. *Learning Re-abled.* Portsmouth, NH: Boynton, 1995.

Emig, Janet. "Writing as a Mode of Learning." *College Composition and Communication* 28 (1977): 122–28.

Evans, Nancy J., Deanna S. Forney, and Florence Guido-DeBrito. *Student Development in College: Theory, Research, and Practice.* San Francisco: Jossey, 1998.

Gardner, Howard. *Multiple Intelligences: The Theory in Practice.* New York: Basic, 1993.

Gordon, Lawrence. *People Types and Tiger Stripes*, 2d ed. Gainesville, FL: Center for Applications of Psychological Types, 1982.

Grimes, "Targeting Academic Programs to Student Diversity Utilizing Learning Styles and Learning-Study Strategies." *Journal of College Student Development* 36 (1995): 422–30.

Houston, Linda S. "Accommodations for Learning Differences in the English Classroom." *Teaching English in the Two-Year College* (Dec. 1994).

Kalivoda, Karen S., Jeanne L. Higbee, and Debra C. Brenner. "Teaching Students with Hearing Impairments." *Journal of Developmental Education* 20.3 (1997): 10–16.

Kolb, David A. *Experiential Learning: Experience as the Source of Learning and Development.* Englewood Cliffs, NJ: Prentice, 1983.

Kutz, Eleanor, et al. *The Discovery of Competence: Teaching and Learning with Diverse Student Writers.* Portsmouth, NH: Boynton, 1993.

McAlexander, Patricia J., Ann B. Dobie, and Noel Gregg. *Beyond the SP Label: Improving the Spelling of Learning Disabled and Basic Writers.* Urbana, IL: NCTE, 1993.

O'Brien, Terrence P., and Mary J. Thompson. "Cognitive Styles and Academic Achievement in Community College Education." *Community College Journal of Research and Practice* 18 (1994): 547–56.

Rothchild, Jacqueline, and William E. Piland. "Intercorrelates of Postsecondary Students' Learning Styles and Personality Traits." *Community College Journal of Research and Practice* 18 (1994): 177–88.

Schroeder, Charles C. "New Students—New Learning Styles." *Change* Sept.–Oct. 1993: 21–26.

7 Writing and Adult Learners

Auerbach, Elsa R. *Making Meaning, Making Change: Participatory Curriculum Development for Adult ESL and Family Literacy.* Boston: U of Massachusetts P, 1990.

Greenwood, C. M. "'It's Scary at First': Reentry Women in College Composition Classes." *Teaching English in the Two-Year College* 17 (1990): 133–42.

Kiskis, Michael J. "Adult Learners, Autobiography, and Educational Planning: Reflections of Pedagogy, Adragogy, and Power." *Pedagogy in the Age of Politics: Writing and Reading (in) the Academy.* Ed. Patricia A. Sullivan and Donna J. Qualley. Urbana: NCTE, 1994. 56–72.

Knowles, Malcolm. *The Adult Learner: A Neglected Species.* 4th ed. Houston: Gulf, 1990.

Luttrell, Wendy. *Schoolsmart and Motherwise: Working-Class Women's Identity and Schooling.* New York: Routledge, 1997.

Miritello, Mary. "Teaching Writing to Adults: Examining Assumptions and Revising Expectations for Adult Learners in the Writing Class." *Composition Chronicle: Newsletter for Writing Teachers* 9.2 (1990): 6–9.

8 Critical Thinking

Blodgett-McDeavitt, Cynthia. "A Profile of Critical Thinking, Problem Solving, and Learning to Learn among Adult and Continuing Education Administrators." Amer. Assoc. for Adult and Continuing Educ. Conf. Kansas City. 1–4 Nov. 1995.

Brookfield, Stephen D. *Becoming a Critically Reflective Teacher.* San Francisco: Jossey, 1995.

———. *Developing Critical Thinkers.* San Francisco: Jossey, 1987.

Elder, Linda, and Richard Paul. "Critical Thinking: A Stage Theory of Critical Thinking." Parts 1 and 2. *Journal of Developmental Education.* 20.1–2 (1996): 34–35.

———. "Critical Thinking: Content Is Thinking/Thinking Is Content." *Journal of Developmental Education* 19.2 (1995): 34.

———. "Critical Thinking: Rethinking Content as a Mode of Thinking." *Journal of Developmental Education* 19.3 (1996): 32.

———. "Critical Thinking: Using Intellectual Standards to Assess Student Reasoning." *Journal of Developmental Education* 18.2 (1994): 32–33.

———. "Critical Thinking: Why Teach Students Intellectual Standards?" Parts 1 and 2. *Journal of Developmental Education* 18.3 (1995): 36–37 and 19.1 (1995): 34–35.

Golub, Jeff. *Classroom Practices in Teaching English.* Urbana, IL: NCTE, 1996.

McLaughlin, Margaret A., Patricia T. Price, and Mildred Pate. "Using Whole Language to Incorporate African American Literature into Developmental Reading/Writing Classes." *Teaching English in the Two-Year College* 22 (1995): 173–78.

Meyers, Chet. *Teaching Students to Think Critically.* San Francisco: Jossey, 1986.

Meyers, Chet, and Tom Jones. *Promoting Active Learning: Strategies for the College Classroom.* San Francisco: Jossey, 1993.

Middendorf, Marilyn. "Bakhtin and the Dialogic Writing Class." *Journal of Basic Writing* 11.1 (1992): 34–46.

Sirc, Geoffrey. "The Autobiography of Malcolm X as a Basic Writing Text." *Journal of Basic Writing* 13.1 (1994): 50–77.

9   Collaborative Learning

Bruffee, Kenneth A. *Collaborative Learning: Higher Education, Interdependence, and the Authority of Knowledge.* Baltimore: Johns Hopkins UP, 1994.

Clark, Milton J., and Carol Peterson Haviland. "Language and Authority: Shifting the Privilege." *Journal of Basic Writing* 14.1 (1995): 57–66.

Dale, Helen. "Collaborative Research on Collaborative Writing." *English Journal* 83.1 (1994): 66–70.

———. "The Influence of Coauthoring on the Writing Process." *Journal of Teaching Writing* 15.1 (1996): 65–79.

Hacker, Tim. "The Effect of Teacher Conferences on Peer Response Discourse." *Teaching English in the Two-Year College* 23 (1996): 112–26.

Holt, Mara. "The Value of Written Peer Criticism." *College Composition and Communication* 43 (1992): 384–92.

Ott, C. Ann. "Collective Research at an Urban Community College." *Teaching English in the Two-Year College* 24 (1997): 7–13.

Schaffer, Jane. "Peer Response That Works." *Journal of Teaching Writing* 15.1 (1996): 81–90.

Smagorinsky, Peter. "The Aware Audience: Role-Playing Peer-Response Groups." *English Journal* 80.5 (1991): 35–91.

Strong, Gregory. "Teaching Writing with Small Groups." *Thought Currents in English Literature* 66 (1993): 129–52.

Wallace, David. "Teaching Collaborative Planning: Creating a Social Context for Writing." *Making Thinking Visible: Writing, Collaborative Planning, and Classroom Inquiry.* Ed. Linda Flower et al. Urbana, IL: NCTE, 1994. 48–66.

10   Technology

Adler-Kassner, Linda, and Thomas Reynolds. "Computers, Reading, and Basic Writers: Online Strategies for Helping Students with Academic Texts." *Teaching English in the Two-Year College* 23 (1996): 170–78.

Conference on Basic Writing—Home Page. <http://www.asu.edu/clas/english/composition/cbw/>.

Harris, Mark, and Jeff Hooks. "Writing in Cyberspace: Communication, Community, and the Electronic Network." *Two-Year College English: Essays for a New Century.* Ed. Mark Reynolds. Urbana, IL: NCTE, 1994. 151–62.

Hawisher, Gail E., and Cynthia L. Selfe. *Critical Perspectives on Computers and Composition Instruction.* New York: Teachers College P. 1989.

Hawisher, Gail E., Cynthia Selfe, Charles Moran, and Paul LeBlanc. *Computer and the Teaching of Writing in American Higher Education 1979–1994: A History.* Norwood, NJ: Ablex, 1996.

Hobson, Eric H., and Karen Richardson Gee. "Ten Commandments for Computer-Assisted Composition Instructors." *Teaching English in the Two-Year College* 21 (1994): 224–30.

Mabrito, Mark. "Electronic Mail as a Vehicle for Peer Response: Conversations of High- and Low-Apprehensive Writers." *Written Communication* 8 (1991): 509–32.

Marx, Michael Steven. "Computers and Pedagogy: Distant Writers, Distant Critics, and Close Readings: Linking Composition Through a Peer-Critiquing Network." *Computers and Composition* 8.1 (1994): 23–39.

Meem, Deborah. "The Effect of Classroom Computer Use on College Basic Writers." *Research and Teaching in Developmental Education* 8.2 (1992): 57–69.

Posey, Evelyn J. "The Widening Gulf: Computer-Enhanced Instruction on the Developmental Writing Classroom." *Teaching English in the Two-Year College* 21 (1994): 231–37.

Selfe, Cynthia. "Technology and Literacy: A Story about the Perils of Not Paying Attention." *College Composition and Communication* 50 (1999): 411–36.

Taylor, Todd. "Computers in the Composition Curriculum: An Update." *Writing Program Administration* 20 (1996): 7–18.

Thompson, Diane. "Electronic Bulletin Boards: A Timeless Place for Collaborative Writing Projects." *Computers and Composition* 7.3 (1994): 43–53.

11 Writing and Race, Class, and Gender

Annas, Pamela. "Style as Politics: A Feminist Approach to Teaching Writing." *College English* 46 (1985): 360–71.

Balester, Valerie. *Cultural Divide: A Study of African-American College-Level Writers.* Portsmouth, NH: Boynton, 1993.

Bernstein, Susan Naomi. "On Teaching, Meditations and Invitations." *Journal of Developmental Education.* 3.2 (1998). 3 August 1999 <http://inet.ccp.cc.pa.us/vpacaff/divess/jde/snb.htm>.

Blake, Francie. "Identity, Community, and the Curriculum: A Call for Multiculturalism in the Classroom." *Journal of Developmental Education* 2.2 (1997): 3–7.

Cochran, Effie Papatzikou. "Giving Voice to Women in the Basic Writing and Language Minority Classroom." *Journal of Basic Writing* 13.1 (1994): 78–91.

Cushman, Ellen. *The Struggle and the Tools: Oral and Literate Strategies in an Inner City Community.* Albany: State U of New York P, 1998.

Dean, Terry. "Multicultural Classrooms, Monocultural Teachers." *College Composition and Communication* 40 (1989): 23–37.

Delpit, Lisa. *Other People's Children: Cultural Conflict in the Classroom.* New York: New P, 1995.

DiPardo, Anne. *A Kind of Passport: A Basic Writing Adjunct Program and the Challenge of Diversity.* New York: NCTE, 1993.

————. "Narrative Discourse in the Basic Writing Class: Meeting the Challenge of Cultural Pluralism." *Teaching English in the Two-Year College* 17 (1990): 45–53.

Fox, Helen. *Listening to the World: Cultural Issues in Academic Writing.* Urbana, IL: NCTE, 1994.

Gibson, Michelle. "An All-Too-Familiar Paradox: Familial Diversity and the Composition Classroom." *Writing on the Edge* 7.2 (1996): 19–30.

Gilyard, Keith. *Voices of the Self: A Study of Language Competence.* Detroit: Wayne State UP, 1991.

Hourigan, Maureen. "Re-visioning Basic Writing." *Literacy as Social Exchange: Intersections of Class, Gender, and Culture.* Ed. Maureen Hourigan. Albany: State U of New York P, 1994.

Jordan, June. "Nobody Means More to Me Than You and the Future Life of Willie Jordan." *On Call* Ed. June Jordan. Boston: South End P. 1985. 123–39.

Lu Min-zhan. "From Silence to Words: Writing as Struggle." *College English* 49 (1987): 437–48.

————. "Professing Multiculturalism: The Politics of Style in the Contact Zone." *College Composition and Communication* 45 (1994): 442–58.

Patthey-Chavez, G. Genevieve, and Constance Gergen. "Culture as an Instructional Resource in the Multiethnic Composition Classroom." *Journal of Basic Writing* 11.1 (1992): 75–96.

Raimes, Ann. "Out of the Woods: Emerging Traditions in the Teaching of Writing." *TESOL Quarterly* 25 (1991): 407–30.

Rich, Adrienne. "Taking Women Students Seriously." In *Lies, Secrets, and Silence: Selected Prose, 1966–1978.* Ed. Adrienne Rich. New York: Norton, 1979. 237–45.

Royster, Jacqueline Jones. "When the First Voice You Hear Is Not Your Own." *College Composition and Communication* 47 (1996): 29–40.

Sadarangani, Umeeta. "Teaching Multicultural Issues in the Composition Classroom: A Review of Recent Practice." *Journal of Teaching Writing* 13.1–2 (1994): 33–54.

Villanueva, Victor Jr. *Bootstraps: From an American Academic of Color.* Urbana, IL: NCTE, 1993.

Wallace, David, and Annissa Bell. "Being Black at a Predominantly White University." *College English* 61 (1999): 307–27.

12 Teaching ESL

Benson, Beverly, Mary P. Deming, Debra Denzer, and Maria Valeri-Gold. "A Combined Basic Writing/English as a Second Language Class: Melting Pot or Mishmash?" *Journal of Basic Writing* 11.1 (1992): 58–74.

Carroll, Pamela Sissi, with Frances Blake, Rose Ann Comalo, and Smaddar Messer. "When Acceptance Isn't Enough: Helping ESL Students Become Successful Writers." *English Journal* 85 (1996): 25–33.

Nelson, Marie Wilson. *At the Point of Need: Teaching Basic and ESL Writers.* Portsmouth, NH: Heinemann, 1991.

Ransdell, D. R., "Important Events: Second-Language Students in the Composition Classroom." *Teaching English in the Two-Year College* 21 (1994): 217–22.

Robinson, William S. "ESL and Dialect Features in the Writing of Asian-American Students." *Teaching English in the Two-Year College* 22 (1995): 303–09.

Smitherman, Geneva. "CCC's Role in the Struggle for Language Rights." *College Composition and Communication* 50 (1999): 349–76.

Wilson Nelson, Marie. *At the Point of Need: Teaching Basic and ESL Writers.* Portsmouth, NH: Heineman, 1991.

Zamel, Vivian. "Strangers in Academia: The Experiences of Faculty and ESL Students across the Curriculum." *College Composition and Communication* 46 (1995): 506–21.

13 Placement and Assessment

Anson, Chris M. "Portfolios for Teachers: Writing Our Way to Reflective Practice." *New Directions in Portfolio Assessment: Reflective Practice, Critical Theory, and Large-Scale Scoring.* Ed. Laurel Black et al. Portsmouth, NH: Boynton, 1994. 185–200.

Bartholomae, David. "The Study of Error." *College Composition and Communication* 31 (1980): 253–69.

Belanoff, Pat. "The Myths of Assessment." *Journal of Basic Writing* 10.1 (1991): 54–66.

Cameron, Thomas D. "A Responsible Evaluation Instrument and Its Impact on a Developmental Writing Program." *Teaching English in the Two-Year College* 20 (1993): 313–23.

Haswell, Richard, and Susan Wyche-Smith. "Adventuring into Writing Assessment." *College Composition and Communication* 45 (1994): 220–36.

Haviland, Carol Peterson, and J. Milton Clark. "What Our Students Tell Us about Essay Examination Designs and Practices." *Journal of Basic Writing* 11.2 (1992): 47–60.

Herter, Roberta. "Writing Portfolios: Alternative to Testing (Research and Practice)." *English Journal* 80.1 (1991): 90–91.

Hilgers, Thomas. "Basic Writing Curricula and Good Assessment Practices." *Journal of Basic Writing* 14.2 (1995): 68–74.

Hillenbrand, Lisa. "Assessment of ESL Students in Mainstream College Composition." *Teaching English in the Two-Year College* 21 (1994): 125–30.

Lindemann, Erica. "What Do Teachers Need to Know about Linguistics?" *A Rhetoric for Writing Teachers.* Ed. Erica Lindemann. New York: Oxford UP, 1987. 93–116.

Miraglia, Eric. "A Self-Diagnostic Assessment in the Basic Writing Course." *Journal of Basic Writing* 14.2 (1995): 48–67.

Sommers, Nancy. "Responding to Student Writing." *College Composition and Communication* 33 (1982): 148–56.

Sweigart, William. "Assessing Achievement in a Developmental Writing Sequence." *Research and Teaching in Developmental Education* 12.2 (1996): 5–15.

White, Edward M. "The Importance of Placement and Basic Studies: Helping Students Succeed under the New Elitism." *Journal of Basic Writing* 14.2 (1995): 75–48.

———. "Responding to and Grading Student Writing." *Assigning, Responding, Evaluating: A Writing Teacher's Guide,* 3rd ed. New York: St. Martin's, 1995. 122–48.

———. *Teaching and Assessing Writing.* San Francisco: Jossey, 1994.

Wiener, Harvey S. "Evaluating Assessment Programs on Basic Skills." *Journal of Developmental Education* 13 (1989): 24–26.,

Yancey, Kathleen Blake. "Looking Back as We Look Forward: Historicizing Writing Assessment." *College Composition and Communication* 50 (1999): 483–503.

14 Basic Writing and the Writing Center

Boyd, Richard. "Imitate Me; Don't Imitate Me: Mimeticism in David Bartholomae's 'Inventing the University.'" *Journal of Advanced Composition* 11 (1991): 335–45.

Harris, Muriel. "Talking in the Middle: Why Writers Need Writing Tutors." *College English* 57 (1995): 27–42.

O' Hearn, Carolyn. "Recognizing the Learning Disabled College Writer." *College English* 51 (1989): 294–302.

Tassoni, John Paul. "The Liberatory Composition Teacher's Obligation to Writing Centers at Two-Year Colleges." *Teaching English in the Two-Year College* 25 (1998): 34–43.

Supplemental Section: Teacher Research and Basic Writing

Though none of these texts fits precisely within the thematic arrangement of *Teaching Developmental Writing: Background Readings,* each is a useful resource for those who teach developing writers. They are included here for further reference as you plan, teach, and evaluate your basic writing course. Many of these resources draw strong links between teacher research and the problem-posing pedagogy presented in several of the articles in *Teaching Developmental Writing: Background Readings.*

Atwell, Nancy. *In the Middle: Writing, Reading and Learning with Adolescents.* Portsmouth, NH: Boynton, 1987.

Brandt, Deborah. *Literacy as Involvement: The Acts of Writers, Readers, and Texts.* Carbondale: Southern Illinois UP, 1990.

Calkins, Lucy McCormick. *The Art of Teaching Writing.* Portsmouth, NH: Heinemann, 1994.

Croake, Edith Morris. "Toward a Mentoring Program for New Two-Year College Faculty." *Teaching English in the Two-Year College* 23 (1996): 304–11.

Daiker, Donald A., and Max Morenberg, eds. *The Writing Teacher as Researcher.* Portsmouth, NH: Boynton, 1990.

Graves, Donald H. *A Fresh Look at Writing.* Dallas: Southern Methodist UP, 1991.

Greene, Brenda M. "Empowerment and the Problem Identification and Resolution Stratgies of Basic Writers." *Journal of Basic Writing* 11.2 (1992): 4–27.

Haswell, Richard. *Gaining Ground in College Writing.* Dallas: Southern Methodist UP, 1991.

Hillocks, George. *Teaching Writing as a Reflective Practice.* New York: Teacher's College P, 1995.

Horner, Bruce. "Discoursing Basic Writing." *College Composition and Communication* 47 (1996): 199–222.

Knodt, Ellen Andrews. "Taming the Hydra: The Problem of Balancing Teaching and Scholarship at a Two-Year College." *Teaching English in the Two-Year College* 15 (1988): 170–74.

Laurence, Patricia, Peter Rondinone, Barbara Gleason, Thomas J. Farrell, Paul Hunter, and Min-zhan Lu. "Symposium on Basic Writing, Conflict and Struggle, and the Legacy of Mina Shaughnessy." *College English* 55 (1993): 879–903.

Lewiecki-Wilson, Cynthia. "Professing at the Fault Lines: Composition at Open Admissions Institutions." *College Composition and Communication* 50 (1999): 438–62.

Lu, Min-zhan. "Conflict and Struggle: The Enemies or Preconditions of Basic Writing?" *College English* 54 (1992): 887–913.

Lytle, Susan L. "Living Literacy: Rethinking Development in Adulthood." *Linguistics in Education* 3 (1991): 109–38.

Maher, Jane. *Mina Shaughnessy: Her Life and Work,* Urbana, IL: NCTE, 1997.

Minot, Walter S., and Kenneth R. Gamble. "Self-Esteem and Writing Apprehension of Basic Writers: Conflicting Evidence." *Journal of Basic Writing* 10.2 (1991): 116–24.

Neumann, Anna, *Learning from Our Lives: Women, Research, and Autobiography in Education.* New York: Teacher's College P, 1997.

Reagan, Sally Barr. "Warning: Basic Writers at Risk—The Case of Javier." *Journal of Basic Writing* 10.2 (1991): 99–115.

Stuckey, J. Elspeth. *The Violence of Literacy.* Portsmouth, NH: Boynton, 1992.

Stygall, Gail. "Resisting Privilege: Basic Writing and Foucault's Author Function." *College Composition and Communication* 45 (1994): 320–41.

Tate, Gary, Edward P. J. Corbett, and Nancy Myers. *The Writing Teacher's Source Book.* New York: Oxford UP, 1994.

Acknowledgements (continued from page iv)

Stephen D. Brookfield, excerpt from "Understanding Classroom Dynamics: The Critical Incident Questionnaire," from *Becoming a Critically Reflective Teacher* by Stephen D. Brookfield. Copyright © 1995 by Jossey-Bass Publishers. Reprinted by permission.

Conference on College Composition and Communication, "Writing Assessment: A Position Statement from the Conference on College Composition and Communication." *Teaching English in the Two-Year College*, October 1995. Copyright © 1995 by the National Council of Teachers of English. Reprinted with permission.

Yu Ren Dong, "The Need to Understand ESL Students' Native Language Writing Experiences." *Teaching English in the Two-Year College*, December 1999. Copyright © 1999 by the National Council of Teachers of English. Reprinted with permission.

Linda Elder and Richard Paul, "The Elements of Critical Thinking (Helping Students Assess Their Thinking)." Appeared in <http://www.criticalthinking.org>. Reprinted by permission from the Foundation for Critical Thinking, P.O. Box 220, Dillon Beach, CA 94929, <http://www.criticalthinking.org>.

Andrew Fleck, "Instructional Note: 'We think he means . . .': Creating Working Definitions through Small Group Discussions." *Teaching English in the Two-Year College*, December 1999. Copyright © 1999 by the National Council of Teachers of English. Reprinted with permission.

Jacob C. Gaskins, "Teaching Writing to Students with Learning Disabilities: The Landmark Method." *Teaching English in the Two-Year College*, May 1995. Copyright © 1995 by the National Council of Teachers of English. Reprinted with permission.

Dianne Goode, "Creating a Context for Developmental English." *Teaching English in the Two-Year College*, March 2000. Copyright © 2000 by the National Council of Teachers of English. Reprinted with permission.

Ann E. Green, "My Uncle's Guns." *Writing on the Edge,* Vol. 9, No. 1, Fall/Winter 1997/98. Reprinted by permission of the author.

Kay Harley and Sally I. Cannon, "Failure: The Student's or the Assessment's?" Copyright © 1996 by *Journal of Basic Writing,* The City University of New York. Reprinted from Volume 15, Number 1, by permission.

bell hooks, "Embracing Change: Teaching in a Multicultural World," from *Teaching to Transgress: Education as the Practice of Freedom,* Routledge, 1994. Reproduced by permission of Taylor & Francis, Inc./Routledge, Inc., <http://www.routledge-ny.com>.

Glynda Hull and Mike Rose, "This Wooden Shack Place: The Logic of an Unconventional Reading." *College Composition and Communication,* October 1990. Copyright © 1990 by the National Council of Teachers of English. Reprinted with permission.

Mary K. Jackman, "When the Personal Becomes Professional: Stories from Reentry Adult Women Learners about Family, Work, and School." *Composition Studies* 27.2, Fall 1999, pages 53–67. Reprinted with permission.

Loretta Frances Kasper, "ESL Writing and the Principle of Nonjudgmental Awareness: Rationale and Implementation." *Teaching English in the Two-Year College,* February 1998. Copyright © 1998 by the National Council of Teachers of English. Reprinted with permission.

Valerie Ann Krahe, "The Shape of the Container." Appeared originally in *Adult Learning,* March/April, 1993. Reprinted by permission of Valerie Ann Krahe, Instructor in English, McDowell Intermediate High School, Erie, PA.

William B. Lalicker, "A Basic Introduction to Basic Writing Program Structures: A Baseline and Five Alternatives." Appeared in *Conference on Basic Writing: Basic Writing e-Journal,* Summer 2000. Reprinted by permission of *BWe,* <http://www.asu.edu/clas/english/composition/cbw>.

Ellen Mohr, "The Writing Center: An Opportunity in Democracy." *Teaching English in the Two-Year College,* May 1999. Copyright © 1999 by the National Council of Teachers of English. Reprinted with permission.

Janice Neuleib and Irene Brosnahan, "Teaching Grammar to Writers." Copyright © 1987 by *Journal of Basic Writing,* The City University of New York. Reprinted from Volume 6, Number 2, by permission.

Sarah Nixon-Ponder, "Using Problem-Posing Dialogue in Adult Literacy Education." Appeared originally in *Adult Learning 7.2,* November/December, 1995. Reprinted by permission of the author.

Rei R. Noguchi, "Teaching the Basics of a Writer's Grammar," from *Grammar and the Teaching of Writing.* Copyright © 1991 by the National Council of Teachers of English. Reprinted with permission.

Richard Raymond, "Building Learning Communities on Nonresidential Campuses." *Teaching English in the Two-Year College*, May 1999. Copyright © 1999 by the National Council of Teachers of English. Reprinted with permission.

Daniel Royer and Roger Gilles, "Directed Self Placement: An Attitude of Orientation." *CCC* 50.1, September 1998. Reprinted with permission.

Gregory Shafer, "Using Letters for Process and Change in the Basic Writing Classroom." *Teaching English in the Two-Year College*, March 2000. Copyright © 2000 by the National Council of Teachers of English. Reprinted with permission. "Negotiating Audience and Voice in the Writing Center." *Teaching English in the Two-Year College*, December 1999. Copyright © 1999 by the National Council of Teachers of English. Reprinted with permission.

Mina P. Shaughnessy, "Some New Approaches toward Teaching." Copyright © 1994 by the *Journal of Basic Writing,* The City University of New York. Reprinted from Volume 13, Number 1, by permission.

Susan Stan and Terence G. Collins, "Basic Writing: Curricular Interactions with New Technology." Copyright © 1998 by *Journal of Basic Writing,* The City University of New York. Reprinted from Volume 17, Number 1, by permission.

Marilyn Sternglass, "The Changing Perception of the Role of Writing: From Basic Writing to Discipline Courses." Appeared in *Conference on Basic Writing: Basic Writing e-Journal,* Summer 2000. Reprinted by permission of *BWe,* <http://www.asu.edu/clas/english/composition/cbw>.

Kay Thurston, "Mitigating Barriers to Navajo Students' Success in English Courses." *Teaching English in the Two-Year College*, September 1998. Copyright © 1998 by the National Council of Teachers of English. Reprinted with permission.

Constance Weaver, "Teaching Style through Sentence Combining and Sentence Generating," from *Teaching Grammar in Context* by Constance Weaver. Copyright © 1996 by Constance Weaver. Reprinted by permission.

Smokey Wilson, "When Computers Come to English Class." *Teaching English in the Two-Year College*, May 2000. Copyright © 2000 by the National Council of Teachers of English. Reprinted with permission.